READING, WRITING, AND SPEECH PROBLEMS IN CHILDREN AND SELECTED PAPERS

Strephosymbolia.

A "Temporal cross section" of the theory of reading disabilities as of. July 1925.

... Thus strephosymbolia would be envisaged as of no relation to right and left handedness in the ordinary sense (though it may prove to be more common in the left handed) nor to the question of fixed dextrad or sinistrad orientation of written languages but rather as due to a failure to establish an exclusively unilateral dominance by adequate training for elision of obverse sensory engrams so that in using visual material from the associative level the lead is an inconsistent and confusing one.

Samuel Torrey Orton.

July 12th 1925.

Reproduced from manuscript by Samuel T. Orton (reduced in size)

Reading, Writing, and Speech Problems in Children and Selected Papers

Samuel Torrey Orton

Foreword by
Richard L. Masland

8700 Shoal Creek Boulevard
Austin, Texas 78758

The PRO-ED Classics Series

Series Editor
Donald D. Hammill

Printed in the United States of America

Library of Congress Cataloging in Publication Data

Orton, Samuel Torrey, 1879–1948.
    Reading, writing, and speech problems in children and selected papers / Samuel Torrey Orton; foreword by Richard L. Masland.
        p.   cm.   — (The PRO-ED classics series)
    Rev. ed. of: Reading, writing, and speech problems in children. c1937.
        ''Works by Samuel Torrey Orton'': p.
        Bibliography: p.
        Includes indexes.
        ISBN 0-89079-179-1 : $24.00
    1. Learning disabled children—Education.   2. Child development. 3. Children—Language.   4. Remedial teaching.   I. Orton, Samuel Torrey, 1879–1948.   Reading, writing, and speech problems in children.   II. Title.   III. Series.
LC4704.079 1989   88-30734
371.9—dc19   CIP

8700 Shoal Creek Blvd.
Austin, Texas 78758

10 9 8 7 6 5 4 3 2 1   88 89 90 91 92

CONTENTS

PART I. READING, WRITING, AND SPEECH PROBLEMS IN CHILDREN

PART II. SELECTED PAPERS BY SAMUEL TORREY ORTON

FOREWORD

By Richard L. Masland

Fifty years have passed since Samuel Torrey Orton published the first edition of his pioneering study, *Reading, Writing and Speech Problems in Children*. Over 20 years ago, a collection of his papers, written from 1925–1946, was published posthumously by his widow, June Lyday Orton. These works are reprinted as Parts I and II in this volume.

The intervening years since Orton wrote about language learning problems have seen great advances in our understanding of the structure and function of the human brain. Nevertheless, Orton's remarkable observations and conclusions continue to provide valuable insights into the characteristics, nature, and remediation of developmental alexias, agraphias, apraxias, aphasias, word deafness, and stuttering.

Throughout his work Orton emphasizes the diversity of the symptomatology that these conditions exhibit and the need for individualization of analysis and treatment. He notes that "each case of developmental delay forms an individual problem" and that "we are all prone to search for a simplified and universally applicable formula, but no such general 'method' can be defined" (p. 86 in this volume).

Orton observed a disorder, or rather a peculiarity, of cerebral dominance leading to interference in right-left discrimination in many dyslexic children. Furthermore, family histories often revealed unusually large numbers of relatives with mixed cerebral dominance, left-handedness, or various forms of language disability. Because of the frequency of poorly established cerebral dominance associated with disturbances of right-left discrimination and sequencing problems, developmental variations in hemisphere preponderance were thought to be an underlying cause in many cases.

Orton rejected Hinshelwood's thesis that "word-blindness" results from congenital malformation of the left angular gyrus—the seat of word storage in the brain. Evidence at that time suggested that the two hemispheres were identical at birth and equally capable of supporting normal language functions. Subsequent studies have shown, in fact, that asymmetries in the language areas are significant, and that, indeed, in most people, the left hemisphere can support stronger language functions than the right.

Furthermore, recent anatomical studies of brains of dyslexic subjects have demonstrated areas of malformation or underdevelopment in crucial areas of the dominant hemisphere. These same studies also suggest that underdevelopment of one area may be associated with overgrowth of others. Viewed in this light, Orton's thesis of a structural imbalance between the two hemispheres, which he presented in *Reading, Writing and Speech Problems in Children,* is once again timely.

Orton's papers, published in 1966 as the Orton Society's Monograph #2 under the title *"Word-Blindness" in School Children and other Papers on Strephosymbolia (Specific Language Disability—Dyslexia) 1925–1946,* provide a deeper examination of Orton's thinking about dyslexia and other disorders of written and spoken language. In these papers he develops the theory that dyslexia may be accounted for by a physiological process dependent upon delayed maturation of one or another of the brain functions required for reading.

His emphasis on the physiological nature of the disorder and his demonstration that it was remediable by appropriate diagnostic and educational approaches had a profound and continuing impact, especially when he used dramatic case studies to demonstrate the devastating secondary damage caused by misunderstanding and inappropriate management.

The theoretical basis for Orton's explanation of the nature of dyslexia has been a source of continued controversy. He was impressed by the frequency with which dyslexic individuals made two related types of errors—the reversal of symbols, such as *b* and *d*, *p* and *q*, and words, such as *was* and *saw,* and the tendency to read words or parts of words from right to left. Orton also noted the tendency of some to use mirror writing. He concluded that most of the other difficulties of dyslexic children were secondary to these basic problems of reversals and sequencing difficulties.

Orton developed a neurophysiological explanation for these phenomena. He noted that the two hemispheres of the brain are symmetrical and postulated that the sensory information (engrams) would be represented in each hemisphere in equivalent but mirror–image (antitropic) patterns. However, language functions depend upon only one "dominant" hemisphere. Thus, the comprehension of the written symbol can occur only when the engram, or sensory trace, of that symbol in one or the other hemisphere becomes associated with the language centers on the left.

Confusion, Orton believed, would occur when clear-cut hemispheric dominance failed to be established. Without this, "the immediately successive linkage between the sensory stimulus (printed word) and its meaning (concept) which constitutes reading" could not take place ("Methods for Diagnosis and Treatment of Cases of Reading Disability," 1928). Reading disability, he theorized, is "probably dependent on failure of constant selection of either the right or the left sensory record in the brain" ("The Relation of the Special Educational Disabilities to Feeblemindedness," 1929).

Orton noted that in many of his cases disorders of spoken language development were very significant. While denying that these atypical forms of maturation had a "pathological" basis, he did not deny the existence of a strong hereditary factor that must have a structural basis.

Orton's papers on "Special Disability in Spelling" and "Special Disability in Writing" (written with Anna Gillingham) provide models for thorough case studies. They outline approaches to intervention that should be understood by every student of dyslexia.

Since Orton's time, three discoveries have both strengthened his concepts and required that they be modified. The first is the discovery that whereas the left cerebral hemisphere is "dominant" for handedness, language, and similar sequential activities, the right hemisphere is superior in pattern recognition, orientation, and other functions requiring parallel processing. These findings tend to strengthen Orton's concepts, since the establishment of an association between the visual stimulus, most effectively analyzed in the right hemisphere, and the linguistic counterpart, stored in the left hemisphere, could easily be seen to predispose to uncertainty of cerebral dominance, especially if the language function were poorly established in the left or if the spatial skills in the right hemisphere were strongly developed.

The second important discovery is the finding of Geschwind and Levitsky of significant structural asymmetries of the human brain. Specifically, the planum temporale—that area most directly involved in the analysis of auditory input—is ordinarily much more highly developed on the left than on the right. This finding establishes a structural basis for the physiological asymmetry noted by Orton.

Finally, and most important, has been the demonstration by Galaburda and Kemper that anatomically observable irregularities occur in the development of the brains of dyslexic individuals. In a sense, these findings support the view of Hinshelwood that dyslexia is attributable to a developmental anomaly. On the other hand, they also support the view of Orton that "other areas would be competent to assume the function." The most striking finding of Galaburda and Kemper is not the presence of minor irregularities of development on the left side, but rather the evidence of compensatory overgrowth on the right. As a result, instead of the usual asymmetry, the planum temporale on the two sides is more likely to be equal in the brains of dyslexic individuals. This finding provides anatomical support for Orton's thesis of confusion of cerebral dominance. It provides similar support for his observation that many individuals who are deficient in language skills are superior in other areas of intelligence.

The new findings highlight the fact that the brilliant insights presented by Orton as a result of his meticulous case studies are still illuminating the discoveries of those who are continuing his work.

Richard L. Masland, MD
President, World Federation of Neurology
H. H. Merrit, Professor of Neurology,
   Emeritus
Columbia University

PREFACE

This volume contains the work of Samuel Torrey Orton that earlier appeared in two books. The first, *Reading, Writing and Speech Problems in Children*, based on the Thomas W. Salmon Memorial Lectures at the New York Academy of Medicine, was published in 1937 by W. W. Norton and Company, Inc. June Lyday Orton renewed the copyright in 1947. Norton continued to distribute the book under special arrangement with The Orton Dyslexia Society until 1987. In that year the Society and PRO-ED agreed to include the work in the PRO-ED Classics in Special Education Series along with papers from *"Word-Blindness" in School Children and Other Papers on Strephosymbolia (Specific Language Disability—Dyslexia) 1925–1946*.

The latter volume was compiled by June Orton in 1966 and contained Orton's papers that deal with the causes, nature, and treatment of language learning disorders. The Orton Society, as it was then called, published the papers as its Monograph #2. Recognized by students of dyslexia as seminal works in the field, these papers have been out of print for some years.

The Orton Dyslexia Society, noting renewed interest in brain research and neurological studies that seek to uncover the links between cerebral development and language ability, believes that a new generation of readers will welcome the chance to read these two books by Orton, here bound in a single volume. While the historian will find in Orton's writings the evolution of the mind of a scientist whose concern for the total child makes him a man apart in his times, medical researchers, educators, and psychologists will find much in these two works that confirms present-day theories and studies.

Several people have played key roles in the effort to reprint these classics. Special thanks are due Sylvia O. Richardson, MD, who was instrumental in bringing The Orton Dyslexia Society and PRO-ED together in this endeavor. Margaret Byrd Rawson and Richard L. Masland, MD, wrestled with the selection of papers to appear in Part II, and Rosemary F. Bowler undertook the preliminary editing of the papers and served as liaison between the Society and PRO-ED.

The Orton Dyslexia Society

A Biographical Sketch of
Samuel Torrey Orton
by June Lyday Orton

It was in Iowa in 1925 that Dr. Samuel T. Orton began his studies of children with specific language disabilities and called the attention of his colleagues in neurology and psychiatry to the large numbers of pupils otherwise normal in every respect who were retarded in their educational and personality development by a special difficulty in learning to read. Dr. Orton subsequently originated a combined medical-psychiatric-educational approach to the diagnosis and treatment of children with developmental language disorders which challenged the prevailing currents of thought in each of these disciplines.

Sporadic cases of "congenital word blindness" had been previously reported in the medical annals, chiefly from abroad, describing individuals who had never been able to learn to read and likening them to certain aphasic adults whose language function had been more or less permanently impaired by brain damage.

In psychiatric circles attention was being given to children through the organization of child guidance clinics with the new "team" concept of psychiatrist, psychologist, and psychiatric social worker, all of whom were generally committed to the principles of emotional causation for the many problems of childhood, including poor school performance.

Educational surveys were already bringing to light a surprising number of very poor readers among high school students and an even larger percentage among delinquents, while the educators were vigorously defending the fairly new "whole-word" or "sight" method of teaching reading and the ultra-progressive schools were expecting their pupils to acquire reading incidentally through other activities of their own choice.

In marked contrast to all this came Dr. Orton's new and successful approach to a certain type of reading difficulty as a specific learning disability with a genetic, physiological background, one which he

---

Note: This was the late Mrs. Orton's introduction to the original monograph published by the Orton Society in 1966.

demonstrated would respond to a broad but precise program of educational remediation based upon an individual diagnostic study of each case. How this all happened can be surmised perhaps from the following biographical sketches and then compared with his own statement of the development of his psychiatric philosophy which follows them.

SAMUEL TORREY ORTON was born in Columbus, Ohio, on October 15, 1879, of New England ancestry. His father, Edward Orton, LL.D., was a fifth generation descendant of Thomas Orton who migrated to America from England in 1641 and settled in Windsor, Connecticut. He was a noted scientist and educator who became president of Antioch College in Ohio and the first president of Ohio State University, later serving as Ohio State Geologist for twenty years. Samuel T. Orton's mother, Anna Davenport Torrey, was born in Millbury, Massachusetts, not far from the 1640 settlement of her English forebears, the William Torreys. She was a younger sister of Mrs. Alphonso Taft, who became the mother of William Howard Taft, President and Chief Justice of the United States, and of Horace Dutton Taft, founder and headmaster of Taft School at Watertown, Connecticut, where young Sam Orton completed his high school courses.

"Samuel T. is fitting for college and expects to study either medicine or mechanical engineering," wrote Edward Orton in 1896 concerning his son's future. Although the young man chose medicine and made it his life career, his mechanical bent perhaps accounted for his persistent search to discover how things worked, most of all, the human brain. His recreation was in designing and building—boats, tennis courts, gardens, garages, laboratories, hospitals—and in inventing better methods and techniques, from ways of pouring slabs of cement to staining and cutting brain sections for the microscope. He always loved to explore nature, observing, naming and classifying rocks and plants and butterflies from the time he was a small boy tagging along after his father on geological expeditions. While in college he spent two summers with the Ohio State Archeological Society digging in Indian mounds, and his study of the pathological changes in the bones of these early inhabitants formed the basis of his first scientific paper, written while still in medical school. He enjoyed hunting and fishing, played a good game of tennis and even football in his earlier years, and always seemed active and energetic, physically and mentally, in spite of a rather frail physique and many illnesses. His insatiable interest in things about him carried over to people. He added to his store of information wherever he went through easy conversations with a plumber or a president, a small boy or a senior scientist. He admired all forms of good workmanship but he was intolerant of careless techniques or any display of pretentiousness, and he would never compromise on a matter of principle.

After graduating from Taft School, Samuel T. attended Ohio State University for four years and then entered the University of Pennsylvania from which he received his medical degree in 1905, and an honorary doctorate in science forty years later. He also earned a master's degree from Harvard University. He was a member of Alpha Omega Alpha, an honorary medical fraternity, and the honorary scientific society, Sigma Xi.

Always interested in pathology and stimulated by such professors as Dr. Simon Flexner at Pennsylvania, Dr. Orton had the opportunity for further training in that field under the eminent Dr. Frank B. Mallory at the Boston City Hospital, of whom he once wrote, "Meticulous technical methods and the most careful morphological observations were the religion which Mallory instilled into all of his students." There he also came under the influence of Dr. E. E. Southard who was specializing in the pathology of the nervous system and later gave him the opportunity for an extended research study of a hydrocephalic brain in his laboratories at the Danvers (Mass.) State Hospital. Another Massachusetts hospital which attracted leading neuropathologists was the Worcester State Hospital and after working for three years in the West, Dr. Orton came there to serve as its pathologist from 1908 to 1912, following Dr. Adolph Meyer by a decade. During this period he also taught courses at the Harvard Medical School and at Clark University until 1913 when he arranged to go to Breslau, Germany, for study in the laboratories of Dr. A. Alzheimer.

Upon his return, Dr. Orton was appointed pathologist and clinical director of the Pennsylvania Hospital for Mental Diseases in Philadelphia where he was involved in many professional activities from 1914 to 1919. Although never a prolific writer, he usually managed to publish at least one scientific paper each year and the titles in his bibliography suggest the development of his interests during this period. (See Appendix [2].) Then came a move westward again with the opportunity to build and direct a State Psychopathic Hospital at Iowa City, Iowa, and head the department of psychiatry in the medical school of the State University of Iowa. There he spent the next eight years (1919–1927) and began his work with children with language disabilities.

Dr. Orton made sure that the new hospital provided ample space for his laboratories as well as facilities for the best care for his patients and he extended its services through an outpatient department with a staff which included psychologists, social workers, speech therapists, and others in related fields who worked with both children and adults. Courses were given to students in psychology, sociology and other departments of the University and consultations were held with many of the state institutions. Dr. Orton had always been active in promoting mental health activities, and in September, 1924, he presented a report at the Iowa State Conference of Social Work as chairman of the mental hygiene committee on "The Problem of the Feebleminded", covering in depth the social, legal, genetic, medical, psychological, psychiatric, and research areas involved. In view of his later work with children with learning problems, it is interesting to note that he stressed the fact that the so-called feebleminded were by no means a homogeneous group and urged the consideration of the individual's special abilities rather than his defects as a guide to his vocational training. At this same meeting, Dr. Orton proposed "A Mobile Psychiatric Unit as the Most Feasible Method of Meeting Iowa's Mental Hygiene Needs." Four months later he was out in the field with such a unit conducting a clinic in Greene County, Iowa, upon the invitation of its local doctors, welfare agencies, and school authorities.

Thus the stage was set for the entrance of "M.P.", the sixteen-year-old youth from a rural school who was referred because "he seemed bright but couldn't learn to read", the prototype of the hundreds of other "word-blind" children to whom Dr. Orton was to devote the next twenty years, indeed the rest of his life.

"M.P." presented a special challenge to this neuropsychiatrist who was very familiar with the clinical symptoms and the brain pathology in adults who had *lost* their reading or speech through brain injuries—cases of acquired word-blindness, receptive and motor aphasia, etc., and Dr. Orton arranged to study the boy extensively at the hospital. The Greene County clinic soon discovered a number of other pupils who were blocked in their educational progress by specific retardation in learning to read. Dr. Orton became impressed by the extent of the problem, and particularly by the serious effect upon the personality development of children with this unrecognized and untreated handicap. His further studies of these cases led him to reject the older theories that some obscure brain defect or brain damage was the cause of "congenital word-blindness", as it was called, and he offered instead a physiological, functional explanation which carried with it a favorable prognosis. He saw in the reading disability a maturational deviation in language development which offered possibilities for specific remedial training and the relief of the emotional reactions in the children resulting from their anxiety and frustration. Noting especially their characteristic confusions in direction in their efforts to recall letters and words, he coined the term *strephosymbolia* (twisted symbols) to describe their difficulty.

Dr. Orton immediately envisaged in broad outlines a research program which was to extend far into future years and included: further investigation of the characteristic symptoms of the reading disability by controlled studies of larger numbers of children; experiments with teaching methods in harmony with neurological concepts—the therapeutic test; the extension of studies to related types of childhood language disabilities and apraxia, and underlying all, basic research in the physiology of the brain. Such a program was started the following year under his direction with a two-year grant from the Rockefeller Foundation (1926–1927) which also enabled the mobile mental hygiene clinics to continue. Comparative studies were made of the reading performance of a large sampling of normal and retarded readers from a variety of sources and a group with specific disability were successfully taught in a summer session at the hospital by his research associate in psychology, Miss Marion Monroe. Studies in stuttering were undertaken with Lee Edward Travis, Ph.D., a speech pathologist. Research in cerebral physiology was started on animals in his laboratories by a brain anatomist, with Dr. Lauretta Bender working on a correlated project in Holland. Lack of continuing research funds, however, prevented the fulfillment of this part of the program, to Dr. Orton's great disappointment, and together with certain issues over university policies, brought about his resignation from the hospital and the medical school in 1927.

The next twenty years of Dr. Orton's professional life were to follow quite a different course. Leaving the security of full-time hospital and medical school positions, he came to New York City in 1928 to open his own office for the practice of psychiatry. He was president-elect of the American Psychiatric Association in which he had long been active and he soon was given an appointment as neuropathologist at the New York Neurological Institute and a part-time professorship in neurology and neuropathology in the College of Physicians and Surgeons of Columbia University. Other responsibilities came with his election to the presidency of the American Association for Research in Nervous and Mental Disease in 1932 and continued editorial work on the *Archives of Neurology and Psychiatry* and the *Bulletin of the New York Neurological Institute,* which he was active in starting. But his interest in specific language difficulties persisted and in addition to seeing an increasing number of children with language and educational problems in his private practice, he was able to organize two more research programs, again with help from the Rockefeller Foundation.

The Language Research Project of the New York Neurological Institute was carried out under Dr. Orton's direction from 1932 to 1936, with a research associate in neurology the first year, Dr. Earl Chesher, and one in psychiatry, Dr. Paul Dozier, for the remaining time. A succession of assistants with training in various fields, mostly volunteers, made up of the rest of the staff, with help for several months from Dr. Edwin Cole, a Boston neurologist. Diagnostic and treatment procedures were developed and tested with large numbers of children,

xvii

and some adults, who presented a variety of language problems—reading, spelling, handwriting, auditory comprehension, speech development, stuttering, and certain language disorders associated with brain injuries. Although lack of funds and lack of space brought this project also to an untimely end, the knowledge acquired about language disabilities was widely disseminated through those who had participated in its program, developing in different ways in different places. Miss Anna Gillingham continued to consult with Dr. Orton on prediction and prevention experiments, and some ten years later she formulated her manual on remedial training with Miss Bessie Stillman. This she afterwards developed as the "alphabetic method" of teaching all beginning readers.

Dr. Orton's third research program, financed by the Rockefeller Foundation from 1939 to 1944, was directed toward further investigations of children with special difficulty in learning motor skills, and involved slow-motion pictures and other studies of apraxia, carried out by Dr. David Wright at a boys' school in Connecticut. But this program was interrupted midstream by World War II. Dr. Orton's medical assistants went into military service and could not be replaced. He then transferred his research program to the Institute of the Pennsylvania Hospital in Philadelphia, making weekly visits there throughout the difficult winter of 1943–1944. One of the few gains from the wartime displacements was the coming of Katrina de Hirsch from England to New York City, where Dr. Orton found her experience with aphasic patients and her insights into the developmental language disorders of children a most welcome contribution to the field.

Dr. Orton once commented: "The physician brings to his task a feeling of personal responsibility to the patient indelibly impressed upon him as part of the heritage of medicine." (American Psychiatric Association presidential address, 1929.) This quality was outstanding in all of his work with the language disability children, together with his doctor's insistence upon a thorough individual diagnostic study before making any recommendations for treatment. A great deal of his time was devoted to conferences with parents and tutors and he worked incessantly to seek out and develop new resources to meet the educational needs of his patients, in schools and camps, in kindergartens and colleges. He gave talks to school faculties and parent-teacher groups, lectures to speech classes, courses for tutors and teachers, and seminars for the former members of his research staff, in addition to addressing many medical meetings in neighboring cities and states. Although he always declared himself unqualified to discuss general educational procedures for the average child, he did not hesitate to speak with authority about the responsibility of the educators as well as the doctors for "these certain children with certain developmental language disorders'' and his very detailed, practical recommendations in written reports, conferences, and follow-up studies earned their respect and appreciation as he repeatedly demonstrated how the medical and the educational specialist could work profitably together for the benefit of the child. He also kept careful medical records with special attention to family histories on the 2000 or so private patients whom he saw during his twenty years in New York.

Most of Dr. Orton's talks were given from notes, often illustrated with lantern slides, and were not recorded, but some were transcribed in the proceedings of medical meetings or published in professional journals which provided reprints. These were useful in furnishing information about the language disabilities to his many correspondents from all over the United States and abroad and constitute the bulk of this present collection of his papers. When urged to write a book on language problems, Dr. Orton would always protest that he did not know enough about the subject yet, sometimes adding wryly, ''Let my students do it.'' The book came about inadvertently, however, with the Thomas W. Salmon Memorial Lectureship award in 1936. This entailed Dr. Orton's giving three consecutive lectures at the New York Academy of Medicine which were then printed by the lecture committee as a book of three chapters under the title, *Reading, Writing and Speech Problems in Children* (W. W. Norton & Co., Inc., New York, 1937).

Dr. Orton was married twice. His first wife, Mary Follett Orton, died in 1926, leaving him with three children: Samuel Torrey Orton, Jr. and Sarah Patterson Orton, twins, and Mary Follett Orton. He was married to June Frances Lyday of Detroit, Michigan, in 1928, at the beginning of his New York work in which she was thenceforth associated.

On the first of October, 1948, Dr. Orton announced his retirement from active practice, with anticipation of completing his country home, ''Hwimsy'', which he had enjoyed planning and building over a period of years. But during a visit there the very next day he suffered a fall, resulting in a broken hip and subsequent kidney and other complications. He was taken to St. Francis' Hospital in Poughkeepsie, New York, where he died six weeks later, on November 17, at the age of sixty-nine. Burial was in Columbus, Ohio, the place of his birth.

At a memorial dinner for Dr. Orton in New York City a year later, The Orton Society was founded by a group of his former associates and was dedicated to carrying forward the work for children with specific language disabilities in his scientific and humanitarian spirit.

REFERENCES

NATIONAL CYCLOPEDIA OF AMERICAN BIOGRAPHY. James T. White and Co., New York, 1930.

Orton, Edward, LL.D. *AN ACCOUNT OF THE DESCENDANTS OF THOMAS ORTON OF WINDSOR, CONNECTICUT, 1641. Columbus, Ohio, 1896.*

Orton, Samuel T., M.D. *The Philosophy of Psychiatry in PSYCHIATRY AND THE WAR, Ed. Frank J. Sladen, M.D., Charles C. Thomas, Springfield, Ill., 1943.*

Ross, Ishbel. *AN AMERICAN FAMILY, THE TAFTS. World Publishing Co., Cleveland, Ohio, 1964.*

WHO WAS WHO IN AMERICA, Vol. 2, p. 406. The A. N. Marquis Co., Chicago, Ill., 1950.

PART 1

◇——————————————◇

*Reading, Writing,
And Speech Problems*

FOREWORD

The commanding position which Dr. Thomas W. Salmon made for himself in American psychiatry both during the war and in the years that followed in his professorship at Columbia imposes a responsibility of no mean magnitude on the recipient of the lectureship created in his honor and in his memory. Nor is this obligation in any way lessened by the outstanding place occupied by those who have given the first three of these memorial lectures.

In the present volume the writer offers a necessarily condensed summary of the findings of a ten-year period of intensive study of some disorders in the acquisition of the language faculty encountered by certain children, as interpreted from a much longer period of interest and study from the literature, in the clinic, at the autopsy table and in the laboratory, of cerebral localization and of the aphasias. The work with children was begun as an outgrowth of an experiment with a mobile Mental Hygiene Unit organized and sent into the field under the writer's direction by the Iowa State Psychopathic Hospital in 1925, and was extended there for a time under a generous grant from the Rockefeller Foundation. From 1930 to 1936 it was continued as the Language Research Project of the New York Neurological Institute, again with aid, during the lean years, from the Rockefeller Foundation.

These last six years of observation and experiment have broadened our experience with diagnostic methods, have served to control the efficacy of training techniques, and have extended therapeutic aid to several hundred children suffering from language delays and disorders. An epitome of the yield of the whole ten-year period is here presented for the first time.

Since any disorder in the normal acquisition of spoken or written language serves as a severe hindrance to academic advancement and often also lies at the root of serious emotional disturbances, the studies here recorded may prove of interest to teachers and parents as well as to physicians, and therefore this presentation has been simplified in so far as its content would permit. The inclusion of some technical words has, however, seemed unavoidable, and for this reason a brief glossary of such words has been appended.

3

INTRODUCTION

Man's dominant position in the animal world rests largely if not entirely on his possession of two facilities: first, his ability to make use of sounds, markings and gestures for the purpose of communicating with others of his kind and as a background for his own ideation and, second, the very high degree of skill which he has developed in the use of his hands since they were freed from the duties of support and locomotion by the abandonment of the arboreal habit and adoption of the erect posture.

In most of the simpler functions of the nervous system man seems to be definitely inferior to some one or another of his animal competitors. Mention need only be made here of the superiority of most mammals in the sense of smell, of the strikingly greater acuity of vision possessed by the soaring birds of prey by virtue of their second macula, of the exquisite vibratory sense of many fish, and of the fact that certain insects—notably the honeybee—are capable of responding to light waves in the ultra-violet which are well beyond the range of human vision. It is therefore of arresting interest to note that in the two faculties whence man's superiority derives—speech and manual dexterity—a highly novel physiological pattern has been evolved in the brain whereby the functional control of these faculties is restricted sharply to one of the two cerebral hemispheres—a plan of activity in sharp contrast to that existing in the lower functional units of the central nervous system where exact bilateral symmetry is the rule.

That the higher animals other than man possess a means of communicating with each other is obvious, but the content of such communication is limited strictly to the transfer from one to another of the feeling tone of the moment. Considerable confusion has arisen in discussions of animal "language" because of failure clearly to recognize this limitation. Thus the emotional state of the animal is expressed in the sounds which it emits or the bodily postures which it exhibits and one who is well acquainted with his dog, for example, can tell by either the bark or the postures whether it be excited or angry or forlorn.

5

Nor has man lost this facility of communicating feeling tones. Indeed in early infancy this "animal language" is his only equipment and almost from the beginning the baby shows a high degree of the capacity to react in harmony to the emotional state of his mother or his nurse and is able also to give expression to many types of his own feelings so accurately that the experienced mother can very often tell from the sound of the child's cry alone whether he be hungry or frightened or in pain. Volume, pitch, and timbre of the voice, the occurrence of vibrato and a wide range of associated movements of the face and body all play their part in this emotional expression which is never entirely lost from human speech, although the extent to which it is exhibited varies markedly with the individual, with race, and with training. As might be expected from its long phylogenetic ancestry this form of expression which depicts the feelings has become very deeply rooted in the nervous system and may today be characterized as subserved by an instinctive or reflex mechanism which requires no training. Cannon and his co-workers have demonstrated that, in the cat, centers which are capable of controlling emotional expression are to be found in the thalamic region which is a part of the nervous system far older phylogenetically than is the true brain. Emotional expression is well developed in earliest infancy while the cortex is still extremely immature, as well as in cases of very marked defect in the development of the brain. Indeed certain rare cases of deformity in which a child is born without any brain whatsoever (anencephalic monsters) have been able to cry and to exhibit the appropriate accompanying facial expression. Conversely, emotional expression is usually retained late in the dementias and is often to be seen preserved in full vigor in extensive aphasic syndromes.

In man, however, in contrast to all other animals, another form of communication has evolved and it is this which primarily interests us here. This is symbolic language, in which a sign or a series of sounds has come to serve as a substitute for an object or a concept and can thus be used as a means of transferring ideas rather than mere feeling tone to a second individual. As mentioned above, that fraction of our language which deals with emotional expression is instinctive and requires no instruction, but it is obvious that if symbolic language is to carry meaning between two individuals they must both learn to associate the same symbol with the same object or idea, and thus it is that we find this form of language always dependent upon training. The acquisition of verbal language understanding and response by the normal child is such a gradual and effortless process that it is sometimes difficult to appreciate that this is a result of specific teaching until we remember that the child learns the language, be it English, French or German, to which he is exposed, while his emotional expressions are so independent of teaching as to be universally understandable.

Communication of meaning may be accomplished by spoken sounds, by written or printed characters, or by symbolic gestures, and thus we may delineate the language faculty as the capacity to understand the spoken word and to reproduce it verbally, the capacity to understand the written word and to reproduce it, and, less commonly used, the ability to understand and to reproduce gestures which carry specific meaning as in the sign language.

As already mentioned, that part of the language faculty which deals with the emotional moment probably has a very long phylogenetic history extending well back into the animal series. As measured by this, symbolic language is without doubt a relatively recent acquisition although it still is of an age to command respect. We know nothing with security about the time of development of speech or of sign language, but the earliest known fossil skulls of man give evidence of a brain development which would have been sufficient for such needs and man as far back as we can trace him already knew how to fashion crude weapons, so we may assume that the skills needed for symbolic gestures were already at hand and Sir Richard Paget has offered an interesting thesis that the sign language was the first form of symbolic language to be developed and that spoken language was largely an outgrowth therefrom. Studies of the brain case in fossil man show not only that his brain was greatly enlarged in size over that of the anthropoids but that this expansion had taken place in the frontal and parietal lobes which include all the critical areas which subserve both spoken and written language in modern man. The exact age of these examples of fossil man cannot of course be determined, but they probably extend back at least a half a million years. Sign language was extensively used by the American Indian for intercommunication between tribes who had a large number of different dialects, but in most races which have developed a spoken language it has undergone degeneration almost to the vanishing point if, as Paget believes, it was the origin of the spoken form. In contrast to the probable great age of spoken language, and possibly also of sign language as well, written language is probably only a few thousand years old.

The development of speech in the child is generally believed to go through several stages. The first of these is the lal or babbling period during which the infant produces many vowel sounds usually linked with a consonant and often with the same consonant repeated after the vowel. Labial consonants predominate and pure linguals are less frequent. The second stage is that of echolalia or echo speech which is characterized by an immediate repetition of words heard but without any understanding of their meaning and without the ability to reproduce them except as an echo. Usually the period in which the echo speech is used exclusively by the child is quite short and any considerable elongation of this period is apt to be indicative of a delay in the maturation of the higher form of speech although a minor degree of echoing may persist for some time along with the beginnings of real speech. Clearly this ability to echo even quite complex word sounds is still a very lowly form of integration of the motor speech mechanism with the auditory centers since no association is built with meaning. Its interest for us lies in the fact that it is often stated that comprehension of the word, that is lalognosis, precedes its reproduction. Obviously this is not true of echolalia as quite a range of complicated motor patterns are involved in the echo process long before any recognition of their symbolic meaning occurs. This question as to whether the understanding of words precedes the development of speech need not detain us here, however, as it is quite evident that children follow no general rule in this regard since we see in childhood—and indeed in adult life also—individuals with poor word memory and paucity both of understanding and of speech, others with good understanding but poor expression, and finally those with a quick ear for words and a facile tongue for their repetition but with very little comprehension. In some children the understanding of the spoken word clearly precedes the development of their speech; in others the reverse is apparently true.

As we have stated, the infant's instinctive or reflex capacity to communicate its emotional states is present from the beginning of its independent life but gradually there is evolved an association of certain word sounds with objects of the environment and as this symbolic speech increases, the child's dependence on emotional expression is reciprocally reduced. The character and efficiency of the training methods employed at this point are a cardinal factor in the degree with which the emotional expression will be inhibited, but other variables also enter here. Thus the child who is delayed in his development of verbal symbolism will continue to use, over a longer period and to a greater extent, his emotional expression and naturally demands and receives a greater share of maternal protection than he would were he better able to understand commands and express his desires. Many such obvious psychological factors—especially those affecting emotional maturation—as well as many environmental influences play an important role in the development of language, but even after making abundant allowance for all such variations it is apparent to the critical observer that there are striking inherent or constitutional differences in certain children, apart from those of general intelligence, which markedly influence their acquisition of the language function, and it is toward the better understanding of these differences and of their most satisfactory treatment that the studies which are reported in this volume were directed.

We are all familiar with the progress from the echo period to the use, first, of nouns, then verbs, and later sentences, and the gradual lengthening of the sequences of words and phrases which characterize development at this period. In the average child this increasing familiarity with the spoken word both for understanding and response forms the only development in his language function during the first six years of his life. By the time he has reached school age it has been estimated that the normal child has an understanding vocabulary of several thousand words. This forms the foundation on which he must begin, at the age of six or thereabouts, to erect an entirely new form of language—reading and writing—if he is to take his place in the literate world. In the occasional very precocious child, reading and writing can be taught much before the age of six, but taking our school population at large, attempts at teaching graphic language before this age are unprofitable and it seems probable that it is this fact which has determined the age of six for an introduction to formal academic training. It may therefore be pertinent to inquire whether the cortices of the angular gyrus region have reached a sufficient anatomical or physiological maturity before this period to make reading and writing practicable. If this should prove to be the explanation it would constitute an interesting ontogenetic parallel with the relative age of spoken and written languages.

◆   ◆   ◆

CHAPTER ONE

LANGUAGE LOSSES IN THE ADULT AS THE KEY TO THE DEVELOPMENTAL DISORDERS IN CHILDREN

Most of our knowledge of the cerebral physiology of the language faculty is derived from studies of the symptoms which follow injury or disease of the brain in the adult. Thus the extent and character of a disturbance in speech, in reading or in writing which follows damage to the brain may be studied and after the patient's death the brain may be removed and carefully dissected to determine just what parts of it have suffered injury. Such an approach of necessity limits our investigations to the slow accretion of facts gathered by many investigators and over a long period of time and is obviously much less precise than the direct experimental attack which is possible in many fields of medicine. Moreover, it is beset with many inherent difficulties. Neither injury nor disease is apt to be limited by anatomical boundaries, and in both the damage to the brain is very prone to overlap two or more areas of the brain which have quite different functions and hence to lead to confusion in interpretation. One of the commonest causes of such partial brain destruction is the blocking of an artery with consequent starvation and death of the nerve cells and fibers in the area which it fed, and since there are few arteries of any considerable size in the brain which do not serve more than one functional brain area, the effect of such vascular disease is usually complex. Moreover, the majority of the vascular accidents which lead to blocking of an artery are the result of arteriosclerosis which is a diffuse process involving many arteries so that more than one area of damage is very often found in such cases. Again, arteriosclerosis of the brain vessels is a slowly progressive disease and new areas of destruction and new resultant symptoms may occur and interfere seriously with interpretation unless the studies of the patient's speech have been made shortly before his death.

A second common cause of brain damage is by the growth of a brain tumor, and here the results are apt to be even more confusing because the damage is produced in part at least through the pressure exerted by the growing tumor, and such pressure effects may be transferred to other parts of the brain than those where the tumor is growing and hence give rise to misleading or confusing symptoms. Direct injuries of the brain through wounds which break or penetrate the skull are sometimes circumscribed but not uncommonly they also spread over areas of the brain which have two or more functions. Not infrequently we see transient disturbances in speech or reading occurring in patients with high blood pressure which are probably due to a spasm of a small artery. These attacks which are commonly described as a threatened stroke are, in the writer's experience, very apt to be highly selective in the sense that they disturb only one fraction of the language faculty but they do not as a rule result in permanent damage to the brain cells so that the exact locus of the brain areas involved cannot be established with certainty if an autopsy should be performed later.

In recent years, as brain surgery has advanced, operations for the excision of malignant brain tumors have often included removal of large parts of brain substance adjacent to the tumor and careful studies of the symptoms shown by these patients after operation are opening a new avenue of information. Unfortunately here again it is often very difficult to be sure of just how much of the brain substance has been removed, since a tumor—particularly a slowly growing one—may often cause marked pressure displacement of brain substance without interfering seriously with its function and it is therefore at times impossible to determine whether a given area has been removed or had been crowded aside before the operation.

Animal experiments are of no value in this problem since even the highest of the apes lack the very functions and to a large extent the brain areas in which we are interested and, moreover, it is a well established fact that the physiological activities of the brain of one phylum cannot be used for interpretation of those of another. Many observations point to the fact that there is a progressive concentration of functional control in the true brain as the animal scale is ascended and that some functions which in man are exclusively resident in the brain cortex, in some of the animals are partly at least governed by lower nerve centers. In man's brain, for example, the optic thalami—two large collections of nerve cells lying at the base of the true brain—have been reduced as far as vision is concerned to nerve relay stations between the eyes and the cortex, and will not serve for vision, whereas in the dog—an animal relatively high in the scale—experiments have been recorded indicating that the thalami will serve to discriminate between light and dark, and in birds and reptiles almost all of vision is controlled by these structures and very little by the brain cortex. A comparable situation is to be seen in control of motion. In man, destruction of the brain cortex of the motor area causes a complete and permanent paralysis of voluntary movement of the corresponding muscles; in the anthropoids a minor amount of recovery of voluntary motion takes place after destruction of the motor cortex, while in the lower monkeys recovery after such destruction is practically complete. Failure to understand that the brain of man is, except in name, not the same functional organ as that of the lower animals has led to much loose thinking and many futile attempts to discuss human brain physiology on the basis of findings in the white rat or other experimental animal.

Still another obstacle to the study of the cerebral physiology of language arises from the fact that in the normal adult the various functions which make up the language faculty—speaking, reading, writing, etc.—are so closely interlinked both in learning and by usage that any interference with one seems prone to cause disturbance of others. Thus, loss of the capacity to read, for example, without some degradation of speech is exceedingly rare. It is probable that a large individual variation enters here also and that those who have been extensive readers and have stocked their vocabulary largely through this route would show a different degree of speech disorder resulting from a loss of reading than would those who have learned words chiefly by ear. Such factors cannot at present be evaluated but the element of a common approach to words through both vision and hearing would not appear, of course, in the congenitally deaf or congenitally blind and studies of disturbances in symbolization comparable to the aphasias in such cases should prove progressively informative.

A close cooperation between the clinic and the laboratory is essential to progress here. All too often reports are to be found in the literature of cases excellently studied from the clinical standpoint but with exceedingly inadequate anatomical reports, and again we see extensive anatomical studies carried out on cases with a very meager clinical background. Both approaches are arduous and time-consuming and rarely indeed does the busy practicing clinician have the time and opportunity to study these cases with the care that must be given them if they are to be made to give their greatest yield, and this applies with almost equal force to the laboratory investigations where really thorough studies of one case from the localizing standpoint require a major time allotment both by technicians and microscopist. The greatest promise for progress in this complex field of research would seem to rest in especially created and endowed institutes for brain study such as are already to be found in several European centers.

Because of difficulties of investigation such as those mentioned above, the problem of disorders in the language function in the adult is far from being a completed study, but an enormous amount of medical literature has nevertheless accrued during the last seventy-five years and from this and from the writer's own experience in the clinic and laboratory we may select some facts which are believed to be of importance in understanding the obstacles which are encountered by certain children in gaining a normal mastery of spoken and written language.

The first of these is that the locus of an area of brain destruction is of much greater import in determining a language disorder than is the amount of brain tissue destroyed. Thus a very small area of damage in the angular gyrus region may result in a complete loss of the ability to read and write and a marked disturbance in speech as well, while a much greater destruction of tissue in, for example, the frontal region of the brain may give no demonstrable disorder in language. Moreover, when we consider certain critical loci there is no direct relationship between the amount of tissue destroyed and the gravity of the symptoms, as a small lesion in the angular gyrus may give as widespread a language disorder as that which follows one twice its size. Clearly this does not harmonize with the older views of strict cerebral localization of functions, which held that the angular gyrus and its neighboring brain convolutions serve as the storehouse for the visual memory of words. The discrepancy sometimes found here between the small volume of tissue destruction and the extensive loss of function points clearly to the conclusion that we are dealing with a disturbance of cerebral physiology rather than a destruction of areas of registration. Again these facts are clearly out of harmony with Lashley's unfortunate misinterpretation of his earlier experimental material which led him to advance the thesis that the volume of brain tissue destroyed is of more significance than the area involved.

UNILATERAL CEREBRAL DOMINANCE

A second interesting fact and one which seems to be of major meaning to us in understanding the language disorders of children is that one side of the brain is all important in the language process and the other side either useless or unused. So striking is this that we know that a very small area of destruction in an appropriate area of the controlling or dominant hemisphere of the brain will give rise to extensive loss in speech or reading while an equal area of destruction in exactly the same part of the nondominant or subjugate hemisphere will be followed by no language disorder whatsoever and indeed will often give no recognizable symptoms. This concentration of the whole control of speech, reading and writing in one half of the brain bears an intimate relation to the development of unilateral manual skill in the individual and is the unique physiological pattern mentioned earlier in this volume as the special attribute of those faculties which have done most to give man his commanding position in the animal world. Many of the higher animals show traces of a preferential use of one side of the body. For example, a dog may consistently use the same paw for scratching at a door or a cat may always choose the same paw in reaching through the bars of its cage for food and a race horse when starting to run will quite consistently lead with the same foot. In all of these examples, however, the responses are so simple that the contralateral pattern may easily be substituted and indeed often is if the conditions preceding the act be slightly altered. It would be interesting to know whether any differential effect of right- or left-sided brain lesions could be demonstrated on the much more complicated behavior patterns which could be taught to the higher primates, but so far as the writer is aware no such experiments have been recorded and the weight of current evidence is that the animals below man do not exhibit that unilateral cerebral dominance which forms the hallmark of the language faculty.

In considering this striking fact of the functional supremacy of one brain hemisphere, however, it is essential that we bear in mind not only that it is clearly demonstrable only in man but that even in man it is only in the language faculty and the more intricate manual skills that this specialization is to be found and that, for many of the simpler activities of the brain, the relation of the two hemispheres to each other, while a variable one, is quite different from that underlying speech, reading and writing. Thus the two hemispheres operate quite independently of each other in the control of motion so that damage to the brain cortex of the motor area will regularly give rise to a paralysis of voluntary motion on the opposite side of the body only and destruction of similar areas of both hemispheres would be necessary to completely destroy this function. This is also true of that part of the sensations of pain, touch, temperature and kinaesthesis which reaches the brain cortex and which informs us as to the place of origin on the body of these sensations. In vision the situation is somewhat complex due to the fact that the human eye is equipped with two seeing mechanisms—one for quick scanning vision of a broad field and one for more accurate intake of detail in a much narrower range. The first of these— the peripheral retinal field—is organized like the motor centers as a crossed but independent mechanism so that damage in one hemisphere results in a loss of vision on the opposite side and the patient can no longer see ''out of the corner of his eye'' in that direction. This is the condition known technically as hemianopsia. In the second visual apparatus—central or macular vision—which gives us the finer detail of things seen and most of our ability to distinguish colors, the two hemispheres seem to work as a unit so that the stimuli received by either eye are fused into a single impression as shown by Sherrington's classical flicker experiments with binocular vision. In the matter of hearing, our information is not quite so precise as it is in vision, but the general opinion is that here, as in central vision, either of the two hemispheres may serve interchangeably with each other. When those parts of the brain cortex which serve as the terminus of nerve paths from the eyes and ears—the so-called arrival platforms—have been destroyed in both hemispheres of the brain, we encounter the conditions known as cortical blindness and cortical deafness, respectively, in which no conscious vision or audition is possible although the eyes and ears are normal.

These lowest anatomical centers, as so far described, are however only the first step in the brain's use of visual and auditory data, and studies of cases with differently placed brain injuries show us that it is possible for a patient to see and hear and yet to be unable to understand the meaning of objects seen or sounds heard. These conditions are those which are called visual and auditory agnosia and the patients are said to be suffering from mind blindness or mind deafness.

The capacity to comprehend the meaning or purpose of objects seen and to understand the various sounds of the environment is usually retained, however, in patients who have lost the capacity to read or to understand the spoken word, and thus we see that there are three steps or levels in the degree of physiological complexity with which the brain makes use of incoming data represented in vision by, respectively, 1st, cortical blindness—in which there is no conscious vision; 2nd, mind blindness—in which the patient can see so that he does not collide with things in moving about but is quite unable to recall the purpose or use of the objects seen; and 3rd, word blindness—in which there is no loss of vision or of the capacity to recognize and interpret objects, pictures, etc., but in which the printed word no longer brings its meaning. The comparable conditions in the field of hearing are cortical deafness, mind deafness and word deafness. Destruction of the appropriate cortex area in both hemispheres is necessary before cortical blindness or cortical deafness occurs, and while there is some difference of opinion among investigators here, the majority of students of this problem believe that bilateral destruction is necessary at the second level also before mind blindness and mind deafness result; but all neurologists are agreed that a lesion in one brain hemisphere—providing it be the dominant—is sufficient to cause the disorders of spoken and written language.

Studies of the comparative anatomy of the brain have demonstrated that the striking enlargement which has taken place in man's brain when compared to that of the highest animals is not merely a general increase in total brain volume but is a disproportionate expansion of the third level type of cortex in which are to be found those areas whose integrity is essential for the proper functioning of the language faculty. In the brain of the monkey, the cortex devoted to the first level of vision covers a much larger relative area than it does in the human brain and the cortices of the second and third level are comparatively restricted. Figure 1 is a conventionalized drawing of the two sides of the left hemisphere of a human brain showing the major anatomical subdivisions or lobes. The occipital lobe serves vision exclusively. The temporal lobe is largely auditory although some parts of it probably subserve smell as well. The parietal lobe serves for the reception, registration and elaboration of the senses of touch, pain and temperature and of muscle, tendon and joint sense (kinaesthesis). The functions of the frontal lobe are not completely understood but it contains all of the mechanisms for the elaboration and control of voluntary movements. Certain higher mental attributes have been assigned to this region by various authors but as a whole it may be loosely considered as primarily the executive division of the brain. The limbic lobe has to do with smell and taste and possibly certain of the sensations arising within the body. The parts of the human brain which have undergone the greatest relative expansion as compared to that of the highest primates are the frontal lobe and that area in which the parietal, occipital and temporal lobes meet.

While the separation of the sensory functions into three stages or levels of elaboration, as given above, rests primarily on the study of the symptoms resulting from brain disease or injury, it also receives support from microscopic studies of the brain cortex, which reveal differences in the size, number and arrangement of the nerve cells and fibers by which the brain areas subserving these various steps can be distinguished from one another, or to express this in another way, the brain shows structural as well as functional differentiation of these three levels. Figure 2 shows the distribution of the three types of cortex from the structural standpoint which are to be found in the occipital pole or visual area of the brain. The first area—V-1—is known as the area striata because of the presence of a white band of nerve fibers which is so prominent that the confines of this type of cortex can be readily determined by the naked eye. Surrounding this is the "common occipital" cortex—V-2—which grades off with less sharp demarcation into the third or parietooccipital type—V-3.

Another striking confirmation of the existence of the three steps in brain function comes from studies of maturation or ripening of the brain cortex. In the embryo and infant, before a given brain has matured, the nerve fibers lack the fat-like sheath or insulation which is later deposited around them. This fatty sheath is called myelin and the ripening process is spoken of as myelinization of the fibers. The myelin

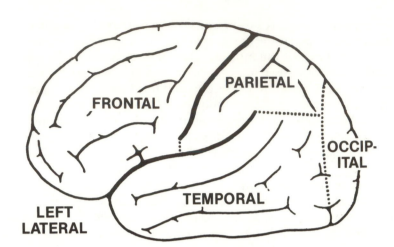

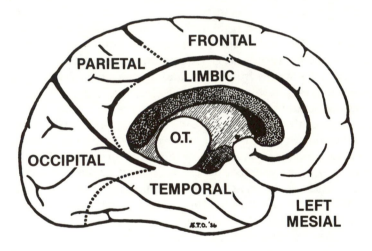

Figure 1. A conventionalized map of the outer (lateral) and inner (mesial) surfaces of the left hemisphere of the human brain showing the location of its major subdivisions or lobes.

sheaths can be readily stained by appropriate methods and thus the progress of the ripening process can be followed by studies of a series of brains from embryos, stillborn children, and infants. Flechsig applied this method and found that maturation proceeds in three distinct waves covering, in separate stages, those areas of the brain cortex whose destruction leads to the three syndromes of cortical blindness, mind blindness and word blindness and the comparable conditions in audition. Flechsig demonstrated that at the time of birth only the "arrival

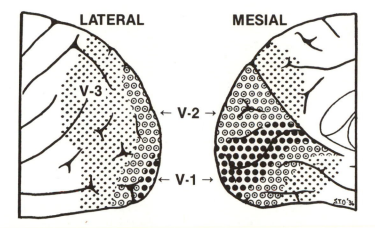

Figure 2. An outline map of the lateral and mesial surfaces of the occipital region of the left hemisphere of a human brain showing the distribution of the three chief types of visual cortex.

platforms'' or first level cortices have received their myelin, that a second period of myelinization follows during the first two or three months after birth which results in the ripening of a second zone of cortex lying near by each arrival platform and that only during the final or third wave does maturation occur in the areas of the third level.

I have emphasized this dissection of the cerebral functions into steps because it offers us some understanding of how a selective loss of reading, for example, in the adult or a selective retardation in learning to read in a child may occur with full visual competence in other regards and thus focuses our attention on the specific and peculiar physiological pattern by which reading and the other language functions are governed.

THE APHASIAS

The term aphasia is one which has undergone considerable change in its scope, and hence a brief outline of its various meanings may be of value to the reader. Unfortunately, the lay press has very widely confused it with amnesia, meaning loss of memory—a very different sort of condition and, of course, an indefensible error. Even in the medical literature, however, there is considerable latitude in the use of the word—aphasia. It is a coined word which by derivation means loss of speech and some dictionaries still confine it to this narrow meaning. In the earlier medical literature it was expanded to cover not only loss of ability to speak but loss of the ability to understand the spoken word, although often these two conditions were differentiated by the use of the qualifying adjectives, motor and sensory, respectively. Because, presumably, of the very close interlinking of the various fractions of the language faculty, a still wider expansion of its meaning has since occurred so that many medical writers of today use it as a broad general term to cover all losses in the use of language including reading and writing as well as speaking and understanding speech. This is quite generally the use which is implied when the word is found in the plural as "the aphasias," while its use in the singular form, generally though not consistently, indicates a restriction of its meaning to the field of spoken language.

There are certain of the syndromes which occur in the broad general group of the aphasias which interest us specifically here because of the close similarity in the symptoms which they show to those exhibited by certain children who suffer from delays or disabilities in acquisition of language. In presenting these syndromes it must be borne in mind that they can be described here only in skeleton form and, moreover, that due to the overlapping of lesions and the interdependence of functions, *pure* cases of these conditions are exceedingly rare if indeed they occur at all in the adult, so that the descriptions given here must be considered somewhat of an abstraction. Again, while we no longer adhere to the strict "pigeonholing" of a function in a given brain area which characterized the earlier studies of the aphasias, but today think in terms of a much wider interplay of various parts of the brain, nevertheless we do recognize that given areas of the cortex may play a predominant part in language understanding and expression and that damage to such an area in the dominant hemisphere will disturb the physiological process underlying a particular fraction of the language process to a much greater extent than it does that of the associated fractions. In this sense, localization of areas critical for different parts of the language function is therefore not only possible but serviceable and from this viewpoint such areas will be nominated with each syndrome discussed.

1. Alexia (Word Blindness)

The first of these syndromes to be reviewed is that of alexia or acquired word blindness. In this condition an individual who has previously been able to read and to write may suddenly lose both of these skills due to damage to the brain, providing that damage occurs in exactly the right locus and in the controlling or dominant hemisphere. The term "word blindness" is to some degree misleading since the individual who has suffered such a loss can still see the word but the grasp at sight of the meaning of the word is gone. Because of the location of the critical area whose destruction results in word blindness or alexia, there is very commonly a hemianopsia or loss of one half of the peripheral or scanning vision. This is not always true, however, and even in those cases in which it exists, central or macular vision which is predominantly used for reading is intact and all other functions of vision except the recognition of words at sight are unaffected. Thus there is no loss in the ability to recognize the meaning and implications of objects, pictures, diagrams, etc., other than words. In brief, word blindness consists in a very highly selective loss of the capacity to recognize at a glance constellations of printed or written letters which before the injury carried with them a specific meaning. Most cases of word blindness can read the individual letters of the word and an occasional patient, by reading each letter aloud and recalling what that sequence of letters spells, may be able to identify some words, but looking at the word as a whole brings no prompt understanding of its meaning. It is not uncommon to find that the patient suffering from word blindness cannot write but yet has not lost his skill in handwriting. The apparent paradox of this statement disappears when we learn that the patient cannot produce anything of his own composition in writing, but has in no way lost his mastery of the writing act since he can copy with ease from the production of another. Such a copy can be made from either script or print and will be produced without hesitation or tremulousness and will conform in all its individual characteristics to the writing of the patient before the brain injury occurred. The outline of alexia as here given is that of a severe case, but many partial or less severe cases are encountered, and even in the severe cases some measure of spontaneous recovery or improvement under appropriate methods of retraining may occur so that a wide range of variation in the degree of the degradation of the reading function may be observed, and some of these are instructive for our purpose. One such variant is that of the individual who can recognize many words at sight and yet has a striking defect in perception of minor differences in form, so that prefixes and suffixes tend to be disregarded or misread. Such patients also have a tendency to omit entirely all the shorter words so that the sentences as read are devoid of conjunctions, articles, prepositions, etc. Other cases may be able to read not only all the letters in a word but can recognize at sight, as an isolated unit, practically every word of moderately difficult material but have great difficulty in grasping the meaning of the sequence of words which constitute the sentence or short paragraph, particularly if the sentences be long or their structure at all unusual.

Spelling as a rule is well-nigh impossible for the patient suffering from word blindness. Oral spelling is apt to be somewhat better retained than written, but large individual variations apparently enter here which may be due to the method by which a given patient was taught spelling originally. In one of the writer's cases the patient had learned to spell in boyhood almost exclusively by the oral method with much competitive recitation of the nature of "spelling bees" in school, and he had retained a considerable measure of this skill orally although his written efforts were crowded with errors in spelling and many of these were of such degree as to warrant the use of the term neographisms to describe the result.

While, as explained above, no area of the brain can be designated as the "center for reading" because of the complexity of the symptoms in every case of alexia, we can nevertheless nominate an area in the dominant hemisphere whose integrity is essential to maintaining a normal reading skill, and this critical area for this fraction of the language function is the angular gyrus and its immediate environs. (Fig. 3-1)

2. Auditory Aphasia (Word Deafness)

A second syndrome of the aphasias which is of particular interest to us is that of auditory aphasia or acquired word deafness. This, again, is a condition resulting from damage to the brain, but only if it affects the dominant hemisphere and is characterized by a loss of the ability to understand the spoken word in persons who have previously been competent in this regard. Acquired word deafness is a part of the somewhat broader syndrome of sensory aphasia and its existence as a pure or isolated condition is to be questioned. However, many sensory aphasics show a more or less complete loss of the ability to understand the speech of others although their hearing is intact. In such cases it is frequently possible to demonstrate by the audiometer that there is no loss either in acuity or range in the auditory function, and moreover a patient with complete loss of the understanding of words may still be able to interpret properly all other sounds of the environment such as the dinner bell, telephone ring, fire alarm, etc., and often apparently derives considerable pleasure from music. In the past there has been very little systematized testing of this stage of the auditory process and the opinion of most observers of aphasia cases as to the integrity of the function of understanding sounds rests on observations of the patient's reaction to casual noises of the environment. To meet the parallel need existing in the examination of the hearing function in children we devised, as a part of the Language Research Project of the New York Neurological Institute, a set of four phonograph records containing thirty-two commonly encountered sounds so that

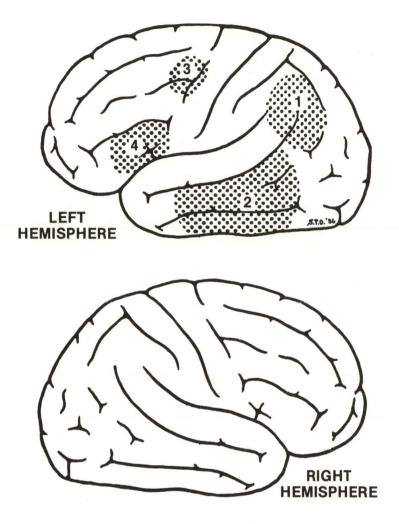

Figure 3. A map of the outer surfaces of the left and right hemispheres of a human brain showing the "critical" language areas. This diagram shows the conditions as they exist in a *right-handed* individual, with the critical areas for language in the left hemisphere only. The four areas are defined in the text.

a more methodical examination of the competence of this function may be made. As a natural corollary of the loss of recognition of spoken words we consistently find in the sensory aphasic a striking distortion in the ability to reproduce speech properly and a very wide range of errors in the words spoken, with frequent misuse of words or mutilations which may even result in a completely unintelligible gibberish—jargon aphasia. Many of these patients can echo words after the examiner although without understanding them, thus conforming with the ability of the cases of acquired word blindness to copy in writing what they cannot read.

The motor speech apparatus is intact in the patient with acquired word deafness and such cases are apt to be garrulous in spite of the fact that their efforts to express themselves rarely carry the desired meaning to their hearers. As these patients are completely cut off from the understanding of both their own speech and that of others and are almost equally handicapped in their expression of their thoughts and desires, it is almost impossible to determine how far the intelligence suffers, but most observers consider that there gradually ensues a true intellectual degradation or dementia although many skills and acquired adaptive reactions may be preserved. In acquired word deafness, as in its counterpart in the visual function which we have already discussed, we find many cases in which the symptoms are less severe than those described above and some of the more severe cases undergo some improvement, so that again here, as in alexia, we find an almost endless variation in the degree of the patient's handicap. In the word-deaf cases, in contrast to the situation found in true organic deafness, raising the voice is of no value. Slow speech delivery and clear enunciation are, however, of major aid to the patient, as is the presentation of ideas, questions and commands in simple grammatical form and in short sentences. Such patients are occasionally able to understand individual words quite well but will fail to follow the meaning when such words are combined into phrases or sentences, or they may grasp short simple sentences correctly but lose the thread when the sentences are longer or more complex grammatically. They can at times carry out each of a number of simple commands if given separately but will become confused if they are given a series of such things to do. With many aphasic patients especial trouble is encountered in using certain word categories as, for example, the pronouns or the prepositions, or they may have difficulty with the comparatives. With others the nouns may make the most trouble—nominal aphasia. Kleist has designated as paragrammatism the type of errors seen in one form of sensory aphasia which is characterized by confusion in the use and order of words and grammatical forms, and Head has called attention to the frequent slurring or complete elision of the smaller words such as articles or conjunctions.

The area of the brain which is accepted by practically all investigators as the critical area for the understanding of words and sentences occupies the second and third temporal gyri. (Fig. 3-2)

The two foregoing groups of the aphasias affect largely, as has been emphasized in their description, the receptive apparatus for words in the field of vision and audition respectively, and result primarily in a loss of the ability to recognize the printed or the spoken word, with secondary or resultant distortions of expression in writing or in speech. These are hence called sensory language disorders, but other losses may occur which lie predominantly or exclusively in executive or expressive control of graphic or verbal language, and these are spoken of as motor disorders of the language function. As with the sensory types, a lesion of the brain involving a single hemisphere is sufficient to cause the motor language losses, but only if that lesion involved the dominant hemisphere.

3. Motor Agraphia

Many authorities question the existence of pure motor agraphia, or loss of the ability to write restricted to the expressive or motor component of this function. Unquestionably part of this doubt rests on an anatomical basis since the critical area for writing is located within a fraction of an inch of the centers which control voluntary movement of the lower arm and hand and only a short distance from the motor speech areas, and few lesions are so circumscribed and so located as to involve the critical area for writing without causing some paralysis of the writing hand or some disturbance of speech or both. However we do see cases in which there is little or no disturbance of speech and in which the actual paralysis of the master hand is too little to account for the extensive loss of writing skill, and yet in which there is no loss in the sensory side of graphic language—that is, no disturbance in the ability to recognize words at sight and to read understandingly, and which can therefore be said to be predominantly cases of motor agraphia although complicated to some degree by a greater or less amount of actual paralysis. Because of the presence of some measure of loss of muscular strength in the hand it is difficult to determine how far skilled movements of the master hand other than writing are disorderd in these cases, but coarser movements of all sorts can be carried out without difficulty and there is some evidence to show that inability to write may be a very highly selective loss not accompanied by the loss of other skills of the hand. The patient with motor agraphia, in contrast to that form of writing disorder which accompanies acquired word blindness, cannot copy, and such letters as he produces in attempts at writing are tremulous and malformed. Oral spelling is not disturbed in cases of this type and one of the writer's patients was able to arrange the letters of the game "anagrams" with sufficient accuracy to indicate that there was no disturbance of his ability in graphic spelling.

The critical area in motor agraphia is described as occupying the posterior portions of the second frontal gyrus and probably parts of the adjacent cortex on the precentral gyrus. (Fig. 3-3)

4. Motor Aphasia

A second disorder of the motor or expressive mechanism of the language faculty is motor aphasia. This is more or less complete speechlessness but without disorder of the peripheral speech mechanism. Again, because of the close juxtaposition of the critical area for this function and those for writing and for control of voluntary motion of the face, arm and hand, cases of disorder in the motor control of speech are commonly complicated by loss of writing and more or less paralysis of the face and hand. When the paralysis involves the muscles used in the various speech acts, an additional element of difficulty in speaking is injected. Paralysis, however, either of the master hand or of the face is not always present in motor aphasia, and frequently it is fugacious and clears up entirely soon after the injury, leaving the motor aphasia more or less in isolation. In contrast to the speech disorder which accompanies a sensory aphasia there is no loss of understanding of the spoken word and while the patient in his efforts to speak often makes use of the wrong word he is usually instantly cognizant of his error and attempts a correction. Except in complicated cases due to extensive lesions there is no loss in reading skill. Writing is frequently lost, but when this is so the disorder is of the motor type and probably due to an involvement of adjacent cortical fields. The patient suffering from motor aphasia as a rule is rather quiet and shows none of the flow of unintelligible jargon which is so apt to mark the sensory aphasic. Echo speech is usually impossible but even in severe cases with almost complete loss of speech for purposeful expression there may be considerable retention of expletives, profanity and words which have come to be associated with the expression of emotion. As a rule, however, these words are produced only under the stimulus of emotional strain. Not infrequently the motor aphasic will retain a few speech sounds or a word or phrase which is produced at almost every attempt at expressive speech. Again, as in the other forms of language disorder, all degrees of the difficulty are to be observed in a series of cases of varying severity or as spontaneous or stimulated improvement occurs. In extreme cases even the speech sounds symbolized by individual letters are lost, but more commonly these sounds can be given as an echo to the examiner or can be called when the printed letter is exhibited, but the formation of words by the blending of such sounds is arduous or impossible. In still milder degrees of the disorder many words can be spoken but the construction of sentences is difficult or impossible. This is the condition which Kleist has called "sentence muteness" and the patient's product is apt to lack many connecting words, giving rise to what the French have called "telegram style" in speech and what the Germans describe as agrammatism.

There is general agreement among students of aphasia that the critical cortex for the motor control of speech is that of Broca's area which is the posterior end of the third frontal convolution. (Fig. 3-4)

5. Apraxia

One further syndrome which will be discussed very briefly here is that of apraxia, which is the loss of a previously acquired ability to carry out intricate skilled acts. As already mentioned, a high degree of manual dexterity is one of man's marks of superiority and, as is the case with the language function, it is so organized in the brain that a unilateral lesion of the dominant hemisphere may lead to a marked degradation in skill. In one of the writer's patients there was a complete loss of the previously acquired ability in the use of the typewriter by the sense of position of the various keys. The patient could still compose the material of a letter, could spell correctly and could hunt out by eye each individual letter on the keyboard and thus make use of the instrument, but her previously acquired and highly cultivated skill in finding the keys with all fingers and without search was gone.

The parietal lobe and particularly those parts of it lying just in front of the angular gyrus region are widely accepted as the critical area for apraxic disturbances. This area is not differentially marked in the illustration.

LATERALITY—(HANDEDNESS, EYEDNESS, ETC.)

In the adult the foregoing syndromes occur almost without exception only when the injury has occurred in that half of the brain which is opposite to the master hand. Indeed, except when a stroke has occurred or other symptoms point to the locus of the lesion, we have no guide whatsoever as to which is the dominant hemisphere except the "laterality" of the individual, that is, his handedness, eyedness and footedness.

The infant at birth starts with no unilateral superiority in control of either hand or language as far as we can determine. This is supported by the entire indifference with which a very young infant uses either hand and by Pierre Marie's observation that there is no greater incidence of speech disorder in children who have suffered a birth paralysis involving the right hand than when it involves the left. Marie inferred from this that neither the right nor the left hemisphere is exclusively predestined for control of speech at birth and that if one be damaged the other can take over complete control. Most children do, however, without much question, carry an hereditary tendency to develop the predominant use of either the right or the left hemisphere. This is borne out by genetic studies of the occurrence of handedness in families and by the persistent appearance of left-handed individuals in all races in spite of many generations of directive training and strong social pressures toward the right hand, and by the relative proportion of left- and right-handedness in the general population which conforms quite closely to that which would be expected if the tendency toward right-handedness serves as a dominant hereditable factor in the Mendelian sense.

Handedness, however, is so freely open to the influence of training that the resultant patterns which one finds are a combination of the hereditary bent and the effects of training. Both of these factors will vary in degree. We know today from experimental genetics that it is only when crossings of homozygous or pure stocks take place that the typical Mendelian segregation of opposite characters occurs. When crossings are not between pure stocks but rather include a long series of matings which are promiscuous so far as a given set of opposing characters is concerned, varying degrees of intermingling of these characters will occur which are technically known as "intergrades." Obviously the question of handedness has not entered into human matings in the past and we might therefore anticipate intermixtures between right- and left-sidedness which we call "motor intergrades."

Not only will the hereditary tendency toward use of the right or left hand vary with the degree of this process of intergrading, but the training which each such individual receives is also a highly variable factor. For the most part this tends to lead the individual toward the right hand, first, because the great majority of people are right-handed and naturally assume that their children are also going to be, and second, because there exists no inconsiderable amount of prejudice against left-handedness, which in many instances is so strong as to amount to the belief that the left-hander is abnormal. This prejudice is reflected in the derived meanings of the Latin word "sinister" and the French "gauche." There is certainly no justification for this belief and there is reason to believe that a high degree of specialization in either hemisphere makes for superiority and that the good left-hander is therefore not only not abnormal but is apt to be better equipped than is the indifferent right-hander. The rigor of training to which a left-handed child is exposed is also a great variable extending all the way from simple measures such as transferring the spoon from the left to the right hand while the child is learning to eat to more drastic procedures such as tying up the left hand so that the right must be used. It is rare indeed that training is exerted to produce a left-handed individual, but three cases have come to the writer's attention where this was true. One was an instance in which the mother herself became confused while facing the child across the table as to which was the child's right hand, and persistently insisted on the use of the spoon and other implements in the child's left hand. The other two were both boys who were trained from early childhood toward left-handedness by their fathers with the intent of developing them into baseball pitchers. Neither boy succeeded in acquiring a good left-handed pitching skill.

We will exclude from this discussion those cases in which disease or accident to the brain in childhood has brought about an early shift of the handedness pattern, since they form an exceptional group by reason of the fact that the integrity of the brain structure has been altered and the shift is usually to be looked upon as the result of a preferential use of the least damaged side of the brain. Accident to the hand or arm, however, or infantile paralysis, which does not involve the brain, not infrequently enforces a change in handedness which is quite comparable in its results to that brought about by enforced training, since there is here no change in the integrity of the brain mechanisms, and we have seen complications associated with shift of handedness so caused quite comparable to those which may follow efforts to change the natural handedness of a child by disciplinary and training methods.

STUDIES IN LATERALITY

While our whole knowledge of unilateral cerebral dominance rests on the study of the aphasias and subsequent investigation of the brain, yet, as suggested above, we are limited in our clinical studies of children to observations of the laterality of the child, and these have been found to be much less easy than might have been anticipated. We are accustomed to think in terms of clear cut preferences for the right or the left hand and it would seem, therefore, that a determination of the preferred hand would be a relatively easy matter. Our findings, however, do not conform to this and it has become necessary to use a battery of tests, and even when these have been applied the interpretation of the examiner based upon his experience with a considerable number of children is often necessary before a conclusion can be reached.

There are three factors entering into the question of laterality—eyedness, footedness and handedness. Eyedness, or the selection of one or the other eye chosen whenever the individual is compelled to use only one, as in looking through a knothole in a fence, for example, is not so widely recognized as handedness but it is probably of equal importance. It is not so susceptible to training but the writer has so far encountered at least one case in which there was a clear cut story of a purposeful shift in eyedness. This was an instance in which a boy found himself in difficulty in using the rifle because of his right-handedness and left-eyedness. Since eyedness is not so readily affected by training some have thought this to be a better guide to the inherent or native sidedness than is the master hand. Parson, particularly, championed this viewpoint and went so far as to hold that all left-eyed and right-handed individuals were native left-handers who had been shifted by training, and further held that the sighting eye determined the master hand. Unfortunately for this thesis it does not explain the group with the obverse pattern—those who are left-handed and right-eyed, nor does it explain the large number of individuals who do not have a strong predilection for either eye in sighting. Extensive studies in eyedness in the past few years have brought us to the belief that no one test is to be trusted, and have also demonstrated that there exists a complete and graduated series from the strongly right-eyed to the strongly left-eyed individual, with all stages and degrees of amphiocularity represented in between. We have used quite a wide variety of tests of eyedness—toy microscope, toy telescope, peep-hole toys, hole-in-card test, kaleidoscope, Miles' V-scope, Parson's manoptoscope, etc., and have come to the conclusion that no one test can be said to be entirely trustworthy and that some such wide battery as that listed here must be used. One of the tests most extensively used and often exclusively depended upon in psychological laboratories, that is, Parson's manoptoscope, has proven in our hands the least trustworthy and the most apt to be at variance with the other tests of the battery. Those tests of the series in which one hand is used to raise the test object, i.e., the telescope, kaleidoscope, peep-toys, etc., bring in the factor of handedness which may apparently in amphiocular cases lead to a choice of the corresponding eye. As a balance against this, the hole-in-card test has been used with the card held first by the examiner for several trials and with the hole as nearly in front of the bridge of the nose as possible. After this, the card is held by the patient first in his right hand, then in his left and finally in both hands. Not infrequently this will reveal the influence of the hand used, as when the card is brought to the right eye with the right hand and to the left eye with the left and with neither eye promptly chosen when both hands are used.

Gould believed that the eye with the better vision determines a superiority of the corresponding hand and claimed that the right eye has the better acuity in 94% of all infants and that this determines the high proportion of right- as compared with left-handedness. Our own findings do not permit of comment on Gould's statement concerning infants but we have encountered a number of cases of children in whom definitely poorer vision was demonstrable not only on the side corresponding to the handedness but in the eye used for sighting, that is, the master eye, as well and, moreover, as Wile has pointed out, Ballard's statement, that the same proportion of right- and left-handedness occurs among the congenitally blind as among the seeing, is a trenchant objection to both Gould's and Parson's belief. Some anatomists have called attention to the frequency with which the occipital pole—the visual sphere—of the brain is apparently somewhat larger on the left than on the right, and this has been held to be in support of the view that visual dominance precedes and may determine handedness. In the writer's experience this has not proven a dependable guide and one factor which may be misleading here is the very frequent distortion from a true ellipsoidal outline which is to be found in human skulls and brains. In many instances where one occipital pole seems to be better developed, a compensatory bulge will be found in the contralateral frontal pole suggesting strongly that the whole brain is somewhat askew and that the better development of the occipital region on one side may be more apparent than real. This distortion sometimes favors one side and sometimes the other but again as far as the writer's observations go, it does not correlate with the handedness to the individual.

It is interesting to note that in spite of the extended discussion which has been given to the problem of the master eye, almost all observers have been thinking in terms of visual acuity and almost no attention has been given to the fact that using the eye for sighting is primarily a function of motor control rather than of vision. To sight, we attempt to brink the center of the macula, the pupil and the object of regard into line, and quite obviously this is an act dependent much more directly on the skillful use of the extraocular muscles than it is on the clarity with which the object itself be seen, unless indeed there be very marked differences in the visual competence on the two sides. This view of ocular dominance conforms to our findings that unless the difference in refractive errors be great they play little apparent part in the choice of a master eye and that the eye preferred for sighting may actually have the greater error. Consideration of the dominant eye as dependent on the more ready use of the ocular muscles on one side brings this subject into immediate and close relation with the greater muscular skill developed by the master hand and limits interpretations based on vague concepts of visual superiority.

Footedness is not so important as eyedness and handedness, although fixed patterns of selective choice are not infrequently found in hopping, kicking a football, starting up a flight of steps, mounting a bicycle, using the coaster brake, etc., and when such selective choices occur they are generally, although not consistently, on the same side as the master hand.

In studies of the handedness of an individual, both history and tests are of importance. We have made it a practice to take a history of the developmental period from the parents of others who have been associated with the child at this stage, and also to question the patient himself with regard to his current practices, asking him to demonstrate whenever possible his choice of hand in everyday activities such as the use of a comb, toothbrush, eating utensils, baseball bat, tennis racquet, saw, hammer and other tools and implements. Both types of histories may be instructive although they are occasionally misleading or contrary. From the parent, inquiry is made concerning three points in particular: first, whether there was any delay in establishing a choice of a preferred hand beyond the period when the average child makes such a selection; second, whether any efforts, rigorous or mild, were made to encourage or enforce the use of either hand, and third, whether the patient showed any undue clumsiness in acquiring such skills as buttoning clothes, tying shoelaces, using eating utensils, etc. Occasionally a parent has become somewhat sensitive concerning earlier efforts to direct the child's handedness and is not quite frank concerning the measures adopted, but much more commonly the history is misleading because of poor observation. In one such case a child, who proved both by observation and by test to be electively left-handed in everything except three activities in which he had been definitely trained, was reported by his mother to be entirely right-handed. His mother came of a family with considerable left-handedness and had no prejudice against it and I believe was entirely sincere in this statement. And, moreover, his nurse had also entirely overlooked the fact that he preferred his left hand. Because of this factor it is sometimes advisable to plan a period of observation of the child in his home for a week or more during which the parents are instructed to watch him with care and to note particularly his preferences in those acts in which he has not received instruction.

Occasionally the child's training has been left so entirely in the hands of a nurse or maid who has later left the family's employ that it is impossible to get a history of the early development and the parents are quite unaware as to whether an effort has been made to change his spontaneous handedness tendency. The fact that left-handedness has often been associated in the minds of the uneducated with misfortune, as in the Irish use of the word *kithogue* is to be remembered here and many nurses will, on their own responsibility, attempt to ward off such evil from their charges. In the case of older children or in large families, the parents' memory is usually increasingly unreliable and the patient's own history should then be taken to determine his actual preferences in all sorts of activities in which one hand alone is used. Here we find the effects of training are very much to the fore and frequently the child will remember definite efforts on the part of some adult to establish one or the other pattern for him in certain selected activities. Thus one boy, who is a confirmed sinistral in all activities except golf, tells of the difficulty he had in learning this game because no left-handed clubs were available and he also adds, quite pertinently, "It is my poorest sport." Occasionally mere example will suffice to fix the right- or left-hand pattern. This was strikingly brought home to the writer by the story of a friend in the West who during his college days made quite a name for himself as a pole vaulter. He was entirely right-sided— hand, foot, and eye—except for his pole vaulting in which he used the left-hand position. To account for this he described his first contact with this sport. A group of athletes gave an exhibition in his home town during his senior year in high school and among them was a pole vaulter who happened to be left-handed. The observing boy was instantly enamored of this sport and throughout the summer, in imagination only, was running down the field carrying the vaulting pole in the left-hand position. When in the following fall he entered college, the track coach, finding him right-handed in other things, made vigorous efforts to teach him the right-hand position in vaulting, but to no avail. He had so fixed the motor pattern during his summer of contemplation that the substitution of the other was impossible and the coach ultimately gave up his efforts and let him go forward as a left-handed vaulter. This history is recited primarily to show the relatively small amount of influence which is required to cause a change in pattern in some individuals and hence the insecurity of an opinion based on other than extended tests, history and observation.

Occasionally a child is encountered who is so obviously eager to prove to the examiner that he is entirely right-handed that the account which he gives of his own preferences and even his showing on the tests must be discounted to some extent. Such an attitude does, however, suggest strongly that someone in his environment has influenced him in favor of the right-sided pattern. Again, children who are neither predominantly right- nor left-handed may have an unusual amount of difficulty in learning which is right and which is left, and their verbal account of their handedness preferences may be at striking variance with a simultaneous demonstration of their habitual choices.

Many are conscious of this confusion and will give a history of difficulty in following directions involving turns to the right and to the left.

As a compliment to the history of past development and recognized preferences, tests of current skills are of importance to establish the actual status of the moment. Quite a wide variety of tests may be employed, even for comparatively young children. Showing movements, both those of the overarm throw and the underarm toss, are of value in showing the relative facility of use of the muscles of the shoulders and upper arms of the two sides. Tests such as putting pegs in holes, counting with the finger push comptometer, and others of this general nature should also be included to determine the relative skills of the two hands in such movements and also so that a comparison may be made between the skills of the shoulder and arm movements and those of the hand and fingers. At the same time observations should be made as to the relative degree of ease and grace in carrying out these activities. In order to minimize the effect of training we have found it wise to include in the battery of motor tests an element of novelty free from the effects of training or practice as far as this is possible, and we have devised and adapted apparatus for this purpose, but if the choice of tests in common activities be broad enough they seem to meet the need as well as more elaborate apparatus.

Many statements are to be found in the literature concerning the superior strength in the master hand, and this has been tested by the use of a pair of dynamometers used first simultaneously in the two hands and then one at a time in each hand. We have found no consistent relation between strength of arm and the master hand except when the latter has been well established and has long done the major part of the manual work, and we consider this factor too unstable to be of value.

For a time it was hoped that an electrical study of the action currents of the forearm would prove a dependable guide to the inherent native handedness pattern of a given individual. This was based on the work of Golla in London who, by using two galvanometers, found in a left-handed individual that there was a tendency of the action currents of the left arm to precede in time those of the right when both hands were closed simultaneously. Travis and the writer carried out some further observations along this line on a small series of stutterers and normal speakers some years ago in the Iowa Psychopathic Hospital with what looked at the time like very promising results. A much larger series has now been studied including pure right- and left-handed individuals and some who were left-handed in all spontaneous activities but used the right for certain trained skills, notably writing, and including individuals with and without various types of language disorders. In this study much better instruments were provided in the laboratories of the Language Research Unit of the New York Neurological Institute, and not only was the series of cases investigated much larger and more carefully selected but the number of readings in each case was considerably greater. The results were disappointing in that it was found that while Golla's formula of a slight precedence in time of arrival of the action currents on the master side was often correct, yet there were so many exceptions that the use of this test to determine the inherent pattern in any given individual could not be depended upon and the method has had to be discarded as a diagnostic procedure. It is to be noted, however, that this method which is dependent on readings of the action currents in the forearm is subject to general uncontrollable sources of possible error, and that direct registration of the electrical activity in various brain areas such as is made possible by the new electroencephalograph offers promise of excluding these errors and may give us trustworthy and valuable results in this and certain kindred problems in the language disorders.

MOTOR INTERGRADING

A large number of children have now been studied with extensive histories and by batteries of tests for both eye and hand preferences. Most of them came from the selected group which was referred to our laboratories because of some form of developmental defect in language. This series shows quite a number who were entirely right-sided and some who were entirely left-sided, but in addition it includes a great many whose motor patterns showed a striking mixture of right- and left-sidedness. Some, for example, were right-handed and left-eyed; some left-handed and right-eyed; some indifferent in their handedness and amphiocular. In some, moreover, the large movements of the shoulders such as are used for throwing were much more skillful and graceful on the left side, while the finer movements of the hands such as are used in writing were better on the right. This is a situation which one is apt to encounter in a left-handed child who has followed his own bent in throwing but has been taught to use his right hand for writing and drawing. In still other children there was no frank intermixture of right and left patterns but much less than the amount of difference between the skills of the two sides usually found in the strongly right- or strongly left-handed individual.

Another factor which we found complicating the study of handedness preferences was that in some children in this group with mixed motor patterns, especially the younger ones, there was a striking lack of stability in their choices. The same test repeated on different days not infrequently gave opposite results, and in certain cases observation of the child in his home showed a decided preference for the left hand on some days and an equally selective choice of the right on others. Again, in several children, we have observed what appears to have been a spontaneous shift from left- to right-handedness occurring without any demonstrable external influence. This has appeared at various ages but most frequently between the ages of two and three and the ages of six and eight, which constitute the two critical periods in language development which will be discussed later in this volume.

While the majority of our cases are those of children who have come to us because of delay or disorder in the development of some phase of the language faculty, we have also carried out the same tests of handedness and eyedness on a limited number of adults who gave no history of language difficulties, and we have found instances of crossed and mixed patterns among them also, so that we feel that the occurrence of motor intergrading is by no means to be considered a fixed measure of the ability to acquire either manual or linguistic skills. It is, we believe, to be looked upon as evidence of the absence of a sufficiently strong hereditary tendency to establish a clear cut selective preference for one side in all motor acts but since such intergrading will include all degrees of intermixture there will be many individuals who exhibit some evidence of mixed sidedness and yet who have met with no difficulty in acquiring either complex motor acts or spoken or written language.

One of the outstanding characteristics of the individual who is endowed with a very strong tendency toward the use of either the left or the right hand is his persistence in adhering to his natural preference in spite of the environmental pressures brought to bear. Examples of this are to be seen in many left-handed people who have been forced to learn to use the right hand for writing in school but who, as soon as this pressure has been relaxed, have reverted to writing with the left hand because of greater ease and speed. When we consider this, the occurrence of a group of children who exhibit little bent toward either the right- or left-hand pattern in spite of the usual exposure to training and of another group who start with a slight preference for the left but even with the most moderate pressure are led to shift to the right, is, we believe, strong evidence that this group of mixed, crossed, and undecided patterns indicates the presence of an inherent variable here, and our findings in this selected group of children seem to be explicable only on the existence of a graded series of sidedness preference extending all the way from very strongly right-sided individuals to very strongly left-sided ones and with all degrees of intermingling in between. This is what might be anticipated as the result of intergrading between two genetic factors leading respectively to left- and right-sidedness.

Granting a striking variation in the strength of the hereditary tendency, lt is obvious that the results of various training methods on different children will like-wise be a variable, and this we believe is the unquestionable answer to the very wide difference of opinion which exists as to the influence of an enforced change in the child's natural handedness inclinations. A long and bitter battle has raged about this question and both extremes of opinion still find vigorous protagonists. There are those who feel that no harm can ensue from making every child conform to a right-handed pattern, and indeed in many schools today no child is permitted to write with his left hand. At the other extreme are those who feel with equal conviction that every effort at shifting a child from his natural patterns will result in some one or another sort of difficult.

The great degree of individual variation which has become increasingly apparent as our studies of laterality have progressed makes it clear that no dogmatic general answer can be given to the question as to whether a left-handed child should ever be trained on the right side. The question can be answered only for a given individual after tests and observations of the child himself, and even then it is sometimes necessary to experiment with a period of training and, in one or two instances, such an experimental period demonstrated that our first opinion based on history and tests was not leading to the expected results in training and it was necessary to change the program completely. One other factor which must be considered here is the age of the child. As will be elaborated in a subsequent chapter, there are certain periods in a child's development—notably between two to three, and six to eight years of age—which are critical in the development of the language function, and interference with inherent handedness patterns at these times seems much more prone to give rise to difficulties than at others. There is abundant evidence, for example, that shift of handedness enforced by injury in the right arm of a right-handed adult will have no demonstrable effect on his speech, whereas a comparable situation arising during one of the two critical periods just mentioned is very apt indeed to be followed by a speech disorder.

In the group of children who, however, are clearly not developing a selective skill in either hand or in whom the balance is comparatively close, it seems highly advisable to increase definitely both the skill and the habit of use of the hand on the side which has the greater capacity, if this can be determined. When the balance is fairly equal, preference is given to the training of the right hand in most cases. Concerning those children, however, who show an early and distinct preference of their own for the use of either hand, we feel that the only logical plan is to permit them to follow this physiological bent without outside interference, which at best is probably guided largely by prejudice, One occasionally finds parents or teachers who are attempting to train a child towards complete ambidexterity, overlooking the fact that with man's development in manual skill, which we mentioned at the outset of this volume as one of his two great advances over the lower animals, we find an increasing tendency towards the preferential use of one hand or the other. Although we have seen many children who exhibit a high degree of ambivalence between the left and right hands, they have commonly shown less than the usual skill for their age in the more intricate movements of either, and we have encountered none in whom true ambidexterity could be said to exist, that is, where all skills on the two sides were not only equal but also highly developed. There seems to be a fair uniformity of opinion in the literature that the so-called ambidextrous person is usually a native sinistral who has acquired through training a considerable measure of skill in certain right-sided activities, and our experience would tend to confirm this. In many of these cases, it is true, training on the two sides has not resulted in any demonstrable harm to the individual but the much higher degree of the motor skill generally exhibited by "pure" right- and "pure" left-handers leads to the conjecture that even the very skillful ambidextrous individual might have been still more facile had he been trained electively in accordance with his natural physiological bent.

The very close parallelism which exists between the symptoms to be seen in adults who have suffered a loss in language as a result of brain injury and those to be seen during the development of the language faculty in some children suggests very strongly that we are dealing with a disturbance of the same physiological process in both instances and, since in the adult such a loss occurs only when the lesion is in the master hemisphere, our attention is naturally directed to those factors, open to our observation and study, which tend to determine the choice and establishment of unilateral brain control. For reasons which are too technical to be reviewed in detail here, the hypothesis that these developmental disorders in acquiring the language functions are the result of faulty development of particular brain areas (agenetic cortical defects) is no longer tenable, while the existence of demonstrable mixtures between right and left motor preferences with a strong familial background implies that comparable intergrading may exist between the critical areas for the various fractions of the language faculty in the two hemispheres of the brain, thus giving rise to a series of developmental disorders in language, a description of which will form Chapter Two of this volume.

◆　　◆　　◆

CERTAIN DISORDERS IN THE DEVELOPMENT OF LANGUAGE IN CHILDREN

The first part of this volume reviewed very briefly some of the disorders which follow small areas of destruction of the brain in the adult after language has been acquired, and it was pointed out that these losses of language occur only when the master half of the brain is affected and that the only guide we have as to whether the right or left hemisphere of the brain is operating as the master half in the normal individual is his "sidedness" as shown by his handedness, footedness and eyedness. A summary of studies in sidedness in a large number of children and adults was offered which indicates the existence of a wide range of variability in the establishment of the master hand and eye. Since the principle of functional superiority of one brain hemisphere is operative in the control of the language function in the normal adult as well as in determining a greater capacity for the acquisition of skilled acts on one side of the body, we may safely assume that a variability exists in the establishment of the unilateral patterns in language development in the child comparable to the demonstrable variation found in the motor patterns.

Discussions in the medical literature of the past bearing on the syndromes of defect or delay in language acquisition in childhood have for the most part stressed the inherent or hereditary factors involved, and the term congenital has come into wide use to differentiate these disorders as met in the growing child from the comparable conditions which result from brain injury or brain disease in the adult which are described as acquired syndromes. While the importance of heredity is clearly recognized and accepted here, nevertheless we feel that use of the term congenital tends to overstress the inherent difficulty and to underemphasize the many environmental factors, both specific—such as methods of teaching—and more general—such as emotional and social forces—and we therefore prefer the use of the term developmental to congenital since it may be said to include both the hereditary tendency and the environmental forces which are brought to play on the individual.

DESCRIPTION OF SYNDROMES

I. Developmental Alexia (The Reading Disability)

The first of the syndromes of delay or disorder in language acquisition, encountered by certain children, to be discussed here is that of developmental alexia (congenital word blindness, strephosymbolia, specific reading disability). This was first described by Morgan in England under the name of congenital word blindness but Hinshelwood, an English opthalmologist, gave us the first intensive study of the condition in a monograph published in 1917. A number of children were referred to Hinshelwood because of their lack of progress in learning to read and because it was thought that this might be caused by some disorder in vision. This did not prove to be the case, but in his critical study of these children Hinshelwood placed emphasis on two very pertinent facts: first, that there are often several such cases in one family, and second, that the symptoms which they show are very closely parallel to those which appear in adults who have lost the capacity to read because of injury to the brain. At that time studies of the adult cases had pointed out the critical relation which the angular gyrus of the dominant hemisphere bears to loss of reading skill and this brain area was considered to be the storehouse for visual memories of words. Basing his deductions on this, Hinshelwood hypothecated a congenital defect of development (agenesis) of this particular area of the brain in such children. There has been no evidence forthcoming to support this defect hypothesis since Hinshelwood's time, and there is much to be said against it. In the first place, such areas of agenesis are of comparatively rare occurrence and are not met with in a general autopsy service with anywhere near the frequency with which the cases of reading disability are to be encountered among children. Secondly, if it be true as Marie reported that there is no higher incidence of speech disorders in children born with a right hemiplegia than in those with a left, and if Marie's assumption from this, that when one hemisphere is damaged before speech is learned the other can take its place, is correct, it would then require a lack of development in the angular gyri of both hemispheres to satisfy Hinshelwood's hypothesis, and such bilateral agenetic defects are exceedingly rare. Finally, as our studies of cerebral functioning have progressed, we have been led to discard the older concept of the angular gyrus region as a brain area in which more or less photographic visual memories of words are stored and have come to realize that the process of reading is a much more complex activity requiring the physiological integrity and interplay of many brain areas although the angular gyrus and its adjacent cortex in the dominant hemisphere still bear a critical relation to this function, as we have seen in our review of acquired alexia.

The term congenital word blindness as used in medical literature to describe the reading disability is misleading, first since it tends, as discussed above, to overemphasize the inherent factor and second since there is no true blindness in the ordinary use of this term nor, indeed, is there even blindness for words. This can be readily demonstrated by the fact that cases with severe reading disability can copy words correctly which they cannot read at all. In other words, the word is seen but not recognized. The writer, in 1926, in the course of an intensive study of several cases of this disorder noted a striking tendency to distorted order in the recall of letters shown in the attempts of these children to read a word or to spell it and offered the term strephosymbolia—meaning "twisted symbols"—as more descriptive of the symptomatic condition than is congenital word blindness.

In his monograph Hinshelwood attempted to separate the more extreme cases of reading disability and would restrict the term congenital word blindness to those in whom the difficulty in learning to read was "so great and so unusual that it could be regarded without any exaggeration as an abnormal or pathological condition." He did not, however, offer any usable criterion as to how such a separation of the pathological cases could be made, and our experience in studying and retraining several hundred such cases over a period of years has convinced us that the strephosymbolics cannot be so divided but rather that they form a graded series including all degrees of severity of the handicap.

Because of this wide variation in the expression of this disability no attempt will be made here to describe all the variants but the syndrome will be presented as seen in two very characteristic forms of the disorder: first, that of cases seen very early before the influence of training has too far altered the picture, and with them that of very severe cases where attempts at training have had little influence; and second, that of mild or residual cases where reading has been acquired but to so poor an advantage that failures in secondary school and college may be definitely referred to this educational shortcoming.

Obviously there are multiple causes for a delay in learning to read. Marked defects in vision may underlie such a difficulty and should be thoroughly investigated and, if present, corrected. Defects of hearing have also been encountered which have led to poor auditory discrimination of words and in some cases poor reading has seemed to have its roots in residuals of an uncorrected word deafness which is to be discussed later herein. General intellectual defect is also a frequent cause of failure in reading. Emotional disturbances, such as antagonisms toward a particular teacher or general apathy toward all school work, or lack of adequate disciplinary training at home, may all play their part in giving rise to a slow start in this academic need. When, however, all of such factors are excluded, there remains a group of very considerable size in every school who have shown no evidence of any delay or abnormality in either their physical, mental, or emotional development until they have reached school and are confronted with reading, and then they suddenly meet a task which they cannot accomplish.

When seen early—that is, during the first two years of exposure to reading, usually between the ages of six and eight—the earmark of the specific reading difficulty is an inability to learn to recognize words at sight as readily as do the facile readers. The more rapid learners in this field of education are no brighter on the average than are some of the reading disability cases, and indeed some of our very severe strephosymbolics when measured by all available tests rank high in intelligence. The writer, for example, has studied one boy who was reading almost nothing and spelling less, after three years in school, who passed intelligence tests with a quotient of 145 and gave every evidence in every other field except his reading, spelling and writing of being a "near genius." Thus intelligence does not always correlate with reading skill, and in any group of nonreaders all ranges of intelligence are to be found as they would be in any casually selected group of children. A word of caution must be offered here, however, and that is that poor reading comprehension forms an integral part of the general picture presented by children with dull normal intelligence and those of the defective group, so that failure in learning to read with understanding must not be considered a specific disability unless it is distinctly out of harmony with the child's skill in other fields—notably the ability to learn by hearing and to master arithmetical concepts. A simple method of showing quantitatively the specific character of the retardation which occurs in children suffering from developmental alexia is by means of an educational profile on which are entered the child's grade, actual age, mental age and his accomplishment in standard tests of arithmetic, reading, spelling and writing. Three such charts are given in Figures 4, 5 and 6. Much more striking contrasts are available in our records in cases of older children suffering with extreme degrees of this disability, but such cases are relatively rare and the three presented here have been chosen to show the characteristic picture at three age levels in the more commonly encountered cases of moderate severity. In each profile, "Grade" refers to the placement given the child at school, "C.A." indicates chronological age, while

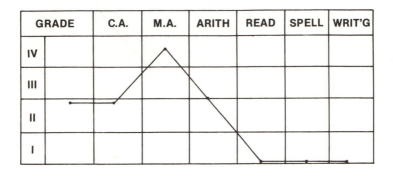

Figure 4. Educational profile of an eight-year-old left-handed boy with a superior intelligence but a retardation in reading, spelling and writing, typical of strephosymbolia in younger children. C.A. indicates chronological age. M.A. indicates mental age.

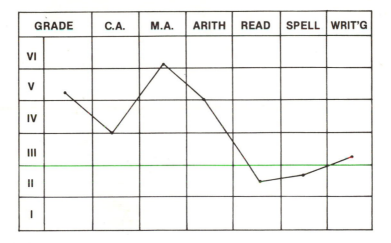

Figure 5. Educational profile of a ten-year-old right-handed girl with a moderate degree of strephosymbolia. Abbreviations are the same as in Figure 4.

"M.A." gives the mental age as determined by a Stanford-Binet examination. It will be noted that all three of these cases were children of superior intelligence, and it may be added that they came from educated families and good schools. The standings given in arithmetic, reading, and spelling were obtained by averaging two or more standardized tests in each of these subjects, and the grade in writing is that of writing speed as determined by the Ayres scale.

Usually the auditory development of these children has been quite normal. There is no defect in the acuity of hearing; they have learned

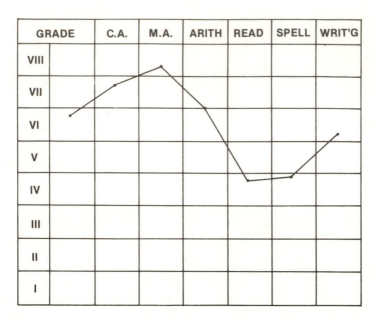

GRADE	C.A.	M.A.	ARITH	READ	SPELL	WRIT'G
VIII						
VII						
VI						
V						
IV						
III						
II						
I						

Figure 6. Educational profile of a fourteen-year-old right-handed girl with a moderate degree of strephosymbolia. Abbreviations are the same as in Figure 4.

to differentiate and interpret the various sounds of the environment; understanding of words has been good and they have learned to speak at about the usual age. Some indeed are exceedingly keen in the auditory field and are able to memorize pages of their readers from hearing their classmates recite, so that their own inability in reading may be hidden from the teachers for a time. As they progress, however, they outrun this skill and it soon becomes apparent that the word which they see does not bring recognition in spite of the many times which it has been shown to them. Under such circumstances, reading very often takes on largely the qualities of a game of guessing at words, or the child will offer a word with no likeness in form or suitability in context to that which he is attempting to read. Sometimes, indeed, a highly imaginative child will concoct a whole story bearing no relation to the words on the page before him beyond one or two initial or key words which he cleverly weaves into his own production. In very severe cases, the child may remain practically at this level for years unless appropriate methods of training are adopted. Such children are usually avidly interested in stories, both those told to them and those read aloud, and although this is a valuable means of developing their auditory vocabulary and providing factual data of which they would otherwise be deprived because of their lack of reading ability, a difficulty sometimes enters here in that much reading aloud is apt to develop the interests of such a youngster far beyond the point which he will be able to reach in reading for himself for several years.

Vision in the group of nonreaders at large is not defective. Minor errors of refraction and muscle imbalance are encountered here as they would be in any group of children but no more frequently, and some of our extreme cases of strephosymbolia have vision which is far better than the average of those who are learning to read with ease. We have not had the opportunity to check the strephosymbolics from the standpoint of relative size of the retinal images in the two eyes (aniseikonia) but we feel that the demonstrable fact that their difficulty lies in recalling previous exposures of the word rather than in seeing it, permits the practical exclusion of this factor as of importance. Our observations on the presence of suspenopsia and on the capacity for binocular fusion and stereopsis show no consistent deviation in the children with a reading disability from the normal variation to be found in these functions in good readers.

Functions other than reading but which incorporate a visual element are usually entirely normal. For example, visuomotor coordination may be excellent as is shown by superiority in various games requiring close control of movement by vision, such as baseball or tennis, and by the interest and ability which the strephosymbolic frequently shows in intricate handwork. Visual recognition of objects, of places, and of persons is quite normal, and interpretation of pictorial and diagrammatic material is frequently very good. Sense of direction is also often well developed as in the case of one boy with such a marked reading difficulty that he could not understand any of the signboards along the way, who had nevertheless memorized routes so that he was the trusted family guide for automobile trips.

That there is no true blindness for words as the older nomenclature would suggest is clearly emphasized by the fact that these children see the word and will make an attempt to read it although such an effort commonly does not bring correct recognition, and this is still further brought into relief by the fact that many of these non-readers are able to copy correctly words which they cannot read. This is particularly well demonstrated in certain instances by asking the child to copy and later to read short nonsense syllables in which the element of past exposure and hence an unknown measure of familiarity does not enter. Even the confusing b's and d's are copied perfectly although often presenting a hopeless confusion when read.

While the early cases of strephosymbolia and those of more extreme severity often have learned to read very little indeed, nevertheless an observation of the type of errors which they make in attempting to read is instructive. In the beginning we find a very wide range of letter confusions—*b*'s mixed with *h*'s; *m, n* and *u* are confused, etc. Such confusion is present in practically all children in the very beginning but the more facile readers very quickly straighten them out and even the reading disability cases, with a little teaching, soon get most of the letters properly associated with their names, with the notable exception of those letters which are similar in form but reversed in orientation, that is, *b* and *d* and *p* and *q*. In some of our more confused cases difficulty has been encountered in telling *t* from *f*, and *a* from *s*. This will be more readily understood if the imprint of the lower case type for these letters is examined in the mirror, as this brings out similarities which might quite escape us otherwise. Not infrequently children who have been struggling with their *b*'s and *d*'s and have learned to tell them apart when they are isolated may easily be led to exhibit their uncertainty by the exposure of a word containing one of these "twin letters" but which otherwise is like that of a more familiar word which contains the other. Thus children who have often seen the word "big" but are not so well acquainted with "dig" will often read both as "big." As a rule *b* and *d*, being more frequently met, are more readily straightened out, and it is not uncommon to find a child who can differentiate these two letters in all except the most treacherous associations but who still has trouble with *p* and *q*, and indeed it may be fair to raise the question as to whether this confusion may not have given rise to the admonition "to mind your *p*'s and *q*'s."

In the poor readers, reversible words also form a serious stumbling block; "was" and "saw," "on" and "no," "not" and "ton," are inextricably mixed. There is also a marked tendency to twist around a pair of letters in a word, leading to confusion between such words as "from" and "form," "calm" and "clam," etc. Or occasionally the reversal of one syllable of a word occurs as when "tarnish" is read as "tarshin" or "ratnish," or there may be a reversed assembly of two syllables of a word, each of which has been read in the proper direction, as when "repast" is read as "ast-rep." One striking fact about this reversal tendency is its instability. The letter *b* is sometimes *b* and sometimes *d*; "was" encountered several times in the same paragraph may come back as either "was" or "saw" with no consistency. As the child grows older and progresses somewhat in his ability to solve these puzzles of direction, and especially when he begins to make use of the context to determine his choices between two possibilities, the use of three- and four-letter nonsense syllables and combinations constructed of two, three, or four such syllables will frequently uncover a tendency to reversals which has to a considerable extent disappeared from familiar words. While these errors are to be observed by listening to the child's reading, they can be graphically shown in written productions to good advantage. Figures 7 and 8 are examples. In Figure

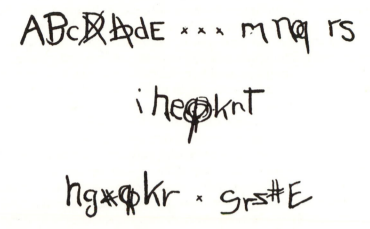

Figure 7. Graphic evidence of the confusion between *b* and *d* and *p* and *q* in the writing of an eight-year-old boy with a marked reading disability.

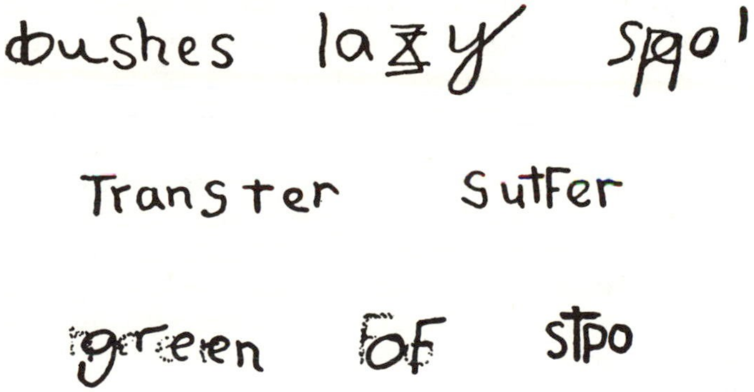

Figure 8. Confusion in the orientation of letters and in direction of writing from the work of a ten-year-old strephosymbolic girl.

7, the boy attempted, when writing the alphabet from memory, to dodge the confusion between the lower case forms of *b* and *d* by using capitals. When asked to write the small letters, he produced a *b* for a *d* but saw his error and corrected it. When he came to *p* and *q*, he fired both barrels at once and had to omit the second of this pair. In writing to dictation of the letter names the fourth symbol in the second row was produced when *p* was dictated, and this also applies to the corresponding symbol which appears in the bottom row when he was writing letters in response to dictated sounds. In Figure 8, the difficulty in deciding which orientation to use is evident in the *b* for *bushes*, the *z* of *lazy* and the *p* of *spoil* which were the three words dictated for the first line. The second line shows trouble with the *f* and *t* as described above. The child could spell both *transfer* and *suffer* orally without error. It may be noted here that in the second *f* of *suffer*, she has avoided the puzzle presented by the lower case forms by using a capital F. In the bottom line can be seen the tendency to backward progression and distorted order. In writing *green*, this girl produced *neer* before she saw her error and partially erased it—leaving, however, "ghosts" of the letters which could be traced for the illustration. Similarly, *of* was written first as *Fo*, again using the capital, and then changed to *oF*. The last word in this line was meant for *stop*.

A further fact of interest in the poor readers is the facility which some of them show in reading reversed or mirrored print. Printed material may be shown to a child so that he sees it in a mirror, or text may be produced in reverse on the typewriter by inserting a sheet of carbon paper face up, thus producing a mirrored copy on the back of the overlying paper, or better still, type can be secured from type-founders which give a mirrored imprint, which are called offset type, and test cards printed from these. In rare cases the skill of a child in reading these sinistrad words or sentences is better than his ability with material printed in the dextrad or ordinary direction, and this may extend to both speed and numbers of words correctly read. More commonly, however, the child requires a longer time to read the mirrored passage but very frequently shows a relative skill in this if the ratio of the time required for reading comparable paragraphs in both directions be taken and compared with that of normal readers of the same age, grade and intelligence. The data for determining this relative skill were published as part of the studies in the reading disability carried out in Iowa several years ago.

Occasionally the same factor of reversal which is to be seen in reading also causes trouble in arithmetic. The child may misread 12 as 21, for example, or may get into difficulty with the direction to be followed in carrying when adding, or in borrowing when subtracting. Compared with the number and length of the sequences of letters to be remembered in order to recognize words, however, those of arithmetic are simple and are usually quickly straightened out although the tendency to miswrite 12 as 21 is apt to persist after its recognition is secure, much as the tendency to miswrite a *b* or a *d* often remains long after the child can discriminate by eye between them. Usually the arithmetical processes do not make serious trouble for the children who are nonreaders, if they have normal general intelligence, and they frequently present a striking contrast in their ability in handling numbers and their difficulty in mastering words. With those children who have spent several years in school without recognition of their reading disability or without adequate retraining, it is not unusual to find on standardized tests that the results in arithmetic are several school grades ahead of those in reading and spelling. As would be expected, however, the poor reader is seriously handicapped in understanding the directions on such tests and can often make comparatively little headway with the story or reasoning type of problem as contrasted with his ability in simple computation. To obtain a just estimate of the arithmetical ability it is obviously necessary to read the problems aloud to the child, and when this is done the prompt and accurate answers often demonstrate that an apparent difficulty with the problem type of examination rests in its reading requirements and not in the ability to handle the arithmetical concepts. We have encountered a few strephosymbolic children, with superior intelligence, who were failing in arithmetic as well as in reading in the upper grades, but this appeared to be directly attributable to poor teaching or to a demonstrable emotional factor in the situation and in every case in which special tutoring was provided for the arithmetic as well as for reading, the arithmetic responded quickly whereas the reading was found to require special methods and a much longer period of remedial training.

Spelling forms an almost insuperable obstacle to the strephosymbolic child. Since his memory of the word picture is not exact enough to serve as a basis for its recognition when *seen* again as in attempting to read, it is not surprising to find that the much more accurate recall needed for reproduction also fails, and in greater degree. With very severe cases and with untreated moderately severe cases observed during the first two or three years of school, there is usually no progress in either reading or spelling which can be measured by standardized tests. With cases of less severity and when proper treatment has been instituted, progress is made in both subjects but the ability to recognize words almost always outruns the ability to reproduce them correctly so that spelling as a rule lags considerably behind reading. Moreover, unless very careful attention by appropriate methods be given to spelling as well as to reading, the child may progress very little in the former. These children can often learn to spell words by rote auditory memory but this is apt to be very short lived, so that repeated drilling by spelling lists of words out loud often has very little permanent effect. Occasionally the rote memory will carry a considerable list of words for a time so that in some instances one finds the child able to spell all of the words of his current school grade but exceedingly defective in those of the earlier grades, long since forgotten. Errors may be of equal number and degree in both oral and written spelling or one may be harder than the other. When this is the case it is usually the written spelling which is the more difficult. The errors which are made in spelling are of many varieties but it is of interest to note that here also, distortions in the order of recall of the letters belonging in a word are outstanding and that among these are to be seen typical confusions between *b* and *d*, and *p* and *q*, as well as reversals of paired letters, syllables and whole words, such as are to be found in the reading errors. Not infrequently one encounters a child who gives no history of delay in acquisition of silent reading understanding but who does have great difficulty with spelling. Usually, in such cases, tests of *oral* reading capacity show many deficiencies in this technique and the character of the spelling errors suggests strongly that this disability rests on the same basis as does that which usually accompanies the severe reading disorder. Figure 9 shows the educational profile of a case of

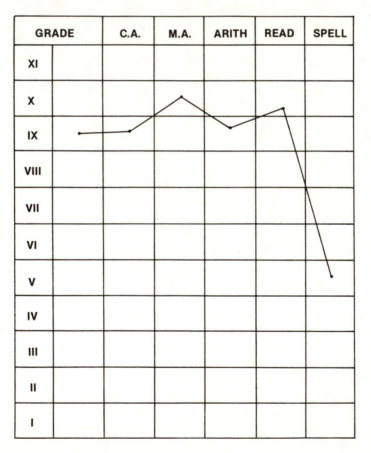

GRADE	C.A.	M.A.	ARITH	READ	SPELL
XI					
X					
IX					
VIII					
VII					
VI					
V					
IV					
III					
II					
I					

Figure 9. Educational profile of a fourteen-year-old boy with a special spelling disability. C.A. indicates chronological age. M.A. indicates mental age.

special disability in spelling. This was a boy who gave a history of a very slow start in learning to read although, as the profile demonstrates, he had finally gained a good skill in this. His oral reading was still poor as it is apt to be in the poor spellers. The headings in this figure are the same as those explained in connection with Figures 4, 5 and 6.

In extremely severe cases of strephosymbolia the visual recall of the details of the word may be so defective that unless the child has been taught the phonetic values of the letters, he is quite hopelessly at sea in spelling and some of his attempts produce the most bizarre results. The product may be so unlike the word attempted as to constitute a true neographism and a whole composition of such words presents a startling appearance. A classical example of this is a school composition offered as a description of the British Campaign of 1777 in the American Revolution which was handed in by a boy of sixteen years of age who had never learned to read. This is produced in facsimile in Figure 10. When this boy was permitted to dictate his compositions, he produced a creditable performance, showing that the ideas were there and also the words to express them, but when he attempted to write down what he had just dictated the same sort of errors appeared as are found in this composition. This is shown in Figure 11. Thus it is apparent that the linkage or association between the component sounds of a word and the proper letters to represent them was as defective as was that between the letter and its proper sound, as shown by his complete inability to read any but a few familiar words and his utter helplessness with nonsense syllables. He was, however, able to copy from print into his own characteristic script in practically letter perfect form although he understood nothing of what he was writing. His copying is shown in Figure 12.

The handwriting of children with a reading disability is a variable. Not infrequently they show evidence of a much greater difficulty in acquiring printing or writing than would be expected from their dexterity in other manual skills, and hence fall clearly in the group of special writing disabilities which will be discussed later in this volume. Others, however, encounter no such selective obstacle and learn to write without undue difficulty.

Studies of laterality in the cases of developmental alexia have shown a very considerable number of crossed patterns between handedness and eyedness, as well as other forms of motor intergrading, but this is by no means without exception and we have encountered extreme cases of the reading disability in children who were right-sided as well as in those who were completely left-sided. Manual dexterity is variable in the group but often is quite highly developed. This is also true of general athletic skill and we find no motor problems consistently associated with the reading disability. Since developmental alexia is

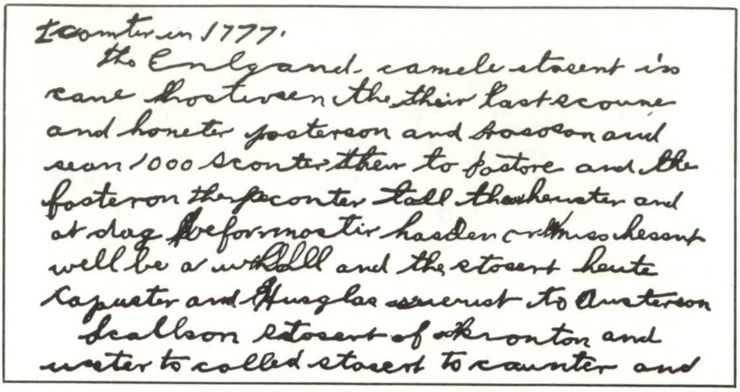
Icomter in 1777.
the Englgand camele stoeent iss
cane hostiveen the their last ecoune
and honeter posteroon and Aosoeon and
sean 1000 Sconterther to fastore and the
fosteron the facconter tall thashenater and
at dag Beformoastir hasden or the so hessont
well be a whildl and the stoeert heute
Capuater and Hugglas assenust to Anteraon
Scallson Estoeent of Akronton and
waster to called stoeert to caunter and

Figure 10. Unintelligible neographisms produced by a sixteen-year-old boy with a severe reading disability. This material was submitted as a composition descriptive of the English campaign in 1777 in a high-school course in American History.

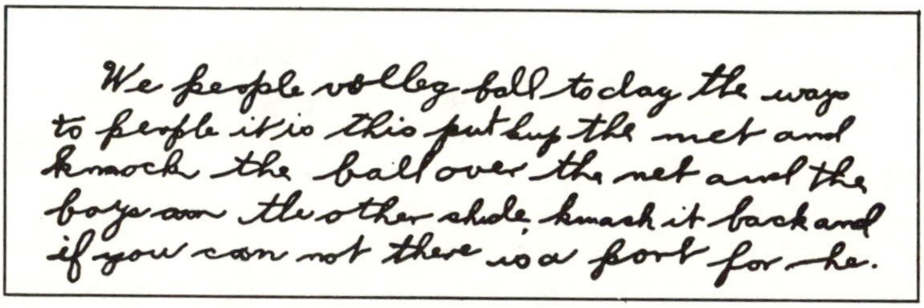
We pefple volleg fall today the ways
to perfle it is this put bup the net and
knock the ball over the net and the
boys oon the other shde knash it back and
if you can not there is a port for he.

Figure 11. A simpler composition by the same boy who produced Figure 10. He first dictated the material which he intended to write, which was as follows: We played volley-ball today. The way to play it is this—put up the net and knock the ball over the net and the boys on the other side knock it back and if you cannot, it is a point for him.

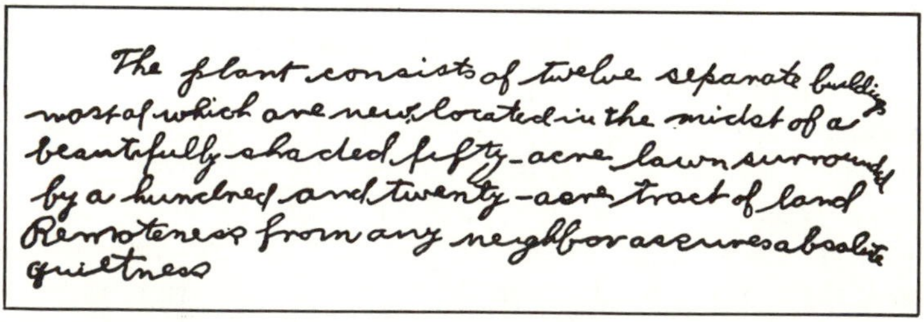
The plant consists of twelve separate bulldings
most of which are new located in the midst of a
beantifully shaded fifty-acre lawn surround
by a hundred and twenty-acre tract of land
Remoteness from any neighbor assures absolute
quietness

Figure 12. Copying from print into script by the same boy who produced Figures 10 and 11. The marked contrast between copying and propositional work is seen by comparing this with Figures 10 and 11.

primarily a difficulty in recognition and hence falls in the category of sensory disorders, the problem of the child's handedness is of no importance from the standpoint of retraining unless there be a coexistent writing disability, speech defect, or apraxia. The presence among the reading disability cases, however, of a large number of children who show mixed or crossed motor patterns is considered suggestive evidence that as a group they belong among the intergrades, and this is borne out by the fact that the family history in by far the great majority of cases shows the presence of left-handedness in the stock and very often language disorders of one sort or another in other members of the family as well.

The milder cases of strephosymbolia gradually learn to read, but usually very poorly as compared with the accomplishment of others of their age and general intelligence. As they progress in school work, both the volume and the intricacy of the reading demands increase to the place where they surpass the child's ability, and academic progress may then be definitely blocked. Thus we meet these cases failing in the secondary schools and even in college through inability to read with sufficient speed to cover their assignments or through difficulty in understanding the material which they have studied because of misreading of words. Upon tests of silent reading comprehension these pupils occasionally come up to the norms for school children of their age but usually fall considerably below the expected achievement for their intelligence and general background. Silent reading, moreover, permits of skimming to grasp the general intent of a sentence or paragraph without the necessity of reading every word with understanding, and when the pupil is confronted with the much more precise task required by reading aloud many errors come to light and not infrequently some of these are of a nature to explain difficulties in understanding the content. Confusions of words with somewhat similar configurations and not too dissimilar meanings are frequent, as when *house* is read for *home*, *sugar* for *syrup*, etc. Reversals such as we see in the younger children are rare although they occur occasionally even among the college students and can sometimes be brought out by the use of compound nonsense syllables when they are not to be seen in reading meaningful words. Misreading or the omission of small words is common, and this often will completely change the meaning of the text. Not infrequently questions concerning the meanings of words which have been misread or mispronounced will disclose serious confusions between words which are roughly similar in appearance, and at times the problem of competence of auditory discrimination will arise as when words which sound somewhat alike are also confused. In one fourteen-year-old girl, for example, the word *phenomena* met in print was read as ''fmonia'' and when she was asked at a subsequent visit what was meant by "fmonia" she parried with the question, "Do you mean the liquid or the disease?" Obviously her interchange of *phenomena* and *pneumonia* was the result of their visual similarity while that of *pneumonia* and *ammonia* rested on their auditory likeness. From all of these she had constructed the neologism "fmonia" which might serve for any of the three. Comparable confusions are in some cases very numerous as, for example, when *deference* is read as *difference*, *laughter* as *loiter*, *flock* as *float*, *experiment* as *experienced*, and *aggregation* as *exaggeration*. These and many others appeared in the oral reading of a fourteen-year- old boy with superior intelligence but with a residual strephosymbolia. At this age it is often impossible to say how much of such confusion results from faulty recall of the precise details of the printed word and from failure to learn its spelling and how much may represent a residuum of a complicating auditory word difficulty.

Among the older children—of late secondary school or college age— who give a history of a clear cut early reading disability, we have met several who have learned to read individual words accurately and who have acquired a good vocabulary but who have great difficulty in gaining the meaning from reading of long sentences or paragraphs. Not infrequently such a patient will be able to define accurately and without hesitation all the words in the material read and yet fall to grasp the significance of the sentences into which they are combined. The oral reading in such cases is apt to be a jerky, word by word procedure with very little of the emphasis demanded by major and dependent clauses, giving the impression that while each unit of the longer phrases and sentences is grasped, the grammatical sequence and hence comprehension are far from facile. These children complain of the time required to cover reading assignments with understanding and of the frequent need of rereading or even of more or less analyzing their required reading before being able to comprehend it thoroughly.

Spelling constitutes a major hurdle to children of this group. It is not uncommon to end their achievement in this subject lagging five or more grades behind their placement in school and their accomplishment in mathematics. Usually it is from one to several years below their silent reading ability but is apt to be much nearer the rating which they achieve in oral reading tests. Sometimes the words which make them the most trouble are the smaller words which they should have learned during their earlier years in school. Their errors are of the same general order as those of the younger children, notably misplacements and the choice of the wrong diphthongs or phonograms to represent a sound, showing their difficulty in the visual recall of the exact word picture. Reversals are not an outstanding feature but they are not uncommon. Often a misspelled word is recognized as such by the child with the remark, "I can see that it isn't right but I can't see what's wrong with it." Erasures and changes are frequent and many times a word that is correctly spelled upon the first attempt "looks wrong" to the child and he will add a few extra letters for good measure. As with the younger children, an occasional individual of this older group will show an extreme disability in spelling without the poor reading which more commonly accompanies it. No essential difference has been found in the type of errors made by these two groups of bad spellers. When the reading is not involved, there will be no difficulty, of course, in learning from books, but these children are heavily penalized in their written work because of their poor spelling, which may actually prevent their papers from being accepted, no matter how excellent they be in other respects.

These older children with a history of serious delay in learning to read while in the lower grades usually encounter trouble again when they take up the study of foreign languages. With many of them the ability to learn by ear is sufficiently well developed so that they have little or no trouble learning to converse in French or German, but the reading, writing, spelling and formal grammar that usually form so large a part of the instruction in preparatory school and college courses offer much the same sort of obstacles which the child met when he was first assigned similar tasks in learning English. Often when a new language is begun the first step is that of teaching the characteristic phonetic values of the letters of the alphabet in that tongue, and this occasionally makes the learning in the new language easier than might otherwise have been true, but by and large the borderline strephosymbolic is not a good prospect for the learning of new languages and his path is apt to be thorny particularly if, as sometimes is the case, he is at work in several of these new subjects at once.

Among the children of secondary school age who have been studied because of scholastic failures which were out of harmony with their general promise and their accomplishments in other than linguistic fields, we have met some with a degree of difficulty on the expressive side which has seemed very much more severe than would be expected from their apparent understanding. In a few this has involved both spoken and written expression but in the majority it has been much more prominent in writing. The poor spellers as a group are usually also poor in grammar, punctuation, sentence structure, etc., and occasionally this is so severe and so at variance with the understanding of printed material, with the general intelligence and maturing judgment of the individual, as to raise the question as to whether or not it may constitute a specific disorder in verbal expression comparable to acquired agrammatism. When severe, the condition serves as a decisive handicap in written examinations, and when it interferes with both oral and written expression the chance of a satisfactory adjustment in either academic or social activities is distinctly limited. Such cases form one of the more recent extensions of our studies in the language delays, and methods for a satisfactory approach to their diagnosis are still in a highly experimental stage, but they are a group of great interest and no little challenge.

The children with a specific reading disability are almost never interested in reading for pastime. Their whole tendency is to turn to athletics or mechanics or social activities as an outlet and it is not uncommon to find a child almost up to college age who has read practically nothing except those books which have been required in the school courses. Indeed, one of our college patients won a prize in a book-review contest when in high school by presenting a clever theme entitled "I Have Never Read A Book"! Naturally the restricted intake through lack of reading over a long period strikingly limits the store of words available for expression. The occasional individual may compensate to some degree for this by facility in the auditory field and so develop a good speaking vocabulary, but usually both spoken and written vocabularies are poor, and written compositions and examinations on which so much of academic progress depends fall far below the pupil's probable potentialities had his training from the beginning been suited to his needs. Long experience with indifferent academic success or failure in spite of hard effort may eventually dull the zest for learning even in the most conscientious pupil, and we find many of these older students apparently acquiescent to their status as failures or near failures in each succeeding.class, although sometimes their ambition does withstand their discouraging experiences and they persist in the conviction that they will master their difficulties in time and often optimistically present plans to study law or medicine although at the age of nineteen or twenty they are still deficient in most of their high school work. Their rating on intelligence and scholastic aptitude tests, which are usually composed largely of linguistic material, frequently drops below that obtained in earlier examinations but often is found to be higher than their output in the classroom would lead one to expect. It is frequently hard to determine in these older cases how much of the current difficulty is due to residuals of strephosymbolia and how much to poor early training. Typical reading troubles are often reported by the parents to have been suspected them in early school years but to have been either overlooked or underestimated by the school, or left uncorrected for one reason or another. In other cases there is a history of some extra help having been given to a child by various teachers in the lower grades and of considerable repetitive tutoring and intensive cramming of special subjects during vacations after the pupil has advanced into the secondary schools, but with no recognition of the fact that a fundamental language difficulty may underlie failures in such subjects as history and French, for example.

The presence of residuals of an old reading disability, expressing themselves in slow and inaccurate oral reading, considerable difficulty in grasping the meaning of even moderately complex material read silently and difficulty with spelling and written expression, often brings up the question of how far advanced academic education will be really profitable. Most parents want their children to finish high school or preparatory school and to make at least an attempt at college. The rigidity of college entrance examinations together with the foreign languages which are required for admission often serve to prevent such a student from going to one of the larger colleges and, unfortunately, the smaller colleges are not infrequently those which have clung most closely to the classical tradition and whose curriculum therefore is heavily laden with languages, while the sciences, in which the pupil would have the best chance of success, are not so freely available. In some cases, the experimental, so-called progressive colleges have admitted these students without the usual entrance requirements in English or foreign languages, but here independent and creative work is highly stressed and the boy or girl who is unfamiliar with books, who cannot cover a large amount of collateral reading and who is inept in written expression, is again faced with obstacles which are often insurmountable. In two such cases where the students' interests were primarily in drama, their difficulty in oral reading prevented them from successful competition in the tryouts for parts in dramatic productions. When the language problem is recognized for the first time at the high school age, there has often accrued so great a deficit in familiarity with words through lack of reading, which may in turn have seriously interfered with the development of understanding, that the question must often be raised as to whether this can be overcome by even the most careful retraining program in time to prepare the pupil for college before he is far past the usual age for it, and whether or not the same time spent in vocational training or on a job would not in the long run put him much further ahead than an effort at collegiate education.

To summarize briefly the clinical picture of strephosymbolia we may say that we are here confronted with a group of children presenting all degrees of difficulty in learning to recall a printed or written word with sufficient accuracy to recognize it (reading) or to reproduce it (spelling). While some children who show this syndrome may also exhibit concurrent disorders in other fields of language as, for example, in learning to write or in an adequate mastery of spoken language, yet many of them show no such complications and the most searching examinations reveal no other deviations in the function of the brain except this difficulty with the recall of word pictures, and hence they are much more selective than the "purest" of cases of alexia in the adult in which a certain measure of interference with other functions than that of reading is always to be observed if the examining methods be exhaustive enough. In this respect developmental alexia is unique and may indeed in time come to be recognized as a pure syndrome which will warrant further study for a better understanding of the acquired condition as well as for its own inherent interest and its great practical value to education.

2. Developmental Agraphia (Special Writing Disability)

Another group of children find special difficulty in learning to write. This may, as has been mentioned, coexist with the reading disability and the associated trouble with spelling, but the writing disability is also encountered not infrequently as an isolated developmental disorder. This special difficulty in learning to write may exhibit itself in one of two ways. In the first, the child may be able to form letters well and produce a neat and acceptable writing from a qualitative standpoint, but the process may be so slow as to constitute a definite obstacle to school advancement. An example of this type is the case of a boy who was quite unable to finish more than half of any class assignment requiring writing although what he did complete was neatly and accurately done. He was quite regularly receiving grades of about 50% on his written work, which represented an almost perfect mark for the amount of ground which he had been able to cover in the time allowed for each examination. Figure 13 shows the educational profile of such a case. This was a fifteen-year-old left-handed boy who was taught to write with his right hand and, while the product was of fair quality, he was able to produce while copying only the number of letters per minute that are to be expected of an eight-year-old as measured by the Ayres Handwriting Scale. The second type of this disability is that in which the quality of the writing suffers. In speed, these latter children are variable; some of them are slow, as well as poor writers, while others achieve a good speed but the quality of their product is far from acceptable and often quite illegible.

In many cases of this difficulty there is a history of a shift from the left to the right hand in early infancy, or an enforced training of the right hand for writing in spite of a strong preference for the left as exhibited in all spontaneously acquired skills. These shifted sinistrals seem a little more apt to fall into the group of slow writers rather than poor writers, although there is no consistency in this. Figure 14 shows an example of the handwriting of a boy of this group. His left-handedness was recognized and accepted in everything except eating at the table

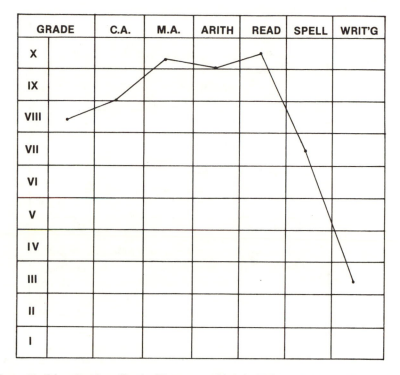

GRADE	C.A.	M.A.	ARITH	READ	SPELL	WRIT'G
X						
IX						
VIII						
VII						
VI						
V						
IV						
III						
II						
I						

Figure 13. Educational profile of a fifteen-year-old shifted left-handed boy with a marked special writing disability. The abbreviations are the same as those in preceding profiles.

and writing, where a right-handed pattern had been enforced. The upper part of the illustration gives inherent evidence of the difficulty he was finding in acquiring an acceptable writing skill while the lower part shows the results after he had been taught to write with his naturally superior hand. In this instance the training of the left hand for writing was not begun until the boy was fifteen yeas old. Sometimes when right-hand training of a natural sinistral has been instituted very early, the usages acquired through a number of years of such training may effectively hide the natural bent, and such cases of ''masked'' left-handedness can often be recognized only by the use of motor tests. Figure 15 shows the handwriting of such a case. Here the boy's tendency to use his left hand had been noted in infancy and he had been purposely trained to use the right. At the time of his examination at the age of eleven, he was considered by his parents, by his teachers and even by himself to be right-handed, but motor tests showed a much better latent skill in the left and he was consequently shifted to that hand in all his activities including writing. The upper half of the illus-

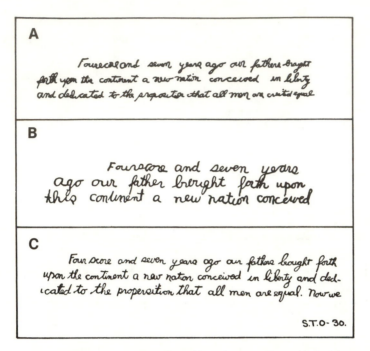

Figure 14. Writing of the same boy whose profile is shown in Figure 13. At A is an example of his right-hand writing when first examined. B shows the product of his left hand at the same time. It was then only one-half as fast as the right. At C is shown the effect of two months' training of the left hand for writing. In this time it had acquired the same speed as the right hand.

tration shows a fair sample of his writing after five years in school. The lower half shows the product with his left hand one year later.

It is not infrequent to find that a left-handed child, when he first starts to write, produces everything in the mirrored or sinistrad form, and indeed there is some reason to believe that this is the natural or spontaneous direction for the left-handed. Figure 16 is an excellent example of this. At the top of the figure is shown the product of a six-year-old left-handed boy writing with his left hand and showing almost complete sinistrad reversal. It may be noted that in the fifth word— the article *a*—he was in some confusion and produced a doubled letter, while in the next word, which is "pet," he has spelled it both ways as t-e-p-e-t and in the last word on that line he has reversed his direction. The lower part of the figure shows his writing—still with the left hand—one year later when dextrad progress had been acquired and dextrad orientation in all the letters except the *b*'s in "rabbit." In addition, however, to the fact that the left-handed child probably has to acquire an orientation and progress opposite to that which would be

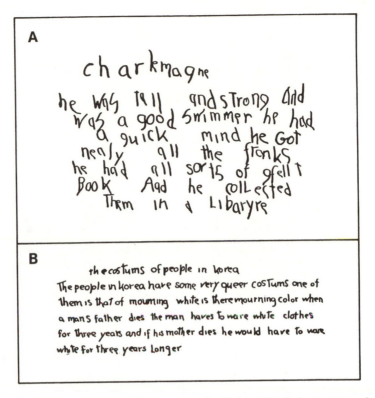

Figure 15. Special writing disability in a "masked left-hander," eleven years of age. At A is shown the product of his right hand after five years of intensive training while B shows his left-hand writing one year later.

most facile for him, he is all too frequently met by another difficulty in that the paper is put before him in the same position in which it would be placed for a right-handed child, which forces the left-hander to adopt the cramped and awkward position so often to be seen. The proper position to prevent this trouble will be discussed later in this volume.

In addition to the frank left-handers and those whose left-hand tendency has been masked by early training of the right, we have seen a number of patients who were indifferent in their handedness and who had less than the average skill in finer movements of the hands and fingers of either side and whose poor writing seemed to rest on this basis. In some of these the difficulty extended to the learning of any new manual manipulation and was extreme enough to be likened to an apraxia; in others it was sharply restricted to the movements of writing and it was among these later that two interesting clinical obser-

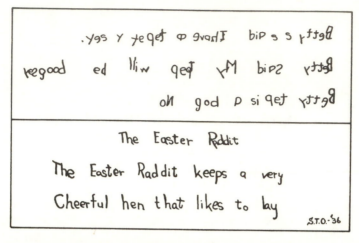

Figure 16. Writing of a left-handed boy. At the top in his spontaneous mirror-writing produced during his first year in school. Below is his product one year later when everything except the confusing *b*'s and *d*'s had been reoriented. Both examples were produced with his left hand.

vations were made. In one girl of eleven it was possible to demonstrate a high degree of dexterity in the finer movements of the fingers and the hand for a wide variety of activities, including the use of the pencil for drawing. She was able to draw each letter, singly, with ease and nicety, but the process of blending the letters into words with anything like acceptable speed for her age had resisted years of hard work on the part of both herself and her teachers. In the course of a routine examination of her skills, however, it was found that while she could not write successfully in the dextrad or ordinary direction with the right hand and showed no skill in writing in either direction with the left, yet she could, without practice, produce quite a respectable product with her right hand if written in the sinistrad or mirrored form. Figure 17 shows this girl's product. At A in the illustration is shown a sketch made from objects in her home which indicates a clever use of the pencil. At B is a sample of her usual writing in the dextrad form. At C is shown a part of her first attempt at mirror writing. If the reader will examine this before a mirror, its quality as compared with the dextrad will be immediately seen. Not only, however, was the quality good, but writing in this direction was also a much more facile procedure. Another patient who showed this symptom in striking form was a twenty-one-year-old medical student who had never been able to learn to write acceptably in the ordinary direction. With plenty of time and in simple material he could write so that it could be deciphered, but under pressure for time, as in taking notes in college, or when the prop-

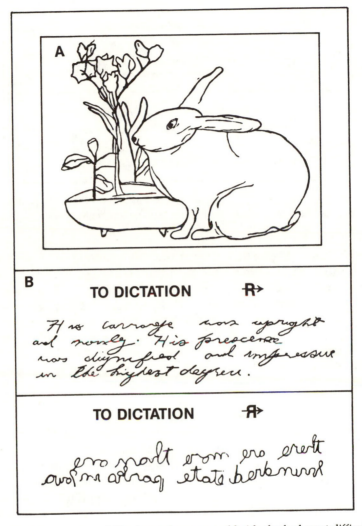

Figure 17. Mirror-writing ability in an eleven-year-old girl who had great difficulty in learning to write in the dextrad direction. A further explanation of this figure is given in the text.

ositional element was marked, as in answering examination questions, his writing was not only illegible to others but he himself could not read it. He was right-handed and possessed of at least the average manual dexterity as evinced in the dissecting room and in laboratory manipulations. Again, in this case, no latent writing skills were found in the left hand, but from the very first trial he was able to produce a legible and really quite creditable script in the mirrored form with

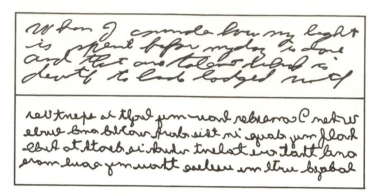

Figure 18. Mirror-writing with the right hand produced by a 21-year-old student with a marked specific writing disability. Further explanation is given in the text.

his right hand. Figure 18 shows at the top a sample of his writing to dictation which is more legible than the average of his propositional efforts, and below, a sample of his mirror writing produced within a week after his first introduction to this procedure. Again, if the reader will examine the lower part of this illustration with a mirror, the contrast between the product in the two directions will be strikingly apparent. A number of others of our specific writing disability cases have shown this symptom in varying degree of perfection, but so far it has not appeared in those cases in whom motor skills were clearly below average on both sides. The capacity to write in the sinistrad form is not an unusual accomplishment and one occasionally meets an individual who can write in either direction with either hand with almost equal skill. Figure 19 shows an example of this. The interest in the mirrored writing in the special disability cases, however, rests not so much on the presence of this skill as the fact that it was acquired without training and without practice during the long period when the patient was struggling unsuccessfully to acquire the dextrad or ordinary form of progress. This fact is worthy of especial note.

A second interesting fact observed in certain children who were having great difficulty in learning to write was the capacity to produce a somewhat better formed and more regular hand while their eyes were directed away from the paper or while they were blindfolded than while they were watching the writing hand. Figure 20 gives a fair example of this. Our attention was directed to the possible confusing element brought in by current visual impressions by a study in the Language Research Laboratory of the Neurological Institute of a case of aphasia following a fracture of the skull and damage to the brain. This patient was entirely unsuccessful in copying various geometric figures on the

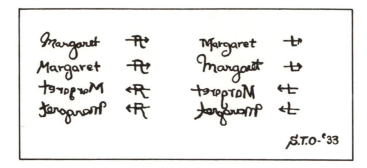

Figure 19. Skillful writing in either direction and with either hand. The initials indicate the hand used and the arrows show the direction of writing.

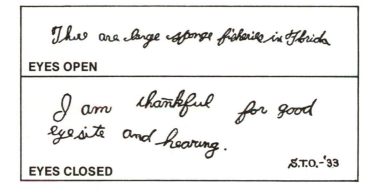

Figure 20. Contrast between writing while watching paper and while blindfolded, produced by a thirteen-year-old boy.

board while looking at them but could study such a design for a moment, close his eyes and then product a highly satisfactory replica.

The special writing disability in those cases which are not the result of faulty training, enforced shift of handedness, or marked motor intergrading, and which is not associated with reading or spelling disability, again exemplifies, even more clearly than does strephosymbolia, that the developmental disorders of language in children may exist in much purer form than do the comparable syndromes resulting from brain damage in the adult since *acquired* motor agraphia without other complicating disorders (notably of speech) is so rare that many authors deny its existence as an entity.

3. Developmental Word Deafness

There are cases described in the medical literature under the name of congenital word deafness but they are few enough to have been looked upon heretofore as decided rarities. The presenting symptom in these cases is a difficulty in recognition of the spoken word and a consequent delay and distortion of speech, but with normal hearing. As with the term word blindness, "word deafness" is misleading since it can be clearly shown that typical cases of this nature have normal hearing throughout the whole of the audible range and can hear the word accurately but do not understand it.

In these children as in adults with acquired word deafness, the audiometer gives an entirely normal picture. There is, moreover, no difficulty with the understanding of sounds of the environment—bells, whistles, etc.—other than words, and this condition forms therefore a very close analogy in the auditory field to strephosymbolia in the visual, in that there is no trouble with reception nor is there any difficulty with the elaboration of sensation until the word level is reached, but here the sharply defined disorder appears. When word deafness is suspected, careful tests of hearing are of utmost importance. With older children a test of the complete audible range on any standard audiometer is possible.

In very young or distractible children such tests are of course out of the question, and we must depend on our observations of their reactions to tuning forks, music and other sounds, and here a real difficulty enters through the presence of a condition which is apparently that of auditory inattention. Such youngsters at times react to various sounds and at other times pay no attention whatsoever to sounds of even greater intensity, and this is particularly true of spoken words. With the normal growing child, during his period of acquisition of word understanding and of speech, we expect a fairly close attention to words which are spoken to him, and even very active young children usually can be interested in nursery rhymes or stories read aloud to them. Apparently, however, in the children of the group which we are now discussing, the spoken word does not serve to attract attention freely. If the spoken word carries no meaning, it is easy to see why the child does not react to it. Indeed the sounds of speech around him would be disregarded as adults disregard the sounds of traffic or other adventitious noises of the environment. Occasionally this factor is so striking that a real question arises in the minds of the parents and others who are working with the child as to whether or not a true deafness is present.

True deafness, whether peripheral or central, does not belong in the category of disorders which we are discussing here. It forms a special and well developed field of study with its own methods of treatment, and such cases may therefore be excluded from our discussion. Audiometer tests, however, occasionally bring to light a special form of partial deafness which must be carefully differentiated from word deafness. This is the so-called high frequency deafness in which hearing is normal or nearly so for all pitches of the audible range except a few. The term "high frequency deafness" is not quite exact since occasionally lessened acuity may be found for only the lower pitches, as for example in bass deafness, and possibly the term "regional deafness," suggesting a reduced acuity in one region of the audible range, would better describe the condition. However, the higher frequencies are involved more commonly than the lower and the term high frequency deafness has already acquired wide usage. When such partial deafness involves those notes produced by vibration rates between 512 and 2048 double vibrations per second, which fall in the range required for spoken language, some difficulty with understanding may be encountered because the child cannot hear all of the sound units in a word. More commonly, however, enough sounds are caught to permit the understanding to develop with little or no serious interference, but defects appear in the child's speech. Generally, as shown by the audiometer curve, the hearing acuity drops sharply as the higher pitch ranges are reached and the defect in learning to speak is characterized by the elision particularly of those sounds which in themselves are high pitched, such as s, f, th, etc. Differentiation of the short sounds of the vowels a, e, i and u where the differences lie largely in the high-pitched overtones is also apt to be very defective. Children with this difficulty learn without instruction to cultivate a visual aid to understanding by watching the lips of the speaker and sometimes become quite proficient as lip readers. This reinforcement of hearing by watching the speaker is probably far more extensive in normal individuals than we usually appreciate since we all are apt to make use of it when listening intently to a voice which is faint or when in the presence of considerable noise. Advantage may be taken of this fact in examining children who have a speech disorder in which high frequency deafness is suspected, by having them echo after the examiner non-familiar material such as nonsense syllables, first while facing the examiner and watching his lips and then with their backs turned. Very often there is striking contrast between their capacity to echo the material under these two conditions. When a child is old enough to be given the audiometer test there is no difficulty whatsoever in the diagnosis of this condition. Before that, it is sometimes very hard indeed to say how much of a true regional deafness exists, how much word deafness, and how much a habit of auditory inattention. Figure 21 shows the audiogram of a typical case of high frequency deafness. The presenting symp-

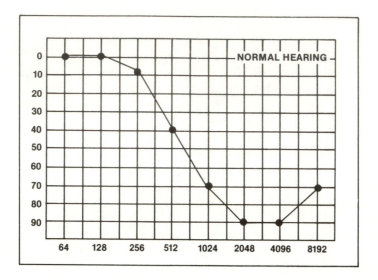

Figure 21. Audiogram in a case of regional deafness of the high frequency type. The numbers in the vertical column at the left indicate sensation units. The numbers below indicate pitch as represented in double vibrations per second. The dots on the heavy line show the loss in hearing units for each pitch as found in this particular patient. The critical zone for speech lies between 512 and 2048 d.v. per sec.

tom in this case was that of a speech defect rather than understanding. It will be noted that hearing is normal for notes up to 128 double vibrations per second. At 256 there is a slight loss in acuity while between 512 and 2048, which is the range used in speech, there is enough reduction to constitute a 50% loss as calculated by the Western Electric Audiometer scale.

Verbal understanding forms so large a factor in the acquisition of concepts and hence in the development of the intellect that anything interfering with the registration of words and their subsequent recall will of course sharply limit the mental development, and an, as yet, unanswerable question arises when we attempt to differentiate developmental word deafess, in its severe forms, from general intellectual defect. If a child is really deaf and is recognized as such, he can by appropriate methods be taught concepts and his intellect will continue to develop. When, however, the child obviously can hear, such methods will not be employed and if he does not learn the names of objects and concepts of his environment he may fail to develop mentally and become truly feebleminded by deprivation. Our studies of this group are as yet rather few but have led us to believe that word deafness may be at the root of many cases which are now classed as feebleminded and may also be the basis of the failure to develop speech in some of the so-called hearing mutes in institutions for the deaf and dumb. Minor degrees of this sort of a difficulty shown in a marked tendency to misuse words through confusion with those of somewhat similar sound are to be seen on every hand. Typical of course is Mrs. Malaprop. Traces of word confusions like those seen in developmental word deafness are not infrequent in cases of the reading disability, as was indicated in the discussion of that condition.

In the majority of those cases where we believe this form of disorder to underlie a lack of normal language development and which were seen as young children, there has been a marked overactivity. The child, while inattentive to speech, is by no means inert but seems bent on investigating the environment to the best of his ability by vision, by touch, and at times even by smell. While speech is usually greatly delayed in its appearance, it does evolve slowly and at this stage there is a marked tendency to a prolonged period of echolalia and a prolix use of the small and often defective vocabulary which is available. In this there is an interesting parallel to the verbosity and paraphasia of the sensory aphasics in adult life. As these children grow older a variable degree of understanding of spoken words is attained, and here again it is note-worthy as in the case of the reading disabilities that the ability to understand individual words often far outruns the capacity to grasp the meaning of equally simple words when combined into sentences, particularly if the sentence be long or if the form of its presentation be somewhat unusual. The rate of intake of meanings is slow, as shown by the much better ability to understand if the speech delivery be deliberate and the words carefully enunciated. Often one simple command will be carried out promptly and correctly, while if a series of equally simple tasks be requested only one will be attempted and even that may end in failure. The verbal output of these older cases is marked by many errors both of pronunciation and of grammar. Omissions of some of the sounds of the word are very frequent. As examples of this may be quoted "spense" for "expense," "minds" for "reminds," "post" for "suppose," "irresing" for "interesting" and even such extreme contractions as "flushey" for "flying ship." Parts of words may be distinctly distorted by the substitution of other sounds, as in "astinkly", for "distinctly," "repeller" for "propeller," "atween" for "between" and "ensify" for "emphasize." Confusions of properly enunciated words also appear as when "destruction" is used for "construction," "disaffection" for "defective" and "disgusting" for "discussing." There is also a tendency to drop out words from common phrases as when "quite a many people" is used for "quite a good many people" and "all sudden" for "all of a sudden." True neologisms also may appear, such as "ardless" used for "astronomer" and "phiages" for "physiologists." The varying forms of verbs seem to be especially difficult, leading to such expressions as "I have spoking," "They did all they can" and "thinking about to use" (using). Most of the examples of errors given here were from the speech of an extremely interesting boy of eighteen with normal hearing throughout the whole range as tested by the audiometer, normal understanding of sounds other than those of speech and normal appreciation of intensity, pitch and rhythm as shown by the Seashore musical appreciation tests, but a striking difficulty in both the receptive and reproductive functions when dealing with the spoken word.

Most of the children whom we have studied and whom we believe to belong in this category of developmental word deafness have given a history of marked delay in the time of development of speech and a striking lack of preferential choice of a master hand, and on testing have shown a definite "motor intergrading." The majority of those who were old enough to have made any efforts at reading have shown serious confusions of the strephosymbolic type when they encountered this subject. History of left-handedness or of some form of special language disability has been present in the families of most of these cases.

4. Developmental Motor Aphasia (Motor Speech Delay)

A fourth group of cases of developmental disorder in which we have been interested is that of children who are very slow in the development of speech and who usually show marked disorder in their speech as it develops but who have, in contrast to the word deafness cases, a good understanding of the spoken word. Their attention is usually quickly caught when they are spoken to and they often will listen carefully to what is said to them although they are somewhat more apt to be interested in doing things than in listening. They do not, however, show the striking degree of auditory inattention which is present in the word deafness cases, and would not be apt to be confused with deaf children. They use their hands freely in pointing to objects to obtain their desires but we have never seen any indication of the development of true symbolic gestures as in a sign language. They make efforts at verbalization in which they have a varying degree of success. In one four-year-old boy who probably belongs to this type there were no consonantal sounds at all in his attempts at propositional speech. He could echo quite a number of consonants after the examiner as separate phonetic units but could not use them either as blends with vowels in echoing or in his own efforts to talk. These children usually recognize their own speech errors to some extent and will not accept as correct a word pronounced by the examiner as they have given it, and this sometimes forms a diagnostic point of some value since it is in sharp contrast to the situation in the word deaf cases. Most of the children in this group are late in beginning to talk and likewise late in developing a preference for either the right or the left hand, and by the motor tests they usually show marked intergrading. In a few of our cases, history has been obtained of an abrupt onset of mutism after speech had started to develop, coinciding in time with efforts to train the child away from the preferred left hand. In one small boy such training efforts were accompanied by the development of a jargon which could not be understood at all but which cleared up strikingly as soon as he was allowed to use his left hand freely again in all of his activities.

These children with good understanding of the spoken word, but with little or no speech of their own, would seem to be closely analogous to cases of motor aphasia as seen in the adult. Milder cases apparently clear up spontaneously and such instances may be the source of the advice so frequently given to parents by their friends, "Let him alone and he will grow out of it." When speech is spontaneously acquired in these children, its development is apt to be very rapid, but a certain measure of speech defect often persists in the form of a lisp or a defective r or other infantilisms, and in several of our cases stuttering has appeared from the beginning of speech. Moreover, many of the child's early social adaptations will be seriously interfered with if he cannot talk freely with other children of his age. He is apt to be over-protected in the home because of his disability and often exhibits a marked emotional over-reaction to his feeling of frustration on vainly attempting to make himself understood, so that early speech training, which has given great promise in this type, would seem to be definitely indicated.

5. Developmental Apraxia (Abnormal Clumsiness)

The fifth group of cases to be discussed is that of developmental apraxia (congenital apraxia). The recognition of this type of individual goes back at least to Galen who spoke of some children as being "ambilevous," that is, doubly left-handed. Except for the unjustified implication as to the general unskillfulness of left-handers, this characterization fits the situation well. These children seem to be equipped with a lack of skill on both sides comparable to that of the left hand in a strongly right-handed person. The inability in this condition is for the carrying out of any complex trained movements whether they be of hand, foot, or body, and the question might be raised as to why this syndrome is included in a description of the developmental language delays. Two considerations have led to such inclusion. First, an acquired apraxia may result in the adult from a unilateral brain lesion, providing that lesion affect the dominant hemisphere, thus placing the control of highly skilled movements in the same group physiologically as the various language functions; and second, the difficulty of learning complex movements which characterizes the apraxias may extend to the motor patterns of both speech and writing as well as to the movements of the body and the extremities, and hence lead to specific language disorders in the motor or expressive field.

As stated above, there is a notable absence of skills on either side in these children and usually in spite of extended training there is a strong suggestion of a very close balance between the two hands. Motor tests often also show an amphiocularity or a lack of ability in monocular sighting by either eye. Such children are often somewhat delayed in learning even the simpler movements such as walking and running, and have great difficulty in learning to use their hands and to copy motions shown to them. They are slow in learning to dress themselves and are clumsy in their attempts to button their clothes, tie their shoes, handle a spoon, and in other simple tasks. One such boy recently studied had been slow in learning to walk and was awkward in his gait. He had mastered with some effort the riding of a three-wheel velocipede but the bicycle proved too much for him. Roller skating was likewise impossible for him as was baseball and almost all of the games of boyhood. In his case, his difficulty in learning motor patterns extended also to speech and writing. His speech was clipped and slurred, and although he could make all the sounds necessary for most words, his ability to blend them into a word and to use them properly in speech was very poor. In writing, neither hand had very much to recommend it and much effort over several years had failed to produce an acceptable penmanship. Although twelve years of age and equipped with normal intelligence, his motor patterns, on either side, were those of a much younger child and showed a marked intergrading.

6. Stuttering in Childhood

The last condition which we will discuss is that of stuttering. When encountered in the adult, stuttering has accumulated so great an emotional overlay that the problem of its genesis and treatment is much confused. This is a natural result of the experience of the individual who had been blocked, by reason of his impediment, from free social intercourse and who has very often indeed accumulated a heavy load of inferiority and a fear of speaking. In by far the great majority of stutterers, however, the difficulty with their speech began in childhood, and at the time of onset of stuttering the picture is very different from that seen in the adult. The emotional and personality factors which are so striking later and which have led many observers to classify all stutterers as neurotics, are notably absent in childhood. Many early stutterers when seen within the first year of their difficulty show no demonstrable deviation in the emotional sphere and present no history of environmental or psychological difficulties which seem at all adequate to explain the disorder. For this reason and since this volume deals largely with the developmental period of language, attention will be given here only to the phenomena of stuttering as they are seen in early childhood.

It may be wise to recapitulate briefly here some of the neurological characteristics of the stuttering episode. Two types of muscular spasm are to be observed, a tonic contraction of the muscles which results in a complete block of speech and which is sometimes called stammering, and the clonic or repetitive spasm which gives rise to the typical stutter. There seems no valid reason to attempt to separate these two conditions since close observation will show them to be intimately intermingled in almost all cases. The chief seat of these spasms is the speech musculature, broadly envisioned, including the breathing apparatus, the larynx, and the muscles of the lips, tongue, and face, but the spasms are by no means limited to this field, as during blocked effort at speech it is often easy to see that many other muscular fields are in a greater or less degree of tonic spasm. The clonic spasms also may overflow into channels other than those actually needed for speech, giving rise to clonic movements of quite distant muscular groups. Occasionally also this motor overflow may result in short, jerky movements of the arm, foot, shoulder, or head which might very easily be interpreted as the movements of chorea or St. Vitus' dance. Differentiation from chorea is, however, simple since the movements here described are consistently associated with an effort at speech and often occur only while the child is actually blocked by a spasm, whereas true chorea shows no such association with the speech effort. These muscular responses in fields other than those employed in speech are, however, an exception, and commonly the more readily observable abnormal motor responses are limited to the face and particularly to the lips and tongue. Here a very wide variety of movements may be observed, for the most part represented as fragments. Thus at times during an effort at speech one may recognize movements of sucking, spitting, biting, laughing, crying, smiling, etc. Their range is very much wider than that of the sucking movements which have been so selectively stressed in some interpretations of their genesis.

When classified by the time of onset of the disorder, stuttering children fall into two main groups. Many show a speech impediment from the time they first begin to talk, that is, from two or three years of age; others develop a normal and facile speech which continues so until the sixth to eighth year, when stuttering begins. If we consider what is happening to the child's language development in these two critical periods we see that during the first—that is, at the age of two or three—he is just beginning to establish his habits of speech and also of handedness. Some delay in both the beginning of speech and in the preferential use of either hand is common in the history of children who begin to stutter at this age. The second critical period occurs when the child is just beginning to learn his graphic language—reading and writing—and beginning to integrate these new unilateral brain functions with his speech which is still in a somewhat formative stage.

It is very common to find a considerable measure of special writing disability coexisting with stuttering. Many childhood stutterers apparently have as much difficulty in acquiring writing as they had in speech. With that group of children whose stuttering started early, that is, with their first efforts at speech, a typical reading disability also frequently develops when they first enter school. This has occurred often enough in our series of cases so that we feel that special attention should be paid to the early reading training of a child who has been or is a stutterer.

When we classify the childhood stutterers on the basis of history and examinations of eyedness and handedness, we find that they fall into four main groups. The first is that in which an enforced shift from the left to the right hand has been carried out by parents or nurse. The second is comprised of those who have been slow in selecting a master hand and who on examination show marked motor intergrading. In the third there is no history of handedness shift and no evidence of intergrading on examination but a very strong family history of stuttering. The fourth group consists of cases in which there is no history of shift and no evidence of intergrading and which are said to be the only cases of stuttering in the family. In an occasional case no pertinent family history can be obtained but in the majority of instances of these apparently sporadic cases, disorders of the language faculty of other types or the presence of a familial tendency toward left-handedness can be found by proper inquiry. Stuttering in children has no true counterpart in the syndromes caused by lesions occurring in the adult brain.

7. Combined or Mixed Syndromes

Emphasis has been given in the description of several of the foregoing developmental syndromes to the fact that they may be very highly selective and in this regard much more nearly approach the abstraction of a "pure" condition than do those which follow a lesion of the brain in the adult. In passing, mention has also been made of the occasional appearance of two developmental disorders in the same individual. Thus the child who stutters with his earliest speech is quite apt to encounter specific trouble with reading when he reaches that point in his schooling, and even more commonly will show a measure of the special writing disability. Inaccuracies in the auditory recall of word sounds comparable to a mild degree of word deafness have been identified as a complicating factor in many cases of the reading disability and even more strikingly in errors in spelling, as when a child mispronounces a word and then spells it as he has pronounced it. More serious combinations also occur, however. In those cases of severe word deafness which we have been able to follow into school, as well as in several which we have had under our own guidance in retraining, a strephosymbolic disturbance of comparatively severe grade has been revealed by their approach to reading and writing. When both of these conditions exist the problem of language training is doubly complex and the outlook for good intellectual progress is not particularly bright. Some of these children are skillful with their hands and do quite well in manual occupations. Some, however, exhibit a measure of apraxia as well as word deafness and strephosymbolia, and here practically every channel of competition and advancement is blocked. At present it appears that any one of these major disorders may be strikingly improved by means of careful, detailed, individual diagnosis and appropriate instruction, but where all three pathways—the visual, the auditory, and the kinaesthetic—partake in a developmental delay or disorder, the task of training becomes almost too intricate for our present understanding and techniques.

HEREDITARY FACTORS

The occurrence of a case of developmental delay in acquiring language carries no interference as to the intellectual status of the family from which it sprang, nor would our observation indicate the presence of any consistent neurotic taint in these families. Among our patients are to be found the sons and daughters of successful doctors, lawyers, ministers, scientists, writers, linguists, college professors and businessmen. One factor to be found in these families which is of specific interest to us, however, is the frequent occurrence of two or more cases of language disability in the same family. This has long been noted in the past but always, we believe, with regard to the occurrence of the same syndrome in closely related individuals, that is, congenital word blindness in one family, stuttering in another, etc. Bearing in mind the hypothesis that these various language disorders may stem from a common origin and that this may be the result of intermixture of right- and left-sidedness tendencies, our case histories have for a number of years inquired not only into the whole range of language disorders discussed in this lecture but also into the presence of normal left-handers in the family, and when this is done the familial factors are much more impressive than when the history is limited to the occurrence of any one syndrome in the stock.

Certain of the disorders under discussion may follow true to type in a given family so that stuttering may occur in several subsequent generations, as may the reading disability, without the appearance of other frank disorders. In the great majority of such cases normal left-handers will be found in the same families, however. As with any recessive hereditary character, this may be difficult to trace, since few family records are complete enough to ascertain the facts beyond the living generations and even here the early facts of development of the older members of the family may have been forgotten and their natural bent may have been markedly altered by training. One interesting story comes to memory in this connection. This was a family in which a child had encountered a severe reading disability and in which no instance of left-handedness could be recalled. Somewhat later, however, the family visited the Scottish castle which was the ancestral home of the mother's forebears, and found everything there the reverse of the common building practice and clearly designed to meet the needs of a race of left-handed warriors, and the countryside was filled with tales of the left-handed McD's.

No dogmatic statement can be made concerning the method of inheritance of these disabilities since the information concerning the family backgrounds is too fragmentary for a careful analysis. However, it may be said that all of these difficulties in acquiring language are more frequent in boys than in girls. Our earlier work indicated that in strephosymbolia the ratio is about 3½ to 1 and the distribution among stutterers is approximately the same. This preponderance in males suggests a sex-influenced factor, although it is clearly not sex-linked. In our group of stutterers the transmission has been somewhat more frequent by the male parent while in strephosymbolia it seems somewhat more apt to follow the female line. These statements are tentative, however, and must await wider observations and analysis. The incidence of left-handedness and several varieties of language disorder in certain families is shown in Figure 22.

Since it has been necessary again to bring into our discussion the factor of left-handedness, it would seem wise to repeat the previous statement that there is no real reason to consider the straight left-handed individual in any way inferior to the right-handed except by reason of those inconveniences which are forced upon him by the

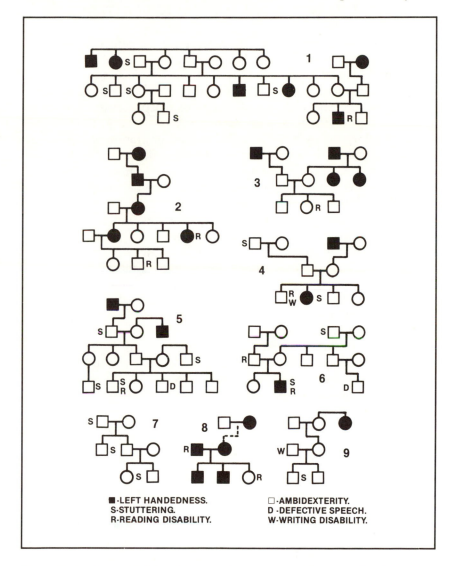

Figure 22. Incidence of left-handedness and several types of language disorders in nine selected families.

custom and usage of the right-handed majority. It is only those in whom the tendency toward some measure of left-sideness is present, but not in sufficient strength to assure complete unilateral superiority of the right hemisphere of the brain, in whom trouble may ensue and who form a fertile soil for the disturbing effects of misguided training.

EMOTIONAL REACTIONS AND BEHAVIOR PATTERNS

Since the children on whom our observations are here recorded were in the great majority of instances referred to us solely because of language delays or disorders, they form an unselected group as far as personality types and emotional and behavior problems are concerned, and we have seen a wide range of reaction patterns such as would be anticipated in any group so chosen. Because, however, of the cardinal importance of taking into consideration in any properly planned course of retraining, the emotional makeup of the child and his reaction to his particular disability, we have in history taking and in examination included as complete a study of the personality development of the child and the outstanding environmental factors in his situation as circumstances permitted. Especial attention has been given in each case to ascertaining whether there were any deviations in emotional development before the onset of the language difficulty and whether there has been any marked change in the child's behavior reactions at school or at home in the years that have followed. We have found, as would be expected, that there is a very considerable variability in the individual reaction to a given handicap dependent not only upon diverse factors in the child's own make-up but also upon the social, economic and educational status and ambitions of the family. It is obvious, for example, that a boy whose life ambition is to become an undertaker's helper and whose family approves this choice, as was the case with one of our patients, will not suffer from a reading disability so severely as will one who is bent on following his father into medicine, law, or teaching. Pressures arising within the family circle through competition with brothers and sisters may also influence his reactions. It is not uncommon to find a youngster who has shown no special concern over not being able to read in his second or third year in school until a younger brother or sister entering the first grade and finding reading easy is able to surpass the older brother in a few months and then the trouble begins. The stress placed by the school on the child's disability also constitutes a definitive factor, and the general educational philosophy of the school as well as the achievement of the child's class as a whole and the personality of his individual teachers must be estimated in the evaluation of his emotional reactions.

As the child who carries any form of unrelieved language handicap grows older, there naturally ensues an accumulated emotional overlay which in many instances makes any effort to assign etiological significance to either the organic or the emotional factors that are then apparent in the situation as purposeless as attempting to allot preeminence to either the warp or the woof of a piece of cloth. From our experience with nearly a thousand cases of the various types of these development disorders it becomes clear that no generalization concerning the appearance of emotional disturbances in the various syndromes under discussion is possible. We may, however, briefly review the reactions which we have met most frequently in association with each disability when seen early in its course.

The *reading disability* cases as a group form a clear cut example of the appearance of emotional disturbances which are purely secondary to the academic obstacle. The majority of these children have exhibited no deviation in either their emotional or intellectual development up to the time they have encountered reading in their first or second year of school. Indeed, the usual story of parents and other observers is that of an entirely normal, healthy and happy child up to the age of six or seven, who entered upon his school life with eager anticipation and had no difficulty in adjustments throughout the nursery school or kindergarten periods. The primary teachers may, moreover, have made no attempt to force him to read, but no matter how carefully the school attempts to capitalize those things in which the child is successful and minimize his failures, he cannot be shielded from making a comparison of his own between the rate at which he is learning to read and that of his classmates, and he tends to develop an entirely natural feeling of inferiority as a result. At first this may be limited strictly to the subjects of reading and spelling and if proper treatment for these delays is instituted early it will not extend beyond this boundary and will also be rapidly eradicated there with progress in the remedial work. When, however, proper treatment is not instituted or the handicap is entirely disregarded because of the "laissez faire" attitude adopted by many schools, the feeling of inferiority is very apt to extend to other fields so that the child approaches every task with the expectation of failure, and all of his school work may lag seriously behind. At times indeed this may tincture his whole reaction pattern. One of my third grade pupils who could read nothing and whose younger brother in first grade was learning to read easily, when asked to help his father with some simple tasks around the house, replied, "Oh, I can't do that, Dad, you know I'm a dumb-bell." In others a generalized feeling of depression has developed with unwonted tearfulness both at home and at school or an attitude of extreme dejection.

We have studied a number of children in whom the failure has led to a striking emotional blocking of expression. This also is at first apt to be restricted to reading and spelling and the child will talk freely and easily about his arithmetic or the facts that he has learned in his geography class but will stop abruptly the moment reading becomes the topic. At times this blocking extends to all his work at school and may even include the athletic program there, so that the boy cannot be led into any discussion of school or its activities. Not infrequently the child shows on the surface a cultivated indifference which masks the depth of feeling which exists toward his reading trouble until this is revealed by the marked relief of emotional tension which follows the beginning of successful treatment. Occasionally the strephosymbolics show a definite frustration reaction when their repeated attempts at reading have been unsuccessful, although they seem somewhat more apt to attempt to cover up their shortcomings and evade as many reading demands as they can. We have seen others who have reacted to their difficulty by the adoption of a boisterous, swaggering attitude, assuring us that reading was their favorite and best subject in spite of the fact that they were failing completely in it. Emotional instability resulting in the so-called "nervous" or "high-strung" reaction pattern in which distractibility and difficulty in concentration are outstanding has been observed in some of the reading disability cases, but except in the few in whom this was traceable back to infancy, this tendency has promptly disappeared with the institution of a successful program of reading. We have not observed any tendency toward seclusiveness and phantasia or the presence of abnormal fears or undue dependence on maternal protection as characteristic of the strephosymbolics. Indeed, time and again, the parents report that the child with the reading disability is the best adjusted and the most dependable member of the entire family group.

With the cases of reading disability encountered somewhat later in their school progress, the feeling of inferiority is apt to be marked as a result of their repeated failures, although this may to some extent be offset in those who have a good innate intelligence and are able to compete successfully with their fellows in mathematics and science. Compensations of this and other types, such as good athletic skills and social acceptability, naturally play a large part in determining the severity of the inferiority reaction in a given child. When an adequate program of retraining has been instituted and is proving to the child that he can make progress against his mysterious handicap, the inferiority feelings usually gradually evaporate. While carefully guided retraining has been successful in a technical sense in teaching reading to those who have even severe degrees of strephosymbolia, one might almost say that the greatest profit from such a program comes not so much in the reading advance, which at best must be slow, as in the effect which this improvement brings about in the child's personality. Relief from emotional tension, a generally more buoyant frame of mind and regained self-confidence are by-products of no mean value.

The cases of selective *writing disability* show no striking emotional accompaniment. These children are usually somewhat ashamed of their lack of writing skill and often no little puzzled by it, particularly when they are deft in drawing or in using tools, but as a rule this defect is not so consistently exposed to others as is a difficulty with speech or even one in reading, and ordinarily there is engendered in the child no striking emotional deviation. Nor do they as a group show any personality characteristics which mark them off from any chance group of children except in the cases of those in whom the writing disability exists as a complication of others of these difficulties such as an ability to read, a speech defect, or an apraxia. If very severe in degree, however, it may lead to failures in written examinations which the child may consider unjust, and he may develop a resentment toward his teachers or a feeling of frustration.

Since the beginning of the handicap assessed against the child in *developmental word deafness* reaches so far back into infancy, it is difficult to determine what characteristics are innate in this group and what are developed as a result of the defect. We will therefore merely describe the emotional patterns which we have observed without attempt at assigning them value. As a group these children are very slow in gaining a normal measure of independence from their parents, and several whom we have seen have been quite fearful of any strange person or situation. Negativism beyond that which might be due to failure to comprehend spoken commands has not been found with any consistency in these cases. Temper tantrums of an explosive sort have been observed as a part of the behavior pattern in several word deaf children. It would seem as though the earlier infantile pattern of screaming to gain a desire has persisted here through lack of the normal substitution of the growing ability to express desires in words. One boy of eight who had a marked deficit in word understanding launched a vigorous and somwhat successful physical attack on the headmaster of his school when criticized for the infraction of minor rules. Extensive experience in retraining this boy over a considerable period of time uncovered no tendency toward recurrence of this type of outburst when care was taken to make sure that the boy understood just what was asked of him and why, and our ultimate interpretation of his assault on the headmaster was that of a belligerent panic in the face of a verbal criticism which he could not readily understand. The notably bellicose attitude toward his fellow pupils contained in the history of one of our cases of severe high frequency deafness with considerable interference with word perception again seemed to link this pugnacious behavior with difficulty in understanding spoken words.

In cases of word deafnes, maternal overprotection as judged by standards for other children is usual and would seem to be a natural consequence of the longer period of dependence on others through which these children must pass before gaining sufficient mastery of words for understanding or for self-expression. Naturally, a mother who realizes that her child is not developing as he should and cannot make his wants known to others will continue to anticipate his needs, and this in turn minimizes the child's necessity for speech and in such a situation it not infrequently becomes necessary to place the general training of the child in entirely new hands before specific measures aimed at his disability can be profitably undertaken.

In sharp contrast to the cases of special reading disability, these children with an obstacle to the understanding of the spoken word do not seem to show any marked feeling of inferiority. Unless a considerable measure of spontaneous improvement occurs or unless training methods prove efficacious, they suffer from a progressive deficit in the concepts and ideas which are ordinarily absorbed without effort through conversation with others, but they seem to lack insight into this defect very much as the generally defective children do. There does not seem to be, however, in those whom we have studied, any retardation in emotional maturation or any serious fault in judgment such as accompanies feeblemindedness. Within the limits of their understanding they give the impression of being rather competent individuals.

Since the word deaf child cannot understand the speech of others and cannot express himself he is rather apt to play alone when young, but this does not seem to be an inherent seclusiveness and some of this group have shown definite social inclinations and a tendency toward garrulousness within their limitation.

The cases of *motor speech delay* which we have studied have shown a quiet, friendly shyness. They are quite ready to respond to advances from others and do not actively withdraw from social contacts, but their difficulty in expressing themselves naturally prevents them from taking the initiative toward making new friends among children or adults. As a group they have shown no abnormal fears nor signs of marked seclusiveness, although their difficulty in making themselves understood often leads to marked frustration reactions and occasionally to related explosive behavior. There is naturally a tendency for their mothers to look after them closely because of their inability to talk and sometimes a reluctance to undertake any disciplinary training since a two-way discussion of situations is impossible, but on the whole they do not appear to be inclined to be overdependent or very different, emotionally, from other children of their age.

The children with *developmental apraxia* are cautious in undertaking new motor activities, but in view of their disability this appears more in the light of a good understanding of their own capacities than as an abnormally fearful disposition. They all show as they grow older a marked feeling of inferiority but it must be borne in mind that in all athletic activities they *are* inferior so that such feelings are closely akin to insight. Some of them are very persevering in their attempts to overcome their handicap and reasonably successful in doing so. The apraxics occasionally are apt at scholastic work and gain a variable degree of compensation from this. They are often socially acceptable to the group in spite of their gawkiness and apparently are not inherently seclusive.

The picture in *children who stutter* shows a striking contrast to that in adults with this impediment, as has been stated previously in this volume.

In the younger group—those who begin to stutter with their first efforts at speech—there is no consistently unusual trend in emotional development. They are not as a rule overdependent on their parents or antagonistic to them; they develop the usual interest in social contacts with other children of their own age and are not emotionally unstable except for an occasional explosive outburst as a result of the frustration of their efforts at speech. These explosions, however, are impersonal and not aimed at parents, teachers, or companions and give the impression of a form of protest to their disability. In contrast to the emotionally equable temperament of the majority of these children they show a rather marked degree of hyperkinesis or motor tension. Their movements are apt to be abrupt and sometimes jerky in character so that they are frequently descrbed as "nervous" children. Some of these movements are directly associated with the speech effort and are to be considered as associated movements or motor overflows which have already been discussed, but there is in addition a tendency for the stuttering child to display a considerable degree of general motor activity. It would seem important to differentiate this form of "nervousness" from the emotional lability which also goes under the same rather vague term.

In the older group—those whose speech difficulty first develops from six to eight years of age—there is usually a history of entirely normal development—physical, emotional, and intellectual—up to this critical age, and commonly there is no history of adequate trauma either physical or psychological to account for the onset of the stuttering. Usually during the first year or more of their speech disorder they show none of the personality scars which characterize the adult with this affliction. As a group they are not unusually fearful—indeed some are adventurous—nor is there at first any evidence of the fear of speaking which may be so prominent later. They often on the contrary are naturally talkative and very persistent in their efforts at speech and in no wise inhibited from making an attempt to talk, although some of those whose disorder is characterized by long blocks in which no sound is forthcoming seem to be more prone to submit resignedly to the difficulty in talking and to curtail markedly their speech output. Clearly the problem in these childhood stutterers is far different from that of adults who stutter, and calls not only for specific treatment of the disorder itself but for measures aimed at the prevention of the various personality disorders and emotional maladjustment which bulk so large in the picture of this condition when seen in the adult.

CHAPTER THREE

♦　　♦　　♦

INTERPRETATION AND TREATMENT OF CERTAIN DISORDERS OF LANGUAGE IN CHILDREN

In the first chapter of this volume certain of the disturbances of language which follow injury to the brain in the adult were briefly reviewed and attention was called to the arresting fact that these disorders may follow a lesion in one hemisphere of the brain but only if it be the master half of the brain which is injured. It was further pointed out that our only guide to the master hemisphere in the adult was his laterality, and observations in children were reported which indicate a wide range of variability in establishing a clear cut laterality as measured by tests and history of development of handedness, eyedness, and footedness

In the second chapter five syndromes of delay or disorder in the acquisition of language were described—developmental alexia, special disability in writing, developmental word deafness, motor speech delay, and stuttering—and one other—developmental apraxia— which follows the same unilateral pattern of organization in the brain although it does not always interfere with language development. In all but one of these six disorders, viz., stuttering, it was pointed out that the symptoms observed are a very exact counterpart of those seen in the corresponding syndromes in the adult, suggesting strongly that the determiner for these disabilities in childhood is very closely related physiologically to that which is disturbed by lesions in the critical cortices controlling language in the adult. Since the normal pattern in the adult is a concentration of control of the functions under discussion in the hemisphere opposite to the master hand, and since our clinical observations show so wide a variation both in time and degree in the development of a selective preference for either side in many children, it is suggested that these disorders in language development may derive from a comparable variation affecting the essential language areas of the brain and thus rest on a basis largely physiological in nature and not dependent on defect or destruction of any part of the cortex.

The present chapter offers a discussion of the neurological interpretation of the children's disorders, a general review of the principles on which our experiments in retraining have been founded, and a brief discussion of the specific methods of treatment employed in each syndrome. A word of caution must be entered here, and that is that no general formula can be given which will be applicable to all cases of any of the syndromes discussed. Each case of developmental delay forms an individual problem in which factors derived from the neurological status, the emotional reactions, the educational needs and the facilities for carrying on retraining must be evaluated and a program devised to conform to all of these. This point can scarcely be emphasized enough since we are all prone to search for a simplified and universally applicable formula, but no such general "method" can be defined for any of these syndromes and any attempt to apply such a blanket prescription without thorough diagnosis of the individual case would assuredly lead to error and misguided effort.

INTERPRETATION

As has already been mentioned, these special disabilities occurring in children may show a much higher selectivity than do the corresponding syndromes in the adult. In certain of them, notably the reading disability, we are able to observe the step by step evolution of the disorder from the simplest beginnings, and moreover it is thrown into bold relief against the entirely normal previous progress of the child in his general intellectual and emotional development and against normal or even superior accomplishment in spoken language. Thus the problems presented are much less complex than those encountered in the tangled wreckage of a group of closely interrelated functions such as we see in the acquired aphasias. Apparently in the normal literate adult there is an intimate interweaving between such fractions of the language faculty as reading, writing, spelling, and speaking, which results in more or less functional overlapping, so that the results of even the most restricted brain damage are apt to be complex and rarely if ever do we see pure syndromes such as can be demonstrated in some of the developmental disorders in children. For this reason this group offer a particularly favorable field for investigation of the language function.

From our studies, extending over the past ten years, of the symptoms of the six disorders under discussion we have so far been able to recognize only one factor which is common to the entire group and that is a difficulty in repicturing or rebuilding in the order of presentation, sequences of letters, of sounds, or of units of movement and a brief presentation of our observations of this factor in the various syndromes is presented here because it has served to guide many of our experiments in treatment.

The reading disability cases are sufficiently advanced intellectually when they encounter their trouble so that they can be very intensively studied and it is clear that this disorder is not one of sensory reception but rather of memory. By a variety of tests it is possible to show that these children see the word that they are attempting to read correctly, but that the record left by previous exposures to the same word is not sufficiently clear to suffice for its recognition, as in reading, and still less so for its reproduction, as in spelling. The most apt demonstration of this point is that a child will frequently misread a word which he has just copied correctly and will still more often misspell such a word. When we study the errors made by these children in attempting to read and even more strikingly when we analyze their efforts at spelling, we see that the major interference with the process of recognizing or recalling the word is a failure to repicture the exact order of its constituent letters. As these children are progressively exposed to reading and spelling instruction, especially in the milder cases, this disorderly recall of sequences becomes somewhat less clear cut since they gradually learn to recognize many words correctly, particularly when clues to their meaning are offered in the context. In those children whose training in reading has been exclusively by the "whole word" or "sight method," however, order remains as an obvious difficulty much longer than in those who have been taught the sounds which each letter represents and hence have an auditory clue to the proper sequence. The characteristic confusions by reason of reversed orientation and reversed sequence which lead to the misreading of *b* for *d* and *was* for *saw* form a special instance which will be elaborated later in this chapter.

In the cases of special writing disability in children, as outlined in the previous chapter, there is sometimes difficulty in forming the individual letters but the purer cases are frequently able to form each character exactly and with ease but find an immediate difficulty when they attempt to combine them into sequences, whether connected as in cursive writing or separated as in "'manuscript" writing, and thus, except in those children with an apraxic factor who have a very low degree of skill in finger movements and those whose native skill has been sacrificed through enforced training of the wrong hand, the chief obstacle in cases of the special writing disability is in the formation of sequences of letters by which the word is constructed.

Naturally, since the syndromes of developmental word blindness and developmental word deafness are so closely comparable in every respect, we were led to look for reversals in the order of the speech sounds in cases of the latter condition and a few such distortions have been observed as when a child used the word *naf* for *fan*, for example. Reversed order of parts of the sounds in a word as in *emeny* for *enemy* and *pomerad* for *promenade* is somewhat more common as is the transposition of the two parts of paired or associated words as when "cuff buttons" is recalled as "button cuffs" or when a boy reports that he lives on "Driverside River." This form of error has not been common in our studies however and by far the more frequent type is due to irregular distortions in order of reproduction of the component sound units of a word, often combined with the omission of some of its sounds. Usually the first few sounds are given correctly while those toward the end are distorted in order or slurred or omitted. Occasionally these alterations give rise to neologisms such as those that have already been quoted from the speech of an eighteen-year-old, word deaf boy. While these children show many errors of a wide variety of kinds it is clear that their difficulty is not in hearing and not in the speech mechanism but in the recalling of words previously heard, for the purpose of recognizing them when heard again or for use in speech, and that one of the outstanding obstacles to such recall is remembering all of the sounds in a word and these sounds in their proper order. This can be demonstrated in some cases of developmental word deafness by the fact that the child is able to echo correctly many words which he cannot recall in expression, and indeed a prolonged period of echolalia is common in this disorder. During this period the child automatically repeats many of the words and even phrases and sentences which are spoken to him but which he cannot produce except as an echo. As will be seen, this forms an interesting parallel to the ability of the word blind cases to copy words which they can neither read nor spell.

In the case of vision, which is the function of paramount importance in reading, the correct revival requires proper spatial orientation and spatial sequences—that is, the symbols constituting the printed word must be recalled in the proper order in space—while in audition, on the other hand, we are concerned entirely with a temporal factor—that is, the sounds must follow each other in the correct order in time—and it is the recall of sounds in proper temporal sequence which seems to be at fault in word deafness.

In those children who are delayed in learning to talk but who seem to have a normal understanding of the speech of others, we again meet with a difficulty in sequence building which is as striking as that in any of the syndromes so far discussed from this viewpoint. Mention has already been made, in the description of the syndrome of motor speech delay, of the ability of children with this disorder to echo many sounds which they cannot use in speech. Indeed, many of them can reproduce as an echo all of the sounds of the letters of the alphabet but cannot make use of these same sounds in words and may not be able even to echo short blended series of sounds, and it is this sequential blending which seems to constitute the greater part of their difficulty in acquiring propositional speech.

In the case of children who have great trouble in learning complex patterns of movement—the developmental apraxias—simpler movements are often readily acquired although they may be lacking in grace or smoothness. Here the controlling sensory element is that of kinaesthesis or the registration of movement patterns. In by far the great majority of body movements, while one side is carrying out one stage of the act, the other is cooperating or preparing itself for the next stage or phase and a closely coordinated control of the two sides is essential. In many of the simpler acts, such as walking, there is evidence to suggest that much of this coordination is carried out by the spinal cord and other nervous structures below the level of the brain. When, however, we attempt to interrupt the simple movement pattern of walking and use parts of it to reassemble into a dance step, for example, this new combination is without question controlled by the brain and it is in just such recombinations of simple movement units into new sequential patterns that the apraxic child encounters trouble.

In stuttering children we frequently find true phonetic disorders in that certain letter sounds are imperfectly made or cannot be produced at all, but this is not always true and some of these children have as good a grasp of the process of forming the individual sounds as have normal speakers of the same age. Stuttering is so exceedingly variable in its severity from time to time in the same patient and so strikingly different in its expression in different patients that any general statement is hazardous and may readily be met with exceptions. We may risk this hazard, however, by pointing out that at least a major part of the young stutterer's trouble lies not in saying any one sound but in moving on to the next. Thus while we usually say that the individual is stuttering on the *k* sound in K-K-Katy, he is in reality saying *k* correctly over and over again and his difficulty actually lies in changing from the motor pattern needed for *k* to that necessary for the next sound, *a*. Thus in this disturbance of speech also, the fusing of the simple sound units into word-blends seems to play a prominent, if not the commanding, role.

While this difficulty with the revival of sequences affecting recognition in the two sensory syndromes—reading and the understanding of speech—and affecting reproduction in the motor syndromes—motor speech delay, agraphia, stuttering, and apraxia—is the only factor which we have been able to find common to the symptomatology of the group as a whole, and while it throws little or no light on the genesis of these disorders, yet there are several facts to be observed in the strephosymbolics and the developmental agraphics which challenge us to a neurological explanation. I refer here to the characteristic tendency to reversals in reading and spelling found in the strephosymbolics; to the development, without training, of a facility in mirror reading in the same group, and to the occasional occurrence, again without training, of a skill in mirror writing in cases with a selective writing disability.

The reversals are of two types. First, those in which confusion exists between two letters with the same form but opposite orientation, as when *b* is confused with *d*, and *p* with *q*. These we have called static reversals. The second is when there is an element of sinistrad progression through a series of letters as when *was* is read as *saw*, or *tomorrow* as *tworrom*. These we have called kinetic reversals. The two types are practically always to be found associated in any case of strephosymbolia, but they vary markedly both in their relative frequence and in the resistance which they offer to eradication by retraining. That the reversals play a significant role in strephosymbolia is adequately supported by our earlier studies in Iowa. The errors made by a group of reading disability cases were tabulated and compared with those made by a carefully selected control group of normal readers of the same reading grade and intelligence, and the errors by reversal were found to be significant statistically for the reading disability cases at each of the first four reading grades which were studied. Not only was this so, but the frequence with which errors by reversal appeared in the work of a given case proved to correlate with the amount of his retardation in reading, that is, with the severity of his disorder. In mirror reading likewise, the relative success achieved by the strephosymbolics was significant when compared with a carefully selected control group and it was noted that as the child progressed in dextrad reading, his skill in mirror reading was comparably reduced.

One fact about the reversals which will bear emphasis is the apparent equivalence to the child of the dextrad and sinistrad patterns. Thus there is no consistency in the errors made here and either one of the twin letters may be at one moment called by its right name and at the next by that of its opposite. Again, we must take cognizance of the fact that both mirror reading and mirror writing skills may exist in selected cases as a by-product of their attempts to learn to read or write in the dextrad direction and without specific training in the sinistrad forms. It is evident in the untrained mirror reading skill shown by some strephosymbolics that during attempts to learn to read words in the dextrad direction the brain has registered these words in the sinistrad position as well, so that they have become serviceable for recognition of the mirrored copy, and similarly in certain cases of the special writing disability, while efforts at teaching the dextrad or ordinary direction of writing have met with little or no success, the brain has received and registered the mirrored forms with such fidelity that mirror writing of a very acceptable quality has been possible with no instruction and no practice.

Since in the normal adult the cortices governing the language functions are active in only one hemisphere of the brain, it is pertinent to inquire concerning the physiological conditions existing in corresponding areas of the other half. Here we have very little exact information. The gyri of the nondominant hemisphere corresponding to those which form the critical areas for the control of language are a part of what are known to neurologists as "the silent areas" since injury to them gives rise to no outstanding symptoms. They are however almost, if not quite, as well developed in size and in nerve cell and fiber connections as are those of the dominant half, and we must assume therefore that they receive and register nerve impulses with practically the same freedom as do those of the controlling hemisphere. The fact that the normal functional pattern in control of reading is a strictly unilateral one, as demonstrated by acquired alexia, infers therefore that any registrations which may have occurred in the nondominant hemisphere have been elided or are unused. In recent years there has been a tendency to question the existence of exact sensory records in the brain and to speak in vague terms of dynamic forces here, and the term *engram*, which means a physiological record, is said to have "gone out of fashion," particularly in the psychological literature. However it is self-evident that any form of learning presupposes the storage in the brain of some sort of a record of a stimulus which will permit recognition when the same stimulus is encountered again, and the writer prefers to retain the word engram to define such a record, and the facts which have been recorded here suggest very strongly that engrams exist in the nondominant hemisphere which may, if not completely elided, cause confusion in recognition and recall. This view implies that the records established in the right and left brain hemispheres are oppositely oriented.

Strictly opposite right and left orientation cannot be questioned in the motor structures. That the bones, muscles, joints and nerves of the left arm and hand, for example, are the mirrored opposites of those of the right is categorical, and this strict antitropism or right and left pairing can also be readily demonstrated in the nerve cell mechanisms which control the movements of the limbs. Thus a microscopic examination of the spinal cord at the level at which the motor nerves to the arms arise will show groups of the large nerve cells which are directly in command of muscular movements arranged on either side of the midline in the same number and in the same patterns but in mirrored design. (Figure 23) This same plan is carried out in that part of the brain cortex which in its turn directs the activity of the motor cells in the spinal cord in voluntary motion. Here the giant nerve cells of Betz are arranged in similar order in the two hemispheres but again as strict right- and left-hand opposites. Immediately behind the motor cortex of the brain lies the field in which messages from the skin bringing information as to the place of origin on the body surface of stimuli of pain, touch and temperature are recorded, and in this same general field the kinaesthetic stimuli from muscles, joints and tendons are also received. That the registration of these groups of incoming messages must also be in the nature of right and left oriented engrams is entirely obvious since they must coordinate with the similarly oriented motor mechanisms to give adequate control. Other considerations bear out this statement that the kinaesthetic and common sensory records in the brain are oppositely oriented.

In the field of vision the situation is not so clear, but as far as the gross brain structure in the areas which subserve this function is concerned, there is just as strict right and left pairing as is to be found in the motor and kinaesthetic areas. In other words, the brain contains right and left visual areas which are exactly alike except for their opposite orientation and we feel therefore that the question of the existence in the nondominant hemisphere of engrams of opposite orientation from those in the dominant hemisphere cannot be lightly dismissed as the probable source of the static and kinetic reversals and of the spontaneous ability in mirror reading and mirror writing.

Since the problem of heredity plays such an important part in the genesis of the special language disabilities as well as in the problem of right- and left-handedness it may be well to discuss briefly the ways in which it might operate. We cannot at present accept the hereditary transmission of a purely functional character and believe that the passing on from the family stock of a strong preference for the use of the right or the left hand must rest on the transmission of a better brain structure in the left or right hemisphere, respectively, which in turn leads to the development of a functional superiority. As yet we have no precise knowledge on this point. Many investigators hold that in the adult the hemisphere of the brain opposite to the master hand, which is also the dominant hemisphere for language in almost all cases, is somewhat larger than that of the nondominant. So far as the writer's own studies have gone they do not support this view and we have no accurate information concerning the relative size of the two hemispheres at birth or in infancy. Moreover, size in the brain is a treach-

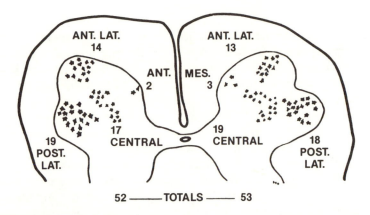

Figure 23. Projection drawing of a cross-section of the spinal cord to show the strict antitropic arrangement of the motor nerve cells of the right and left halves of the cord.

ero᠃ s guide as may be readily seen by consideration of the recorded brა n weights of various men of genius. This is true largely because a very considerable part of the brain's bulk is composed of materials which are not primarily concerned in its functional integrity—notably the fatty insulating sheaths which surround nerve fibers. Functional aptitude is probably dependent more on numbers of nerve cells, richness of their interconnections and abundance of blood supply than on the total size of the nervous organs, and it is therefore quite possible that either the left or right brain hemisphere might be endowed by heredity with a physical superiority over its mate without differing from it appreciably in size. Regardless, however, of the ultimate answer to this question, it is apparent that such structural superiority as is passed on to a given child might encompass the entire hemisphere or might be found in one area only and through usage lead to the development of a functional superiority of the whole hemisphere on that side, or as a third possibility the child might be endowed with a better structure in the cortex of one brain area in one brain hemisphere and in other areas on the opposite side, leading to a difficulty in establishing a complete unilateral superiority in functional use. Some considerations of the clinical observations made in cases of the special disabilities would suggest that the third condition may obtain, but no solution to these problems can be expected until much wider neuroanatomical, neurophysiological and neuropathological studies have been carried out.

TREATMENT

Experiments in treatment were incorporated as an integral part of our first program of research into these developmental delays and disorders of the acquisition of language with the hope that such investigation might throw more light upon the basic problems of their genesis which have already been discussed in this volume as well as with the more practical aim of finding means of aiding these children to overcome their handicaps. These experiments which at first were restricted largely to cases of the reading disability and stuttering were initiated in 1927 in the Iowa State Psychopathic Hospital under a grant from the Rockefeller Foundation. The writer there began the extension of this investigation to the other syndromes and this wider experimental program was carried forward as the Language Research Project of the New York Neurological Institute between 1930 and 1936. Because of the novelty of the clinical material, many cases encountered in private practice have also served as research material both from the standpoint of improved diagnosis and as a means of evaluating methods of retraining. From these varied sources we have now had the opportunity of studying carefully almost a thousand cases representing all ages from the preschool child to the college student and including pupils from public, private and parochial schools and from schools representing every shade of educational philosophy from the most progressive to the ultra-conservative.

As has already been stated, each child presents an individual problem, not only because of the diverse influence of a considerable number of environmental conditions, but also because the relative part played by each of the three major functions entering into the language faculty—vision, audition, and kinaesthesis— varies markedly in different children as does the child's emotional reaction to his difficulty. The first step toward successful treatment therefore must be a careful evaluation of the extrinsic factors—economic, social, educational, etc.— together with an extensive analysis of the status of spoken language, graphic language, motor skills or limitations, and emotional reactions. Our experiences in teaching reading to those children who have suffered from a delay or defect in learning this subject have pointed to the importance of sequence building in such cases and in our experiments in the other syndromes this has led us to look for such units as the child can use without difficulty in the field of his particular disability and to direct our training toward developing the process of fusing these smaller, available units into larger and more complex wholes. A brief review will be given here of the way in which this principle has been applied to each syndrome.

1. Developmental Alexia

The hallmark of the specific reading disability or strephosymbolia is a failure in recognition of a printed word even after it has been encountered many times. Because of this and because the great majority of the children whom we studied had already been unsuccessfully exposed to the sight or flash-card method of teaching reading, we believed it unnecessary to experiment extensively with this procedure and indeed as our observations were extended we came to feel not only that repeated flash exposure of the whole word was not effective but that it might in certain children even increase the tendency to confusion and failures of recognition. Since the majority of the cases of reading disability have shown a normal development of spoken language and could readily understand, when spoken to them, the same words which they could not read, our approach has been an attempt to capitalize their auditory competence by teaching them the phonetic equivalents of the printed letters and the process of blending sequences of such equivalents so that they might produce for themselves the spoken form of the word from its graphic counterpart. Since, moreover, in the greater number of strephosymbolics there is no frank disorder in the kinaesthetic function, we have made use of movement patterns to aid in eradicating confusions between twin letters and in maintaining consistent dextrad progress in assembling the units of the word. Thus in those children with moderate degrees of confusion who are seen during the first or second year of school and even at a much later period in cases of extreme severity, to eliminate the "static reversals" which lead to great insecurity in differentiating *b*'s and *d*'s and *p*'s and *q*'s and occasionally other somewhat less exactly antitropic letter forms such as *f* and *t* and *a* and *s*, the kinaesthetic pattern for each letter is established by having the child trace it over a pattern drawn by the teacher, at the same time giving its sound or phonetic equivalent so that the sound of a letter *d*, for example, is being produced simultaneously with the movement required to draw this symbol. The obvious purpose of this procedure is to fix the association of the sound with the properly oriented letter form, and its efficacy usually becomes apparent shortly after such exercises have been begun by the fact that the child can, by using the motion, consistently differentiate the confused pairs long before he can be sure of them by visual inspection alone. Our first attention is given to fixing the mnemonic linkage between "what the letter says," i.e., its *sound* and the properly oriented printed form, but since the letter *name* must also be available to the child for use in oral spelling, this is also taught in the same way. Ordinarily the tracing while sounding is not indicated for teaching the sounds of the letters other than those mentioned above, although occa-

sionally other letter confusions such as *h* and *k* and *u* and *n* are profitably eradicated by the same procedure. It has proved impossible to
forecast the amount of practice in tracing-sounding which will be
required for a given child. In general, the tendency to confusion in
orientation varies with the severity of the disability but it is also strikingly inconstant in the same child from day to day. Even after the task
of telling the twin letters apart seems to have been mastered, a reversion to the former uncertainty frequently occurs. At times this can be
related to fatigue, to an oncoming cold or to some unusual emotional
stress, but at other times no clear cut reason can be discerned for the
relapse. Since such a resurgence of the difficulty is common, however,
we have found it advisable to check occasionally on the security with
which these letters can be recognized and associated with their proper
sounds and to repeat the tracing-sounding when any hesitation or
uncertainty reappears. The emotional reaction of the child to this process as well as the success of the teacher in interesting the pupil in the
end result of the practice are apparently factors of major importance
in its rapid success.

No attempt will be made here to give details of the exact drill procedures which have been employed in establishing the phonetic basis
for reading. We have tried to avoid overstandardization lest the procedure become too inflexible and be looked upon as a routine method
applicable to all cases of nonreaders, which would be clearly unwise
in view of the wide variation in symptomatology and hence in training needs which these children exhibit. In teaching the phonetic units
we have often found it convenient to use cards, each bearing a single
letter or one of the more common digraphs, phonograms or diphthongs, printed by hand with fairly large rubber type in the lower case
or small letter form. These cards are exposed to the child one at a time
with instruction in "what it says" as well as its name, until he can
give either the sound or name for any of the cards at sight. A question
which often arises here is that of how far differentiation of the varying
sounds of one vowel should be taught, and since our aim is merely
to approximate the sounds closely enough so that a word known by
ear will be recognized when read, we have found the finer distinctions
quite unnecessary and have thus been able to keep the number of
sounds to be learned from undue expansion.

One point of difficulty which we have encountered many times with
the phonetic approach as it is usually taught is the tendency to stress
the vowel component of a consonant sound so that the child produces
bŭ for the sound of *b* with the major accent on the *ŭ*. This frequently
makes trouble at the next step of the process when the blending of
sounds is begun, since "bat" for such a child becomes "bŭ-ă-tŭ."
Purification of the sounds of many of the consonants to avoid the *ŭ*

component is often difficult unless the child be taught from the beginning that *b*, for example, is *bŭ* only when followed by *ŭ*. Practice in combining the consonants with all of the child's available vowel sounds thus becomes the first step in the process of fusing or blending sound units into words.

It cannot be too strongly emphasized that simply teaching the child to be able to give the sounds for each letter of the alphabet and for the phonograms, etc.,is hopelessly inadequate for the needs. We have repeatedly seen children referred to us as reading disability cases with the statement that the phonetic method had been tried but had failed. In these cases examination has revealed the fact that while the teaching of the phonetic equivalents may have been fairly complete, the next and most cardinal step, that of teaching the blending of the letter sounds in the exact sequence in which they occur in the word, had not been attempted or had been poorly carried out. It is this process of synthesizing the word as a spoken unit from its component sounds that often makes much more difficulty for the strephosymbolic child than do the static reversals and letter confusions. Here appear in the early cases and those of extreme severity the confusion in direction of sequences which has been presented as one of the diagnostic signs of strephosymbolia under the head of "kinetic reversals." It has already been mentioned that the two types of reversals do not always appear in the same numerical relation—in some children the *b-d* and *p-q* confusions have been found to be much more frequent than the definite progress to the left in attempting to read a word. However, in all of our very severe cases the tendency to sinistrad reading of parts or all of many words has been striking enough to demand special attention in the retraining program, and this is even more apparent if we add those instances in which distorted order, other than frank reversals, is found in attempts to assemble the sounds of a word. We have found nonsense material particularly helpful with those children who have already learned to recognize many short words at sight but who are insecure at this and apt to misread words by the substitution of another with a somewhat similar general configuration. Nonsense syllables can be constructed of three or four letters and later these may be further combined into longer aggregates and the child is informed that they are not real words and that he must solve them by sounding without attempting to produce anything with which he is familiar.

With those children who are seen in the first year of their schooling and who hence are beginning to blend only very short series of sounds to correspond with very simple sequences of printed symbols we have found that the habit of consistent dextrad progress may develop with the sounding-out process and not require adjuvant procedures, although even in these cases the addition of a single letter to syllables of familiar length or the addition of one or more syllables to the sequence may lead to the appearance of the reversal tendency. Thus a child who has mastered direction in three letter words may have trouble with those containing four or may maintain the proper direction in the first syllable of a dissyllabic word and distort the second part or may follow in the proper direction through each of two syllables but assemble the syllables themselves in reversed order. In attempting to establish the habit of constant progress toward the right in these children, we have again experimented with the employment of movement as a guide and have had them point to the letters of the word with the finger as they progressed with the assembly of its sounds. This method of finger pointing while reading is a spontaneous act with some children and has been criticized as retarding the rate of reading seriously. There remains, however, the very pertinent question as to whether children who use finger pointing while reading are slow readers because of this habit or whether they are slow readers because of strephosymbolic confusions and make use of the finger to overcome their difficulty. It must be remembered here, moreover, that in the case of extreme degrees of the reading disability our choice may not lie between rapid and slow reading but between slow reading or none at all.

In the case of facile readers the acquisition and exercise of this skill brings, without special attention, a considerable degree of association between the printed letter and the sound it represents. It must be remembered, however, that the special reading disability operates as a distinct obstacle to the association process and we have found it is not safe to assume that when the associative linkages are established in one direction they will also be operative in the other. Thus a child may be able to give promptly the sound equivalent of each letter as it is presented visually and yet be quite unable to give the name of the letter or to produce its graphic form when its sound is presented verbally. Since the reading disability cases without exception are poor spellers it has proved advisable to make sure of all of the usable linkages between vision, audition and kinaesthesis while the reading retraining is under way. It has been our experience that if this be not done reading may advance fairly successfully but spelling will make almost no headway or, as in one striking case, oral spelling may be fairly well acquired but written spelling may remain extremely faulty. This was the case of a young girl who had led her class in spelling in Texas but on moving to Iowa was failing consistently in this subject. On inquiry it was found that in Texas the spelling lessons were always recited aloud while in Iowa lists of words were dictated to be written. The child had not formed a prompt and facile association between the letter name and its graphic form, and while she had no writing disorder her attempts at written spelling were filled with errors of substitution and omission.

Spelling in our experience has been much more difficult of acquisition than reading and much more resistant to special retraining procedures. This can be readily understood when we appreciate that a much less exact mnemonic pattern is necessary for recognition than for recall. Misspelled words will often be read by a poor speller without cognizance of the error, or more frequently the child will say that the word does not look quite right although he is unable to see what is wrong with it. Because of this lack of precision in visual recall of a word it is important to make use of the auditory patterns by means of phonetic dissection as a guide to spelling and to make sure that careful auditory discrimination between closely similar sounds be well established. The short sounds of the vowels, notably ă, ĕ, and ĭ are very apt to be poorly differentiated in the speech of the average child and substitution of one of these sounds for another is frequent. Especial attention should therefore be given to the clear differential enunciation of all of the phonetic units. Errors in the pronunciation of the sounds may make relatively little trouble in reading since a word bearing a compromise sound or even a true substitution of one short vowel for another is often still sufficiently close to the auditory memory of it to bring recognition, but in spelling, of course, such substitutions constitute glaring errors. In English spelling, the problem is further complicated by the fact that a given phonetic unit may often be represented in several ways. It is important therefore for the child to learn that the long sound of *a*, for example, may be designated by *a, ay, ai, ea, eigh*, etc., and practice in telling how many ways we can indicate the *a* sound is valuable both for reading and for spelling. Unfortunately for these children, the correct choice usually rests on visual familiarity with the word and, since it is in this field that their handicap lies, even with intensive effort on the part of both teacher and pupil, spelling usually lags behind reading by one or more grades.

Phonetic analysis or sound dissection of words which are familiar by ear and accurately spoken but are misspelled in the pupil's oral or written work has frequently proved serviceable in correcting certain types of errors. This often proves to be almost as difficult a procedure for the child at first as is the opposite process of phonetic synthesis or sound blending for the construction of words from their phonetic units as described above. The spoken word has been acquired in both the auditory memory and in the speech mechanism as a unit and not a blend of its parts and often the child is completely at sea at first as to how to approach the dissection. Occasionally even the breaking up of long words into syllables is difficult or impossible although this seems to be more readily learned than the further step of analyzing the syllables themselves into sounds. This approach to the use of the auditory memory of words as an aid to spelling has been of special value in correcting two outstanding types of errors in spelling—omissions of letters and distorted order in assembling the proper letters. Accuracy of speech is naturally of cardinal importance for this purpose. If sounds are omitted or slurred or improperly differentiated in the child's own speech, this is strongly reflected in the spelling of those who do not have an accurate visual recall of the word's appearance. When, for example, such a boy speaks of the "sopperntendent" of his school, he is apt to spell it likewise. Obviously these processes interact and in those words in which the correct spelling has been acquired there is usually a more accurate spoken reproduction although older patterns of slovenly pronunciation may remain, especially in propositional speech, despite knowledge of the spelling of the word. In many cases, a campaign of speech training for accurate and clear enunciation is indicated. When there is not too great a degree of mispronunciation the child may be taught to take apart the blended word into its constituent phonetic units and to name and write each unit as it is isolated. In those children in whom a direct association has been established between the sound of the letter and its graphic reproduction the step of naming is unnecessary and the child separates the phonetic units and writes a symbol for each. Many children, however, have been so thoroughly trained to link the written form of the letter with its name that it is necessary for them, after dissection of the blend into its components, to assign a letter name to each sound so isolated and then to write the corresponding letter. Our experience here has again emphasized the fact that each linkage of the association process must be checked before it can be trusted. Thus it is not uncommon to find a child who, while spelling a word aloud and writing it at the same time, will give the name of the correct letter and yet produce on the paper an entirely different one.

With the severe strephosymbolics who have spent two or three years in school without progress in learning to read there is often a considerable emotional reaction to the failure and an obvious desire to master, at once, this topic in which their classmates have so rapidly outstripped them, and this has naturally raised the question as to how early in the course of the retraining narrative reading may be introduced. In our experience this has generally been unprofitable until the phonetic foundation is secure and the child has begun to learn to blend successfully so that he can see for himself that there is a way to find out what a word "says" even if he does not recall it from its visual presentation. There will be variations here, of course, dependent on many extrinsic influences, but as a rule those children who have experienced several years of exposure to reading with little or no profit are easily intrigued with the fact that this new task is something in which they are not completely "stymied" but in which day to day progress is obvious to them. When carefully encouraged it is thus usually possible to maintain interest and cooperation until such time as actual reading can be begun. One difficulty is often encountered here which is troublesome to overcome, and that is that during the two or three years in which the child has been completely blocked in reading his interests have been expanding at a normal rate so that one is faced with a boy who can be interested only in fourth grade reading material, for example, and yet whose technical skill in reading would limit him to stories of "the little red hen." This not infrequently offers a real challenge to the teacher to find or devise material with a very simple vocabulary and yet with a sufficiently interesting content so that the child is not disheartened by the "babyishness" of the reading on which he must practice. One danger which arises here and which the teacher must be prepared to combat is that the child stimulated by his success in mastering the phonetic work, may expect too rapid progress in narrative reading and may go through a period of discouragement as he finds that "sounding out," while enabling the reading of individual words, is a very slow process until considerable practice has ultimately fixed the majority of the more frequently encountered words so that they are recognized at sight or can be sounded out so rapidly as to bring almost instant recognition. During this stage of the retraining, the maintenance of the child's morale is extremely important and often presents a problem challenging the ingenuity of the teacher. One measure with which we have experimented to meet this situation is to have the child read part of the story and then to have the teacher read aloud for a time to maintain the interest in the content. It is important, however, to hold the pupil to high standards of accuracy in all of his attempts at oral reading, aiding him only with the words which he is not yet prepared to master by the phonetic approach, in order to prevent a return to earlier habits of guessing or approximation.

In addition to the relief from emotional stress which comes with successful progress in the new way of learning to read, a not unimportant by-product is the change in ease with which the attention can be held and the disappearance of a characteristic motor unrest which is seen in many of these nonreaders. With a number of our cases of strephosymbolia the question has been seriously raised by teachers or parents as to whether the whole of their failure in reading might not be caused by a fundamental defect in the attention. This question arises because of their marked distractibility and their tendency to be constantly squirming or wriggling in their chair when confronted with the—for them—impossible task of recognizing words at sight, although they may work with considerable concentration upon other tasks not involving reading. The initiation of phonetic training—a task which can be mastered—often brings a change in these two factors which is little short of miraculous. The child is not only able but willing to sit quietly through a fairly long drill period with excellent attention, and indeed as progress begins to be obvious the attention is often exceptionally well maintained.

No fixed program has been adopted as to the amount of time to be spent on the phonetic drills. As a general rule, however, it has proved advisable to devote not less than one half hour nor more than one hour daily to this work and even this may be cut into several shorter sessions or divided between time spent on giving the phonetic equivalents for the letter cards and in writing letters from dictation of their sounds, etc. When possible it has seemed wise to have the remedial work incorporated as part of the school day and carried on during the time when the child would otherwise be unprofitably occupied in the regular reading class. This obviates any feeling on the part of the child that he is being punished for failure in reading by having to work after school or during a period which is playtime for the other pupils. Since most of the strephosymbolics have a good auditory memory it has proven valuable at times to offer oral instruction in those subjects which are being covered by the rest of the class and which require reading, such as geography. It is also important at this stage that all of the child's teachers understand his limitations so that he may not be retarded in his learning of arithmetic, for example, by his inability to read the problems for himself, or by reversals in the putting down of a sum correctly added as when 7 + 5 are written as 21 although the child was thinking 12, or by difficulties arising through inconsistency in the direction of carrying or borrowing.

One query which recurs in the discussion of retraining programs is that of how long special work will have to be continued, and to this no definite answer can be given. It is obvious, however, that no miracle such as learning to read fluently in a few weeks or months can be expected and that the program should be planned looking toward two or three years of more or less individualized help with a gradual change in the nature of the remedial work as the child's skills increase and as advances in school grade alter the demands on him.

It will be apparent from the foregoing description of the methods which we have found most successful in retraining children with a severe degree of strephosymbolia that the procedures can only be carried out as a highly individualized program, that is, that the teacher must be prepared to work alone with the child, and this has been found to apply also to those with less extreme degrees of severity who have been overlooked or uncared for during the first years of their schooling, so that there is a striking deficit in both their reading ability and their reading experience. When, however, children who show only mild degrees of the disability are considered, it is pertinent to inquire whether or not treatment in groups may be practicable. One experiment in which these milder cases were segregated from the bulk of the class in the first grade and trained by the phonetic method has been tried and gives promise of considerable success.

For those pupils who, in spite of a moderate handicap in reading, have advanced into the upper grades of grammar school or into junior high school before any effort has been made to correct their disability, as well as for those who have successfully completed the earlier stages of remedial work, oral reading takes an increasingly prominent place in the retraining program. This has usually been dropped out of the school curriculum before these higher grades are reached and tests of the child's ability in this will frequently demonstrate that he has been reading to himself with only an approximation of the correct word sounds and with slurring or omission of many new and difficult words, guessing at the meaning of many of them from the context. If his disability be not severe and he has a good intelligence, he may even be able to obtain passable scores for his age on tests of silent reading comprehension, but he is often unable to make any headway with new or difficult subject material. This sort of reading does not enable him to store memories of words sufficiently clearly to be serviceable in his own speech or writing and he is often at a loss in following some grammatical constructions and in understanding reading material in which practically every word must be grasped for adequate comprehension such as is apt to be demanded of him in his courses in science and mathematics. In such cases, oral reading brings to light many deficiencies in phonetic associations and offers an opportunity to discuss exact word meanings and choices. Reading aloud with emphasis on correct pronunciation and some attention to the construction of exceptional words may also serve as a direct aid to spelling which, in these children, usually lags considerably behind their ability in silent reading comprehension and is much more apt to be found on a level with their ability in oral reading. Study of phonetic choices, word families, spelling rules, prefixes and suffixes, simple derivations and the requirements of grammatical construction have been found profitable at this age.

Unless there be a complicating or associated *motor* disorder such as an agraphia or a speech defect, the problem of handedness is not important in cases of the reading disability. We have found no evidence to show that conversion of a naturally left-handed child to the right-handed pattern plays any part in the genesis of this syndrome and we have also found extreme degrees of strephosymbolia in clear cut dextrals as well as clear cut sinistrals. Since the difficulty can be so clearly related to the sensory cortices there seems to be no good reason for interfering with any pattern of handedness which has been established in the child—be it right or left or converted. Moreover, since the confusions seem to be so clearly referable to the process of recall rather than that of sensation there is, on theoretical grounds at least, no reason to believe that measures aimed at changing the eyedness or those intended to train the eye movements will be particularly profitable, although of course errors in refraction should be corrected with glasses whenever indicated.

One urgent practical question arises in many of these cases and that is, "How far is it justifiable to continue the special training in a particular child?" If the disability be severe or if it has been overlooked for several years, the retraining, to be successful, must be carried out on an individual basis, as has been pointed out, and progress at first is often quite slow. As a consequence, it is a costly form of education and external considerations must be evaluated in determining its practicability in a given case. Here the general intellectual level of the family from which the child comes as well as their economic status must be considered. The relative degree of disability which the child exhibits and his probable latent intelligence, together with his own vocational interests, are also factors of importance in such a decision. However, it must be remembered that reading and writing, while not essential in all trades, are an important part of the equipment in any, and that advancement in almost any occupation will depend in part at least on the possession of at least a reasonable amount of skill with these two fundamental intellectual tools. Moreover, when we see pupils with the reading disability repeating year after year of schooling, the question may well be raised as to whether the tutoring required to give such a child a start in reading might not prove less costly in the long run to both parent and school than are the many repetitions.

It may be noted that the methods recommended here are diametrically opposed to those which are currently in use in many schools. There has been in recent years a striking swing toward the use of the sight or flash-card method of teaching reading and away from the use of phonetics. The writer is not in a position to offer an opinion as to the efficacy of either of these methods as a general school procedure but their effect on children suffering from varying degrees of strephosymbolia has come under his immediate attention and he feels that there can be no doubt that the use of the popular flash method of teaching reading is a definite obstacle to children who suffer from any measure of this disability. We have no new numerical data to offer here since our work recently has dealt exclusively with referred cases and we have made no general surveys of the number of cases of the reading disabilities in schools using different methods. At an earlier period, however, some such surveys were undertaken in Iowa and they indicated strongly that where the sight or flash-card method of teaching reading was exclusively used, the number of reading disability cases was increased by three times that found in schools which used phonetic training for those children who did not rapidly progress by the flash-card method. As a further measure of the comparative efficiency of these two methods of teaching when dealing with a case of specific reading disability, it may be said that we have retrained a number of children who had not progressed beyond first grade reading skills after having spent three or four years in schools where the sight method was used exclusively, and have been able to advance them by two or more reading grades in one academic year by the application of the phonetic method. This has also been true in many cases in which the school program had been previously supplemented by intensive individual work but with no phonetic training or at best very inadequate attempts along these lines. It may also be noted in passing that the great majority of the children whom we have seen have not shown any lack of desire to learn to read although they may have been prevented from obtaining any profit or pleasure from efforts to read by themselves in the past because of their very deficient skills. Indeed, a reading disability may be suspected whenever a child does not occasionally turn to reading for pastime and, conversely, when remedial reading training has been successful in supplying the child with a usable skill, his interest in reading will usually develop spontaneously and he will commence at once to make up for lost time.

It would obviously be advantageous, were it possible, to select those children who have a strephosymbolic tendency at the time of their entry into school, or before, and thus build a preventive program rather than to await the advent of the trouble and then institute retraining. Practically all children, however, show a tendency to confusion of reversible letters and to occasional sinistrad reading of reversible words, and no means have yet been devised which will indicate whether these ambivalent tendencies in visual recall will persist and make trouble or whether they will rapidly disappear. We cannot yet therefore make a selection for preventive treatment but there are certain children who might be said to be under suspicion as potential reading disability cases. These include the stutterers whose impediment began with their earliest speech, children with difficulty in understanding the spoken word, the apraxics, and those who have been very late in making a choice of a master hand. As far as our observations go at present those with good understanding of the speech of others but who are slow in developing their own speech are less apt to encounter trouble with reading than is the case with the other groups mentioned. A family history of left-handedness or of the occurrence of other cases of developmental language disorders should put us on guard for a reading disability, but is of no import as to the outlook in any particular child. Obviously, however, the earlier special measures are adopted for children with special needs, the greater will be the chance of ultimate success, and we feel that no child with average intelligence or better should be allowed to continue into his second year of schooling, if there be tangible evidence of a reading difficulty, without an analysis to determine whether or not he be of the strephosymbolic group so that special measures may be instituted, when indicated, before he suffers the emotional disorders and language deficits which are usually cumulative from this time on.

In the chapter dealing with the various syndromes met in children, we have spoken of cases first seen after they have reached the late years of the secondary schools or the early years of college as cases exhibiting the residuals of a mild strephosymbolia, and almost without exception this is warranted from the standpoint of their educational history since the record of their early school years gives evidence of marked delay in learning to read and characteristic persistent difficulty with spelling. When viewed, however, from the symptomatology as seen in later years, the disorder is often not so much that of recognition of words as it is that of the comprehension of the meaning of series of words forming sentences and paragraphs. Lack of facility in written expression also marks some of these cases and the two syndromes might therefore be better considered as the counterpart in the reading sphere of Kleist's "sentence deafness" and "sentence muteness" with their characteristic paragrammatic and agrammatic defects respectively. Only a very few of our cases of typical strephosymbolics, who were recognized as such at an early stage of their education and who have been retrained in reading, have as yet progressed as far as college, and the number of those who have been studied for the first time after their entry into college is also comparatively small. Retraining experiments are under way in some such cases and with promise of real betterment, but the series is too restricted in number to permit of an expression regarding the best methods of treatment. Our experiments to date have followed the simple plan of a very careful analysis of the language function from both the oral and visual standpoint and the institution of measures aimed at the correction of the more patent shortcomings. This must obviously be a highly individualized program and since it leads directly into questions of nicety of word discrimination, of etymology and of syntax, as well as the ability to select the significant concepts from a paragraph or a chapter, it requires tutors with a considerable educational background of their own. One very serviceable point, however, should be mentioned, and that is that the same student who may fail sadly to grasp the meaning of material which he reads for himself, may be able to understand quite well the same material read aloud to him by someone else. One pupil who had been dropped from college for failure in the midyear examinations of his freshman year was reinstated provisionally under an oral tutorial program and was able to carry his work successfully in this manner and has since been graduated. The whole problem of these older patients, however, is still in a highly experimental stage and forms one of the frontiers for further research.

2. Developmental Agraphia

In those children who have encountered especial difficulty in learning to write either with serviceable speed or acceptable legibility, tests of skill in the two hands find a history of handedness development in childhood are of utmost importance since here we meet many problems primarily motor in nature.

A considerable number of those who have trouble learning to write are frank left-handers who have been taught from the beginning to use their right hands for writing. Obviously many natural sinistrals have acquired a legible and rapid writing with the right hand but there are others in whom speed or legibility has suffered by this enforced shift and still others who write well and rapidly with the right hand but in whom the threshold of fatigue is low or who find that the mechanics of right-hand writing distracts them to some degree from the content of their compositions. There seems to be no age limit beyond which retraining of the left hand for writing cannot be fairly easily accomplished in strongly left-sided individuals. For the right-handed adult, learning to use the left hand for writing is arduous, but it is often surprising how quickly and easily this skill can be acquired even in adult life by a native sinistral. We have recommended a shift to the naturally preferred left hand, with successful results, to several boys in their teens and to one college graduate. The latter was strongly left-sided in everything except writing in which use of the right hand had been enforced from the beginning, he was ambitious to study medicine but had serious misgivings as to its advisability because of the troubles that he had encountered in written work in college and because he felt that the large amount of note taking and written examinations in medical school might prove too much for him. Learning to write with the left hand proved very easy for him and its use lessened fatigue and the tendency to finger cramps strikingly and gave him at least a subjective feeling of much greater ease of expression in written work. Following this shift he entered medical school and is competing there successfully.

Although the experience of the examiner plays some part in determining when a shift to the left hand in such individuals should be recommended, there are no tests or criteria which can be trusted here because of the great variability in the degree of left-hand skill in native sinistrals, and our approach to this problem has been an experimental one. When the history of left-handedness from early infancy is clear and when the left is preferred in other activities than writing and when motor tests show an equivalent or superior skill in finer movements, other than writing, with the left hand, we have advised left-hand writing as a trial procedure for a few months. If in that time the left has not acquired a writing ability equal to or better than that previously attained by the right, the attempt is discontinued. No estimate of the exact time required to learn to write with the left hand can safely be made.

It cannot always be assumed that the left-handed child should be taught to write with the left hand since in some whom we have studied, in spite of marked superiority in all other motor acts on the left, writing proved very laborious and cramped and in a few instances of this type we have recommended a shift to the right hand for writing only, with a subsequent marked improvement in both speed and quality of the product. Such cases illustrate clearly the highly individual character of each writing problem and certain factors observed in these cases suggest that motor facilities alone do not always determine optimum usage but that sensory factors probably also are operative in the acquisition of writing.

As mentioned in the chapter on diagnosis a proper position of the paper and hand will greatly facilitate the acquisition of left-hand writing both in the case of left-handed children who are just learning to write and in the mistrained left-handers who are experimenting with a shift. The proper position of the paper is the exact mirror opposite of that employed for right-handed children, that is, with the top of the sheet inclined toward the *right*. This is of so much importance as a training factor that an illustration of the exact position is given here. (Figure 24) Careful attention to this will permit the child to follow easily across the page without contortion and without dragging his hand through the ink of freshly written lines.

A second factor which is frequently of considerable aid to the left-handed writer is the determination of the easiest and most natural slant and this applies often to right-handed patients also. As a general rule, the right-handed person tends to slant his letters with their top toward the right but this is not consistent and not a few right-handed writers develop a "backhand" or slant toward the left. Conversely, with the left-handers a backhand writing seems somewhat more common but again this is not always so and it has been found very helpful to deter-

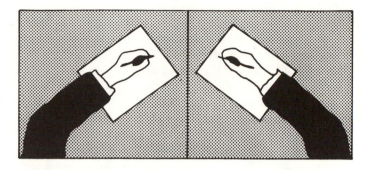

Figure 24. A sketch to show the corresponding positions of the paper and hand for left- and right-handed writers.

mine the slant in which strokes and letter forms can be most easily made. Observations of the natural inclination are made from samples of writing, and to further test this we ask the patient to draw rapidly a series of short lines parallel to each other in the forward slant, in the vertical and in the backhand direction. Similar tests using loops such as those that form parts of letters are also employed and for the older children paper ruled with ink in parallel lines in each of the three slants can be inserted under a thin sheet of paper and experiments in writing following each of the slants are then made. Frequently a strong preference for one or the other pattern will be immediately apparent and it has been found profitable to follow this choice in subsequent training.

While abnormal difficulty in writing is fairly frequently encountered in mistrained and masked left-handers, it is by no means limited to them. It occurs not infrequently in those children who have been slow to choose either hand as a master and in the apraxic children and also in some who seem to have developed early a marked preference for right-sidedness in hand, eye and foot. One very serviceable procedure which we have used with some of the poor writers is that of teaching the child to produce the letter from its "feel" or kinaesthetic pattern rather than by visual guidance. For this purpose the child learns to draw the letter form from a pattern set at a distance and with the paper on which he is writing hidden by a cardboard shield. Once the patterns have been established, practice in this may be carried out with the eyes closed or even blindfolded. The obvious purpose of this method is to train the kinaesthetic patterns so that the hand will more or less automatically produce the letter form without visual control much as the practiced typist finds the proper keys while her eyes follow a manuscript. One noticeable result of practice of this sort is often an immediate relief from the cramped position of the hand and "pencil squeezing" which were apparent before it was instituted. This method proved of value in the retraining of the girl who showed a latent mirror-writing skill and whose product is shown in Figure 17. The patient whose mirror-writing skill is illustrated in Figure 18 was a medical student at the time his disability was studied and no formal retraining was undertaken with him. He was shown, however, that if he inserted a sheet of carbon paper face up beneath the sheet on which he was writing in the mirrored form, it would reproduce the writing in reverse so that he could write in mirror writing on one side of the sheet and turn it over to read it. This was an obvious subterfuge but a serviceable one.

In spite of the employment of the various devices outlined above we have encountered a number of children who progressed very slowly in the acquisition of an acceptable handwriting, and in such cases it may be well to give up the time-consuming writing drills and teach the child to use the typewriter. We have no evidence from our own experiments, however, as to the relative facility with which such children can learn to use this instrument.

In the special writing disability the formation of sequences plays an important part. Many children who can produce each letter symbol quickly and easily in isolation have great trouble in writing words, and this is true whether they be using the cursive or manuscript form. There also is usually much greater difficulty in propositional work than in writing to dictation and this in turn is more difficult than copying. These facts have been considered in planning the school work advised for children who have this handicap as well as in designing the course of their retraining. The first of their practice work has, as a rule, been copying from printed text and only when the mechanics of this have improved considerably have they been asked to write to dictation. We have also advised that these children be excused from all written work if possible in school while the retraining is under way in order that the effect of a careful practice period be not entirely submerged by the need to write under pressure with the rest of the class.

3. Developmental Word Deafness

The number of cases in which word deafness was an outstanding feature and in which we have had an opportunity to undertake experiments in retraining is very small, but the results have been suggestively promising. Starting with the assumption that in this disorder the trouble lay in the recall of sequences of word sounds in the correct time order, comparable to the difficulty in recall of spatial sequences in developmental word blindness, we have undertaken to teach the child orally the separate phonetic units and to purify or correct such as he produced improperly or in confusion and then to proceed through simple blending to short words, at the same time building a visual association of the word with an object of the environment or with a picture to fix its meaning. None of our younger cases in whom we believed word deafness to be a factor has as yet advanced far enough to permit a judicious estimate of the ultimate outcome although some have made good progress. In two older boys, however, in whom the failure of understanding of spoken words was a confronting symptom, a very considerable response has ensued to this program. In both of these cases the value of clear enunciation, the choice of simple words, short sentences and slow speech on the part of the teacher was very apparent. In one case, when the boy was asked the question, "Did you enjoy camp enough this summer to want to go again?", it was met with a blank expression and elicited no response whatever. When, however, this was broken up into the two queries "Did you like camp?" and "Do you want to go again?", the response to both was instant and enthusiastic. With both of these boys their ability to understand a rapid-fire talker was much less than that when the same requests or commands were given by a slow and careful speaker. The older of these boys was seventeen years old when we first saw him but he had reached only about the second grade level in school. A full-time tutor working under the guidance of the Language Research Unit was provided for him and as far as possible all educational procedures made use of objective tasks or concepts while careful training of the speech by phonetic synthesis was also instituted. When he was first seen, this boy's speech was filled with inaccuracies, clipped words, misuse of words and showed frequent neologisms. During a two-year period of such instruction by a tutor the neologisms and mutilated words completely disappeared, he showed a very marked betterment in his ability to comprehend the speech of others as well as to express himself in comprehensible form and his general educational level was raised by four grades or more.

For those children in whom a true regional deafness involving the frequencies within the speech range exists, the special methods employed by teachers of the deaf are indicated and these will not be reviewed here. A word concerning one adjuvant form of treatment may be offered, however, since some of the older patients of this group have learned to read comparatively well and with these selected cases some improvement in the associated speech defect can be built upon the visual memory of the word structure by careful instruction by a teacher versed in phonetic practices. Thus the knowledge of the spelling of the word can be used to implant in the speech of these patients the presence of a letter sound which they have learned to reproduce by kinaesthetic memory but which they cannot hear either in their own speech or in the speech of others.

4. Developmental Motor Aphasia

The children who are very slow in learning to talk and who often show many infantilisms in their speech as well but who have no difficulty in understanding the speech of others have responded to treatment as a rule most encouragingly. In our procedure a careful survey has first been made of the phonetic units which the child can echo after the examiner and where any such units were lacking or faulty they were taught by the methods in common use by teachers of speech. The major difficulty in these cases has been found almost without exception to rest on an inability to blend sounds which can be reproduced in isolation and our experiments have been aimed at teaching the child the simplest sort of blending, consisting at first of only one consonant followed by one vowel until this process has been mastered, when longer sequences are very gradually introduced. For this step we have used both short words and nonsense syllables in order to cover a very wide range of sound blends. Starting with the teaching of whole words, as is so commonly practiced, even though they be short ones, does not seem to be so profitable as this process of beginning a little further back with only two sounds at first and gradually increasing the span. Certainly the initiation of this program should be in the hands of a person experienced in the teaching of speech correction and conversant with the special methods employed in such work. Although later it is probable that the retraining can be carried on by a somewhat less highly trained technical aide, it is nevertheless important that the instructor chosen be someone with clear enunciation and slow, deliberate speech. The propositional element plays a part here comparable to that mentioned in the writing disability and marked defects in this type of speech are to be expected for a considerable period after the child has learned to echo with accuracy and even after he can repeat memorized material without errors. The emphasis in training must in general correspond to these stages of development in the child's speech. The majority of these children are seen at about the age of three or four and frequently the difficulty has improved markedly, either spontaneously or as a result of training, before the child has reached school age. Some of them, however, will enter school before the difficulty has been fully corrected and a moderate easement in the demands for oral recitations is often advisable. A phonetic approach to reading has also proved of value in clearing up residual defects in speech after the child has entered school.

Many of our cases which fall in this group have been children who were also very slow in making a choice of a master hand or who showed marked motor intergrading, and the history of a number who were very ''late talkers', has revealed a close relationship in time between a spontaneous betterment in speech and an increasing tendency to selective use of one hand. We have therefore experimented with a program of training to increase the skills and freedom of use of one hand. Obviously, careful motor tests of handedness and eyedness must precede this in order to determine which hand to train, and not infrequently this will lead the examinee into a dilemma which can only be resolved by experiment. A wide variety of games are useful here, both overhand throwing as with a baseball or darts and underhand tossing as with rope rings or quoits, and indoor games such as jack straws, tiddlywinks, etc., also have been employed. Because of the fact that spontaneous improvement is the rule in these cases and because the motor training has been carried out at the same time as specific speech training, it is impossible to say how valuable the hand exercises have been. However, many of these children with delayed speech of the motor type become stutterers when they begin to talk and handedness training has proven its value in some early stutterers, so it would seem to be indicated. Moreover, the practice in a variety of games will do no harm and is often a distinct asset to the child in his athletic competition with his fellows.

Some of the children with delayed speech but good understanding show such extreme degrees of difficulty in learning other movements that they may be classed among the apraxics. With this group progress in learning the speech blends has tended to be very slow. A few cases have been studied in which handedness training contrary to the child's natural bent has been very closely associated in time at least with a speech regression. One such boy who exhibited a decided preference for his left hand had begun to talk fairly freely when rather rigorous right-hand training was instituted by his parents. This was almost immediately followed by a period of complete mutism which did not disappear until training for left-handed superiority was again instituted.

5. Developmental Apraxia

Among the children finding unusual difficulty in learning patterns of movement is to be found an occasional individual who is a shifted left-hander and who never has been successful in acquiring skills on the right although this may be the side used extensively. Where history and motor tests indicate this to be the case a retraining of the left hand may do much to offset the unskillfulness. A much more intricate problem is presented by the majority of apraxic children, however, since their unskillfulness extends to both hands—they are "doubly left-handed" and often amphiocular as well—and no latent abilities are uncovered by tests in either the right or the left side. The number of cases which we have studied in which apraxia was the outstanding symptom is not large and our facilities for extended experiments in training were not of the best but a few observations and results nevertheless seem worthy of record while awaiting the opportunity to extend this line of research with additional cases and experiments. Our attention has been directed to attempting to determine very simple patterns of movement over which the child has a reasonable mastery, and gradually combining these simpler patterns into more complex and difficult ones. Here again we have been guided by the belief that it is in such recombinations of simple movements that the crux of the apraxic child's difficulty rests.

At times the motor inaptitude seems to involve movements of the body as a whole including such factors as balance and gait and not merely the more complex movements which underlie manual dexterity. These children are often quite proficient in activities such as swimming and horseback riding where the body is supported without so great a need for equilibration, but the gross movements of the body in such acts as walking, running and jumping are very poorly executed. This was the case with one girl of about six years of age who walked with a very clumsy stride and who could "never walk up stairs without stumbling on at least every other step." She also had tried to learn some very simple dance steps from one of her teachers but her efforts in this were far from a reproduction of the demonstrated pattern. To train the stepping movements for stair climbing, two by ten inch wooden blocks were employed and the child was taught to put only the ball of the foot on the block and then to raise the body enough to bring the toe of the other foot clear when it was swung forward. This was practiced on one foot at a time before a second block was added and progressional alternating steps were permitted. Next, the height of the blocks was increased to four inches and gradually a very satisfactory result was attained on the stairs. It may be remarked in passing that the learning of many of our skilled acts depends on visual observation of the movements of others and that these visual models must then be retranslated into kinaesthetic-motor patterns. With this idea in mind, experiments were tried with the dance steps with both the child and her teacher standing before a large mirror so that the teacher's movements were reflected as on the same sides in which the child was attempting to copy them, and this procedure was much more successful than were attempts at vis-a-vis imitation.

It is common to assume that the simple, largely reflex patterns of movement which enter into walking and running, for example, are sufficiently well acquired by the child without training so that in the more difficult sports, such as tennis, attention need be given only to the special instruction for that game and this, of course, is true of most children. In those with a measure of apraxia in their make-up, however, this assumption is not justified and much better headway might be made by spending some time teaching the child how to run and turn and stop without losing balance, before specific training in the sport is begun.

In those apraxic children whose clumsiness is expressed chiefly in learning manual skills, one symptomatic indication would seem to be to raise the level of dexterity in one side above that of the other by games such as those mentioned above, and since no superiority can, as a rule, be demonstrated on either side in these children, we are left with a choice as to which side shall be trained. Under such circumstances our advice has favored the right hand to conform with the more generally used pattern of the community at large.

One issue not infrequently raised by parents of these children is that of what their reaction should be toward the excessive awkwardness which leads to spilled food at table, upset milk glasses, etc. It often helps the parent to understand that this condition may be a real disability and not merely excessive carelessness. Obviously, punishment or scolding for such accidents is not just nor does it seem to be efficacious since too much attention paid to the mishaps may increase the difficulty. How this operates is not clear but it seems to be related to the greater trouble inherent in the propositional or effortful element already noted in the writing disability cases and those with a motor speech delay and which comes into its fullest flower in stuttering. Possibly the best attitude for the parents to adopt is that of tolerant amusement toward each episode but with careful observation of the faulty movements, looking toward sympathetic instruction for their correction.

A considerable measure of feeling of inferiority seems to be unavoidable in the apraxics, especially as these children grow to the age when they enter active physical competition where their limitations must be rather piteously exposed. While the acquisition of skills is arduous for the apraxic, almost any technique can be mastered with sufficient application and practice, and sometimes slow but punctilious training in some one sport or manual craft will serve to compensate largely for the more general awkwardness. Thus, in one of the writer's patients, a question about tennis brought up some obviously rather painful recollections of experiences on the court but the child was prompt to volunteer at this stage that she had by persistence learned to sew quite well. She later brought in a sample of her work which showed almost meticulous neatness and accuracy in stitching. Fortunately, many of the apraxic cases are quite successful competitors in their scholastic work and this is frequently a source of satisfaction which serves as a recompense for their failures in athletics and manual work.

6. Stuttering in Childhood

The childhood stutterers for the purpose of this discussion of treatment must be separated into two groups, viz.—those who stutter from the time they first begin to talk and those whose speech is normal until the sixth to eighth year. In the younger group it is exceedingly important to determine whether a shift of handedness away from the natural inclination has taken place or is under way. Motor tests as well as very careful inquiry into the history is essential here. If the child has been shifted and if the motor patterns are good on the abandoned side, retraining of all unilateral activities in the native hand is always worth the experiment and is often accompanied by a fairly prompt cessation of the stuttering. One of the writer's patients—a boy of three—had stuttered only a few weeks when he was first examined. When the parents were questioned as to his handedness, the mother was sure he was right-handed although the father—questioned separately—described him as "fifty-fifty." Tests and brief observations suggested a strong leaning toward the left hand and the parents were advised to take him home for a week and observe him carefully from this standpoint. At the end of that period, they reported that he used his left hand in all but three activities and in these he was being trained to use his right. These were, however, among the most difficult patterns that he was acquiring at that time. A reversal of these training procedures, that is, a free use of the left hand for all one-sided acts, was followed by a complete disappearance of the stuttering within a few weeks.

Unfortunately such cases as that above quoted have given rise to the frequently heard statement that all stutterers should have been left-handed and ought to be so trained. This rests on a very superficial comprehension of the complexities of the problem of cerebral dominance and of the potential sources of difficulty. In many of our cases there is no superiority of the left hand and no indication of an enforced change from the native pattern. Many of them are marked motor intergrades with no clear preference for either hand, but some find this applies particularly to those with a very strong hereditary leaning toward stuttering—are as clearly as we can determine exclusively right-sided from the beginning.

In those children in whom there is a strong mixture of right- and left-side patterns we have tried to increase the lead of one side or the other by the same training measures which have been described in connection with motor speech delay. In the stutterers this seems to be somewhat more productive than in those children whose speech is late in developing.

In many of this group of younger stutterers and particularly in those who have been slow in learning to speak at all, there are phonetic errors complicating the picture. This varies all the way from one or two infantilisms to imperfections in almost all of the speech sounds. When this is true, accurate phonetic training by standard methods is indicated as the first measure of treatment. From this starting point, practice in blending of the units, starting with very short series and gradually increasing the length of the letter groups has been used with considerable success. Where the handedness is clear and the child is old enough, a beginning may be made in the building of associations between the sound of a letter and its written form. This may serve a double purpose since many of these early stutterers are prone to letter reversals and confusions and not a few of them prove to be typical cases of strephosymbolia by the time they encounter reading.

In the six- to eight-year-old group of stutterers there has usually been a history of normal development and use of speech until this critical period is reached. The chief problem of handedness which has been encountered here is that of right-handed training in writing in a left-handed child or one who is a marked intergrade but with considerable latent skill on the left. Where this is occurring, a retraining of the writing in the correct left-hand pattern is frequently sufficient to cure the stuttering without other measures. In a good many cases, however, the issue cannot be so clearly drawn as this and it is frequently difficult to decide which hand should be used in writing. As with the younger group, training to increase the superiority of the master hand has seemed to be of value, although not quite so markedly so. Where phonetic defects exist, careful training should be instituted to correct the errors and this should be followed by practice in sound blending. The children of this group have not in our experience had much strephosymbolia but they are very prone to have a great deal of trouble with their handwriting, often sufficient to warrant the diagnosis of a developmental motor agraphia. When this occurs, the special methods described under that title have been applied.

When writing has been acquired with moderate speed and skill it can be used to advantage as a training procedure for the stutterer. While the younger group of stutterers are apt to have serious difficulty with reading, the older ones usually learn to comprehend their reading material readily, but oral reading is very difficult because of stuttering in the words being read. In these "reading stutterers" the episodes occur almost exclusively on the initial sounds of the words they are reading and if such a child traces the initial letter of each word with a pencil while he is reading it, he is able to read with few or no stuttering blocks. This "pencil facilitation" for oral reading is at first applied to the initial letter of every word and this makes for a slow, staccato delivery. After some practice in reading by this method, initialing every word, it is usually possible to reduce the use of the pencil to tracing the initials of only every second or third word or only the initial of the first word of a phrase or sentence, until gradually the penciling can be omitted or used only for long or unfamiliar words. It is important in this procedure that the pencil be in motion, tracing the letter, before the speech effort is initiated. If speaking begins first, the penciling will not help. Gradually by this procedure it has been possible in a number of cases to free the reading from stuttering block entirely but the amount of "carry over" which occurs into propositional speech is variable. In some cases no further training of the speech was necessary. Much more frequently, however, the defect remains with little or no improvement in propositional speech even after reading has responded. It is possible to apply the pencil facilitation to propositional speech also, but this is a difficult technique for a child to master and as a rule practice in blending seems to have been equally profitable.

The attitude of the young stutterer is often an obstacle to treatment—he does not permit his handicap to interfere with his activities as a rule and is apt to be either mildly uncooperative or actively resentful of the time asked of him for the training procedures. This frequently is a decisive challenge to the teacher who is working with him and the success with which it is met may determine the outcome of the program to a considerable extent. Home discipline of the young stutterer is important and should be carried out as it would be for a normal child. Too frequently we meet the stuttering child whose difficulty has been blamed on that nebulous quality known as "nervousness," who has been allowed to escape all discipline and who consequently is too poorly controlled to be examined properly or to cooperate in any form of retraining.

It is wise to avoid all strong competition in speech—particularly of the argumentative type—for the stutterer both at home, in school and as far as possible on the playground. The demands for oral responses in school should be reduced to the minimum acceptable or if possible eliminated entirely during the training period and the child should be given the opportunity of writing his recitations or of reciting in private to the teacher. The fact that propositional speech suffers most in the stutterer and that repetitive speech is frequently free of blocks can often be capitalized by permitting the child to commit to memory those recitations from which he should not be excused. Such a child can also often take his share in school plays and other special programs if his part be learned by heart.

The emotional factors must also be carefully studied and the child must be guided through this period to prevent the development of the personality disorders which form so prominent a feature in the case of adult stutterers. The six- to eight-year-old stutterers, and this applies with equal force to the reading and writing disability cases, are old enough and intelligent enough usually to understand a simply phrased explanation of the probable organic genesis of their trouble. They are usually interested in the story of how only one side of the brain works in the language function and intrigued with the idea that the two halves of their brain may be "squabbling over which is to be the boss" and pleased when it is possible to tell them, as it frequently is on the basis of intelligence tests, that their brains are better than average but not working just right for the particular subject in which they have met trouble. This sort of an understanding of how his difficulty may have arisen will often go a long way toward preventing the child from falling back later on explanations based on emotional instability, "nervousness," undue fears or lack of self-confidence which in themselves are not entirely emotionally acceptable and which often seem to operate as a vicious circle.

An even more complete explanation to the parents and to the teachers of the specific nature of all of these difficulties is of prime importance in treatment of the child since the school failures have all too often been interpreted as due to some degree of mental defect or to defective attention or to laziness or to poor training, and frequently with an implication of blame which may very easily foster an unwarranted feeling of guilt in the child or the parent or both.

CONCLUSION

The view here presented that many of the delays and defects in development of the language function may arise from a deviation in the process of establishing unilateral brain superiority in individual areas, while taking account of the hereditary facts, brings with it the conviction that such disorders should respond to specific training if we become sufficiently keen in our diagnosis and if we prove ourselves clever enough to devise the proper training methods to meet the needs of each particular case.

PART 2

◇————————————————————————◇

Selected Papers by
Samuel Torrey Orton

THE PHILOSOPHY OF PSYCHIATRY

◆   ◆   ◆

I do not feel that I am equipped to speak on the Philosophy of Psychiatry, particularly when included in a session under the leadership of Dr. Meyer who is so well prepared for such a task. However, I have been a close observer of the trends of thought which have influenced the development of psychiatry for about thirty-five years and actively at work in certain phases of its field during the same time. This period has been one of marked change in emphasis among psychiatrists and of marked expansion in their fields of interest and endeavor, and I hope that a brief review of my observations during that time may prove of interest.

While still a medical student I became interested in pathology, and on graduation I was fortunate enough to be accepted for a period of training under one of America's best teachers of general pathology, Dr. Frank B. Mallory, at the Boston City Hospital. At the end of that service an opportunity was offered to me in neuropathology, and I spent a short time adding a knowledge of the special techniques of this field and in becoming pretty thoroughly familiar with the problems of cerebral localization under the guidance of Dr. E.E. Southard at the Danvers State Hospital in Massachusetts. Those who had the opportunity of working under Dr. Southard will appreciate how much stimulus and enthusiasm he was able to inject into all of those who had the good fortune to serve with him.

Thus I started with unusually good preparation, and it was a period when neuropathology was thought to offer as much promise in the field of mental disease as its parent subject, general pathology, had held for the somatic diseases. Nisel's method for staining the extra-nuclear chromatin granules in nerve cells was comparatively new and Nisel and Alzheimer had described the histological changes in paresis and had given for that one mental disease a definite diagnostic cri-

Remarks by Samuel T. Orton, M.D. at the McGregor Fund and University of Michigan Symposium, Ann Arbor, Michigan, October 24, 1942

Reprinted from Psychiatry and the War, Ed. Frank J. Sladen, M.D. Charles C. Thomas, Springfield, Ill., 1943

terion. This led to the hope that new methods of staining and finer histological detail would in time reveal structural alterations in other diseases. The older explanations of insanity as being due to magic, the influence of evil spirits, and over-exposure to moonlight had dropped out and the new science of neuropathology was considered the most promising field of exploration.

It was only shortly thereafter, however, that the swing away from the organic or structural causation toward that of functional disorders began to be apparent. There were two reasons for this change. First, the structural attack was not so productive as had been hoped, and it gradually became obvious that the brains of about 80 per cent of our admissions to the state hospitals did not show organic changes pathognomonic for the corresponding clinical pictures; and second, new concepts of the importance of disorders of function began to bear fruit. On the first or negative side of the picture stood such work as that of Dunlap who, after several years of intensive study of the brains of cases of dementia praecox, reported that not only could he find no distinctive pathological picture in them but he could find no way in which they differed from the brains of nonpsychotic individuals. The second or positive side was supported by the studies of Freud and Jung and their pupils. Freud and Jung were at that time sufficiently in agreement to appear on the same platform, and the series of lectures which they gave at Clark University on the invitation of President G. Stanley Hall gave added impulse to the swing of the pendulum toward a functional explanation of many phenomena.

While recognizing the importance of the emphasis so placed on the enormous part played in our behavior by our instincts and emotions, I think it may be fairly said that the swing went to the extreme and gave us a whole generation of psychiatrists who had not even a nodding acquaintance with the structure of man's brain. The discussions at that time would, I think, bear me out in that. There was a great deal of talk about the possibility of lay analysts handling psychotic cases as well as borderline ones, and I even heard a very active and somewhat acrimonious discussion among one of the leading groups of the American Psychiatric Association as to whether we ought not to relegate all the organic psychoses to be studied exclusively by the neurologists, i.e., to group together with the spinal cord and midbrain diseases all that showed a lesion of the brain or cortex, and confine our own interests to the so-called functional groups. The continuation of the study of the brain, of its structures, its functions, and to some extent of its changes and alterations, was turned over during that period very largely, except for a few of us who maintained our old interests, to the physiologists, to the brain surgeons and even to the psychologists.

Another movement which began at about that period was the development of the psychopathic hospital. It had been recognized for some time past that the state institutions, while fulfilling the custodial need very well for the most part, were not the place for the best possible treatment for acute psychotic cases and particularly for borderline cases. Also, there was need for institutions that would segregate the more interesting material for research so that it would not be lost in the maze of large ward groups, and for the expansion of the teaching facilities. These three needs—that of a hospital for treatment, selection of cases for research and of material for teaching—led to the establishment of the genuine psychopathic hospital. Many institutions which were merely receiving hospitals subsequently borrowed that title but were not covering the whole field. The first of the genuine psychopathic hospitals was established here in Ann Arbor under Dr. Albert M. Barrett. Your City and your University may rightly claim to be the pioneers in that regard. The second followed relatively shortly after, with the development of the Phipps Clinic under Dr. Adolph Meyer in Baltimore. The third was that of Dr. Southard in Boston, and it was my good fortune to organize and direct the fourth unit, in Iowa City.

Another movement of about the same time was the tendency toward extension of psychiatric work through mental hygiene societies and mental hygiene clinics. In Iowa we made an experiment in this direction at, I think, quite an early date. Our original experiment was carried out by a group of us from the Psychopathic Hospital staff who had volunteered to go to any community in that state which wanted us and to study cases referred by the doctors, by the courts, by the county social agencies and finally by the schools. We felt we could offer service to these various agencies since our unit was made up of a psychiatrist, a psychologist and a trained psychiatric social worker. The yield was very good, I believe, and we were able to extend it, through a liberal grant from the Rockefeller Foundation, to an enlarged two-year experimental period with the Mobile Mental Hygiene Clinic, as we called it, moving from city to city through the state and studying intensively on the ground, the cases that were referred to us, rather than having them sent to the Hospital in Iowa City.

There was only a growing tendency toward extension of psychiatric interest into the period of childhood, which Dr. White so aptly spoke of as the "golden period of mental hygiene." I think also it was a golden period for research of various types. The interest in children's work has spread very widely and is still actively enlarging. Still more recent is the broadening interest in the application of psychiatry to sociology, both to the understanding of how social factors affect the psychotic disturbance in a given individual and also the influence that psychotic ideas and psychopathic personalities, particularly when they occur in natural leaders of men, may have on society at large.

When I began work at Danvers, Dr. Southard introduced me to a recent book and suggested that a study of the brain of an extreme case of chronic internal hydrocephalus along the same line might be interesting. It was Campbell's Histological Localization of Cerebral Function, and it was, I believe, the first complete map of the human brain based on the histological differences between various areas. This book was followed shortly afterward by much more extensive works by German writers, one of which has since become the popular guide to which to refer in identifying given cortical regions. Campbell's work was much simpler but at the end of the description of each cortex type he reviewed the evidence concerning its function, and it forms, I believe, a much more serviceable chart for correlation of clinical findings. His successors have carried the separation of areas showing minor differences in cellular and fibrous architectonics beyond our ability to subdivide functions with security.

I have carried Campbell's map and its interpretations in mind ever since and have applied it extensively in interpretations. I cannot emphasize too strongly my belief that the enormous organ which evolution has developed in man's head has a much wider part to play in his behavior than that of a generator of emotions, and that a thorough knowledge of the functions represented in each of the various large areas which show a markedly different histologic structure is of enormous value in the study of many clinical syndromes. Moreover, I believe not only that emotional variations may modify the efficiency of the various brain functions, but also that differences in physiological activity of specific areas may generate emotional deviations as well, and that thus observed concurrent emotional disturbances may often be an effect rather than a cause of disordered functions.

One of the best illustrations of this relationship is, I think, to be seen in a critical study of the earliest stages of stuttering—a disorder which frequently makes its first appearance in childhood. When stuttering is studied in an adult who has labored under this handicap all of his life, many neurotic traits are seen which are not obvious in childhood and may quite logically be explained as the results of experience—for example, the withdrawal from social contacts and the avoidance of other situations which require fluent speech—thus fear of the telephone which is a frequent finding in adult stutterers may be a result of past difficulties with that instrument rather than a phobia which causes the stuttering, as it is so often interpreted. Stuttering children, early in the course of their trouble, do not avoid social contacts nor do they fear the telephone, and they do not as a group show any consistent apprehensiveness which might be considered a constitutional factor sufficient to explain the later development of phobias. Indeed many of these children are of a distinctly social, garrulous and venturesome make-up, both before and immediately after the onset of their difficulty. They often exhibit reactions to frustration, when their attempts to speak are blocked, but this would seem to be an entirely logical behavior reaction. Stuttering may, of course, occur in a true neurotic individual, as would be expected in any group selected by including those showing one given type of disorder, but our observations in children have led me to believe that a marked injustice is often done when the presence of stuttering is accepted as *prima facie* evidence of the existence of a neurosis.

In the course of an extended program of research covering a period of about seventeen years, I have also become convinced that certain developmental disorders in childhood may rest not on structural alterations of a given area of the brain but on a failure to acquire the normal physiological pattern of action of that area. This rests partly on our studies of the reading disability—strephosymbolia—and the very close parallel which exists between its symptoms and those seen in acquired alexia in the adult, and partly on the extension of these studies to the problems of developmental aphasia and developmental apraxia. This last syndrome is still a research problem and our most thorough piece of work on it has not as yet been published.

The reasons for accepting a physiological hypothesis concerning the developmental delay of childhood are too varied and too complex to go into in detail within the time allotted here but suffice it to say that they seem to harmonize with modern neurological opinion and to take cognizance of both the intrinsic or hereditary factors and the play of extrinsic or environmental factors and finally to meet the therapeutic test of response to proper retraining methods. While the determining factor seems best explainable on the basis of a faulty physiology we must, of course, grant the emotional factors a prominent place in the picture. I believe that the interplay between these two must always be taken into account. We can no more isolate one from the other than we can discard either the warp or the woof of a piece of cloth. With either gone it is no longer cloth.

Finally, in closing, since our studies point to a failure to acquire the normal adult pattern of unilateral cerebral dominance as the source of the developmental language disorders and of developmental apraxia and since the pattern of control from one side of the brain is also disturbed in injuries to critical areas of the dominant hemisphere, we are hopeful that the somewhat better understanding of the principle of unilateral dominance gained in our studies of the special disabilities of childhood and the methods of retraining derived therefrom which have been so effective, may prove helpful in the rehabilitation of cases with war injuries of the brain. [World War II] We are convinced, as outlined above, that the classifying of all stutterers as neurotics is an error and the assumption that nonreaders are mentally defective can be readily shown to be untenable and we feel sure that some of our observations on right-brained (left-handed) children and on those with mixed or confused dominance could profitably be used for better understanding the troubles which lead, in the Army, to the awkward squad or to the failures of a strongly left-eyed soldier in the rifle pits and that such understanding would in turn be serviceable in the proper assignment for service of these men who do not conform to the more common pattern.

"Word Blindness" in School Children*

♦   ♦   ♦

The material included in this preliminary report has come from several sources but was assembled chiefly during an experimental clinic held by members of the Iowa State Psychopathic Hospital Staff in Greene County, Iowa in January, 1925. Among those children who were reported to the clinic by their teachers as "dull, subnormal, or failing or retarded in school work" was a fairly high proportion whose chief difficulty was in learning to read. Two of these would fit Hinshelwood's criteria of true "congenital word blindness," and one of these two cases (M. P.) also gave bizarre written productions.

Because of his striking disability, M. P. was admitted to the State Psychopathic Hospital, and his case was there studied more thoroughly than was possible in the clinic. The results of this study are here reported in full.

Observations suggesting an explanation of one of the factors in this case are recorded from other cases. These were the presence of mirror reading, mirror writing, and a strong tendency to attempt to read parts or all of a word from right to left and confusion of those letters in which orientation is essential.

Only a few of the studies from the literature of mirror writing and left-handedness have been reviewed in preparing this preliminary report, but these indicate the great frequency of these conditions in "defective" children. The method of writing in alternate directions and

---

*Read at the Fifty-First Annual Meeting of the American Neurological Association, Washington, D. C., May, 1925.

Reprinted from the Archives of Neurology and Psychiatry, November, 1925, Vol. 14, pp. 581–613

with the letters correspondingly oriented as seen in certain ancient documents indicates that our present method of dextrad writing with single orientation of letters has been arbitrarily fixed by custom.

The views on congenital word blindness in the medical literature seem untenable as an explanation of these cases. An hypothesis more in harmony with present conceptions of the aphasias and based on the structural relations and the probable physiologic activities within the visual cortices of the two hemispheres is offered, and a new descriptive term is suggested for this group.

Some points of psychiatric import are suggested. Certain reactions to the disability might readily serve to establish determining character traits. Moreover, it seems probable that psychometric tests as ordinarily employed give an entirely erroneous and unfair estimate of the intellectual capacity of these children.

The implications from the standpoint of education are challenging. If the views herein expressed are proved to be correct by further observation and experiment, there is reason to believe that the majority of these disabilities can be entirely overcome by special training. The methods of training, however, must be developed in consonance with the neurologic background and tested by carefully controlled experiment.

SOURCE OF AUTHOR'S MATERIAL

During two weeks in January, 1925, a mobile mental clinic was held as an experiment in Green County, Iowa, by a group of members of the staff of the State Psychopathic Hospital, consisting of the director of the hospital acting as psychiatrist, the chief social worker of the hospital, a graduate student assistant in social work, the hospital psychologist, and a graduate student assistant in psychology.

Cases were referred to this clinic by four agencies in the county—the physicians, the county attorney, the secretary of the social service league, and the schools. An announcement was made to the school teachers that the clinic would be ready to study pupils who seemed unusually bright and in whom the question of double promotion or enlargement in scope of the school work might be indicated, pupils who presented behavior problems, and those who were considered defective or who were retarded or failing in their school work.

This last group, the retarded, the failures, and those considered by their teachers to be defective proved to be an extremely interesting selection. Altogether 142 pupils of the grade and high schools of the county were studied. Eighty-eight of the 142 fell in the group referred by the teachers as deficient. Psychometric ratings were made of eighty-four of these, but they did not agree closely with the teachers' estimates of the children's abilities.

The distribution of this group by psychometric ratings obtained by individual Stanford-Binet tests was as follows:

Table 1. Psychometric Ratings of Eighty-Four Deficient Students

Very superior intelligence, Stanford-Binet Test, intelligence quotient, 120 or over	1
Superior intelligence, Stanford-Binet Test, intelligence quotient, 110 to 119	0
Average intelligence, Stanford-Binet Test, intelligence quotient, 90 to 109	31
Dull normal intelligence, Stanford-Binet Test, intelligence quotient, 80 to 89	20
Marginal defective, Stanford-Binet Test, intelligence, 70 to 79	18
Moron, Stanford-Binet Test, intelligence quotient, 50 to 69	13
Imbecile, Stanford-Binet Test, intelligence quotient, 25 to 49	1
	84

It is obvious from this distribution that other factors than mental defect were largely responsible for the poor work of these children. Among these factors appeared a special difficulty in learning to read. Fourteen of these eighty-eight children were reported by the teachers as having great difficulty in learning to read or were seen by their grades or by cursory examinations in the clinic to have some special limitations here. One other student referred by his teachers as "nervous" proved to be of this type. Because the method of selection did not specifically call for those with reading disabilities, it is highly probable that this number does not adequately present the whole problem in these schools.

The distribution by grades and intelligence quotients of the fifteen who were recognized as having this disability in greater or less degree was as shown in Table 2.

The two outstanding cases were those of boys about 16 years of age, who had reached the ninth grade, and the degree of their disability was so extreme as to warrant their inclusion in the group of cases described by Hinshelwood (1917) under the name of congenital word blindness. In addition to a practically complete inability to read, one of these two boys (M. P.) had submitted some extremely curious productions as written exercises in school.

STUDY OF A TYPICAL CASE

During the clinic, M. P. was tested by the Stanford-Binet method and showed the following rating: Age, 16 years, 2 months; mental age, 11

Table 2. Distribution by Grades and Intelligence Quotient of Students with Difficulty in Learning to Read

School Grade	Case	Stanford-Binet Intelligence Quotient
First	Merle	103
Second	Dale	91
Second	Francis	122
Second	Douglas	92
Third	Clarke	102
Third	Ludlow	105
Third	Etta	91
Third	Wayne	96
Third	Karl	99
Third	George	75
Third	Derald	102
Seventh	Donald	70
Eighth	John	72
Ninth	Jack	85
Ninth	M. P.	71

years, 4 months; intelligence quotient, 71. During the psychiatric examination which followed, however, I was strongly impressed with the feeling that this estimate did not do justice to the boy's mental equipment, and that the low rating was to be explained by the fact that the test is inadequate to gauge the equipment in a case of such a special disability. Further, it was easily seen that while he was unable to recall the visual impressions of words clearly enough to recognize them in print, he did make facile use of visual imagery of objects of rather complex type. I asked him, for example, questions concerning the adjustment of bearings in the V type automobile engine which required a good visualizing power for answer, and his replies were prompt and keen.

Figure 1 gives below a transcript of a page of one of his written productions, and below, a part of it in facsimile. This was submitted as a composition in American History describing the English Campaign of 1777.

The challenge to interpretation contained in this production, together with the doubts of the accuracy of his mental rating and the general interest of the reading defect, led to his admission to the psychopathic hospital for more extended study and experiment.

Additional tests given in the psychologic laboratory of the hospital gave the following results: The Stanford-Binet test was repeated, but certain alternative tests were substituted; others, when permissible, were given orally, and he was tried by tests higher in the scale. This

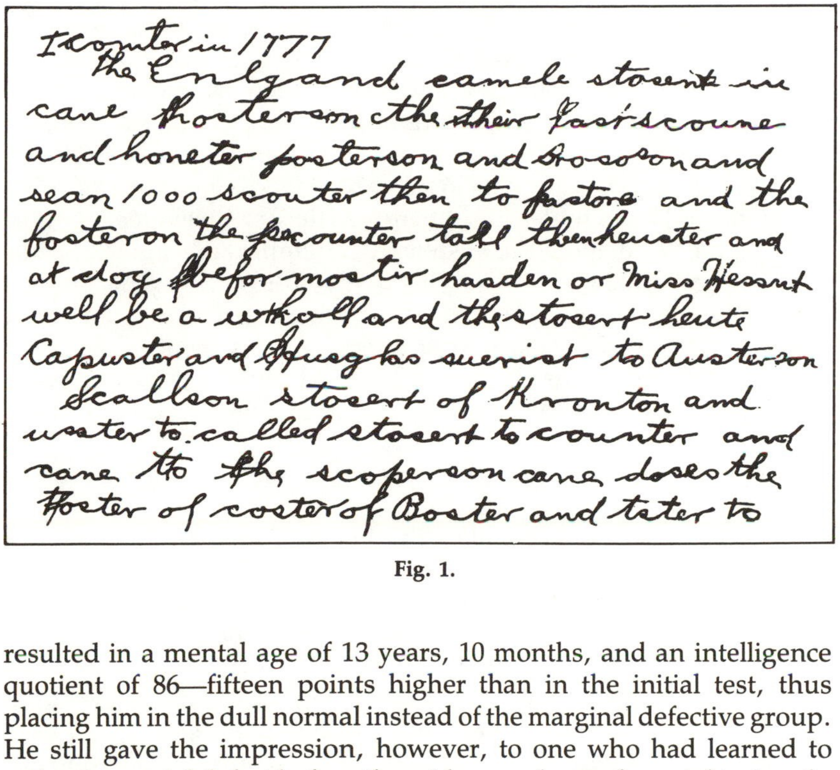

I. Comter in 1777.

The Enlgand camele stosent in cane hosterson the their last scoune and honeter posterson and rososon and sean 1000 scouter then to pastore and the fosteron the secounter tall theen heuster and at dog befor mostir hasden or Miss Hessnt well be a wholl and the stosert heute Capuster and Husglas suerist to Austerson. Scallson stosert of Kronton and usster to called stosert to counter and cane to the scoperson cane doses the toster of the coster of the Boster and tster to last scastorn and to nicast to. But the Anson custome stosent tae the the cashie so the peoper sconer tabe at his the usenter eacet.

Desless of faster to the Last of the scomet of caperson tall the and there can to last a burst Uster and heust Lester and cane to the art last.

Fig. 1.

resulted in a mental age of 13 years, 10 months, and an intelligence quotient of 86—fifteen points higher than in the initial test, thus placing him in the dull normal instead of the marginal defective group. He still gave the impression, however, to one who had learned to estimate mental defect before the widespread use of mental tests, of a much better equipment than even this second rating indicated. By the Pintner-Patterson performance tests, his accomplishment was satisfactory for adults. On twelve of the twenty-two items he earned maximum scores. By the Healy pictorial completion test No. 2 his score was 90 out of a possible 100, which is a superior performance for adults. By the Stenquist mechanical assembly test, No. 1, he earned a score of 82, which would place him on a level with the highest 1 per cent of unselected army draft recruits. He solved the Freeman mechanical puzzle box in 102 seconds on the first trial and 72 seconds on the second, which is a superior performance. Tests with Nagel's color blindness cards gave no evidence of defect in color vision. His capacity to read in a mirror was tested, and it was found that this reversed presentation made no difference in his ease of reading.

As the next step in the study of his case, he was tried repeatedly by the series of tests devised by Head (1920) in his studies of aphasia. The tests of capacity to draw and of the mimeokinetic functions with and without the mirror were tried briefly. The others, however, were carried out repeatedly, and as a result it was obvious that there was no difficulty in the recognition of objects or in calling them by name when visually presented, or in indicating an object by pointing when its name was called. He recognized all of the letters of the alphabet and the arabic numerals promptly and called each by name correctly without hesitation. When names of objects were visually presented, however, there was prompt and correct response in only a few instances, and these usually only in the case of the simplest words. With the longer and less simple words there was delay with evident effort to spell out the word and vocal or subvocal attempts at pronunciation of its letters and syllables, with varying degrees of success. This presentation of words was carried out in three forms: in script, in typewritten words, and by means of black paper letters one quarter of an inch high mounted on white cards. There was no great difference in the ease of reading of any of these, although the gummed letters on cards seemed a trifle easier for him.

He was then tested for his capacity to copy in script from printed text with the result shown in Figure 2.

It will be noted that while there is a certain immaturity about the writing, it is by no means a bad production for a 16 year old boy, and that the copy is practically letter perfect. When asked, however, for the content of what he had just copied, he replied: "I don't know, I didn't read it." He was then asked to read it from his own handwriting, and his pronunciation, reproduced as accurately as I could record it, is shown at the bottom of Figure 2. He produced this slowly and with obvious effort, and in the case of most of the words by sounding out part or all of the individual letters before attempting to pronounce the word as a whole. The similarity of syllabic structure of some of these words to that of the neographisms in his original composition (Fig. 1) is apparent. He was then asked to read the same material from the original printed text, and while his errors were not quite the same, the general character was quite like that from his own copy of it.

A copy of a children's edition of "Aladdin and the Wonderful Lamp" was then given him with instructions to read the first page aloud. His efforts at this are shown in Figure 3. The text is given at the top of the illustration; next is my record of his reading. He was then asked to write the same material from dictation (given two or three words at a

---

COPIED FROM TEXT

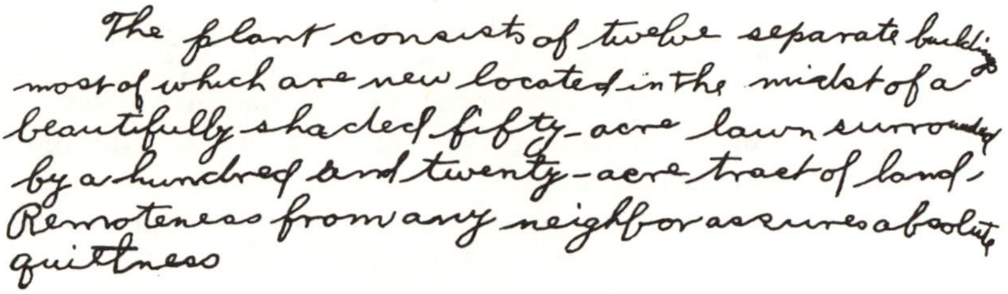

The plant consists of twelve separate buildings, most of which are now located in the midst of a beautifully shaded fifty-acre lawn surrounded by a hundred and twenty-acre tract of land. Remoteness from any neighbor assures absolute quietness

When asked for content he replied—"I don't know—I didn't read it".

READING ABOVE FROM OWN COPY

The prant side of (sounds t-w-e-l-v-e but pronounces) twevel separated building most of which are near located in the most of a booeefer—booeeful should fifty acres lone sardoned by a handered and ten—tendered—across track of long land.

Fig. 2.

TEXT

Aladdin was the son of a poor widow who made her living spinning cotton. When Aladdin was fifteen years old he was playing in the street one day when a strange-looking man stopped and looked at him. He was a wicked African magician who needed a boy to help him, and he thought Aladdin was a nice looking little fellow.

READING (Time 6' 10")

Aladdin was the son of a poor woman who made her livin spinning cotton. When laddin was fighting were old he was playing in the street one day when a standar looking man stepped up and looked at him. He was a wicked African macrican who nidded—needed a boy to help him and he took Aladdin with a nike looking little flune.

WRITING TO DICTATION

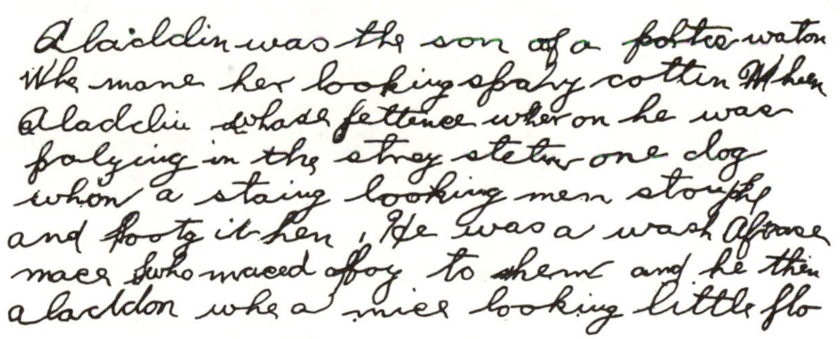

Aladdin was the son of a poor waton who mane her looking spary cotten. When Aladdin whose fettince wher on he was foulying in the stray stetin one dog whon a staing looking men stouffy and footg it hen, He was a wash afonce maee who maeed afoy to shent and he then aladdon whe a mice looking little flo

REPRODUCTION OF ABOVE AFTER READING AND WRITING

There was Aladdin. His mother took in wash—I mean—knitted wool—I mean cotton and he was playing in the street one day and a cross African man rode up and he thought he was good looking so he took him with him.

Fig. 3.

time), and a copy of this production forms the third part of the illustration. After he had attempted to read this material and then had written it to dictation, he was asked to reproduce its contents from memory. The result is recorded at the bottom of the illustration. When questioned as to his inability to remember the material, he replied: "It takes me so long to spell out some words that by the time I read them I forget what was ahead of them."

To test his auditory memory the second page of "Aladdin and the Wonderful Lamp" was read aloud to him, and he was instructed to listen and be prepared to repeat the story. The text was:

> "How would you like to work for me, my boy? I will pay you well," he said to Aladdin. Aladdin said nothing would please him more if his mother would let him.
>
> The poor widow was overjoyed to have Aladdin make some money, and he started next day to work for the magician who treated Aladdin very kindly, giving him lots of fine clothes and paying him well.
>
> Everything went well until one day the magician said to Aladdin: "Come, my boy, I will take you for a walk and show you some very fine things."

M. P.'s reproduction of this was:

> He asked Aladdin if he would like to work for him and said he would pay him. Aladdin said he would if his mother would let him. His mother was glad to have him earn some more money and he went to work for the *musician* who bought him some clothes and paid him. Everything went all right until the *musician* asked him, "When will you take a walk *in the woods* with me and see some fine things?"

It will be seen that this is quite a creditable reproduction of the content of the presented text. Two errors appear—*magician* becomes *musician* and the phrase *in the woods* is inserted.

He was next asked to describe in his own words some of the events of the hospital day, and then to write them down. Figure 4 gives his verbal description and below a facsimile of his writing of the same material, and at the bottom, of his production on writing to dictation.

Several words were next dictated, first as words and then letter by letter, and a written record of them was requested. The whole words were better written than when spontaneously done, and when spelled out letter by letter slowly enough for him to write each letter before the next was heard, he wrote them perfectly. When, however, all the letters of a word were verbally given and he was instructed to wait until the word was spelled completely before beginning to write, his attempts at writing were again full of errors, suggesting an extremely short memory span for series of letter sounds. His span for numerals in other tests was variable, but much better than that indicated for letters.

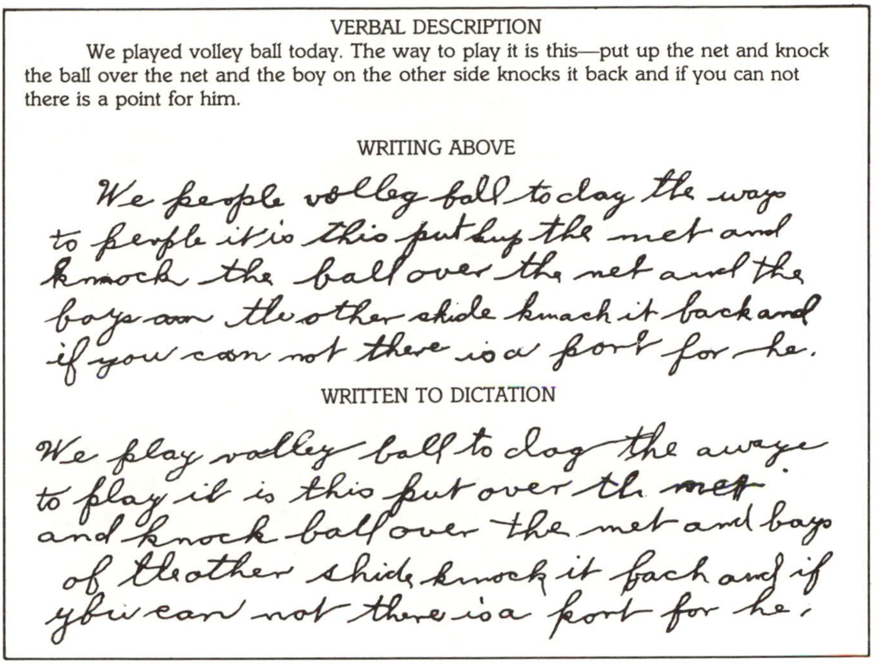

VERBAL DESCRIPTION

We played volley ball today. The way to play it is this—put up the net and knock the ball over the net and the boy on the other side knocks it back and if you can not there is a point for him.

WRITING ABOVE

We people volley ball today the ways to people it is this put up the net and knock the ball over the net and the boys on the other side knock it back and if you can not there is a port for he.

WRITTEN TO DICTATION

We play volley ball to day the awaye to play it is this put over the met and knock ball over the met and bays of the other side knock it fach and if you can not there is a port for he.

Fig. 4.

A large series of separate words made by gummed letters on cards was then prepared, and his ability to read these was tested. Many of these formed series of similar words, such as: *mare, fare, bare, mend, rend, tend, lack, back, hack,* etc. Others were longer common words, like *tonight, today, tomorrow,* and some were two-syllable words in a series, like *target, tarnish, tardy,* etc. These two-syllable words were presented as units and also separated into syllables. Altogether, about 250 cards were used in various ways. Reading of two-syllable words was definitely easier when the syllables were separated, and some words which were impossible for him to read as a whole could be made plain for him by building them letter by letter, using letters mounted on blocks (anagrams). In going over the same series of words day after day, some distinct facilitation was observed, and yet this was irregular, and often words remembered from one day to the next were missed when re-presented on the third day. In one series of sixty-nine simple words, none with more than two syllables, after taking all the time desired for spelling out and corrections, he read only thirty-two correctly.

Recognition of the letters of the alphabet was immediate always, and the name of each letter was correctly and promptly given. When, however, he was asked to sound out the letters as presented, there was evidence of a striking lack of association of certain letter sound with the corresponding letter form. All of these sounds were possible for him and were consistently used in speech, but when a certain printed vowel was presented to him, usually only one of its varied sounds came as a spontaneous response. When pressed for other possible sounds, after considerable hesitation, he usually would offer another; but some of the common sounds of vowels were never produced as a response to visual presentation of the corresponding letters standing alone, although in short words which he could read at sight, he often used all the sounds of each vowel. In the first column of the following table are shown the letters visually presented; in the second, the sound response immediately offered; in the third, the response in answer to the question as to whether this letter might have other sounds, and in the fourth, the common sounds of the letters which were never produced as a spontaneous or requested response to the letter standing alone.

The effect on his reading of this faulty range of sound associations with certain letters is seen in Table 3.

Both of these factors may be seen operating together in such pronunciations as: *twĭvl* for *twelve*, *rĭdn* for *rend*, *tĕgrĕt* for *target*, *blĕwŭ* for *blue*, etc.

A considerable series of three-letter nonsense syllables was also presented by means of the anagrams and gummed letters. In this experiment he was told not to try to find a word with meaning but simply to sound the letter groups as they looked to him, and here again the two elements in his disability mentioned above became evident. Again when trying to read there was a striking tendency to get the sound of a few of the initial letters and then to "jump" at the rest. *Blue* was frequently read as *black* or *blow*. When *check* was presented, he first

Table 3. Letter Test

Letters	When Read	When Questioned	Not Produced	
a	ă	ĭ	ā	ä*
e	ĭ	ē*	ĕ*	
i	ĭ	ī (slow)	....	
o	oo	....	ō*	
u	yŭ	ŭ	ū	
y	wŭ	wĭ	ī*	ĭ
w	wŭ	....	....	
c	k	s (rare)	....	

*These sounds were frequently reproduced in short words which he could read at sight, such as me, bet, my, old, farm, etc.

Table 4. Word Test

Word Presented	Read as
Child	Chĭlled
Chilly	Chĭlwŭ
Twenty	Twĭntwŭ or twentwŭ
Blue	Blwŭ
Ball	Bĕll, bĭll (various times)
Tend	Tĭnd
Dug	Dwŭg
Check	Chŭck
Chock	Chŭck
Bend	Bĭnd
Nice	Nĭke

Table 5. Word Test

Word Presented	Read as
Dug	Gud
Gray	Gary
Tar-nish	Tar-shin
Pardner	Ponder
Mend	Medn
Fend	Fedn
Tomorrow	Tworrom

read it as *chick*. *Chick* was then presented and correctly read, but when *check* was again presented it was read first as *check*, then *chuck*, then *choke*. This tendency was much more pronounced after the tests had been under way for a short time, and apparently increased with fatigue (Table 4).

In his attempts at writing there was also frequent elision of letters resulting in phonic simplifications, which were frequently readily understandable although bizarre in appearance. *Work-up* became *wrkp*, *supper* became *supr*, *dining room* became *dierom*, *cargo* became *crgo*, etc. Several grades of error in writing were observed. Some might rank as extreme instances of misspelling, as *blou* for *blue*, *weit* for *white*, *blak* for *black*, etc. Others show the substitution of other words with similar initial letters, as *people* for *play*, *port* for *point*, *looking* for *living*, etc. Still others show distortions which have almost or entirely lost their sound relation, as *hlo* for *yellow*, *gen* for *green*, *waton* for *widow*, *spary* for *spinning*, *feltence* for *fifteen*, etc. The number of neographisms in any written production seemed to be in indirect relation to the degree of effort expended, and hence to the speed of production. When M. P. was urged to take the time he needed and spell out each word, the product was very much better than when he was told to write rapidly, but some errors crept in even in his most careful work, and such productions were an exceedingly slow and arduous task. Fatigue effects appeared early in these efforts and apparently served to increase the production of bizarre words. There is a striking tendency in his composition (Fig. 1) to repeat new words of almost similar form, such as *hosterson, rososon, fosteron, scoperson* and *toster, coster, Boster, tster*, etc. There was also in his reading of a series of words from cards a noticeable perseveration of letters. *Bend* was called *bĭnd,* and when followed by *lend,* the latter became *blĭnd; rend* was called *rĕdn,* and when followed by *send,* the latter became *srĕdn,* etc. This tendency was never observed when the first word was one which he knew and recognized at sight, so that it seemed as though the unsolved puzzle of a word which did not bring its proper sound association continued its influence on the next presented. The striking neographisms which characterize Figure 1 can probably never be interpreted, as M. P. himself has forgotten the details of the campaign which he had in mind when this was written.

A few brief experiments were tried in training M. P. to learn to recognize some of the simple words that proved hard for him. *Twenty* was one of these, although he read it promptly as *twenty* if spelled *t-w-a-n-t-i*. *Twe* was presented, and he pronounced it *twē*. When urged to try another sound for the *e*, it was produced as *twĭ*. The *twē* sounds were then pronounced for him, and *twen* was presented and read as *twēn*. On urging, it was finally produced as *twĕn*, and then *twent* was offered. This was pronounced as *twĕnt*, but when the *y* was added it was pronounced as *twentwŭ*. *Y* was then pronounced for him as *ĭ*, and he was drilled with *ly, ty,* and *ry*, etc., and again *twenty* was presented, and this time correctly pronounced. This exercise was exceedingly slow—it required eighteen minutes, ten seconds, and while the lesson was retained for one day, on the next it had been forgotten, and *twenty* was again a *twentwŭ*.

Our studies of M. P. show that he made active use of visual images of objects as, for example, in his work with the Healy pictorial completion test. His capacity to copy indicated that his visual equipment was adequate to receive correct impressions of the stimuli and to translate them into one form of motion-copying. He could translate his ideas into speech, and his product here must be considered quite good when allowance is made for the fact that practically his whole vocabulary had been acquired by hearing. He could not, however, translate these same ideas into writing. It is true that with great effort, much expenditure of time and many errors, he could make out many words by reading and could write many correctly, but prompt and facile reading and writing were impossible for him. From his writing to dictation, it is clear that sounds of dictated words did not arouse accurate visual images of letters, except when he laboriously spelled out each word a letter at a time, and even then many were incorrect. His composition suggests that his ideas were even less effective than were dictated words in bringing up the proper visual associations. Conversely, the printed or written word failed to arouse its corresponding concept or its auditory association, so that silent reading as well as reading aloud was impossible for him. Emphasis should be laid, however, on the point that it was in dealing with visual symbols only that this associative difficulty occurred. As our records by the Head tests show, there was no interference with the immediate and correct association of objects with their auditory symbols or of the auditory symbol with the corresponding object. He recognized objects and called them by name promptly and correctly, and also indicated them correctly when the name was called. This analysis would seem to indicate a practically complete failure of association operating electively at the symbolic level between the strictly visual cortices and the great association area, as revealed in his difficulty in reading and, conversely, between the association sphere and the visual areas, as shown by his attempts at writing spontaneously and to dictation.

COMPARISON WITH OTHER CASES

The other fourteen cases of reading difficulty encountered in the clinic were necessarily more hastily reviewed, but from the data obtained from these and a few additional cases seen in the outpatient department and elsewhere, it seems that the tendency to read from right to left leading to confusion of such words as *on* and *no* or *not* and *ton* and the tendency to reversals leading to difficulty in telling a lower case *p* from *q* or *b* from *d* is of constant occurrence in these children and tends to confirm the findings of M. P.'s case.

Some of these subjects were tested with a mirror and were found to read as readily or even more so when the text was seen in mirror image than when seen direct. The motor facility with each hand both in ordinary writing and in mirror writing was also tested briefly in several cases, and some were found who could write practically as well with one hand as with the other. Others showed varying degrees of success in producing mirror writing. Two wrote their names not only in mirrored reversion but upside down as well, and one boy was found who could read at least as easily, if not more so, when the text was upside down and also seen in a mirror. One child, Clarke C, aged 10, with an intelligence quotient of 102, made four mistakes in simple words (*white, bend, nod, dance*) in reading from the printed text directly, but he read the whole sentence of fifteen words promptly and correctly when seen in the mirror. This boy had found the second grade in school very hard, was repeating the third grade, and was reported by his teachers as "naturally dull." Except in his reading, however, he gave the impression of an alert and interested boy, though very slow and insecure in his motor reactions. His own description of his difficulty is worth quoting. "Hardest one (study) is reading. Arithmetic has always been my easiest study. Mother says there is something funny about me because you could read anything to me and I'd git it right away, but if I read it myself I couldn't git it." This aptly characterizes the group. Another, John C., aged 17, with an intelligence quotient of 72, showed a striking insecurity in telling lower case *p* from *q* and *b* from *d*. These letters were mixed both when seen directly and in the mirror, and there was no consistency in his mistakes—in one word *b* would be correctly read, while in the next it would be read as *d*. John formerly stuttered badly and still shows traces of this difficulty. He throws and writes with his right hand, but handles a shovel and pitchfork as a left-handed person would. His father is left-handed in everything but writing. Jack D., a 16-year-old boy in the ninth grade, gave a Stanford-Binet intelligence quotient of 85, which probably does not represent his full capacity, as he has always suffered from a marked reading disability. He showed an additional factor in that *b* and *d* were not only confused with each other, but also with *p* and *q* as though there were a factor of inversion here as well as a mirrored reversal. When asked to attempt to write his name in mirror writing after having seen a pattern so written by the observer, he wrote it as seen in Figure 5.

Fig. 5.   Fig. 6.

His attention was called to the fact that this was upside down, but not a mirror image, and he was asked to try again with his left hand, with the result shown in Figure 6.

As will be seen, the first is inverted, the second reversed.

This inversion in writing occurred in partial form in one other boy, Karl K., aged 9, third grade, intelligence quotient, 99. Copies of his

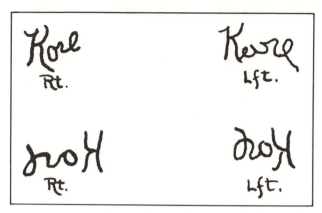

Fig. 7.

direct writing with his right hand and his attempts at mirror writing are shown in Figure 7. In the attempts at mirror writing, he has produced with each hand a mirrored form of *Ka*, but has merely inverted the *rl*.

Karl also apparently had difficulty in both vertical and lateral orientations in reading, as shown by the fact that lower case *p* was often confused with *b* and *d*, although q was consistently recognized correctly. M.R., aged 30, intelligence quotient, 93, came to the out-patient department of the hospital for vocational advice. She had always had difficulty in spelling and in learning things by reading, although she had managed to graduate from college by dint of hard work and possibly some favoring by her teachers because of brighter brothers and sisters who had preceded her. She gave interesting evidence on brief study of the tendency to reversal of direction in reading. She had never attempted to read in a mirror, but on the first trial she read the first five simple words of a printed sentence, the sixth word was *round,* and as this was not immediately recognized, she started to spell it audibly as *b-n* and then stopped as though puzzled. Apparently as long as the words were short and easily read as a whole there was no difficulty with the mirrored images, but when one was met that did not immediately arouse its proper auditory association, she reversed it and began to try to puzzle it out by spelling it backward, suggesting a return to an earlier habit of approach to difficult words.

One of the most convincing observations came from a case, M. O., which was not one of the clinic series. This was a little girl who on her first attempts at writing produced a definite mirrored reversal of each letter with her right hand. It seems axiomatic that the visual image of the letter that was called up by its name, and which must have served as the motor pattern, existed in her brain as the mirrored reversal of that which we consider the correct form of that letter.

Certain additional facts of interest, related to the general problem of cerebral dominance, came out in this group. Many of these children are clumsy with both hands or had been so in earlier childhood. They are often of the motor incoordinate type with evidences of mild apraxia. Some of them have a history of delay in learning to talk and walk and of lack of nicety of balance and consequent frequent falls and of indecision in the choice of the right or left hand in using the knife, fork, and spoon, all of which speak for a definite delay in decisive dominant control of the motor mechanisms. Again, several authors have called attention to the frequent occurrence of stuttering in left-handed children and in those with no established lead, when learning to write with the right hand, and, in some, of the rapid disappearance of this trouble when writing with the left hand is permitted. In our series of fifteen cases of reading disability seen in the Greene County Schools fourteen were boys—a fact of interest in connection with the much greater incidence of stuttering in boys than in girls, and of these fourteen boys there were three who stuttered or who had formerly done so and four others whose speech had a peculiar labored hesitancy quite like that of one who has been broken of stuttering.

LEFT-HANDEDNESS AND MIRROR WRITING IN DEFECTIVE CHILDREN

No attempt has been made in preparing this preliminary report to go into the literature of mirror writing and allied phenomena exhaustively, but a few facts of interest to this study have been encountered. Gordon (1920) reports the finding of an extremely large proportion of left-handed children and mirror writers among the pupils of the special schools for defectives in London and Middlesex. He explains that these schools are not institutions for the feeble-minded but are provided for children "who not being imbecile and not being merely dull or backward are defective, that is to say, children who by reason of mental or physical defect are incapable of receiving proper benefit from the instruction in the ordinary public elementary schools but are not incapable by reason of such defect of receiving benefit from instruction in special classes or schools." It will be seen therefore that he was dealing with children of the ungraded or special-class type rather than defectives as we use the term. Gordon's first observation was that there was a much higher percentage of left-handed children in one of these special schools than in the ordinary elementary schools. He then carried out a large series of tests to determine motor predilection for right or left and found that in schools for the defective the left-handed boys constituted 16.6 per cent, the girls 20.7 per cent, or an average of 18.7 per cent, which he states is more than two and a half times as high as in the ordinary elementary schools. He quotes the proportion of left-handedness in normal persons as found by Ogle as 4.5 per cent, Gould 6 per cent, Jones 4 per cent, Malgaigne 8 to 10 per cent, Hecht and Langstein 12 per cent, and by Masini as 10 per cent. It will be seen that his findings in the defective children are considerably above the highest of these figures. Gordon also studied mirror writing in these children and found that 8 per cent of a total of 1,350 were mirror writers. The product was very good in 56 per cent of these; good in 29 per cent; fair in 7.5 per cent, and bad in 7.5 per cent. Fifty-seven per cent started to write at the right margin of the paper, 13 per cent in the middle and 30 per cent at the left margin. He quotes an interesting remark by the head teacher of one of these schools, who stated that he had frequently noticed a great improvement in a child's intelligence and school work with a natural change of left to right hand. Gordon offers the hypothesis that something has occurred which has interfered with the proper functioning of the dominant hemisphere.

Fildes (1923) has made an extended study of mirror writing. She reports that mirror writing is common among young children and among defective children and varies from an occasional reversal of single letters to complete reversal of all letters and words (true mirror writing) which is comparatively rare. It is found most frequently among the left-handed, but also occurs among right-handed children who have never written except with the right hand. She carried out an extended series of experiments with mirror writers as a result of which she suggests that the main cause for continued error among the defectives is their tendency to repeat a mistake once made in spite of correction. She does not, however, offer any hypothesis to explain this tendency and apparently has not considered the possibility of a mirrored sensory image as the source of this persistence. As a further cause, she hypothecates poor initial observation. That this factor may play some part seems obvious, but that it should be a major factor is out of harmony with the active use of visual images of objects which many of these children show. M. P.'s score, for example, in the Healy pictorial completion test indicates a high degree of keen visual observation. In conclusion, Fildes reports that a tendency to reversal existed in greater or less degree in all subjects tested, both normal and defective, and may therefore be regarded as a common one.

That mirror writing with the left hand is the normal sinistral expression has frequently been recognized. Javal (1909) emphasizes that the complete reversal of direction and orientation of letters is the normal writing for the left-handed and advises that if a patient with a right-sided paralysis or cramp wishes to acquire left-hand writing as rapidly as possible, he should write in mirror fashion. He cites the mirror writing in the manuscripts of Leonardo da Vinci. An interesting account of da Vinci with reproductions in facsimile of some of his mirror writings was published by Caetani (1924) in the *Scientific Monthly*.

Prof. B. L. Ullmann of the State University of Iowa, in a personal communication, has called my attention to some suggestive facts from old Phoenecian, Greek, and Latin inscriptions. The Phoenecian writing, like the Hebrew, ran from right to left and the letter *K—kaph—*in their inscriptions is reversed and appears as Я. When taken into the Greek, however, which was written from left to right, it became *kappa* and took the direction of our own *K*. An exactly parallel situation is found in the contrast between the Umbrian and Oscan Italic dialects which followed a sinistrad direction, and in which the *K*, *S*, *E* and other unsymmetrical letters are written in the sinistral form and the Latin which has a dextrad writing and used a letter orientation like our own. In many of the earliest inscriptions there was apparently great elasticity in orientation so that in some the same letter, such as an *E* for example, appears in both directions in the same inscription. Still more striking is the very old method of writing one line toward the right and then reversing and writing the next toward the left. This gave rise to a back and forth order across the page which was likened to the path of an ox in ploughing a field and hence has been described under the name of bustrophedon or ox turns. The "Old Forum Inscription," of which Huelson (1909) says, "Among all the inscriptions (Latin) preserved on stone, it is certainly the oldest and is not later than the fifth century, B. C.," was a vertical bustrophedon in which the writing on the stone as erected goes from the top down on one line and from the bottom up on the next. The letters, however, are placed as though on a horizontal base line. Figure 8 is a tracing of Huelson's photographic illustration of this inscription on the four faces of the stone, shown in the horizontal position in order to be more easily legible.

As a whole, there is fair concurrence between the orientation of the letters and the direction of the line. The *E*, for example, faces consistently in the direction of writing. With the *A* there is somewhat less certainty. In line 11, for example, the diagonal cross stroke appears in two different letters slanting up with the direction of travel and in two others slanting down. The *S*, however, has apparently become fixed in one orientation throughout the inscription. Lines 2, 4 and 12 are running to the right, and lines 3 and 7 to the left, but the *S* in all has the same form. Another interesting feature is shown by the complete inversion of lines 8 and 9, and from Huelson's numbering of 12 to 15

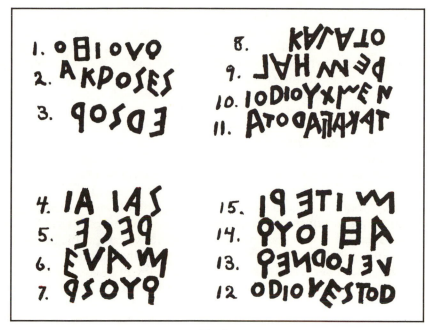

Fig. 8.

one would infer that these were also inverted with respect to the remainder. Professor Ullman further tells me that he has frequently encountered reversals of letter pairs in medieval manuscripts written by one scribe which are consistent enough to be considered characteristic of that individual writer.

Apparently, at one stage in the development of writing the orientation of individual letters was not of great importance, which probably means that the symbol could be read in either direction. The bustrophedon shows that at another stage both orientations were in use in recording and would imply that both left- and right-hand forms of letters assembled in corresponding order could be read by educated persons. The growing fixation of dextral orientation of unsymmetrical letters in dextrad writing as the languages developed would indicate that orientation of letters and direction of writing are intimately connected, but the bustrophedon would indicate that exclusively dextrad orientation is by no means determined by brain capacities, but has been established as a purely arbitrary limitation fixed by custom and education.

Sereni (1923) calls attention to the fact that mirror writing with the left hand is an expression of the symmetry of build of the body. This is obvious when we consider that, so far as the motor mechanisms are concerned, any innervation of the muscles of the left hand will give a motion exactly opposite to that resulting from the comparable innervation applied on the right. Figure 9 shows these relations in graphic form. This again, however, does not take into account the sensory images which serve as the pattern for writing from memory. Writing in either the direct or mirrored form is possible to some people with either hand, and this potentiality is probably latent in us all though difficult to develop because of the exclusive training of one hand for writing. Sereni reported the case of a man, aged 45, who, two years before, had suffered from a trauma to his right elbow, with a temporary loss of the use of his right hand. He learned to write in ordinary form with his left hand, but later he found that he could write in either the direct or mirrored form with either hand. The dextrad writing produced with the left hand was different from that produced with the right, but the mirrored left was like the dextrad right in its strokes, and vice versa. Sereni considers mirror writing as the carrying over, to one side, of a motor process acquired by the other.

Fidles and Myers (1921) have reported a study of a six-year-old boy with a striking tendency toward mirrored reversal of letters and insecurity in recognizing the correct right-left orientation of many of them. He had several left-handed relatives. He had just begun to be taught to write with his right hand, but found difficulty with it, and began to stutter at the same time. He was allowed to write with his left hand, and the confusions of orientation and the disturbance of speech rapidly diminished. Fildes and Myers conclude that the child's early visual experience is probably little concerned with the absolute position of seen objects. His attention is first drawn to form, and his powers of recognition are not gravely disturbed whether that form once learned be represented in the ordinary or reversed or inverted position.

Parson (1924) has recently published a book on left-handedness in which he emphasizes the fact that ocular dominance, i.e., the eye used in fixation, corresponds in all except abnormal cases to the handedness of the individual. His study is based on the results of experiments with the manuscope, an apparatus—sadly misnamed—to determine which is the dominant or sighting eye. Parson apparently holds that the ocular dominance determines both cerebral dominance and the handedness of the individual. His figures are striking in indicating that the facile hand corresponds in side to the eye used in fixation. The selection of one eye as the sighting eye might, however, readily be regarded as a result of the establishment of dominance in one brain hemisphere from other reasons rather than determining it. Parson's manuscope was not available to us until after our observations were complete, and

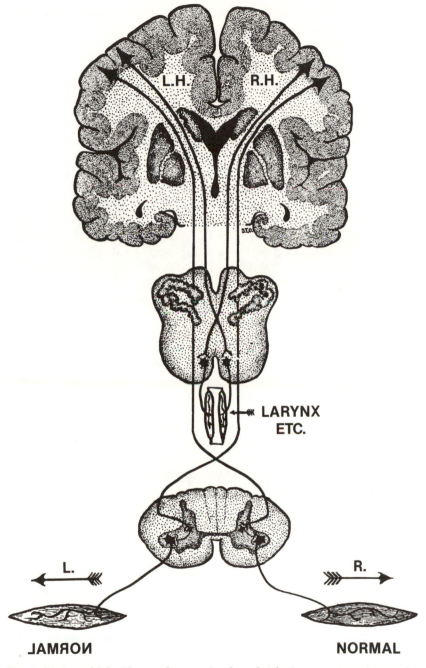

Fig. 9. Motion of left side exactly opposite that of right in response to innervation of muscles.

therefore no tests of his method of determining the dominant hemisphere were made on our material.

CONGENITAL WORD BLINDNESS

In the medical literature we find the first record of a case of congenital word blindness made by Morgan (1896-1897), who reported his observations on a child who could not learn to read, although his vision was normal. He was not mentally defective, and he knew the letters of the alphabet, and Morgan gave to this condition the name of congenital word blindness because of the similarity in many respects to Kussmaul's (1881) acquired word blindness. Hinshelwood published a monograph on the subject in 1917, in which he reported several other cases and discussed them at length in comparison with the acquired condition. Hinshelwood makes a sharp and, I think, unwarranted distinction between mild and severe grades of difficulty in learning to read. He says: "The term congenital word blindness ought to be reserved for those grave cases of defect where the difficulty in learning to read was so great and so unusual that it could be regarded without any exaggeration as an abnormal and pathological condition and where the attempts to teach the child to read by the ordinary methods had completely failed." He also says: "The rapidity and ease with which children learn to read by sight vary a great deal. No doubt it is a comparatively common thing to find some who lag considerably behind their fellows because of their slowness and difficulty in acquiring their visual word memories, but I regard these slight defects as only physiological variations and not to be regarded as pathological conditions." His envisagement of the etiology of true word blindness as here described is that of a defective development, in the early stages of embryonic growth, of the special cerebral area subserving visual memory of words and letters.

Our own studies would lead us to believe that while there may be additional factors in certain cases which serve to determine a greater severity of the disability in a given child, these cases as a whole form a graded series, and it is only the occasional child in whom a fair facility in reading is not ultimately achieved and who would therefore fit in Hinshelwood's group. At the present stage of our study, the factor of reversals of individual letters and the tendency to sinistrad reading of letter groups or whole words seem to characterize all of these cases. How many may show a second factor like that exhibited by M. P. in his faulty range of sound associations with the vowels or like the inversions suggested in Jack D.'s case can be determined only by further study. Hinshelwood's conception of a defective development of the cortex destined to become the center of storage for visual word memories is also out of harmony with the more modern conceptions of cortex function. Marie (1922) calls attention to the fact that an infant with right hemiplegia never presents aphasia, and he believes that the temporal region, the gyrus angularis, and the surrounding zone are not in any sense preformed centers for language, but brain structures adapted by training to that function. Apert (1924), reporting on a case of congenital familial dyslexia, calls attention to the fact that this, like congenital aphasia, is an entirely isolated disability—that is, it is not a part of a general mental defect—and that later the development, which has been checked, recurs. He also has emphasized the fact that children with right hemiplegia are not aphasic, and he expresses the opinion that these developmental delays (hemmungen) are not of anatomic but of functional origin. Pick (1924) lists together mutism, infantile agrammatisms, congenital word blindness, and difficulty in the auditory memory as the underlying conditions resulting in check in development of expressive speech in children. Pick also emphasizes that these are not accompanied by a defect in general intelligence and that after some time normal development proceeds. He states emphatically that these cases are of the group of developmental delays and are not to be considered as defects due to brain lesions.

The evidence available from histologic studies demonstrates that there are three distinct types of visual cortical mechanisms, and the data gathered through correlation of clinical studies with the necropsy findings in cases of focal brain disease indicate that there are three corresponding functional levels. Figure 10 shows the distribution of these three different histologic types of cortex on the mesial and lateral aspects of both hemispheres of the brain.

The first of these levels is indicated in the illustration by solid black and by the name *visual perceptive*. This is the arrival platform, calcarine cortex, or area striata. This last name was given because of the presence of a heavy white band of nerve fibers about midway in the depth of the cortex which sharply demarcates this field and makes it possible to recognize its exact limits with the naked eye. When bilateral destruction of this cortex occurs, there follows complete blindness. The lower reflex centers are still operative, but no visual impressions of any kind enter consciousness or serve as a control of volitional motor responses. These results do not follow unilateral destruction in this field. This cortex was called the visuosensory by Campbell (1905). The term *sensory*, however, embracing as it does the whole receptive and recording mechanism, seems too wide for this restricted functional zone, and I have for some time used the term *visual-perceptive* here. This usage will be explained in the discussion of the next level.

The second level is marked in Figure 10 as the visual recognitive and

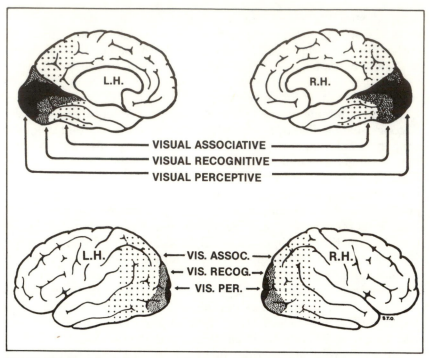

Fig. 10. Distribution of three types of cortex in hemispheres of brain.

shown by the area of stippling. This is the common occipital type of cortex which practically surrounds the arrival platform. The distribution given conforms to that of Campbell's map and quite closely to Brodmann's (1909) area occipitalis, field 18. With extensive losses of this cortex there is retention of mere awareness of visual stimuli but loss of recognition of their meaning. This is the condition known as mind blindness, which can perhaps best be illustrated by the results of Munk's experiments on dogs in which it was first recognized and described. After wide ablation of the occipital lobes, Munk found that his dogs were still able to get about without collision with objects—that is, the animal still retained sufficient control of the motor acts by visual stimuli to guide its movements, but it apparently failed to gain the meaning usually carried by such stimuli. Threats with a whip, sight of food when hungry, or the sight of its master, except when reinforced by additional sensory data from other fields, evoked no responses. Clinical states of similar type in man have since been recorded in numbers, and, from anatomic studies of these, it is obvious that they arise from extensive bilateral destruction of the occipital cortices, but only when there is retention of part at least of the visual arrival platform or calcarine cortex. When destruction is unilateral, this complete loss of the capacity to recognize objects does not follow. This separation of awareness of a stimulus from recognition of its meaning is not so completely accepted by the psychologists, who include both of these functions in the term percept because of the difficulty of separating them by introspection. The evidence from pathology and histology is so clear-cut, however, that I have come to separate these functions and to restrict the use of the term perceptive to that of the first level, i.e., awareness without meaning, and I have so marked the arrival platform on the plate. The second area was called the visuopsychic by Campbell, but the term seems indefensible, and I have used the descriptive term visual recognitive for this level.

The third level—the visual associative—is not to be considered a unitary sensory platform in the sense that it is specifically visual in function, as it is in this great posterior association zone that associative interlinking of the data garnered in various sensory fields probably occurs. This field is indicated in Figure 10 by spaced dots, but the area so demarcated is not intended to show its exact extent or boundaries, but merely to indicate that those cortices of the association zone which lie nearest the visual recognitive field probably play a preponderantly visual part in the associative function. This area as outlined includes part of Campbell's common temporal and parietal areas, and includes Brodmann's area prae-occipitalis, field 19, area occipito-temporalis, field 37, area angularis, field 39, and part of his area parietalis superior, field 7. There is no such clear mark of identification of the recognitive and associative cortices as we find in the white line of the arrival platform, and microscopic analysis of the architectonic patterns is therefore necessary to determine their extent. Lesions of the third level result in the condition known as word blindness, in which awareness of objectivity and recognition of the concrete meaning of objects are both retained, but in which the abstract or associative meaning of the printed word is lost. Here, however, for the first time, we see a sharp difference between the results of lesions in the two hemispheres. In both the lower platforms, extensive bilateral lesions are apparently necessary to destroy the respective functions. In the third level, a unilateral lesion is sufficient but only when it occurs in the dominant or lead hemisphere—the left hemisphere in right-handed persons, and vice versa.

To these three separate levels of the visual function, I think that we may tentatively apply the physiologic hypothesis that each related irradiation from one cortical zone to the next must be simultaneous or immediately successive in time and must be concordant in detail to permit associative linkage. A sensory stimulus which reaches the two arrival platforms results in one conscious impression which we call awareness or the sense of objectivity. We may assume that if the overflow of these impulses into the two recognitive cortices be harmonious in both time and form, the external stimulus will have that correspondence with its respective memory image which constitutes recognition of its meaning. The combined irradiation of the first and second platforms would then result in both awareness of objects and the recognition of their meaning. Activity in the second level aroused by association but without the participation of the first would result in a visual memory, but without the sense of objectivity which characterizes the combined action of both platforms and which serves to differentiate for us the memory image from sensory experience. In the formation of a concept or associative memory, we would postulate the simultaneous or immediately successive irradiation of concordant stimuli into at least three platforms. The arrival platform or visual perceptive would give awareness, the overflow into the recognitive would add concrete meaning of the object or symbol and into the associative would add abstract or symbolic meaning through interlinking with sensory data from other fields.

From the fact that loss of the capacity to read follows a unilateral lesion only when this occurs in the dominant hemisphere we may assume that irradiation is necessary into only one of the two third-level cortices to produce a linkage between visually presented symbols and their meaning. That one or the other hemisphere or one locus in one hemisphere must have an initiatory function for all volitional motor responses seems obvious. Were it not for this placing of the lead or control in one side, the two hemispheres might originate opposed or conflicting responses to a given situation. In man's brain the entire initiatory control of certain major functions, such as speech, writing, and reading seems to be in one hemisphere, as is illustrated by the occurrence of the alpha-privitive symptoms—aphasia, agraphia, alexia, etc., following unilateral lesions. Dominance of this degree has not, I believe, been demonstrated in the lower animals, but some form of initiatory control would seem necessary to prevent confusion of responses such as would result if either hemisphere were competent to lead without reference to the activities of the other.

With the recognition of the dominant part played by the associative cortices of the left hemisphere in right-handed persons, attention was drawn from the function of these areas in the right hemisphere. In every study of the subject of volitional speech, writing, etc., the functions of the various areas in the left hemisphere are discussed in detail, as indicated by clinical correlations, but I do not at present recall ever having seen any attempt to envisage the physiologic conditions existing in the corresponding areas of the opposite hemisphere. Many of these cortical fields in the right hemisphere are listed among the silent areas, and apparently the fact that they are probably activated by incoming stimuli has been entirely overlooked because attention has been directed to the left hemisphere on account of its dominance and the striking results of interference with this dominance by unilateral lesions. When we consider the visual cortices in the light of their anatomic structure, we must remember that here are structures of almost if not quite equal size, extent, and neuron content. In fact, about the only structural difference is that one is the right-left counterpart of the other. I have at my immediate disposal no exact data on the relative weight of the two hemispheres of the human brain, but some years ago, a considerable series of such weights was recorded in the Worcester State Hospital in Massachusetts, and, as I remember these findings, there was rarely a difference of more than 20 to 30 gm. in the size of the two hemispheres, and in several instances this discrepancy was in favor of the right hemisphere from patients who were right-handed, at least so far as writing and the common motor acts were concerned. For many years, as a routine measure, I have cut pieces of cortex from six comparable areas of both the right and left hemispheres, one set as squares and the other as triangles. These blocks have then been embedded in pairs and cut together so that the slide representing the occipital cortex, for example, in a given case will show a square and triangle, from the right and left hemispheres respectively, mounted side by side. Certain cases, of course, such as paresis and the vascular obliterations, will show marked differences in the two sides, and I have never carried through any accurate studies of the number and development of cells in each hemisphere; but the general impression, gained from the study of several thousand such paired sections, is one of comparative equality. If we follow Kapper's theory of neurobiotaxis, we must consider that the cells of the right hemisphere would not have reached this stage of comparatively full development without constant activity, and that their development is the result of irradiation which takes place equally into all parts of both hemispheres; we must further assume that this irradiation into visual areas of the associative cortex of the right (or nondominant) hemisphere forms a mnemonic record there.

The exact symmetrical relationship of the two hemispheres would lead us to believe that the groups of cells irradiated by any visual stimulus in the right hemisphere are the exact mirrored counterpart of those in the left. That simultaneous activity in these antitropic nerve cell groups may still give us a single conscious sensation is shown by Sherrington's (1906) study of a sensory fusion. He studied visual fusion by means of a special apparatus and came to the conclusion that "during binocular regard of an objective image each monocular mechanism develops independently a sensual image of considerable completeness. The singleness of binocular perception results from union of these elaborated sensations." Cases of amblyopia show us that this fusion occurs only when the images strike retinal areas which correspond through associative training, but when the squint remains a new correspondence is ultimately acquired, suggesting that the fusion of the two images into one conscious impression is a function of education rather than of neuron pattern.

I feel that our evidence as to whether the fusion of the results of stimulation of oppositely oriented nerve cell clusters into a unitary sensation is a function of the arrival platform alone or also obtains in the recognitive zone is not quite precise. However, loss of the ability to recognize the meaning of objects (mind blindness) occurs only when there are bilateral lesions of the recognitive zone, which suggests that fusion does occur at this level.

The fact that unilateral lesions in the visual associative cortices result in loss of symbolic meaning (word blindness, etc.) would lead to the conclusion that the mnemonic record contained in the right hemisphere is not requisite for the formation of a symbolic association, and that at this level fusion between right and left mnemonic records does not occur. The tendency common in young children to mirrored or reversed writing, as reported by Fildes, and as seen in our own cases, and the spontaneous production of a mirrored reversal of letters on first attempts at writing with the *right* hand, as recorded in the case of M. O., all point to the existence in the brain of a mnemonic record in mirrored form which serves as the pattern for these motor expressions. Further, the difficulty in our cases of reading disability in differentiating *p* from *q* and *b* from *d* and their tendency to confuse palindromic words like *not* and *ton* and *on* and *no* suggest that the mnemonic record exists in the brain in both orientations.

Letters are in themselves merely objects until they have come to acquire meaning through sound associations or through association in groups of sounds which constitute a word. We would therefore assume that in the process of early visual education, the storage of memory images of letters and words occurs in both hemispheres and that with the first efforts at learning to read the external visual stimuli irradiate equally into the associative cortices of both hemispheres and are there recorded in both dextrad and sinistrad orientation. Images of objects require no definite orientation for recognition or differentiation, but when we are dealing with letters, which have come by custom to be used in one orientation only, it is clear that the orientation of the recalled image must correspond with that of the presented symbol, or confusion will result.

This suggests the hypothesis that the process of learning to read entails the elision from the focus of attention of the confusing memory images of the nondominant hemisphere which are in reversed form and order and the selection of those which are correctly oriented and in correct sequence.

Figure 11 gives a graphic outline of this conception. The symbols indicate the fusion into one sensation which occurs in the perceptive cortical platform and probably also in the recognitive platform. At the associative level, the dominant images are given in bold face and the elided ones in outline. The cortical fields are indicated as in Figure 8, except that the arrival platform is marked by the line of Gennari instead of by the solid black.

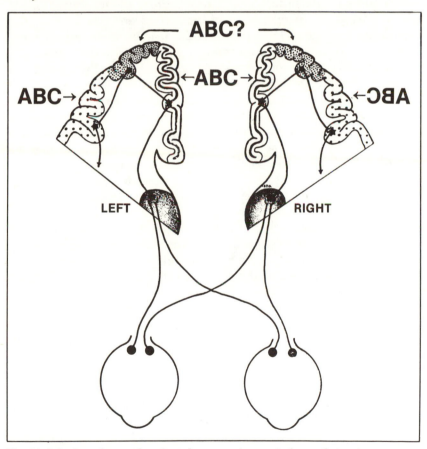

Fig. 11. Selection of correctly oriented memory images in focus of attention.

The frequency, in these cases of reading disability, of reversals of letter pairs (Table 5), such as we see in M. P.'s *gary* for *gray*, of whole syllables, as *tar-shin* for *tar-nish*, or of the major parts of words, as *tworrom* for *tomorrow*, strongly suggests that there has been an incomplete elision of the memory patterns in the nondominant hemisphere, and that therefore either right or left sequence may be followed in attempting to compare presented stimuli with the memory images, and that this leads to confusion or to delay in selection. It seems obvious that such confusion would result in a distortion of the motor output in both speech and writing, and if we assume that the additive function of further associative interlinking with auditory and other sensory images must also be simultaneous or immediately successive, we can readily envisage how delay in selection might interfere with the linking of presented visual symbols with the auditory component of its concept, and hence result in a failure to recognize the meaning, i.e., to read the word as a whole. Most of these children learn to recognize correctly the individual letters and can also read by name and in proper sequence each letter of those forming a printed word, or as in M. P.'s case, can follow the proper sequence in copying. Here the sequence is determined for them by the external stimulus. When, because of failure in training for automatic elision of the obverse record, however, the mnemonic images may be recalled in either sequence, they may fail to correspond with the external stimulus, and delay or confusion will follow and may result, as above suggested, in failure of proper association. That training for elision of one set of images may operate in either hemisphere is obvious when we consider that dominantly left-handed children have apparently no greater difficulty in learning to read than do the dominantly right-handed. Those children, however, who are neither dominantly right-handed nor left-handed, or in whom clear dominance has not been well established before they begin to learn to read, probably have more trouble with reversals of letters. The factor of educational method, which will be discussed briefly later, probably also plays a large part here. Whether other factors enter into the more severe grades of this disability and hence determine a greater permanence of the condition in certain cases cannot be determined without much wider observation and experiment. Such enlargement of the study is projected for the immediate future.

The term congenital word blindness, because of its association with the acquired condition and the implications therefrom, does not seem to be properly descriptive of this disability, and I would therefore like to offer the term *strephosymbolia* from the Greek words, στρέφω, *twist*, and σύμβολον, *symbol*, as a descriptive name for the whole group of children who show unusual difficulty in learning to read. The prefix *strepho* has been chosen to indicate the turning or reversals as it does in the word *bustrophedon*, as illustrated above. *Symbolon* is used in its original meaning of *word, sign,* or *token,* and not as in Finkelnburg's usage in *asymbolia,* in which it included recognition of the meaning of objects as well as of symbols, nor as in the very restricted sense of Oppenheim as a synonym for apraxia. Strephosymbolia thus seems nicely suited to our cases in which our analysis points to confusion, because of reversals, in the memory images of symbols resulting in a failure of association between the visually presented stimulus and its concept.

ERRONEOUS ESTIMATE OF INTELLIGENCE OF DEFECTIVE CHILDREN GIVEN BY PSYCHOMETRIC TESTS

Brief observations on the cases of this reading disability so far studied have brought out several points of psychiatric interest.

It has been pointed out by numerous writers, some of whom have already been quoted in this report, that this difficulty, as is also true of many of the speech and auditory disturbances, is an isolated disability, is not the result of a general mental defect and, further, that often it corrects itself. Nevertheless, there is a strong tendency to characterize these children as *defectives.* This has, of course, been furthered by the belief of Hinshelwood and others that there is here a true focal lack of development in the brain center for visual word memories. Because the term *defective* so constantly implies a general intelligence defect, I have consistently attempted to make use of the word *disability* in describing this difficulty. That the reading disability does not correlate with a low intelligence quotient is obvious from the psychometric ratings of our fifteen cases which show the following distribution:

It can be seen by reference to Table 1 that with only one exception all of the children of the lower grades were in the average normal intelligence group or higher, but that the four in the higher grades were in the marginal defective or dull normal groups. It might, of course, be

Table 6. Psychometric Ratings in Author's Fifteen Cases

Group	Stanford-Binet Intelligence Quotient	Cases
Superior intelligence	122	1
Average intelligence	91 to 105	9
Dull normal intelligence	85	1
Marginal defective	70 to 75	4

inferred from this that only those of inferior equipment failed to overcome their handicap and ultimately to learn to read. I feel, however, from our work with M. P. that this is a distinct problem which will require additional investigation. M. P. had by far the most outstanding case of the series, and I have been far from content, after close personal study, that either the original rating of 71 or the revised rating of 86 really estimated his general intellectual capacity. I think we must therefore challenge the competence of the Stanford-Binet method to give us even an approximate rating in these cases. These children fall in a group of an especial nature more closely comparable to those with true sensory deprivations than to the so-called feeble-minded, and there are apparently three factors here which must be considered in judging the adequacy of the test: First, the ratings given are the result of the application of the test to large numbers of children of each chronologic age. In any such group, unless selected on the basis of a reading difficulty, the number of such cases would naturally be small, and we are therefore comparing these handicapped children with an unlike standard. Second, the material of the test itself consists in part of words which are visually presented, and this penalizes their handicap heavily. This factor was an operative one in the change of intelligence quotient in M. P.'s case from 71 on the first examination to 86 on the second. It would seem that a modification of the method might readily be devised to use only auditory presentation except for those parts of the test that deal with images of objects, such as the ball-in-field test, etc., and that this might readily give a better estimate of their equipment. Third, one path of acquisition of information open to the average child, that of reading, is more or less completely closed to these children. When we realize that M. P.'s disability was so great that practically none of his verbal store had been acquired by vision, we appreciate that his accomplishments in the test are far from establishing as low a capacity as the rating would indicate. This lack of information, however, is not a competent measure of how effectively he can make use of those data which he has garnered by the auditory path.

Several psychiatric reaction patterns were observed in various cases of our series, some of which seem to have a fairly direct derivation from the disability and might readily serve to establish determining character traits.

The first of these was a contented, apathetic disregard of the handicap and its results. M. P. showed this reaction. He was at all times cooperative and entered willingly into all the tests and training experiments, but at no time did he show even a trace of spontaneous interest in his condition or of ambition to overcome his disability. He had apparently made a complete adjustment to his situation and was content to accept himself as others rated him, as different from other boys; but he had apparently developed no particular feeling of inferiority, nor had he suffered from any emotional blocking because of this difference.

The second type was seen only in outline, and no older cases of similar reaction have yet been encountered. This was a mild paranoid reaction toward the teachers on the part of one or two children who felt that they were being asked to do something that was impossible—as it was for them—when they were expected to keep pace with others in their classes in reading.

The third pattern was brought out with extreme clearness in an adult—M. R., aged 30, whose case is briefly quoted above. She not only had a comparatively severe grade of the disability, but was also of that mild motor incoordinate type in whom many exact motor acts are acquired slowly and with difficulty. She had grown up in a family of brothers and sisters who were probably above average in intelligence and dexterity, so that she had been constantly impressed both at home and in school with the feeling that she was not quite the same status as the others of her family. The result of this atmosphere was the development in M. R. of an overpowering sense of inferiority which served as an insuperable obstacle to her own efforts. On first examination, she appeared entirely colorless from the emotional standpoint and was apparently completely submerged by her feeling of inferiority. When, however, her striking reading disability was uncovered, and it was explained to her that this did not necessarily imply a general defect of intelligence, she brightened somewhat, and when she was asked whether she, herself, felt that she was incompetent as her family had led her to believe she replied, *"I do not!"* with the first real emotional response elicited.

The fourth type of reaction was observed in varying degree in several children. This was an emotional blocking. M. O. gave the best illustration of this. After she had been in school for some time—making indifferent progress—her mother observed that she was failing in school on work which she knew and made practical use of at home. The mother asked her specific questions on this sort of material on her return from school one day and received the reply, "I don't know," which had become almost a stereotyped reply to all questions on school knowledge. A few moments later M. O. volunteered the exact information for which she had been asked, and when her mother inquired as to why she had not responded before, she replied, "I can tell you if you will let me tell it myself, but when you ask me I can't tell you anything." This child has since been taught to read with fair readiness for her age, but the blocking of output when anything is demanded as a task or assignment is still very much in evidence in all her efforts.

OVERCOMING OF DISABILITIES BY SPECIAL TRAINING

Little opportunity has as yet been found to review in detail the literature of the teaching of reading, but the hypothesis herein developed
concerning these special disabilities would seem to bear heavily on the
subject of reading as a whole as well as on these particular cases.
Harman (1915) accepts the brain defect hypothesis and calls attention
to the fact that practically all of these children learn the ten arabic
numerals and most of them learn the twenty-six letters of the alphabet
but do not learn to recognize words as whole, and he feels that this
gives the clue to the method for training. He says:

> They must be taught on the plan of the Chinese....A certain mark
> (Chinese character) conveys to the taught child the idea of a house just as
> does a picture or as the symbol 1 does the idea of unity or one. To teach these
> children reading we must fall back on this plan. The word cat must be taken
> as a whole, not as c-a-t = , but the whole thing is the sign for cat. This
> method is known as the "look and say" plan, and when carried out by a
> teacher of intelligence and with great patience, it is possible to teach the
> child to read. In such cases it is obvious that individual teaching is necessary
> to secure any effective progress.

Apparently Harman overlooked the logical absurdity in this. Reading
whole words at a time is a later acquisition than reading letter by letter
and would seem to be the function of that exact cortical area—the
visual memory center for words—which Hinshelwood postulates as
undeveloped, a theory which Harman apparently accepts. Hinshelwood, in discussing Harman's views, states that he is satisfied that
in teaching the word blind to read the old fashioned methods are
preferable to the look and say method or, as it is known in this country,
the flash or sight reading method.

The tentative envisagement of the disability herein outlined would
suggest that the logical training for these children would be that of
extremely thorough repetitive drill on the fundamentals of phonic
association with letter forms, both visually presented and reproduced
in writing until the correct associations were built up and the permanent elision of the reversed images and reversals in direction was
assured. The flash method would seem from this point of view not
only to be inadequate to correct early mistakes in orientation, but also
to put these children under an unnecessary and unjust handicap, at
least until they had acquired the fundamentals in readily available
form. The child has no opportunity to puzzle out whether a symbol
means p or q by the flash method, and many such initial errors might
well be perpetuated. When a child looks at *not* and reads it *ton*, the
teacher's first reaction is that the child in inattentive or is not trying,

and she is apt to apply either discipline or ridicule, which in turn engender an emotional blocking or a feeling of inferiority without, however, correcting the difficulty. These factors are to some extent illustrated in the case of M. O., which has been quoted above in other connections. She started in school in the first grade at 6 in a room in which the flash method of teaching reading was used practically exclusively. She spent two years in this grade and then advanced to the second only after special coaching in the summer vacation period. In this grade she had a more sympathetic teacher who gave her more encouragement, and her progress was more rapid although her reading was extremely slow and insecure. In the third grade, she fell into the hands of a teacher who expressed the idea that M.'s trouble was because she was not trying hard enough and who attempted to stimulate her progress by pressure. During the first few months of this year, M. O.'s emotional blocking became so great that she was definitely losing much that she had had at volitional command during the preceding year. She was withdrawn from school, and her mother was advised to attempt to train her to read by a return to the old fashioned methods of repetitive drill with painstaking correction of mistakes, and after a few months of this training she had practically corrected the whole difficulty. She still has considerable uncertainty, however, in differentiating *on* and *no*, *of* and *for* and other short words which were fixed in confused order for her during her period of flash training. According to our hypothesis, the training should aim at teaching the child to focus the attention on the correct set of images, and for this purpose the repetitive *a-b=ab* sort of kindergarten drill would seem to offer the most promise. The results of this type of training in M. O.'s case are sufficiently encouraging to warrant the extension of experiments along this line.

It would be of great interest to know whether the comparatively high number of cases encountered in our survey result from any particular characteristics of the teaching method in the local schools, and, further, whether a greater proportion of these disabilities is to be observed in those schools using the flash method than is found in those which still adhere to the older drill methods.

In the table giving the distribution of these cases by grades as found in our survey, it is of interest to note that in the first grade there is only one child—here the teaching is of letters chiefly with only a few simple words. In the second and third, however, in which the reading of more difficult words is added, there is a striking increase in number. From here the cases drop sharply except for the four boys in the seventh, eighth and ninth grades. Our series is of course too small for deductions, but this distribution would suggest that the majority of these children make their own adjustment to this difficulty and learn to read without special training. Some, however, do not, and it would seem as if methods could be devised which will teach those with outstanding cases to read, as well as shorten the period of emotional stress in cases of lesser severity. It is obvious, however, that to be effective such methods must be developed in consonance with a sound neurologic background and be adequately controlled by careful observation and experiments in training. This program we expect to extend in the immediate future.

SPECIFIC READING DISABILITY—
STREPHOSYMBOLIA

◆　　◆　　◆

It has long been recognized that there are certain children who have a more or less selective difficulty in learning to read. The earlier observers of this condition, among them Berkhan (1885), apparently assumed that it was related to a general mental defect and described such cases as partial imbeciles (*halb-idiote*). A more or less complete inability to learn to read, particularly when it is associated as it often is with atrocious handwriting and poor spelling, naturally enough would incline the uncritical observer to assume that the child was, if not truly defective, at least not as bright as he should be to accomplish his school tasks. Very often the logic of this explanation forms a typical vicious circle. The child is said to be feeble-minded because he cannot learn to read, and his inability to learn to read is said to be because he is feeble-minded. Gradually, however, case reports of children who were obviously bright in most respects but who could not learn to read or who progressed in reading only with the greatest difficulty were recorded, and in 1896 an English school physician, Kerr, and an English ophthalmologist, Morgan, independently published case reports of reading disability in children of normal intelligence. Morgan considered the condition to be a specific disease entity and gave it the name of congenital word blindness, by which it has been most widely known since his reports. It is interesting to note that much of the early observation in these cases came from the ophthalmologists; naturally, a distorted vision was at once suspected in such cases and the aid of a specialist in this field was sought. A second English ophthalmologist, Hinshelwood (1917), studied a series of cases intimately and compared them critically with cases of acquired word blindness; i.e., the loss of ability to read which follows in certain cases of local brain destruction by hemorrhage, softening tumor, and other destructive organic processes. On the basis of this comparison, Hinshelwood hypoth-

Reprinted from The Journal of the American Medical Association, April 7, 1928, Vol. 90, pp. 1095–1099

ecated a congenital defect of development of the brain area for registration of visual memories of words, and this envisagement of the
reading disability as a result of faulty development of part of the brain
has maintained its influence to a considerable degree in medical circles
to the present time. Many psychologic studies have been made of these
cases and certain observable functional variants, such as unstable
attention and short memory span for letters, have been recorded with
at times an attempt to explain the disability as a result of such conditions. In more recent years, as the views of the functional school of
psychiatrists have spread, their view of the almost universal causative
influence of emotional disturbances has been carried into the field of
children's difficulties of every type, and in the child guidance and
mental hygiene clinics observed emotional variants when associated
with special disabilities have often been assumed to play an etiologic
role.

The assumption of a certain degree of intellectual defect as the
explanation of reading disability is easy of rebuttal but apparently most
difficult of eradication. Many of these children are good at arithmetic;
they do not show any defect in reasoning or in judgment for their age;
they often appear bright and alert and learn very quickly such material
as is presented to them by ear; and some are good spellers. There are,
moreover, a number of cases recorded of individuals who suffered
severely with this disability in their earlier years in school but who
overcame it and ultimately demonstrated a very high degree of intelligence. It should be remarked here that Hinshelwood in his use of the
term congenital word blindness restricted it to a narrow group. He says
that the term "should be reserved for the really grave degrees of defect
which manifestly are the result of a pathological condition of visual
memory center and which have proved refractory to all ordinary
methods of school instruction." Such a criterion is obviously unsound.
No pathologic condition of the visual memory center has as yet been
demonstrated, and "ordinary methods of school instruction" may
cover a multitude of sins.

The assumption of a local brain defect is more difficult to refute. So
far no necropsy reports in cases of congenital word blindness have
been made, and hence no concise information is available on this
point. The assumption rests, however, on the parallelism which exists
between the symptoms of acquired word blindness due to destruction
of parts of the brain after education is complete and the symptoms of
this specific disability. No one can deny that the parallelism is often
very exact, but in the closely related field of speech, Marie (1922) has
called attention to the fact that the results of lesions in adults after
acquisition of speech cannot be directly applied to children in the

plastic period of acquisition. Marie emphasizes that destructive lesions in the so-called speech zone in children do not prevent the acquisition of speech and considers that, in the event of destruction of such areas before training is accomplished, there results an education of other areas for this purpose. This view, together with the facts already quoted concerning complete recovery from reading disabilities of fairly severe grade, must be held to militate against the hypothesis of a congenital brain defect.

In January, 1925, it was my good fortune to direct a mental hygiene clinic in a semirural community in Iowa. To this clinic 125 school children were referred for various reasons, and, of these, fifteen appeared to me not only to be retarded in reading for their age and less apt in this than in their other studies but also to show certain similarities in the errors which they made in attempting to read. One of these cases would fit the measure for the congenital word blindness of Hinshelwood, and the others of the group seemed to form a more or less continuous grading between this extreme and the normal. The group, moreover, showed a distribution throughout a wide range of intelligence and could by no means be looked on as defectives. The distribution, as measured by the Stanford-Binet tests and the range of obtained intelligence quotients, was from 71 to 122. In passing it may not be amiss to call attention to the fact that these tests themselves must be called in question when applied to such a group for three reasons. In the first place, the standards or norms have been determined by application to a large series of children of whom presumably only a small proportion had any reading disability, and hence the standard is an unjust one for them. Secondly, the application of the test itself in places depends on printed material and hence directly penalizes the score of a child who has not learned to read. A third factor that probably also operates is that the intake of a child who does not read easily is naturally much more restricted than that of others, and differences in his word storage as evinced perhaps in vocabulary tests would be expected. That such paucity of word storage and of information ordinarily acquired through reading need not relate to the potential capacity of the individual, an estimate of which is the aim of the Binet methods, is axiomatic. A tentative estimate of the degree of these penalities has since been made. (Durrell n.d.) Another observation of interest in this group was the relatively high proportion of boys to girls—thirteen to two—and this is apparently also true of stuttering.

A short series of tests was carried out in the field examinations in this group of cases, and these were much elaborated by a intensive study of the very severe case seen later at the Psychopathic Hospital. The results of this study were reported by me in 1925. Certain features which seemed to be common to the group were: (1) difficulty in differentiating *p* and *q*, and *b* and *d*; (2) a striking tendency to confuse pallindromic words like *was* and *saw*, *not* and *ton*, and to reverse paired letters or even whole syllables or words in reading so that they were read from right to left instead of from left to right; (3) a considerable degree of capacity to read from a mirror—one boy actually read faster and with less mistakes with a mirror than without, and (4) a greater facility in producing mirror writing, i.e., in writing to the left with complete antitropic reversal of all letters. It was easily demonstrated that these children did not have any visual defect in the ordinary sense and moreover that they did not have any defect in the second level of brain function in the visual field; i.e., they could make adequate and proper use of visual memories of objects, calling the names of objects and pictures promptly and quickly. Indeed, the boy with the very severe degree of reading disability, who could read only a very few simple words correctly although 18 years of age, was able to make a score on the Healy pictorial test (which requires rather judicious use of visual imagery at the objective level) that was equaled only by the record of superior adults.

It is evident that it is at the third level of visual elaboration where association between the printed or written word and its meaning or concept takes place that a dysfunction exists in these cases, which in the very severe case was practically complete. There is no difficulty with auditory memory—indeed, many patients have an unusually keen auditory memory—and concepts are readily built from material presented verbally, but such concepts are not aroused by the visual presentation of the corresponding printed or written word. Some factor has operated here to prevent the normal acquisition of prompt and facile associative linkage between words when visually presented and the corresponding concept and, in reverse order, in many cases, with the associative linkage between the concept and its graphic counterpart, as is shown not only in poor handwriting and misspelling but in extreme cases often by the construction of a wealth of neographisms, as in the case that I reported, (1925).

These observations focused our attention on the third visual elaborative level of the brain as of primary importance in any attempt to understand the physiologic basis of these conditions, and one rather striking difference which is demonstrable between this and the lower levels of visual function seemed to offer a key to the problem. The first level serves to give awareness that a visual sensation comes from without and is not a recalled memory of things seen; in psychologic terms, this level furnishes the element of external awareness in sensation. This function, without much question, resides in the area striata or calcarine cortex of the occipital lobes. The second level, that of objective memories, serves as the storehouse for visual impressions of objects which have been seen. This function probably resides in the second type of occipital cortex which surrounds the calcarine or striate area. Up to this point the two hemispheres of the brain apparently work in unison to produce a single conscious impression; i.e., the messages relayed from the eyes to the two sides of the brain are fused so as to give only one impression. This is brought into relief by the fact that neither of these functions is entirely lost as a result of the destruction of either hemisphere; a bilateral lesion is required to suppress the function of either the first or the second visual platforms. At the third or associative level, however, destruction in one hemisphere may result in complete loss of the associative function, resulting in inability to read (acquired word blindness), while destruction of exactly the same area in the opposite hemisphere will not give rise to any symptoms whatever. That hemisphere in which destruction produces loss of the associative function is called the dominant hemisphere and may be either the left or the right, according to the side which habitually initiates the motor responses of the individual. In other words, it is obvious that the visual records of one side only are used in symbolic association and those of the other are elided or inactive in this process.

Structurally, however, there is no such contrast between the two hemispheres. The nondominant associative area is as well developed in size and complexity as is the dominant, and current neurologic belief (neurobiotaxis) would imply that this silent or inactive area must have been irradiated equally with the active to produce an equal growth. Such an irradiation, moreover, would presumably leave behind it some record in the cells of the nondominant side which one may call an engram. The engram in the nondominant side would be opposite in sign, however, from that of the dominant, i.e., it would form a mirrored or antitropic pattern. Under usual circumstances only one of these reciprocally paired engrams operates in association with the concept in reading, as is shown by the facts of acquired word blindness already cited, and its antitropic or mirrored mate is elided or remains inoperative. If, however, the physiologic habit of complete elision of these engrams of the nondominant hemisphere were not established, their persistence might readily serve to explain the failure to differentiate between *p* and *q* and between *was* and *saw*, and also to account for facility in mirror reading and mirror writing, and thus to explain those confusions of direction which have been extensively recorded in the literature and which as here described seemed to characterize all the cases of my own series. Since this conception of the disability as a physiologic variant differs so widely from the pathologic moment known to result in acquired word blindness, I have felt that the use of the term congenital word blindness was misleading and have offered the term strephosymbolia—twisted symbols—to demarcate better the series of cases showing this typical symptomatology.

This preliminary study thus led me to believe that the reading disability forms a graded series in severity; that it is not generically related to general mental retardation; that it is explainable as a variant in the establishment of the physiologic lead in the hemispheres rather than as a pathologic condition, and, as a corollary of the latter view, that proper methods of retraining, if started early enough, may be expected to overcome the difficulty.

To put these beliefs to the test, funds were asked of the Division of Studies of the Rockefeller Foundation, and a grant was received from it for the purpose of extending our studies. Under this grant the work was carried forward with a group of research assistants in the laboratories of the Iowa State Psychopathic Hospital from January, 1926, until I severed my connection with that institution in October, 1927. The full reports of this work are still in preparation and they will not all be available in print for some time. As a summary of the studies I may say, however, that the tenets of our theorem as given above have been abundantly supported. From those referred by our Mobile Unit, which visited a number of communities in the state, and from those referred by the Iowa City Schools, we found 175 children who were retarded in reading and who constituted a group with selective difficulty in this subject of sufficient degree to be a significant factor in their school progress. These have been checked against similar examinations in 120 normal readers, (Monroe 1928) and they bear out strikingly the importance of the tendency to reversal in the direction of reading as a cardinal factor in the reading disability. Errors in vowels and in consonants and a variety of other observed errors, while needing corrective training, may be considered largely a secondary defect of the learning process resulting from a lack of practice in reading because of the obstacle in recognition interposed by the reversals. In the course of these observations our records have made possible the construction of a series of diagnostic tests which will apparently clearly differentiate cases of this reading disability, even in the lower grades, from the normal readers and at the same time will serve as a guide to retraining methods.

Our extended studies have not only borne out our conviction that these cases form a series graded in severity from the mild case in which spontaneous correction occurs under the ordinary teaching system to the extreme case in which practically no reading facility is acquired without special instruction, but they have also given evidence of the much greater numerical incidence of this condition than has been recognized heretofore. Various authors have estimated the total number of cases at from 1 per thousand (Thomas 1908) to 7 per thousand. (Warburg 1911) Bachmann (1927) notes that this wide discrepancy rests on the range of severity included in the concept of congenital word blindness by various writers. With as loose a concept as that of Hinshelwood there is small wonder that the number of cases reported should vary within wide limits. Our studies are based on objective criteria—the number of reversals in reading, the ratio of mirror reading time to reading time of normally oriented text, the level of reading performance compared with expectations for mental age, and competence in other subjects—and we feel that they give not only a diagnostic selection of the group but also a measure of the severity in individual cases, obviating the necessity of arbitrarily deciding whether difficulty in learning to read in a given case is severe enough to determine its inclusion in the category.

As measured by this standard, the number of cases really takes on numerical importance from an educational standpoint. None of our studies were made with the purpose of an accurate numerical survey in mind, but the indications of our records are that children suffering from this condition in a degree sufficiently severe to be a really significant obstacle to school progress formed at least 2 per cent of the total school population in every community visited, while in some this percentage was more than doubled. This striking difference in numbers we feel to be related directly to the teaching methods employed. Of two communities fairly comparable in the constitution of their population, we found the percentage in one to be more than double that of the other. The school system that gave the lower figure used the modern sight reading plan to some extent; but when children did not advance by this method other procedures, including phonetic methods, were used. In the school with the higher incidence, the children were not permitted to learn the alphabet and hence to attempt phonetic synthesis of words until they had learned ninety words by sight. The enthusiasm with which the sight reading methods are hailed in many educational circles is probably justified for those children who have a well-established unilateral dominance when they begin to learn to read. In them the acquisition of reading seems to be hastened by the sight method. In the children with a reading disability, however, who apparently form no mean fraction of the whole, this method is obviously unsuited and may, we believe, prove a very serious obstacle.

Our concept of strephosymbolia as a physiologic variant rather than as a general mental defect or a specific brain defect naturally gives a decidedly better prognosis, and there is not only good theoretical basis for the belief that the disability can be corrected and the children taught to read, but there is also to be derived from the theory a path of attack for such retraining. If confusion in the direction of reading forms the obstacle to proper association of the presented word with its meaning, the obvious corrective measures should be aimed at training for consistent direction of reading, which probably infers the consistent selection of one of the paired set of visual engrams for associative linkage with the auditory word memories. One very valuable aid immediately suggests itself here, and that is the inclusion of kinesthetic directional training in the building of associations. In general, the reeducation methods which we propose may be said to be based on training for simultaneous association of visual, auditory, and kinesthetic fields; i.e., tracing and sounding the visually presented word and maintaining consistent direction by following the letters with the finger during sound synthesis of syllables and words. This use of the finger seems to be taboo in the modern teaching of reading, and yet it offers a ready means of correcting a tendency to reversals.

Our own retraining experiments are not as yet extensive, but they are exceedingly promising. In one instance, eight children were under individual instruction along the lines here indicated for a period of eight weeks. At the beginning of this experiment the children were retarded in reading below their mental ages on an average of three years. During the six weeks' period, every child of the group gained at least a full year's facility in reading and one gained two years. We have also noted a marked improvement in children's performance in other school subjects as their reading improves under this special instruction.

Another phase of the problem which has interested me tremendously is the relation of a variety of emotional disturbances observed in certain of these children and the effects which such an unrecognized obstacle to progress in school may have on the personality of the child. In my first series of cases I recorded what I thought to be four types of reaction to the disability: the apathetic, the emotionally blocked, the inferiority pattern, and the antagonistic or paranoid. McCready (1926) has recorded his support of this grouping and also reports that he finds the paranoid group furnishing many disciplinary problems in the schools. A further report of our own studies of this phase of the problem is in preparation.

Not infrequently children with marked strephosymbolia are also stutterers. In this connection it is interesting to note that Berkhan (1885) has likened the reading disability and the frequently associated

writing disability to stuttering. From our envisagement of this difficulty as a confusion in cerebral dominance has come also an hypothesis
of stuttering as derived from a comparable difficulty. Reports (Orton
1927; Travis 1927; Travis and Fagan 1928) of our work with stutterers
have just begun to appear in print and others are to follow soon. Here,
again, retraining experiments are not extensive but some of them are
highly suggestive. This phase of the work must, however, be left for a
later report.

Finally, I think that it can be stated today that the reading disability
or strephosymbolia forms a fairly clear-cut clinical entity which can be
diagnosed by appropriate examination methods, that it is not related to
feeble-mindedness and may occur at any intellectual level, and that a
very considerable degree of prognostic optimism is warranted when
proper training is instituted early and is conscientiously carried out.

Neurological Studies of Some Educational Deviates from Iowa Schools*

◆　　◆　　◆

The elementary studies taught in the first years of school are so simple a task for the brighter children that we are wont to consider that any child with an adequate mind even though he may belong to the dull majority should be able to encompass them. In other words we feel that any child who is not grossly defective should be able to learn simple reading, writing, and spelling. In general this is true but like all other generalities it has its exceptions and these exceptions prove to be of unusual interest. The educational deviate is that child who though of average general intelligence yet cannot learn in certain restricted fields such as reading or writing or spelling under the ordinary methods of teaching. That this is a deviation and not a defect is shown by the fact that such children often respond very quickly to methods adapted to their particular learning needs.

As I have elsewhere pointed out (Orton 1929) early academic education consists largely in adding the visual element to an auditory training that is already well under way. Before a child enters school he has already stored by auditory implantation the meaning of many words and has learned to use them as a guide to speech, but he has not as yet learned to build the association between a printed symbol (letter) and a sound or between a sequence of such symbols (word) and the corresponding sequence of sounds which constitutes the art of reading. This requires the conditioning of a new set of reflexes between the visual and auditory spheres—or the building of associations if one prefers—and this process can be shown to occur exclusively at the third or associative level of cerebral elaboration. Children who have the greatest difficulty in learning to read often have good visual control

*Presented before the Seventy-Seventh Annual Session, Iowa State Medical Society, Cedar Rapids, Iowa, May 9, 10, 11, 1928.

Reprinted from The Journal of the Iowa State Medical Society, April 1929

of their hands and can often make excellent use of pictorial material. This renders it obvious that their reading disability is not the result of a visual defect in the ordinary sense, and, further, because of their use of pictures, we can say that there is no abnormality in the function of the second (objective) level of cerebral elaboration. Thus the reading disability may be definitely localized as a defect in the building of association between the visual and auditory spheres at the third functional level and hence is to be regarded as a problem in which an understanding of the neurological background is of great importance.

In January 1925, with several members of the staff of the Iowa State Psychopathic Hospital, I held a clinic in Jefferson, Greene County, Iowa (Lyday 1926), as an experiment in the extension of a mental outpatient service. To that clinic were referred 125 school children who were in some degree problems of various types in the eyes of their teachers. One of these was an extreme case of reading disability or congenital word blindness, and thirteen others seemed to me to exhibit something of the same sort of symptoms as did this outstanding case. Cursory observations of this group were made in the field and the extreme case was taken to Iowa City for more careful investigation at the Psychopathic Hospital, and on the basis of these studies I (Orton 1925) offered a tentative explanation of the reading disability inter- preted by our knowledge of cerebral physiology and also outlined methods for trial in retraining. To enable further study of this problem and to put the training methods to a test, support was asked from the Rockefeller Foundation, and a grant was received which enabled two years of intensive work with a specially appointed research staff. The results of this extended work are naturally too voluminous to be recorded here, but it will suffice to say that my earlier views concerning the disability were amply supported and enough training experiments were carried out to warrant considerable optimism concerning treatment.

In normal children there is usually considerable difficulty in fixing the association of those letters which have two or more sounds such as the s and k sounds of c, the hard and soft g and the varying sounds of the vowels. This will be readily understood when we recall that one of the fundamental rules of the conditioning of reflexes is constancy of presentation between the stimuli to be associated. Where a variable is present the association is more slowly acquired and less fixed. In the reading disability cases such loose linkage between the symbol and its sound particularly in the earlier years in school is very apparent. An explanation of this seems to be forthcoming in the confusion which exists in such cases between reversible symbols such as b and d and p and q. In one of my more recent cases b and d are quite interchangeable so that *baby, bady, daby* and *dady* all spell *baby* for him. This tendency to confusion is of course quite obvious where substitutions such as *d* for *b* are made, but it is also highly probable that a comparable confusion between the correct form and its mirrored image exists with other letters but is not so readily revealed. This confusion is further complicated by a second factor which is a tendency to read in the sinistrad direction. This exhibits itself in confusion between pallindromic words like *was* and *saw, on* and *no, not* and *ton,* etc., and also in a tendency to reverse paired letters within a word as *gary* for *gray, tagret* for *target,* etc. Occasionally one syllable is reversed, as in *tarnish,* read as *tarshin* or the major part of a word may be turned around as when a boy reads *tomorrow* as *tworrom.* These two errors, that of confusion between antitropic images and insecurity in direction of progress, are considered to be the fundamental obstacles to learning to read in the disability cases. The resulting lack of facile association between letter and sound and in building sequences of sounds from grouped letters gives rise to a wide variety of other errors—vowel errors, consonant errors, omissions, additions, repititions, etc., but all of these, I consider to be by-products of the two cardinal ones.

We are thus faced with the problem of explaining why *b* and *d* should be confused by some children more persistently than others and why some should tend to read to the left. The restriction of the disability to the third level of cerebral elaboration considerably simplifies this problem for us. In both the lowest level which gives us external awareness of a sensation (as contrasted to a mnemonic image) and the second level which serves for objective imagery (cf. use of pictorial material as quoted above), the two hemispheres of the brain operate together, and it is only at the third or associative level that a striking difference is found between the right and left hemispheres. Destruction at this level in the leading or dominant hemisphere will result in marked functional loss such as aphasia, agraphia, alexia, etc., while exactly similar destruction in the same area of the nondominant hemisphere gives no clinical result. These facts clearly indicate that for these associative functions the sensory record in only one hemisphere is required and by inference that the record in its mate is elided or inoperative, and our explanation of the confusion which exists in these children between reversible symbols is that the image in the nondominant hemisphere has not been properly elided and hence operates to produce confusion with its opposite which is recorded in the other hemisphere. Further evidence in support of this view is the fairly frequent spontaneous production of mirror writing by these children. Whether or not this factor is the same as that which determines sinistrad progress or whether both may exist independently and produce the most severe grades of disability only when they coexist cannot be answered as yet.

This explanation of the reading defect as a failure to establish complete unilateral cerebral dominance has naturally called attention to other possible expressions of such a condition including developmental apraxia, congenital aphasia, stuttering, and defects of spelling and writing. In one of my Iowa cases a twelve-year-old school girl had led her class in spelling in Texas but on moving to Iowa was failing in spelling. The explanation of this apparent paradox lay in the fact that in Texas her spelling tests were all given orally while in Iowa she was required to write her spelling lessons, and apparently in her particular case the interplay between the visual and auditory was facile in the control of speech but not as a pattern for writing. Again in a case which I have recently seen in Massachusetts a boy read for me two pages of fairly difficult text with only three minor errors, yet on attempting to spell selected words from the same text he made twenty-five serious errors some of which were of quite a bizarre type such as *qulkey* for *quickly* and *trunth* for *through*. Obviously here again the visual records while adequate as a path of intake were not freely enough available to serve as a guide to spelling, and in this particular case there was also a marked lack of visually acquired words carried over into speech.

I think we may assume on a priori grounds that a free interplay between the visual and auditory memories is essential for the acquisition of reading, since the child learns words by ear first and on entering school he merely acquires the means of arousing these verbal memories by way of visual symbols. He knows *cat* as a word sound long before he knows *c-a-t* as its visual counterpart. Again in spelling it is obvious that our ability to recall the silent letters in many words is a function of visual memory. One frequently sees this put to use by insecure spellers who must write out a word and "see how it looks" to be sure of its spelling. Other evidences of lack of a free interplay between these two all important functions is readily observed in both writing and speech defects, but we cannot assume that these children, merely because they differ from the usual, are either less intelligent or less educable. They form the group to which I have applied the term educational deviates to denote those who vary from the standard and who therefore require special methods of training. That this variation is not related to mental defect in the case of the reading disability is abundantly demonstrated by our findings (Monroe 1928) in 175 cases from the Iowa schools in which were represented all levels of intelligence quotients, even as measured by the Stanford-Binet tests which I consider to give a quite inadequate estimate of intelligence in children suffering from these special handicaps.

One of the interesting phases of this work is yet to be reported (Orton and Sprague n.d.). This has to do with the effects on the personality of the child which accrue from an unrecognized handicap. Obviously when a bright child looks at *was* and miscalls it *saw* the teacher or parent is apt to interpret the error as a result of lack of effort or inattention. Later as he falls progressively behind his classmates in reading, he is usually exposed to well-meant but inappropriate pressure by both parents and teacher and also to the characteristically heartless raillery of other children. Several psychiatric reaction patterns to this pressure have been observed, but perhaps the most illuminative fact is the change of attitude which almost always follows when such a child is told that there probably is a real reason for this difficulty and that he is not to be regarded merely as lazy or as a dumbbell.

In my first study of these reading cases in Green County, I was impressed with the large number encountered. Our further studies, however, have shown that that group was not exceptional. In round numbers our findings in Iowa indicate that approximately 10 per cent of all children who are referred to a clinic by their teachers because of poor school work have a varying degree of this handicap, and further that the disability exists in sufficient degree to determine a definite retardation in school progress in at least 2 per cent of the total school population in every community which our Mobile Clinic visited. In one county this number was more than doubled and our interest was naturally drawn to the educational factors which might account for this. The county with the higher number of cases was one in which the sight method of teaching reading was used exclusively at first, and theoretical considerations (Orton 1929) lead us to believe that this pedagogical procedure is in large part responsible for the greater number here.

A number of retraining experiments were instituted at the Psychopathic Hospital and in various communities in Iowa. The methods employed were adopted with a view to the neurological concepts involved and the results give excellent promise that the disability can be overcome by special instruction. These methods as far as they apply to simple uncomplicated reading retardation are discussed in some detail in one of our reports (Monroe 1928). In most instances however one of the most important features of retraining is gaining the confidence and spontaneous interest of the child, and a thorough study of the attitudes and defenses which have been engendered by his difficulties is often of as great value as the actual technical retraining. In cases of retarded speech and developmental apraxia (extreme clumsiness) the problem of cerebral dominance is the cardinal issue, and such children also give promise of great improvement under properly controlled special training. Not infrequently the question of native handedness and the effects of mistraining of a naturally left-handed child are matters of highest import here. In one such case which I have seen since leaving Iowa, a boy of eleven had spent five years of rather unproductive work in an excellent private school. He read with ease and considerable rapidity and was spontaneously interested in reading as an acquisitive method. His speech, spelling, and writing, however, were all on an extremely poor plane and his efforts to express himself were accompanied by an increasingly severe motor overflow which resulted in a condition of exaggerated fidgets and a very apparent heightened nervous tension. Special tests revealed that his best motor facility lay unquestionably in his left hand although he had up until this time been trained exclusively with the right. A shift to the left with other special means of retraining was recommended, and after only eight weeks of intensive work along these lines he shows more improvement in handwriting than he had in the five years of previous training. He is also gaining rapidly in speech, his spelling is improving, and he is under much less nervous tension when attempting to talk.

As a whole these studies which were in very large part carried out on Iowa school children have opened the way to a field of study of really absorbing interest and I think to one of immediate practical importance.

A Physiological Theory of Reading Disability and Stuttering in Children*

♦　　♦　　♦

In 1925 there was published by the writer a preliminary report of a study of a group of children who were retarded in reading and who seemed to him to show a complex of symptoms which differentiated them from normal readers (Orton 1925). At one extreme of this group was a case of such severity that it would be universally characterized as congenital word blindness, while the remainder seemed to form a graded series extending from that to the normal. In the past there has been a tendency to look upon the more severe cases as pathological in nature and the less marked ones as merely cases of slow acquisition of reading, but there has been no criterion by which these two groups could be separated except the opinion of the examiner. In my report it was pointed out that there were certain errors which seemed to characterize the reading attempts of these children and which suggest a physiological rather than pathological basis, and a tentative explanation was offered on the basis of confusion in cerebral dominance. Following that study an extension of these observations was made by a grant from the Division of Studies of the Rockefeller Foundation. This work was initiated in January, 1926, under my direction at the Iowa State Psychopathic Hospital, and continued until October, 1927. For this further study 175 children were chosen who showed a selective retardation in reading below both mental age and school grade placement. By this method of selection there was obtained a group of retarded readers without regard to the character of their reading performance, and to these children was given an examination designed to discover the frequency of certain types of errors in their attempts at reading. As a control series the same examination was

*Read at a meeting of the Boston Society of Neurology and Psychiatry, February 16, 1928.

Reprinted from the New England Journal of Medicine, Nov. 22, 1928 Vol. 199, No. 21, pp. 1046–1052

given to 120 children who were reading with the facility expected for their mental age and grade placement. The results of this work are soon to be published in detail (Monroe 1928), but I may anticipate their appearance by the statement that these studies bear out strikingly my earlier contention that reading disability forms a fairly clear-cut clinical entity which can be diagnosed by the frequence of certain types of errors and that our series of tests will also serve to grade cases according to the severity of their handicap.

The work of retarded readers is characterized by a tendency to confuse letters which are alike in form but different in orientation, as lower case *b* and *d* and *p* and *q*, and by a tendency toward sinistrad reading in which there is either misreading or complete bepuzzlement when confronted with short pallindromes like *was* and *saw*, *not* and *ton*, *on* and *no*, or in which paired letters or syllables or parts of words are read backward as when *calm* is read as *clam*, *gray* as *gary*, *tarnish* as *tarshin*, *tomorrow* as *tworrom*, etc. They further show a markedly greater facility in reading from the mirror than do normal children and often a much greater ability in mirror writing as well. To demarcate this larger group, which includes a much wider range than the earlier category of word blindness, I have suggested the name strephosymbolia (twisted symbols) as a term descriptive of the objective symptoms.

Many other errors are to be found more frequently in the work of the retarded group than in the normals. Here may be mentioned failure to link the proper consonant or vowel sound with its appropriate visual symbol, errors caused by omission or addition of sounds, repetition of parts of a sentence already read, etc., but these I consider to be only a by-product of the failure of proper association due to the confusional element injected by reversals or by insecurity concerning direction of reading. As supportive evidence for the etiological relations of this factor of directional confusion, I may add that our retraining experiments indicate clearly that when this tendency is lessened by special drills aimed at consistent direction, there is not only a marked improvement in ability to read but also a marked change in the error picture presented so that both range and type of errors become more like those of the normal readers.

In my first report I called attention to the rather high incidence of speech disturbances in my series of reading cases and since the concept of confusion in cerebral dominance seemed to offer a point of attack on stuttering also, we have carried out some experimental studies in that field as well.

Stuttering, like strephosymbolia, occurs in graded steps from normal to extreme. The emotional element has received much attention in stuttering and has long been popular as an explanation of its occurrence. It is, of course, true that stuttering is not only more frequent but more severe in embarassing situations and that it rarely occurs in singing or in repetition of material learned by rote. This immediately suggests for us that the difference here is related to the plane of the speech effort rather than to the emotional influence of the environment or the actual emotional content of the speech. This brings into relief the propositional element of speech, and with one exception this seems to be the plane at which stuttering is most severe and most frequent, and it is often of course in embarassing and strange situations that the propositional effort is most stressed. The exception mentioned is oral reading; some stutterers read aloud with relative fluency, but we also have observations in several cases of our series in whom stuttering is much worse when reading aloud than in any other form of speech. A nice formulation of the influence of the propositional element in a somewhat comparable difficulty was given me by a highly intelligent case of writing disability. This was a young man for whom writing in the dextrad direction was very difficult—indeed his product was often quite illegible to himself as well as to others—yet who wrote letters home which his family could read. On question he explained this by saying that when he didn't have to *think* hard he could write better, but when he had to think and write at the same time, as when answering examination questions, he couldn't write so that he could read it himself.

Our physiological studies in stutterers are not all as yet in print but part of this series of reports have appeared (Orton 1927; Travis 1927) and others are to be published soon. In summary we may say that the stuttering act is characterized by a striking failure of orderly integration of the various reflex groups which coordinate in the production of speech. Thus we have records in which the direction of motion of the chest and abdomen are synchronously opposed, the chest inhaling while the abdomen exhales and vice versa, thus counteracting each other so that no breath stream is passing the larynx. Again the larynx, which normally makes many up and down excursions in vocalization independently of the expiratory movements, is seen in some of our records to move in time with the abdomen or with the chest (Travis 1927). We have also found evidence of both tonic and clonic spasms in the muscles of the vocal mechanism during stuttering. The tonic spasms show themselves in both kymographic records of the movements of the chest, abdomen, and larynx and also in the fixed tones which can be shown by plotting photographic records of the speech vibrations (Travis 1927). The clonic spasms are perhaps best shown by the occurrence of a vibrato in the stutterer's speech (Travis 1927). The vibrato is a rapid fluctuation within a narrow range of pitch which is found in singing, in intoning, and probably also in strongly emotionally colored speech but is not found in normal fluent propositional speech.

The relation between stuttering and the enforced training of a left-handed child to use the right hand has been frequently recorded in the literature and naturally our attention turned to the relationship of handedness to stuttering. Many tests have been advanced for the detection of the facile hand, but we soon became convinced that none of the ordinary tests were dependable because of the effects of training and imitation. Many mothers shift children who show a preference for the left hand at a very early age. In one of our cases a little girl started to talk at about the usual period and at the same time gave evidence of selective choice of her left hand. The mother, with that curious reaction which appears to hold left-handedness as abnormal, insisted on the child's use of her right hand with her spoon, etc. Almost immediately the child stopped all efforts of speech and did not begin again for over a year and when she did begin, she stuttered badly. In another case which I have seen quite recently the stuttering was associated with a high degree of strephosymbolia. This was a twelve-year-old boy who started out in infancy to use his left hand and was shifted by his mother. His speech showed no defect until he entered school, where again his left preference was manifest and pressure was necessary to make him learn to use his right hand in writing. Coincident with this new pressure his stuttering began. Today if a pencil is offered to him, he almost invariably grasps it with his left hand and then transfers it to his right. His father is left-handed in everything except writing and the boy carries out most of his motor acts with the left hand. In golf, however, which he has learned from his mother, who is right-handed, he uses his clubs as a right-hander does. In golf this boy shows the effect of imitation, in writing that of enforced training.

An exceedingly instructive description of the influence of imitation was given me recently by a man who had been a pole-vaulter during his college course. In discussing handedness he told me that, as far as he knew, he was naturally right-handed in everything except pole-vaulting and this he did from the left. He explained this by recounting his first contact with this sport when as a high school boy he saw a single vaulter give a demonstration. This athlete was left-handed and from then until he entered college, the boy's imagination turned frequently toward vaulting; as he put it, "I could feel myself running down the field carrying the pole as I had seen it carried, and thrusting it into the ground for the lift." When he finally did appear on the athletic field this preference was so fixed that the coaches despaired of making a right-handed vaulter out of him and let him go ahead as he was inclined. Generally speaking the only motor function which is held to be of real significance as to handedness is that of writing, and, indeed, many hospital records in aphasias and other of the alpha-privative brain diseases (alexia, agraphia, apraxia, etc.) require no further evidence of handedness than that of the writing hand. The practice is so widespread among teachers today, however, of training every child to use the right hand in writing, if it can be done by coercion or wheedling, that very little dependence can be placed on this evidence alone. Much of the aphasia literature must be questioned for this reason and we feel that the ordinary motor tests were far from satisfactory for our purpose.

Golla (1921) has reported finding differences in the time of incidence in the action currents of the two forearms on simultaneous motion which, in his case, were related to handedness. So far as I am aware, neither Golla nor any other observer has followed up this work, but it appealed to us well worth a trial for our purposes. The full results of this work will appear later (Orton and Travis 1929), but in brief we have found that in clearly right-handed normal speakers, the number of times the action currents in the right arm appear first far exceeds the number of times they appear simultaneously or in the left first. In seventeen stutterers, all of whom would be adjudged right-handed by the usual tests, the records are decidedly different. In this group the currents take precedence on the left in much greater number of trials than on the right, and the simultaneous records also outnumber the right markedly. Whether or not these action current patterns give a real indication of the native handedness of an individual remains to be controlled by much wider investigation, but it can at least be stated that our series of right-handed stutterers gave a very different action current pattern than did our right-handed normal speakers. A number of other tests were used, but these need not be detailed here.

Before presenting our current envisagement of the relationship of cerebral dominance to certain of the symptoms reviewed above, it may be well to review briefly certain of our knowledge of cerebral localization and the results of lesions in certain fields.

The central nervous system is divided into two quite symmetrical halves of approximate equality in size. From the gross standpoint, size probably is of very doubtful importance. Variations in weight due to differences in vessels or in amounts of myelin or neuroglia might far outweigh differences in cortical elements and thus mask really significant differences. In general, however, the gross weight of the two hemispheres is the same. Some years ago, at the Worcester State Hospital, I recorded individually the weights of the two hemispheres in a considerable series of autopsies. On reviewing such records of

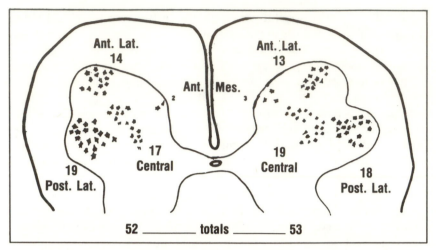

Fig. 1. Projection drawing of spinal cord to show antitropic symmetry.

about 80 brains recently, I found that in the majority of these cases the protocols made record of gross lesions which nullified them for our present purpose, but there were 27 brains which fell in Southard's "normal looking" group. In these the left hemisphere was somewhat heavier in nine cases, the right in eight, and their weight was equal in ten. From the microscopic standpoint we can say with considerable assurance that the two sides of the spinal cord are very exactly alike. Figure 1 is from a projection drawing of a section of the spinal cord chosen from among a set of routine teaching slides. No attempt has been made in this to reproduce exact outlines of cells but their number and position has been carefully followed and the figure speaks for itself. In the brain our information is less exact, but we may safely say that no readily observable differences between the hemispheres occur in lamination, in numbers, in size, or in spacing of brain cells. There are, however, striking differences when we compare the functional activity and relations of the two hemispheres field by field.

The motor cortices are strictly unilateral in their function and they are strictly independent. No further evidence need be cited for this than that of the unilateral paralysis which follows lesions of the contralateral precentral or capsular regions. They are also antitropic, i.e. each is arranged in the mirror pattern of its mate, and I think we can consider it safe to assume that any irradiation pattern of one hemisphere will give a motor response which will be the exact mirror counterpart or antitrope of that resulting from an exactly similar irradiation pattern in the other hemisphere. This relationship is indicated in Figure 2.

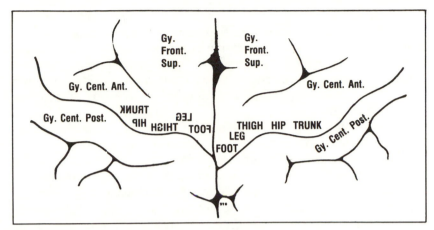

Fig. 2. Antitropic arrangement of functional centers in motor area.

A similar antitropic unilateral independence is to be seen in one sensory cortical field. This is the postcentral zone which is intimately related to the motor area and which probably serves for the registration of the epicritic fraction of the exteroceptive and proprioceptive stimuli brought in through the spinal cord. As in the motor cortex, where separate control of the two paired halves of the body would seem to require separate functional relations, so here in the postcentral cortex the physiological demands would seem to necessitate functional divorce of the two hemispheres. In the case of these spinal receptors it is important for proper responses for the brain to be informed not only that a thumb has been burned but which thumb it is.

In the case of one of the projicient exteroceptors (i. e., those sensory mechanisms which are influenced by stimuli arising at a distance from the body,—smell, vision, and audition,) there is very little accurate information. This is the sense of smell, and the paucity of knowledge here rests in part on the relatively small use that is made of this sense and in part on a lack of interest on the part of recording observers. Of vision and audition we have better information, however. It is obvious that in these two sensations, in order to insure adapted responses to environmental changes, a sensory stimulus arising in one eye must either fuse its charge with that arising in the other eye or enter into rivalry for the control of the final common paths. In certain of the lower animals—notably the achiasmic—rivalry probably occurs, but Sherrington's (1906) careful study of retinal flicker has established fusion as the pattern of the human visual cortex and this is probably also true of audition. That the two hemispheres act as one by thus fusing the effect of bilateral irradiation to produce a single conscious impression seems also well supported by the fact that at the lower levels of sensory elaboration a bilateral lesion is necessary for loss of function. A unilateral lesion causes no demonstrable loss in central vision for example and one side of the brain is apparently no more important than the other in this respect. In audition, likewise, apparently a bilateral lesion of the transverse temporal gyri of Heschel is necessary to produce cortical deafness.

We must, however, bear in mind that there are several functional levels of sensory elaboration in both vision and audition, and, as we shall see, these interhemispheric relations are not alike at all levels. The first cortical platform of vision and audition is the first point of each system at which activity is associated with consciousness. If the arrival platform of both hemispheres (which we have reason to believe is restricted to the calcarine zone or area striata in vision and to the transverse temporal gyri in audition) be destroyed, the results are cortical blindness and cortical deafness, respectively, in which no conscious response to light or sound remains. If, however, these areas be intact but extensive unilateral lesions occur in the higher platforms, the result is mind blindness or mind deafness in which the individual can see or hear things sufficiently to guide coarse motor acts (e. g., avoid collisions) but in which things seen or heard have no meaning. The classical description of Munk's dogs give an excellent picture of this condition in vision. I think that we may assume that this arrival platform or first level of functional elaboration in vision, aside from acting as a very exact guide to motor responses to current sensations, yields in consciousness only that fraction of the visual function which serves to make us aware of the external origin of a sensory impression as contrasted to a mnemonic recall. In psychological terms, it furnishes the perceptive fraction of sensation but not the apperceptive or associative. For these reasons I have suggested the name visuo-perceptive for the calcarine field. (Orton 1925).

When both the arrival platforms and the next adjacent cortical fields are intact but the third level of elaboration is lost by destruction still higher in the cortical pyramid, we encounter the conditions known as word blindness and word deafness, in which vision and audition in the ordinary sense are intact and in which the use of objects and source of sounds can be interpreted but where the printed or spoken word has lost its meaning. Such a patient can recognize objects by vision and put them to their proper use but cannot read their name from print (alexia) and usually cannot call them by name (visual aphasia) or, in the auditory field, he can recognize a voice from the bark of a dog but cannot understand the spoken word.

These losses are exclusively at the third or symbolic level and when they occur they bring into relief the functions which are the additive result of activity at the first and second levels. As we have seen, the arrival platform probably furnishes to consciousness only the perceptive fraction of sensation, but when the second level is also intact there is added to this the recognition of meaning of objects seen but not that of symbols. We have reasons to believe that this second functional addition takes place in the large field of common occipital type of cortex encircling the area striata and for this I have suggested the use of the name visuo-recognitive. It is to be emphasized here, however, that losses do not occur in either the first or second levels of elaboration of the visual or auditory sensory material unless the lesions be bilateral. Not only do the corresponding areas of the two hemispheres at these levels seem to work in unison to produce a single conscious impression, but apparently either is adequate for this result, as is shown by the fact that unilateral lesions do not destroy the function here, and there is no evidence to suggest that either hemisphere is more important than the other. At the third or symbolic level, and here we may include both the sensory input (understanding the spoken word and reading the written word) and its motor congener (speech and writing), the situation is quite different. Here we find that a unilateral lesion is sufficient to destroy the function and moreover that the particular hemisphere plays a deciding part in the result. A destructive lesion in the so-called zone of language which corresponds closely with this symbolic level is only of importance in case it occurs in the dominant hemisphere, and an exactly symmetrical lesion of the opposite or nondominant hemisphere does not result in any observable clinical symptoms. Up to this point our outline has followed the pretty generally accepted views of cerebral function. Although there are many minor differences of opinion in this field, especially as it bears on exact functional localizations and on the predestination of certain cortical structure for certain functions, yet I think the general story as presented would bear the endorsement of the greater number of students of human cerebral localization. Figure 3 is a brain map giving in diagrammatic form the major areas here discussed. This is not intended to represent exact demarcations of these cortical fields. Indeed, except in the case of the calcarine or visual arrival platform, the transverse temporal field or auditory arrival platform, and the precentral or motor area, no abrupt changes of cortex type are demonstrable. The chart does, however, give the general regional distribution and extent of the characteristic cortices. The legend shows in the fourth column the interhemispheric relations which are of so much interest to us in this discussion.

As has been indicated above, however, there is no such striking difference in the structural development of the two hemispheres as we have seen to exist in their functional relations. In general the as-

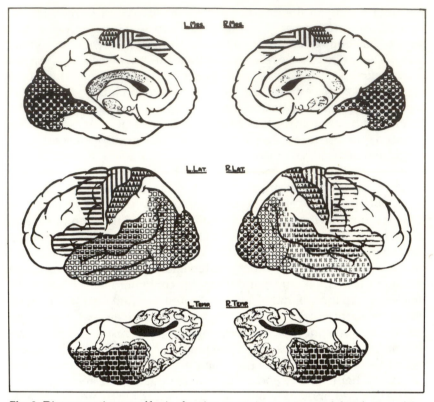

Fig. 3. Diagrammatic map of brain showing approximate extent and distribution of the cortical fields under discussion.

sociation areas of the nondominant hemispheres, resting under cover of their title of silent areas, have received very little consideration. If, however, we are to accept the tenets of neurobiotaxis, which hold that the growth and development of nerve cells is directly related to their irradiation by nerve currents, we must infer that the silent areas of the nondominant hemisphere have received an irradiation approximately equal to that reaching the dominant in order to account for their approximately equal growth. Granting this, I think we may safely assume that such an irradiation will leave behind it a record or engram in the nondominant hemisphere as well as in the dominant. The fact that losses in the language function (verbal understanding, reading, writing, and speech) follow only when the dominant hemisphere is attacked, however, leads us to believe that only that pair of engrams are used in these functions which are recorded in the dominant side. Their counterpart must therefore be considered to be inactive in these processes, i. e., there is elision of one group at this functional level.

There is, however, for some cortical functions strict antitropism (i. e.

right and left pairing) and it is only in those areas where fusion seems to occur (first two elaborative levels of the projicient extero-ceptors) where such apposition is not apparent in function as well as in structure, and many of our data in cases of strephosymbolia offer evidence that this antitropism operates at the symbolic level of the visual field. Here I may quote again the cardinal points which characterize the performance in cases of reading disability;—confusion in orientation, reversal of sequence, mirror reading, and mirror writing.

In skeleton, then, my theory of the obstacle to the acquisition of reading in children of normal intelligence which results in the varying grades of reading disability is a failure to establish the physiological habit of working exclusively from the engrams of one hemisphere. As a result there is incomplete elision of one set of antitropic engrams and there results confusion as to direction of reading which serves as an impediment to facile associative linkage with the auditory engrams, which, during the learning years at least, carry the meaning.

In stuttering the details are not quite so well elaborated, but there are several facts of suggestive interest here. We can demonstrate in stutterers a striking disintegration of the reflex units which should operate in harmony in speech. While certain of these coordinations might superficially be likened to the results of cerebellar dysfunction, we do not encounter true stuttering as a result of acquired cerebellar lesions, and the observed facts of the aphasias lead us to believe that the extensive and complicated integrations of speech are a function of the cortex and that sensory engrams of both visual and auditory implantation form an important pattern storage for the control of speech. Confusion in choice of antitropic engrams here also might result in failure of accurate synthesis of the reflex patterns which enter the speech act. The connection here is not so direct, but the frequent association of change of handedness, especially in writing, with stuttering is suggestive, as are our observations of stuttering during oral reading, our records of action current patterns, and the results of some of our experiments in treatment of stutterers.

Whether or not the theoretical outline for the two conditions of reading disability and stuttering here presented will stand the test of further study and more intimate knowledge of brain function and brain structure, we can at least say that this physiological concept offers a much more hopeful prognosis than that of the agenetic focal brain condition which has been its chief precursor as a theory of the etiology of word blindness or than the most equally intangible emotional variant which has held sway in stuttering. Our new envisagement also has suggested some distinctive lines of experimental attack on retraining which we have already found highly effective in overcoming the reading impediment and very promising in stuttering.

THE NEUROLOGIC BASIS OF
ELEMENTARY EDUCATION*

◆　　◆　　◆

Education in the broader sense is to be looked on as the whole of the process of training a child, beginning with earliest infancy, and thus including the extremely important period of preschool training as well as academic education in its ordinary usage. Before a child enters school he has acquired a large storage of word meanings which have been implanted by way of the auditory path and which serve him as models for speech. He has thus already learned to use the third cerebral level of elaboration by way of the auditory mechanisms, but in the visual field he has not progressed beyond a use of the second elaborative level. He does make use of visual material controlling movement, and use of visually acquired objective data and associations have been formed between objects which he has seen and their names, thus linking the second visual level with the third auditory, but there has not as yet been any training for association of a symbol with its corresponding sound (letter) or of the association of a series of such symbols with the series of sounds forming a word which constitutes reading. One may thus look on the task of early académic education as chiefly the addition of the visual element to the auditory training which has already been begun at the third level.

The evidence of the existence of three progressive steps in cerebral elaboration of sensory material is to be derived from the study of acquired neurologic disturbances resultant on brain damage, such as cortical blindness, mind blindness, and word blindness, and is also reinforced by studies of failure of acquisition of the third level function. This source of illuminative material stands out clearly in cases of strephosymbolia. These children have a good visuomanual association

*Read before the Fifty-Fourth Annual Meeting of the American Neurological Association, Washington, D. C., May, 1928.

Reprinted from the Archives of Neurology and Psychiatry, March, 1929, Vol. 21, pp. 641–646

and are hence often dextrous in the use of their hands; they may also make good use of pictorial material, but fail entirely in ability to understand the meaning of words from printed symbols. In one case which I have already reported (1925), a boy, aged 17, with good manual control, showed unusually good use of pictorial data. He gave a rating by the Healy pictorial completion test that ranked with the highest 10 per cent of normal persons; in spite of this evidence of good vision at the lower levels of elaboration he could read only with the ability of a child in the first grade. A similar difference between the availablity of visual and auditory material at the third level shows strikingly in many cases of special spelling disability, certain writing defects, and in certain stutterers whose handicap is more strikingly apparent in attempting to read aloud than when attempting propositional speech.

The neurologic background of elementary education seems to have been almost entirely overlooked in current educational circles. The methods employed in teaching today are apparently largely determined by the results of average accomplishment in large groups of children and do not seem to have taken cognizance of the fact that certain children with good intelligence may deviate from the average in their ways of learning, so that pedagogic methods which may advance the class as a whole much more rapidly may yet serve as an almost insuperable obstacle to children within that class. Since elementary education consists of the establishment of association (or, if one wishes, the conditioning of reflexes) at the third level of visual elaboration and aims at the free interplay of visual and auditory implantations in control of both speech and writing, it would seem that the neurologic background may offer invaluable aid for the selection of those children who differ from the average in learning requirements and may also suggest special methods for their education.

INTERACTION BETWEEN THE AUDITORY AND VISUAL SPHERES

A facile interaction between the auditory and visual spheres is obviously necessary for reading. The visually acquired material must form a quick and secure association with the word meaning which has previously been implanted by the auditory path in order that the meaning of the printed word may be understood. A failure of this prompt linking results in strephosymbolia. That the visual factor is also operative in spelling is obvious when one recalls that it is only by visual implantation that one is able to remember the silent letters in words. Again, as the child progresses in school, reading forms one of the main pathways by which new words are implanted. That such words are useful in speech will, I think, be immediately apparent to any one who can recall his own hesitant attempts at the pronunciation of the word which is simple to him in reading, but which he has never heard pronounced by another. Neither the visual nor the auditory path will suffice alone for the cultivation of a vocabulary as higher levels of the educational plane are reached, and I believe that both operate together in the control of both speech and writing, although the importance of either is apt to be dependent on the quality of the speech and on the type of implantation which has preceded it. Thus Lincoln's vocabulary has been held as a striking example of the influence of early reading on later speech habits.

My studies to date of special difficulties in the field of arithmetic are by no means sufficient to form an opinion concerning the interplay between the visual and the auditory here, but the spatial element of the decimal system and the progressional element in addition, sub-traction, multiplication, and division would all seem to indicate the need of cooperation between the visual and the auditory in the ac-quisition of even the fundamentals of this subject.

There is one fundamental necessity for the easy establishment of an association or for an easy conditioning of reflexes. This is constancy of presentation of the stimuli to be so linked. When there is much variation either in form or in time of presentation the linking is loose or is not established. The effect of this, I think, is to be seen in normal children who have much more difficulty with those letters which have a varying sound value, such as the s and k sound of c, the hard and soft sounds of g and the various sounds of the vowels. In normal children one observes that error in vowels are much more frequent than those of the consonant sounds which are associated with a single symbol, such as t, f, l, n, and b. Children who are later to become secure readers, however, overcome this difficulty relatively quickly, but it remains to a noticeable degree in those children who later show specific elements of reading disability. Children suffering from strephosymbolia show a weak and insecure association between the symbol a and the sounds ā, ă, ä, and often confuse the short sounds of ă, ĕ and ĭ. Another factor which stands out with prominence in these children is the striking tendency to confuse b and d and p and q. Sometimes these pairs of letters are consistently interchanged so that b is always read as d, but much more often the b and d have an equivalent value. In one of my recent cases, b and d were so completely interchangeable that *baby*, *bady*, *daby* and *dady* all meant *baby* to the subject. There is here appar-ently a complete equivalence of either letter and its mirror counterpart. Sometimes, however, the children do not show this facility for substituting one letter for another, but when either letter is encountered they show bepuzzlement, and the same indecision as to what a letter means is found in connection with other letter symbols which cannot be confused by reversal. I think, therefore, that while the confusion between the symbol and its mirrored counterpart is easily demonstrable with *b*, *d*, *p* and *q*, it probably also operates with other letters, resulting not in an interchange, but in a puzzling indecision.

Another interference with the normal processes of reading is seen in a striking tendency toward sinistrad progress within the word, which is one of the characteristic earmarks of strephosymbolia. Such sinistrad reversals in direction are to be seen fairly frequently in practically all young children who are just starting to read, but those who acquire reading readily soon correct this tendency, while in those with a reading disability this continues to show itself in a variety of ways. Sometimes the whole word is read in reverse direction and *was* becomes *saw*, *on* becomes *no*, *not* becomes *ton*, etc. Again most of the word may be read correctly but a pair of letters is reversed as when *gray* is read *gary*, and *target* is read as *targret*, etc. Such words as *calm* and *clam* form almost insoluble puzzles for these children. Occasionally, children who have learned to read with considerable facility exhibit this reversing tendency strikingly in their attempts at oral or written spelling. No matter how one may look on the problem of cerebral localization, the major fact of antitropism of the two hemispheres remains, and the sinistrad progress is the natural expression of right hemispheric activity as dextrad progress is that of the left.

I think that one may now postulate from a study of the product of a large number of cases of reading disability and a somewhat smaller number of spelling defects that there are in all probability two factors operative here: (1) a tendency toward confusion in mnemonic recall between the original symbol and its antitrope, and (2) a tendency toward sinistrad progress within a word. The first of these, which is a static or orientation factor, I relate to an uncertainty of constant selection of the engram of one hemisphere. The second, which is a kinetic or progressional factor, is more closely related to the normal direction of progress for the left-handed. I cannot as yet speak concerning the relative frequencies or the relative severity of these two factors, but apparently the children who suffer from the most severe handicap in reading exhibit both factors to a considerable degree, and it is possible that either of these alone may form a minor obstacle to reading progress, but that severe reading disability rests on their coexistence. There is also some suggestive evidence that these two factors may be separately inherited.

Many other types of errors in the reading attempts of these children are to be observed. They may make many errors in pronunciation of vowels. They often omit or add letters, words, or parts of words. They frequently substitute complete words or repeat parts of them over and over again. All of these I now hold to be by-products of the fundamental difficulties in association resulting from the confusion and reversals which operate to prevent facile association between the visual and auditory spheres, but do not in any measure show that such association is truly defective or that it cannot be adequately established by proper methods. This conception, as will be seen, immediately takes the reading problem out of the sphere of pathologic conditions and limits it to a physiologic failure and thus to a problem of adequate training.

REINFORCEMENT OF THE ASSOCIATIVE PROCESS

Other things being equal, reinforcement of the associative process by means of a third sensory channel should secure a more adequate implantation and hence an easier association. With this general principle in mind, I have recommended the simultaneous tracing and sounding of a letter over its visual symbol. This differs to some degree from most of the previously used kinesthetic methods in that kinesthesis has been used chiefly for the purpose of aiding the visual implantation. Since, however, the aim is for greater facility of association between visual material and its auditory counterpart, it seems wise to link these together, using kinesthesis as the bond. The mechanics of this process, as carried out, is for the child to trace in script (or in the so-called manuscript writing) a written form, by which the visual is presented, and at the same time to sound the letter or word. Both the name of the letter and its phonetic equivalent should be thus linked to the visual symbol in order that the child may be taught to recall the name of the letter for purposes of oral spelling and the sound of the letter for purposes of constructive reading. The consistent motor drill of this kinesthetic method also aids markedly in written spelling, and has been used in a few cases for the correction of an isolated spelling defect.

The emotional variants, which are so frequently to be found in these children, I consider to be in large part a secondary result of the handicap rather than a causative factor. Granted an obstacle to reading progress which neither the teacher nor parent can understand, it is easy to see how a situation of extreme emotional tension for the child may arise. This emotional overloading is further fostered by the characteristically cruel remarks of other children. Another situation which frequently brings an obvious additional emotional stress is that which arises when a younger brother or sister is rapidly surpassing in reading capacity the child who is suffering from this handicap. From these emotional stresses, there may arise a variety of reactive patterns in the children, which are to be discussed elsewhere (Orton and Sprague n.d.). These reactions are frequently of prime importance from the standpoint of treatment, even though in our current envisagement they are not of etiologic rank. It is highly important that the child's cooperation and willingness to work be encouraged, and this can often be done only if his emotional antipathy toward a subject in which he has met with a serious obstacle is overcome.

I think it has been demonstrated, in most instances at least, that the physiologic variant which causes the reading disability can be overcome by proper training. As will be seen, this possibility of training holds a challenge to the view of inherent psychologic types. In the past one has been wont to look on certain persons as primarily visual or primarily auditory in their mental processes, and the tendency has been to think of these as inherent patterns and to fit the training of the child for the use of that pathway which is the most facile. If, however, one can increase the facility of interchange between the visual and auditory, the logical point of attack in training should be not the most facile but rather that which shows the least facility. In the past, it has frequently been recommended that a child with a quick auditory memory but with poor visual acquisition of words should be prepared for a vocation in which most of his social intercourse will be by way of the auditory pathway. Today, I think, there is an open question whether training should not focus in such a child on the visual in order, so far as possible, to enrich the use of the lesser sphere and thus give him a much more rounded acquisitional capacity. The demonstration of the possibility of training in such cases also offers a strong challenge to the much looser psychologic concept of persons of the nonverbal type. This is particularly true of children who have an apparently quick mind, but who show traces of a special disability both in reading and in the use of visually acquired material as a guide to speech. When one comes to consider such combinations of special disabilities, one is near to the problem of the feeble-minded. I feel sure today that when a reading disability or a speech difficulty (particularly of the type of developmental delay in speech) or a developmental apraxia exists in a child as an isolated defect, the condition is to be looked on as potentially correctable. When, however, two or more of these defects are present in the same child, the picture, both in general and by means of the results of mental tests, is characteristically that of feeble-mindedness. How far training is possible in children showing two or more of these defects cannot as yet be answered, but in one case of this nature in which the child is now under retraining, definite progress has been made in a few weeks.

THE "SIGHT READING" METHOD OF TEACHING READING, AS A SOURCE OF READING DISABILITY

◆   ◆   ◆

I feel some trepidation in offering criticism in a field somewhat outside of that of my own endeavor but a very considerable part of my attention for the past four years has been given to the study of reading disability from the standpoint of cerebral physiology. This work has now extended over a comparatively large series of cases from many different schools and both the theory which has directed this work and the observations garnered therefrom seem to bear with sufficient directness on certain teaching methods in reading to warrant critical suggestions which otherwise might be considered overbold.

I wish to emphasize at the beginning that the strictures which I have to offer here do not apply to the use of the sight method of teaching reading as a whole but only to its effect on a restricted group of children for whom, as I think we can show, this technique is not only not adapted but often proves an actual obstacle to reading progress, and moreover I believe that this group is one of considerable educational importance both because of its size and because here faulty teaching methods may not only prevent the acquisition of academic education by children of average capacity but may also give rise to far-reaching damage to their emotional life.

The sight reading method (or "look and say" of the English) has been credited with giving much faster progress in the acquisition of reading facility than its precursors, and this statement I will not challenge if the measure of accomplishment be the average progress of a group or class. Average progress of large numerical units, however, makes no allowance for the study of effect in individuals, particularly if certain of them deviate to some degree from the others in their methods of acquisition and therefore in their teaching requirements. To the mental hygienist whose interest is focused on the individual

Reprinted from The Journal of Educational Psychology, February 1929

and his problems rather than on group progress, the results as determined by average accomplishment are of little value whereas the effect
of a given method on the individual child is all important.

Outstanding cases of so-called congenital word blindness—a complete inability to learn to read—have been recognized and studied for a
number of years at first chiefly by physicians. It has also been recognized by teachers and psychologists that there is a large group of
children who have a much greater difficulty in getting started in
reading than would be expected from their ability in arithmetic, from
their ease in auditory acquisition, and from their general alertness. In
the past there has been a tendency, at least among medical men, and to
a considerable degree among psychologists as well, to exclude the
minor cases of slow learning in reading from the category of congenital
word blindness. This largely derives from the work of Hinshelwood
(1917) who made the first extensive study of these cases following the
pioneer work of Kerr (1896) and Morgan. (1896) Hinshelwood's statement in this is "... the rapidity and ease with which children learn to
read by sight vary a great deal. No doubt it is a comparatively common
thing to find some who lag considerably behind their fellows, because
of their slowness and difficulty in acquiring their visual word memories, but I regard these slight defects as only physiological variations
and not to be regarded as pathological conditions. It becomes a source
of confusion to apply to such cases as has been done of late the term of
'congenital word blindness' which should be reserved for the really
grave degrees of this defect which manifestly are the result of a
pathological condition of the visual memory center and which have
proved refractory to all ordinary methods of school instruction."

Unfortunately, Hinshelwood's criterion is a double one, neither part
of which can be looked upon as of sufficient diagnostic accuracy to
establish a clear-cut entity. Not only has no pathological condition of
the visual memory center yet been substantiated in such cases, but
there are certain neurological and clinical data which suggest that no
such condition exists. Again, the "ordinary methods of school instruction" does not prove to be an accurate measure. Such methods vary
widely and our own figures indicate that the number of children who
show a significant handicap in reading is to some degrees related to the
teaching method in use. Bachmann (1927) has called attention to the
looseness of the concept of congenital word blindness and related to
this the striking variation in the frequency of such cases as recorded by
various authors. Without some fairly clear objective symptoms on
which to establish the entity, the choice of cases to be included
naturally rests on the judgment of the examiner as to the severity of the
disability. My own initial work (1925) in this field led to a firm con-

viction that we were dealing here, not with two separate groups—a physiological and a pathological—but that those children who were specifically retarded in reading (thus excluding cases of general mental defect) formed a graded series extending from the normal to the extreme and that they showed consistent characteristic performance which not only would serve for diagnosis but which also was highly suggestive of the reason for their lack of progress and which gave excellent cues to methods for retraining. I was convinced not only that the specific reading disability formed an entity of much greater numerical importance than had been recognized before but that it was (even in the extreme cases) an obstacle of a physiological nature rather than a pathological condition and that therefore adequate special methods of teaching should correct it.

I cannot here go fully into the details of the anatomical background for our present theory of this disability but some presentation is necessary in order to illustrate the basis for the criticism of teaching method which is here offered.

Only a small portion of the retina of the eye is used in acquisition of reading. This is the focus of central vision or the macula lutea, so called because it is seen as a yellow spot in ophthalmoscopic examinations. The rest of the retina receives only general and less detailed impressions coming from outside the rather small area to which we are directing our attention. This point is noteworthy because the nervous connections of these two divisions of the retina are quite unlike. The peripheral retina or outer zone has connections with only one-half of the brain (there are some complexities here but these need not concern us). The macula lutea, however, which receives impressions with greatest detail and which is hence used exclusively in learning to read, has a double connection with the brain. The nerve fibers arising here divide and one-half of those starting from each macula go to the visual area of the hemisphere of the brain of the same side and the other half to the corresponding area of the opposite hemisphere. Thus impressions received by either eye or by both eyes are relayed simultaneously to both hemispheres of the brain. This double implantation does not give us a double sensation in consciousness, however, as a touch on both thumbs would do. The simultaneous activity of both areas results in our seeing but a single image. The visual sensation, however, is not a unitary function. There is apparently need for the simultaneous or additive activity of several parts of the visual cerebral mechanisms to complete the linkage of a printed symbol with its meaning and the steps in this process are shown in relief by differential losses such as are seen when certain parts of the back of the brain are destroyed by disease.

When all of that part of the brain which has to do with vision is destroyed the individual becomes totally blind. The eyes, however, are not damaged, they can still be moved, they will turn toward a sudden sound, and the pupils will respond by closing and opening to increase and decrease of the amount of light which strikes them. This condition is known as cortical blindness to differentiate it from blindness due to disease of the eyes or optic nerves. We may, however, see things surrounding us with sufficient clarity to avoid colliding with them, that is to guide our general body movements but without being able to appreciate the meaning of things which we see. This was first demonstrated by Munk in dogs in which much of this part of the brain had been removed. They were able to avoid collisions but did not recognize their master or even food by sight alone and did not cringe from a whip. To this condition Munk gave the name of mind-blindness and its parallel has since frequently been recorded in cases of disease of the human brain.

Apparently at the first level the visual area of the brain serves as a very accurate guide to motion and it probably also furnishes the element of awareness of the external origin of a sensation (as contrasted to a memory). In psychological terms it furnishes the pure perceptual element to sensation, but simultaneous or additive activity in other higher level visual areas is requisite to attach meaning and again we know that this is not accomplished in one step. If destruction of brain tissue happens in a certain area there results a condition in which the patient not only can see correctly but can also understand the meaning of objects seen, but in which the ability to read the printed or written word is entirely lost. That vision in the ordinary sense is normal is shown by the fact that such a patient can copy printed material but cannot read either the original or his copy. Thus we see from these differential losses that the process of linking a printed word to its meaning passes through at least three stages of elaboration in the brain before it is completed.

There are differences, however, in the brain destruction necessary to produce losses at these different elaborative levels. Destruction in one hemisphere only is not sufficient to produce either cortical blindness or mind blindness. At these first two levels of elaboration, that is in perception and recognition of the meaning of objects, apparently destruction must involve the areas subserving these functions in both hemispheres before their loss results. The two hemispheres are apparently of equal importance here as it apparently makes no difference which side is effected; i.e., either hemisphere is alone adequate for these functions. Exception must be taken to these statements in the case of peripheral vision but, as noted before, this is not of interest to us here since central vision is used exclusively in learning to read. When we come to the third plane of elaboration, the situation is strikingly different; this is the level at which the written or printed symbol is linked with its meaning and hence it is variously described as the associative, concept, or symbolic level. Here not only is damage to one hemisphere sufficient to destroy function, but it makes a difference which hemisphere is affected. If the hemisphere which is known as the dominant happens to suffer, a complete loss of this function results and the patient becomes word blind. If, on the other hand, the damage occurs in the other hemisphere—the nondominant—nothing apparently happens. So entirely without a result is a destruction here that this area of the brain takes its place with certain others among those which the surgeons called the silent areas of the brain. Obviously, the visual records implanted in both halves of the brain are not requisite for reading. This situation also exists in the field of understanding of the spoken word and of speech and of writing. In all four of these functions destruction in the dominant hemisphere in the so-called language zone is meaningful while destruction in exactly similar parts of the opposite hemisphere is meaningless.

Thus we learn to understand, to read, to speak, and to write words from sensory records or engrams of one hemisphere only. This fact is so striking that we have been prone to overlook what must happen in the inactive side. We believe today that the completed growth and development of nerve cells is largely a result of stimulation. If cells do not receive stimuli they do not reach their full development. The two sides of the brain do not show much, if any, difference in size or complexity and certainly no such difference as we see in function as outlined above. To account for equality of growth we must accept equality of stimulation—equal nervous irradiation of the two sides— and if they are equally irradiated, records must be left behind in each; i.e., engrams must be formed in the nondominant as well as in the dominant hemisphere. To account then for the difference in effect of damage in the two sides we must assume that the engrams of one side become the controlling pattern through establishment of a physiological habit of use of that set and that the other set of recorded engrams is latent or elided. Variations in the completeness of this physiological selection, i.e., failure of elision of the nondominant engrams, forms the kernel of my conception of the reading disability. Such a theory conforms nicely to our observations that these cases are not to be divided into two categories, that is, cases of word blindness and cases of slow acquisition of reading, but that they form a series graded in severity according to the degree of confusion which exists in choice of engrams, and it also offers an explanation of certain errors and peculiarities which characterize their performance.

The two halves of the body are strictly antitropic, that is, reversed or mirrored copies of each other. The muscles and joints of the right and left hand, for example, are alike but reversed in arrangement. This is also true of the groups of nerve cells in the spinal cord which control the simpler motor responses (spinal reflexes) and also of the cells in the brain which combine or integrate these simpler spinal units into more complex acts. The movements of the left hand, therefore, which are the exact counterpart of the right will give a mirrored result. Thus, the movements of sinistrad (mirror) writing with the left hand are exactly comparable to those of dextrad writing with the right hand, and it seems therefore highly probable that the engrams which are stored in the silent areas of the nondominant hemisphere are opposite in sign, *i.e.*, mirrored copies, of those in the dominant. If then these opposite engrams are not elided through establishment of consistent selection from one hemisphere we would expect them to evince themselves by errors or confusion in direction and orientation, and this is exactly what we find in cases of delayed reading.

This description is really putting the cart before the horse as our observations of tendency to reversals came first and the theory developed therefrom, but this method of presentation has been adopted for the sake of clarity. Many workers with word blind children have noted their tendency to reversals but none, so far as I am aware, have offered an adequate explanation of it.

My original studies in a small group of cases convinced me that there are certain symptoms in reading disability which seem to characterize the whole group and these were confusions between lower case *b* and d and between *p* and *q*; uncertainty in reading short pallindromic words like *was* and *saw*, *not* and *ton*, and *on* and *no*; a tendency to reverse parts of words or whole syllables as when *gray* is read as *gary*, *tarnish* as *tarshin* and *tomorrow* as *tworrom*; a greater facility than usual in reading from the mirror, and frequently a facility in producing mirror writing. These observations have been adequately supported in an extended study of a much larger group of cases. Many other types of errors are to be found in the performance of retarded readers, but they appear to me to be secondary effects due to the failure of association which has resulted from the obstacle presented by confusion in direction. The relation of the cardinal symptoms to the theory as above outlined is obvious and I think has direct bearing on the teaching method. Visual presentation will, hypothetically at least, result in the implantation of paired engrams and certain other factors must determine which of these is selected for associative linkage. What these factors are as a whole, we cannot consider here although it may be well to suggest that heredity probably plays a part in the establishment of dominance here comparable to that which it plays in stuttering and in left-handedness. Undoubtedly training influences may be brought to bear on this process of choice, however, and from the theoretical standpoint the most promising of these should be that of kinesthetic training by tracing or writing while reading and sounding and by following the letters with the finger (a method under taboo today) to insure consistent direction of reading during phonetic synthesis of the word or syllable.

Under a grant from the Rockefeller Foundation, an extended field study was carried out in 1926-27 in Iowa by the organization, as a part of the research work of the State Psycopathic Hospital, of a Mobile Mental Hygiene Unit to visit schools in various communities and a Laboratory Unit to study selected cases more intensively. Fuller reports of these studies are to appear elsewhere but certain observations may be quoted here. In my original group of reading disability cases, I was surprised at the large proportion of these children encountered. Fifteen out of one hundred twenty-five children sent by their teachers to our experimental field clinic for a variety of problems seemed to me to show evidence of this trouble (Lyday 1926). In our extended work we have found in every community visited no less than two per cent of the total school population to be retarded readers showing this characteristic picture. Our studies were not carried out as a survey and hence these figures probably fall far below the actual numbers. There was however a difference in the numbers of cases encountered in certain communities which seemed to bear directly on the subjects here considered. Of two communities of about the same constituent population, in one we found about two per cent of the school population to be retarded in reading to a significant degree and to show symptomatic evidence of the specific disability, while in the second we found more than double this percentage. In the community with the lesser number of cases, sight reading methods were employed but when children did not progress by this method they were also given help by the phonetic method. In the town with the larger number, no child was given any other type of reading training until he or she had learned ninety words by sight.

Aside then from theoretical considerations, this strongly suggests that the sight method not only will not eradicate a reading disability of this type but may actually produce a number of cases. Moreover, our retraining experiments (Monroe 1928) seem to indicate clearly that such children can be trained to read properly with adequate special methods devised to eradicte the confusion in direction and in orientation and this has also been borne out by the remedial efforts of other workers.

Our studies of children with reading disabilities has also brought to light certain other aspects of the problem which are of educational importance but which cannot be elaborated here. Among these were notably the effect of this unrecognized disability upon the personality and behavior of the child. Many children were referred to our clinics by their teachers in the belief that they were feeble-minded, others exhibited conduct disorders and undesirable personality reactions which upon analysis appeared to be markedly secondary to the reading defect and which improved markedly when special training was instituted to overcome the reading disability.

In brief, while sight reading may give greater progress when measured by the average of a group, it may also prove a serious obstacle to educable children who happen to deviate from the average in the case of establishment of a clear-cut unilateral brain habit. These physiological deviates form a graded group extending in severity from the normal to extreme cases (congenital word blindness). They can be detected by appropriate examinations and trained to overcome their handicap by specific methods of teaching. While the number of children who suffer from such a severe grade of the disability as to be practically uneducable by ordinary methods is quite small, the number in whom the disability exists to a sufficient degree to be a serious handicap to school performance and to wholesome personality development probably is of real numerical importance, and moreover there seems to be reason to believe that even those who make a spontaneous adjustment without special training, and thus learn to read, may never gain a facility in this accomplishment commensurate with their ability in other lines.

FAMILIAL OCCURRENCE OF DISORDERS IN ACQUISITION OF LANGUAGE

◆　　◆　　◆

That the problem of a preferential use of either hand for complex purposeful acts is not based on any superiority of that arm and hand has long been recognized. Also it is readily demonstrable that there is no anatomical difference between the two sides at the lower motor (i.e., spinal cord) level at all comparable in degree to the striking difference in skill between the two hands (Orton 1928). That this difference in motor facility rests on a differential use of the two cerebral hemispheres is emphasized by the intimate relationship of handedness to the loss of certain language functions in cases of brain damage by injury, tumor, hemorrhage, etc. I refer here to those cases which may be spoken of as the alpha-privative group of brain disorders—aphasia, alexia, agraphia, and apraxia. While there is much contention among neurologists as to the exact interpretations to be applied here, one fact stands out in sharp relief, and that is that a focus of destruction on one hemisphere of the brain is sufficient to cause any of this group of disorders providing it be in the so-called dominant or lead hemisphere, and that similar damage may occur in the opposite or nondominant hemisphere with no demonstrable symptoms resulting. As a clear-cut example of this unilateral importance I may cite a case reported to me by a friend and colleague. This was that of a boy of fourteen who suffered a depressed fracture of the skull in the left occipital region. An operation was performed to remove the bone fragments, and the underlying brain was found to be so badly softened that it could be removed by a suction apparatus, and a sharply circumscribed defect was left 4 X 2 X 2 cm. After the operation his symptoms cleared up except that he had largely lost the capacity to read and write. Further evidence of the functional importance of one hemisphere has been demonstrated in cases in which an American brain surgeon has removed completely the right hemisphere in patients with

Reprinted from Eugenics, April 1930 Vol. III, No. 4

inoperable brain tumors, following which the patients suffered no loss in language or intelligence.

Losses in the language function due to brain injury have attracted much interest from neurologists in the past, and the literature bearing on them is enormous. A somewhat comparable symptomatology is to be seen in many children, without any evidence of brain damage and with good intelligence, who have great difficulty in learning in some one particular branch of language. These children constitute the group known as the special educational disabilities, and their problem has largely occupied my time for several years. Following an intensive study of a few cases I (Orton 1925) offered an explanation of the obstacle to those whose difficulty was that of learning to read, based on the theory of a failure to establish a clear-cut unilateral dominance leading to confusion in recall which interfered with reading acquisition. Since that time a large series of cases has been intensively studied amply supporting the symptomatology on which this theory was offered (Monroe 1928). Studies in stuttering (Orton, Travis et al. 1927–28–29) were also undertaken to determine if possible the part played by cerebral dominance in this speech disorder. In cases of delayed development of speech and of striking inability in writing and in spelling, this view also offers much of interest and probable significance.

The specific reading disability we have shown to be characterized by confusions between *b* and *d* and *p* and *q*, by sinistrad progress in reading parts or all of words and by a facility in mirror reading. In many children it can be shown not only that *b* and *d* are confused, but that they are entirely equivalent, and the child may use either interchangeably with the other so that he is quite unable to pick the proper form from such a series as *baby, bady, daby,* and *dady,* and so that in writing he frequently substitutes one for the other even in double letters as when *rudder* is written *rudber*. This confusion is held to rest on the fact that lower case *b* is practically the reversed or left hand pattern of lower case *d*. In this instance as in that of *p* and *q* the mirrored form is that of another letter and hence its miscalling shows what is happening. Additional evidence strongly suggests that this same reversed recall also plays a prominent part in slow learning with many other letters but does not identify itself to us so readily because the reversed form of most letters is not like that of any other. The second factor, that of sinistrad progression in reading a sequence of letters, shows itself clearly in the very common confusion between *was* and *saw, on* and *no* and other short pallindromes. It is not limited to these however and may be seen in reversals of paired letters as when *calm* is read as *clam* or *orphan* as *rophan;* and in reversals of syllables which may affect one syllable only of a word, as when *target* is read as *tarteg;* or it may affect both by reversal in direction, though assembled in proper order, as when *tarnish* is read as *ratshin;* or it may affect only the order of assembling as when *repast* is read as *astrep*. Occasionally the first letter alone may have its proper position and all the rest be reversed as when *done* is read as *deno* and *tomorrow* as *tworrom*. Many other errors such as those of vowel sounds, omissions of parts of words, and misreading of consonants enter into the picture and often lead to reading errors which form an entrancing challenge to understanding. If *blind* be read to the left and the *n* miscalled a *u*, it becomes *build*. Reading *card* backwards with a twist in the sequence of the *a* and *r* produces *bark*. When *target* is read from the left and the *at* dropped it becomes *tegr*, and since this carried no meaning the child offered *tiger*. When the first syllable of *target* is reversed and the *g* given its soft sound the word becomes *ratchet*.

MIRROR READING

The third earmark of the retarded readers is their facility in mirror reading. Since they are slow readers both with and without the mirror their proficiency in reading the reversed form cannot be directly compared with that of normal readers of the same age, but if the ratio of time for reading in the ordinary form to reading in the mirror be taken, it can be shown that those who have encountered a serious obstacle in learning to read recognize the mirrored form proportionately much more quickly than do the good readers. Moreover the ratio is in fairly direct relation to the degree of their handicap and indeed severe cases sometimes read more rapidly with the mirror than they can without.

Because of the characteristic reversals of direction shown in these cases, I have offered the term strephosymbolia (twisted symbols) for the group, and I believe that this disability rests largely if not entirely on the failure to acquire the physiological habit of leading exclusively from either cerebral hemisphere and that the confusions which exist and which block progress in reading skill are due to an inadequate elision of the engrams in the nondominant side of the brain. This view, as will be seen, implies a physiological rather than the pathological basis for this disability which was the earlier view of Hinshelwood, who hypothecated a congenital defect of development of the area of the brain destined for the storage of word memories. The physiological view seems well supported by the striking improvement in these children when taught by methods properly adapted to their needs. Thus one of my cases who had learned only a very few two- and three-letter words during three years in a high grade private school gained four years of reading skill during one year of special retraining.

Attention has lately been directed to the comparative frequence of left-eyedness in the reading disability cases. By eyedness we mean a preferential choice of one or the other eye in sighting at a distance. This can be easily determined and some writers have held it to be a causative factor. It is of unquestioned frequence, but in my own series of cases I have seen both right-eyed and left-eyed children and some who were amphiocular; all of these patterns have been found in combination with both right- and left-handedness and with so-called ambidexterity; thus I am inclined to look upon it as merely one of the methods of expression of cerebral dominance and of no greater diagnostic value than several others.

Delay in learning to talk well beyond the usual age period for acquiring this function is not uncommon. This is often one of the first signs observed by the parents in a child who later shows a markedly defective mentality. It is occasionally seen in children who have suffered birth injuries and sometimes obviously rests on defective hearing, especially if this be of central origin. A special group of children has been recognized, however, who seem as bright as others of their age, who hear easily and understand what is said to them readily, but who are very slow in talking. When speech is acquired by those of this group it usually develops rapidly and it may not go through all of the developmental stages of the usual acquisition period. My own observations in this type of case are not very extensive, but in those which I have seen there has been an obvious, equal delay in developing a preference for either the right or the left hand except in those activities where training has determined it.

In stuttering, a wide range of abnormal motor responses of the breathing, vocal, and articulatory mechanisms has been recorded, and various drill methods to correct faulty breathing and faulty phonation have been devised on the assumption that these were the cause of the stuttering. Modern neurological knowledge, however, indicates that such faults are not resident in these lower functions but that they probably arise from faulty integrations or faulty syntheses of normal lower patterns and that the proper integration of such reflex patterns into the orderly sequence of the speech act is resident solely in the language zone of the brain; hence it is here rather than in the control of breathing e.g., that we must look for the origin of stuttering. This, together with recorded observations of the occurrence of stuttering when left-handed children were forced to write with the right hand and its disappearance when left-handed writing was permitted, led us to study this phase more closely.

From the beginning of this work we were impressed with the great difficulty in determining the natural bent or physiological handedness of an individual after he had been exposed to various forms of training. Golla in England has recorded that when the action currents from both forearms were impressed on sensitive galvanometers and a left-handed patient was asked to close both hands simultaneously, the galvanometer connected with the left arm registered the action current effect first. Travis and I applied this method to a series of stutterers and a series of normals by means of two multiple vacuum tube amplifiers and two magnetic phoneloscopes and found that the action current patterns of right-handed stutterers were strikingly different from those of right-handed normal speakers. In the normal speakers the action currents appeared first in the right arm in 81.18 per cent of the trials, first in the left arm in 8.91 per cent, and simultaneously in 9.91 per cent In the stutterers, all of whom were right-handed as determined by all ordinary tests, they appeared first in the right arm in only 15.58 per cent of the trials, first in the left in 53.28, and simultaneously in 31.14 per cent Not infrequently in young stutterers who have not been exposed to much pressure in training for the use of either hand a very striking parity in the skill on the two sides can be demonstrated. This I have met especially in those who have stuttered from the beginning of their speech efforts.

AN EXAMPLE

One girl of twelve who has always stuttered was able to write on the blackboard with both hands at the same time with her eyes closed and in either direct or mirrored form and in all combinations of these, viz., direct with the left hand and mirrored with the right etc., and in all with a very close similarity of product. This child had always been left-handed and was being trained as such. The situation here is obviously different from that in those cases where speech is clear at first and the stuttering begins later. Sometimes this may be associated with quite early training of the child as in one of my cases, a boy of three, who had been stuttering only two weeks when I first saw him. On asking the parents about handedness the mother replied, "He is right-handed in everything," but the father thought he was about half and half. After a period of one week of close observation the parents returned with the story that the boy used his right hand in only three activities, eating, throwing a ball, and digging in the sand, and in all these he had been trained by his elders. In everything else he made use of his left hand, and in a cinematographic picture of him, feeding chickens at the age of two, he was seen to be holding the pan in his right hand and scattering the grain with his left. The parents were advised to retrain him entirely as a left-hander and within two weeks his stuttering had stopped. More frequently the stuttering starts early in the school period and often it is associated with the mistraining either by design or through oversight of a naturally left-handed child.

Special disabilities in writing are not infrequently encountered. In some, as in certain stutterers, the problem seems to rest on the use of the wrong hand. One such case, a boy of eleven in the fifth grade of a very good private school, had made very poor progress in writing; he was also an exceedingly bad speller, stuttered a little, and was looked upon as an extremely nervous child. When tested for his writing facility with both hands with pencil and paper the product was not strikingly different, but when tested at the blackboard with his eyes closed his left-handed writing was distinctly superior. Retraining was immediately begun and with one year's subsequent training his writing with the left hand was far ahead of the product of his right after five years of drill. In another of my cases, a medical student, writing with either hand in the dextrad or ordinary direction was next to impossible. He could write simple home letters and accustomed phrases so that they could be read, but when attempting to write and think, as he put it, at the same time, his efforts were scarcely decipherable. On examination, however, it was found that even without training he was able to write quite legibly and freely in the mirrored form. To make available to him this latent capacity, we suggested the use of a sheet of carbon paper upside down under the sheet on which he was writing. When he then wrote in mirrored form on one side, the carbon paper copied it in reversed or dextrad form on the other side, and his product could therefore be easily read by turning over the sheet. Both the father and paternal uncle of this case also suffered from a striking writing disability.

Spelling errors are so common that difficulty in this regard is often considered as not of serious moment, but a true selective spelling disability may occur of such severity as to form a decisive handicap. In practically all cases of strephosymbolia, as outlined above, there is a marked defect in spelling comparable usually both in degree of severity and in kinds of errors to the handicap in reading. In extreme cases the attempts at writing words may give a product which is wholly illegible. A striking example of this was offered by a sixteen-year-old boy who had reached the seventh grade in school but whose reading capacity was that of a first grade child. An excerpt from a school composition in American history describing the English campaign of 1777 read in part as follows:

I. Comter in 1777.

The Enlgand camele stosent in cane hosterson the their last scoune and honeter posterson and rososon and sean 1000 scouter then to pastore and the fosteron the secounter tall theen heuster and at dog befor mostir, etc.

ISOLATED

Marked defects in spelling, however, may also occur as an isolated disability in good readers. Many interesting errors show themselves here. Most frequent are those which are comparable to the errors in reading, confusions of *b* and *d*, and *p* and *q*, reversals in sequence, errors in vowels, omissions of letters, etc. One seven-year-old second grade boy, when asked to write the alphabet dodged the *b-d* pitfall by using a capital *B*. When he came to *d* he again used the capital and when asked to write the small letter he first produced a *b* which he then crossed out and wrote a *d*. In writing *p* to dictation he recorded beautiful evidence of his insecurity. He made two vertical strokes with three loops to the right and two to the left, thus leaving his guess at three to two in favor of the correct form. An eleven-year-old boy in writing both *way* and *by* started with the *y* first; in writing *baby* produced *bady* which was then corrected, and in writing *liberty* started *led*, saw the error and crossed it out, then wrote *lebatry* with the *r* and *t* reversed in position, again saw his error and crossed it out and wrote *lebarty*, and made a final correction by writing *e* over the *a*. Many other interesting misspellings are to be seen. The sound of *w* is often taught as that of *oo* so that the child is taught to pronounce *went* as though it were *ooent*. This has occasionally carried over into spelling so that one boy writes *news* as *nwz* and another, *school* as *skwl*.

One of the current methods of teaching reading also apparently plays a prominent part in some spelling errors. Certain children who have been taught by the sight reading method have only short words to represent certain sounds so that they do not know any symbol for the long *u* sound except *you* for example. This produces such spellings as *egyoucaytion* for education, *dockyoument* for document, and *tacksaytion* for taxation. One boy read hostility as *hostlostily* and on question as to how he got this he replied, "I don't know *h-o-s-t*, but I do know *l-o-s-t* so I took the *l* off and put an *h* on." Apparently the *lost* was still reverberating when he reached the *l* in hostility. It would seem obvious that the training which this child received in reading by word units rather than by letters or by syllables has provided him with exceedingly clumsy tools to accomplish the analysis of new words. The relationship of cerebral dominance to misspelling is not so clear as in certain other disabilities but the similarity of many errors with those of the reading disability is extremely suggestive here.

Cases of developmental apraxia have also been recorded in medical literature. I have found a history of unusual clumsiness and difficulty in learning trained movements to be of quite frequent occurrence in a number of cases who later encountered difficulty in speech and in reading and believe it to have significance in this regard. A comparable difficulty in copying movements of others, such for example as dance steps, is occasionally seen in older children, and in one I found that while direct mimicry of a movement pattern was difficult and clumsy, yet imitation could be carried out with much greater grace and freedom when the pattern was seen in reverse before a large mirror.

My current belief is that the major part of these special disabilities rests on the basis of a failure to establish a clear-cut unilateral brain control at the highest elaborative cerebral level and that they are due to an interplay between the hereditary patterns of the child and the methods employed in his training. Aside from the inconveniences impressed on a left-handed person by customs largely devised for the right-handed there seems to be no valid reason to consider one motor pattern as better than the other, and I believe that the child who is clearly left-handed—i.e. right-brained—in everything, will not encounter much more difficulty in learning than the clearly right-handed. Between these two extremes, however, there appears to be a group of considerable size in whose members variants in the establishment of unilateral control occur, and these children encounter obstacles which can only be overcome by methods of teaching specifically adapted to their needs.

Left-handedness has formed a topic of considerable interest from the genetic standpoint and Hinshelwood and others have emphasized the familial occurrence of the reading disability. My own family studies have so far been rather cursory but even in this incomplete form I think they show an interesting interrelation between many of the special disabilities discussed above; I am therefore offering this as a suggestion that the genetic problem here is not simply that of left-handedness but the much more complicated one of cerebral dominance with its many forms of expression.

THE CHARTS

The charts which follow show the data available in my case records in eight families. The disabilities are distinguished thus: S = Stutterer, L = Left-handed, A = Ambidextrous, R = Reading Disability, W = Bad Writer.

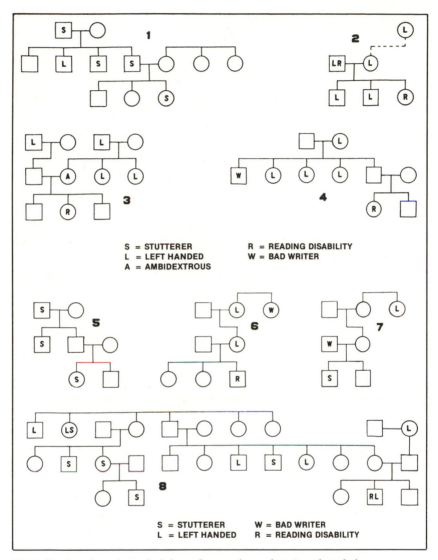

Fig. 1. The heredity of speech defects. See text for explanation of symbols.

In Family 1 the patient was a girl of eleven who had stuttered from her earliest efforts at speech. She was left-handed in most things but showed a noteworthy parity in writing simultaneously with both hands in either dextrad or sinistrad forms. Her father, one paternal uncle, and her paternal grandfather stuttered. The uncle is said to have been "broken of left-handedness" and another uncle is left-handed.

Family 2 is that of a small girl with an extreme case of reading disability. She is amphiocular,—that is she uses either eye interchangeably in sighting through a hole in a card. She has shown little preference for either hand but has learned to write with her right hand. She has two left-handed brothers. Her mother is left-handed. Her father started as left-handed, was shifted to the right, but went back again and now can do about equally well with either hand. He is a poor speller, a slow reader, and has always encountered difficulty with language. Mathematics is easy for him. The mother's grandmother was also left-handed.

Family 3 is that of another girl with a marked reading disability. She is considered right-handed and uses this hand by preference in writing and other trained movements, but she is left-eyed. Her mother is ambidextrous and two paternal aunts and both grandfathers are left-handed.

Family 4 is that of another girl with a severe degree of reading disability. She is right-handed in writing and most other manual things but prefers to bounce a ball and throw with her left. She is right-eyed. Her three paternal aunts and her paternal grandmother are left-handed and a paternal uncle is an extremely bad writer and was very backward in school although he has since been very successful.

Family 5 is that of a three-year-old girl who had just begun to stutter occasionally. She used her right hand in most trained acts but was also quite facile with the left. She was amphiocular and this was easily observable because of a crossing of the eyes which made it possible to see readily which was leading. Thus while working with a pencil part of the time the right eye was focused on the task and the left turned in, but part of the time this order was reversed. Her father is said to be right-handed in everything except throwing a ball. Her paternal uncle has stuttered badly from childhood and her paternal grandfather stutters slightly.

Family 6 is that of a boy of nine with great trouble with reading. He is left-eyed. He uses the pencil in his hand but his efforts are laborious and his product poor. In other things he also uses his right hand by preference. His mother is left-handed and had considerable difficulty in school. His maternal grandmother is left-handed and a maternal great-aunt is a "very poor writer."

Family 7 is that of a sixteen-year-old boy who stutters rather badly. He uses his right hand by preference in writing, throwing, tennis, etc. He is left-eyed. His father is said to be an exceedingly poor writer, to be very nervous when he tries to write, and to restrict his efforts in this regard largely to the signing of his name. The boy's maternal great-aunt was left-handed.

Family 8 is that of a nine-year-old left-handed boy with a rather severe reading disability. His left-handedness was recognized early and he has always been encouraged to use that hand. He is also left-eyed. As the chart shows, his paternal grandmother was left-handed and there is marked occurrence of both left-handedness and stuttering in his mother's family.

My records so far are obviously inadequate to serve as a basis for opinion regarding the nature of transmission of these variants. In one family which is not charted here speech disorders, represented by both delayed speech and stuttering, seem to have been passed by un-affected daughters to their sons, but in others this is obviously not true. One fact of interest here is the numerical relation of the sexes in certain of these language disorders. Stuttering is recognized as much more frequent in boys than in girls although the proportions given vary considerably according to different authors. In an intensive study of a group of one hundred and seventy-five cases of the specific reading disability we found three and a half times as many boys as girls.

CONCLUSION

In closing I would like to repeat that in many children the deter-mination of the native handedness is not easy and that the many rule-of-thumb tests are far from satisfactory, especially after the child has been exposed to either purposive or accidental training. In the study of the majority of cases of language disorders due to brain injury recorded in the medical literature this question has received rather scant attention, and often the sole criterion for handedness is that of which hand was used in writing. With the widespread tendency of mothers to train their children to be right-handed and the equally wide demand by school teachers that every child be taught to write with his right hand if it can be done, it is obvious that many of our case records may be misleading in this regard, and I believe that this must also be taken into account in the study of the genetics of left-handedness.

SOME STUDIES IN THE LANGUAGE FUNCTION

♦   ♦   ♦

An interest of many years standing in the problem of aphasia and the other syndromes that I have been accustomed to call the alpha-privative group (aphasia, agraphia, alexia, apraxia, et al.) has led during the recent past to an intensive study and, I believe, to a some-what better understanding of the disorders and delays in the acquisition by children of the various fractions of the language faculty and to methods of treatment which are, in many instances at least, proving their efficacy.

In these disorders of acquisition we meet syndromes which very closely approximate the losses of a previously acquired language facility which follow lesions of the brain in the adult. The close symptomatic similarity between children who could not learn to read and cases of acquired alexia in adults led Hinshelwood to classify the former under the name congenital word blindness. At the time of his studies, acquired alexia was considered to be due to a destruction of that particular cortical field which served as the "center for visual memory of words," and he made the assumption that in congenital word blindness there is a failure of development of the cortex destined to serve as the visual word center. I need not here go into the reasons which have altered our thinking from that of the strict predestined pigeon-holes of the cerebral localization of that day to our present somewhat more elastic views. It may suffice however to say that Hinshelwood's assumption in this particular seems no longer tenable. There is no precise evidence to support such a focal agenesis and much to suggest that, did it occur, adjacent brain areas would be competent to assume the function. Moreover there seems to be reasonable ground to assume a physiological disorder rather than an obligate structural defect in explanation of these cases. There remains however so instructive a similarity of symptoms between failures of acquisition and loss of

Reprinted from the Proceedings of the Association for Research in Nervous and Mental Disease, Vol. XIII, 1932

language that I believe that no study of either can be considered complete without a comparable investigation of the other. The delays and failures in acquisition offer one great advantage over the alpha-privative syndromes in the investigation of the normal physiological processes, since they are often limited quite sharply to one fraction of the language faculty and hence bring out the failures in associative integration in bold relief in a way that will be encountered only in the rarest of cases of the alpha-privative group. On the other hand, they are not usually associated with disease processes which are apt to lead to death and thus do not supply opportunities for autopsy control of out clinical studies.

CEREBRAL DOMINANCE

The one outstanding peculiarity of the cerebral patterns underlying language in the adult is that of the much greater physiological importance of one hemisphere than of the other in this faculty. This is the phenomenon of unilateral cerebral dominance. Stated briefly, in the adult losses in the capacity to understand the spoken word, to reproduce it, to interpret the graphic word, or to reproduce it may or may not occur following destructive lesions of certain brain areas, dependent on whether or not the master hemisphere is involved. The master hemisphere is usually indicated by the master hand, but here many uncertainties appear because of the existence of many mixed patterns and because of the influence on handedness imposed by early training. Most notably does this last factor affect the hand used for writing, which is the commonly accepted criterion of the handedness pattern of an individual in hospital records.

In addition to the group of functions above outlined as constituting the language faculty, viz., understanding and reproducing both spoken and graphic words, certain other functions apparently are controlled from the master hemisphere. Here we may mention the conscious representation of the body image, of which Schilder has told us, and many of the more complex postural and motor patterns whose disturbance is seen in the apraxias.

The principle of unilateral physiological superiority in the adult brain can be held to be established, however, only in these more intricate patterns of integration and obviously does not obtain at the projections levels. It is scarcely necessary to review for this volume the strict heterolateral and independent function of the two hemispheres in the hemianesthesias, the motor paralyses, or the hemianopsias. In macular vision we find a double implantation, both hemispheres being irradiated from each macula by virtue of the dichotomy of the fibers from the ganglion cells of the retina underlying each macular area. In the auditory field our knowledge is much less precise. This function is generally thought to operate as a bilateral mechanism and hence to be comparable with macular vision. Certain recent observations made in my laboratory suggest tentatively, however, that the capacity to judge correctly the direction from which a sound has come may be a unilateral function, while total acuity and especially that part which deals with the higher pitches of the speech range may require bilateral integrations. Should these as yet very sparse observations be confirmed by further studies they would form an exceedingly interesting analogue of the plan of organization of the peripheral and central retina. On the whole, the auditory functions seem to have been subjected to much less critical analysis than their importance would justify.

Between the projection levels, however, and those in which the physiological superiority of one hemisphere is generally accepted lies a sort of no man's land which receives relatively little attention in the literature of the aphasias, although its disorders are frequently recognized when they exist as an isolated clinical picture. I refer here to the agnosias or disturbances of function of what may be called the second level of cerebral elaboration. The segregation of three distinct stages of elaboration of sensory material in the visual sphere is clearly indicated in our terminology by the three clinical concepts described as cortical blindness, mind blindness, and word blindness. Comparable terms for the auditory sense are found in cortical deafness, mind deafness, and word deafness. In the kinesthetic field the corresponding words for the first two are hemianesthesia and astereognosis. I know of no single word to represent the loss of the derivatives of this sensory field at the third level.

The second level of the kinesthetic function has taken a place in methods of examination and as a localizing index in studies of the aphasias, but I feel that the corresponding stages of elaboration of the visual and auditory sensations have received far too little attention. Critical studies of the integrity of this level in these two functions are not only very rare in reports of the aphasias but even our testing methods are deficient in this respect. What series of aphasia tests, for example, aims at the investigation of the patient's retention of the normal capacity to differentiate among the multitude of meaningful sounds other than words?

Support for the existence of such a second level or intermediate stage of integrative complexity comes from many sources—anatomical, phylogenetic, and pathological—but perhaps it may be briefly illustrated by the contrast between visual agnosia and alexia (or between mind blindness and word blindness). The visual agnosic is not blind since avoidance reactions are intact, although he interprets nothing of what he sees except its position. That this is not a more fundamental loss, i.e., a true dementia, is shown by the prompt recognition of the purpose and use of objects when examined by touch and kinesthesis. The alexic patient, on the other hand, shows an extensive visual familiarity with objects although he is unable to recognize the graphic characters which serve as their symbols.

Cases with the alpha-privative syndromes, however, rarely exhibit as clear-cut pictures as do those with defects in the acquisition of language in children. Indeed, the restriction of functional defect following a brain lesion to one fraction of the language faculty is so rare that one frequently finds the statement in the literature that there is no such condition as pure word blindness or pure word deafness. This is not so in the delays of acquisition. In uncomplicated cases of strephosymbolia (or the specific reading disability), for example, it is possible to show that there is active use of many visual patterns much more intricate than those of the avoidance reactions which we, by analogy with mind blindness, relate to the first level and yet the visual mechanism fails strikingly at the third or word level. Let me sketch here a composite picture of a case of this nature drawn from the experience gained in intensive studies of several hundred strephosymbolics.

A HYPOTHETICAL CASE

I have chosen a boy to represent this hypothetical patient since the reading disability is more than four times as common among boys as among girls. He is almost nine years of age and is just finishing his third year in school but is failing in all of his work except his arithmetic which he does well. His father is a college professor and his mother a college graduate and the home environment is conducive to an intellectual interest. Inquiry into the family history reveals several left-handed or partly left-handed individuals in immediate or collateral lines, among whom is the patient's brother who learned to read at an early age. The parents assert, however, that the patient himself has never shown any preference for the left hand and our observations of his common motor patterns as well as of his acquired skills and his eyedness all bespeak a clear dextrality. The history of his development gives no evidence of delay in sitting, creeping, walking, or talking. He has suffered no head injuries or very severe illnesses. He has learned easily by ear and his vocabulary is good for his age.

Until he entered school he had been looked upon by his parents and also by less interested observers as a more than usually alert and intelligent boy. In school he did quite well in the first grade and his capacity to learn by ear and thus to keep in touch with the class room material through the recitations of others quite misled his second grade teacher as to the really serious nature of the difficulty he had encountered in learning to read. In the third grade, however, this became increasingly apparent and his parents were advised to take him to an oculist on the natural assumption that he was "not seeing his words correctly." He is quite a leader in athletics and very fond of manual arts of all sorts and the school reports a good natural aptitude in this direction. He has a frank and open personality and a cheerful disposition until the school subjects of reading, writing, and spelling are mentioned and then we see evidence of a strong emotional reaction and he remarks, "I guess I'm a dumbbell 'cause I can't learn to read." Questions about arithmetic bring out no such feeling of discouragement.

When we examine him we find a lad who, in spite of his inability to read and the consequent penalty assessed against him in many standardized testing techniques, still makes a rating of above average intelligence. His intelligence quotient by the Terman modification of the Binet-Simon tests is 120, giving him a mental age of ten years and nine months. He shows no hearing defect. Audiometer tests place his hearing well within the limits of normal acuity with both ears. He has learned the meaning of a multitude of sounds in addition to those required for oral communication and he has stored memories of spoken words in good measure, serving the purpose of recognition of words when heard and as recall patterns which he uses in his own reproduction of them in speech. There are some slight inaccuracies here due to the omission of the minor modifications of the spoken word which follow familiarity with its spelling. He makes, for example, a rather poor differentiation in ordinary speech between such closely similar sounds as those of the short vowels $\breve{\imath}$, $\breve{e}$, $\breve{o}$, and $\breve{u}$, and between some consonants such as t and d, and f and v, but these would be caught only by the trained and expectant ear and his enunciation in general is precise enough to lead to easy recognition of his words by others. He is able to echo accurately speech sounds devoid of association when they are spoken by the examiner as nonsense syllables. Extensive somesthetic tests are quite within normal limits. He has a well developed stereognostic capacity and is quick to learn new motor patterns as evinced by his athletic prowess, his mechanical skills, and by pertinent laboratory tests. The accuracy of his movements in all of these fields (e.g., hitting a pitched ball, sawing to a line, or with the "steadiness tester") bespeak a good control of motor responses by the visual mechanism.

When he was sent to the ophthalmologist at the suggestion of his teacher he was carefully examined both with the ophthalmoscope and by refraction tests and was discharged with a clean slate. Perimetric examination shows no restriction or indentation of the visual fields and there is no defect in color vision. His use of certain types of material gained through visual experience is accurate and certain. He does very well in the Healy Pictorial Completion

Tests and perceives and correctly interprets an unusual amount of detail in the pictures which are presented to him in the course of the Stanford-Binet examination. He is observant of objects and quick to see the relation of parts in mechanical problems and can repicture spatial relations in new problems when they are verbally presented. His visual memory for places is so good that he is the most trusted guide of the family group in retracing routes on their automobile trips.

When we test him in reading, writing, and spelling, however, we meet for the first time in any of the fairly exhaustive examinations evidence of a condition distinctly out of harmony with his age, his intelligence, his alertness, and his skill in other fields. Although he is completing his third year in school, he obtains only a low first grade rating by standardized reading tests. Not only is he quite incapable of reading the words of the third grade assignments but he misreads many of the simpler words as well. At this age, he reads only a few words backwards and can distinguish b's from d's and p's from q's without error when given ample time, but he remembers having had great trouble in telling them apart in earlier years. When confronted with a word beginning or ending with one of these "twin" letters, however, which is less familiar than another word of exactly similar spelling except that a b takes the place of a d he is still apt to misread that letter. For example, he is quite at home with the word dog but does not know bog as well and when bog is presented he reads it promptly as dog. When assigned the task of cancelling all the mirrored or backward letters from a card on which both the ordinary and the mirrored forms are printed he makes a number of errors. One or two dextral forms are cancelled and several sinistral forms are overlooked. He takes a long time for this comparatively simple work and shows evidence of uncertainty and occasionally reaches a decision only after tracing the letter forms with his finger, thus selecting from the kinesthetic rather than from the visual clues. When he is asked to read from a card bearing a first-grade test paragraph printed with reversed type, he requires only about three times as long as he does to read a paragraph of comparable difficulty printed in the usual dextrad direction. Since those children of his age who have learned to read readily take about ten times as long for this task, our boy is seen to have a demonstrable mirror reading facility.

His spelling is atrocious. Such as he has shows efforts at phonetic reconstruction with very little evidence of recall of the appearence of the word. Since he has been in a school which stresses the "sight method" of teaching reading and in which phonetic training is taboo (until he takes up French or Latin), he has a very inadequate knowledge of which letters to choose for the sounds of the word which he has in mind and is thus enabled to misspell one word in two ways at once: first, by failing to recall its appearance and, second, by choosing the wrong letters to express his auditory memory of its parts. This produces the most bizarre results—often true neographisms.

His writing likewise lags strikingly. His manual dexterity however shows no impairment. He cannot only draw very good pictures but he can draw each letter of the alphabet rather nicely and he can copy from printed text into his own hand with accuracy and with considerable neatness. When attempting to write to dictation or in original composition, however, his uncertainty of spelling leads to a slow and laborious production with many changes and erasures. Among his errors, in both dictated and spontaneous writing, are an occasional *b* substituted for a *d* and a not infrequent reversal of a pair of letters or a whole syllable. Some of these errors are noticed by him and are altered or erased but most of them escape visual recognition. The stock of words which he can recall in graphic form is so small as to rank his writing capacity with that of a first-grade child.

I have drawn this composite sketch for you to show the completed picture as I have pieced it together from the study of many cases, and while it is confessedly a synthesis I believe it to be only slightly, if at all, idealized. To recapitulate this story we may say that we find no difficulty of any type recognizable by our present methods of examination in the general intellectual level of such a boy or in the auditory, somesthetic, or motor fields. In his visual capacities we find him well equipped as far as the usual eye examinations are concerned, able to use his vision skillfully as a guide to motion and to have stored for practical use a wealth of visual memories of form, size, color, and spatial relations of objects and of his environment, but quite unable to use these visual accomplishments in reading and writing.

Further evidence of the availability of a wealth of visual material when reading has been lost is to be found in many cases of the alpha-privative syndromes although here it is seldom so clear-cut as that quoted above. The alexic patient can no longer read words but usually can and does make use of a wide range of visual memories below the word level both in recognition and in recall. A striking example of this has recently come to my attention. The patient was a woman past middle age who had suffered from a vascular accident and as a result showed a considerable degree of aphasia and an almost complete alexia and agraphia. When she was preparing to come to the hospital for a period of study she wanted to give her maid instructions for the packing of a traveling bag. She could not give the list of articles verbally nor could she write it spontaneously although she knew exactly what she wished to take with her. Some one had, however, given her a set of aphasia cards and from the pictures on one side of these cards she selected those representing the articles she desired. Then turning over each card she copied the name of each article and appended a number to indicate the units wanted. The copy made from print was produced in script and in her accustomed hand. There was no evidence of hesitation or uncertainty apparent in the product. She had constructed a complete and legible list in a good script. Here again we are confronted with a patient who was unable to read but who could still use pictures of objects as symbols and could even write from copy although she could not do so by recall of previously implanted patterns.

Clearly the complexity of the visual material available both to this patient and to our strephosymbolic is far above that which can be allocated to the known functional perquisites of the first or arrival platform of vision, and yet in both the function of the third or word level of visual elaboration is almost completely disordered.

An unsolved problem of localizing value further emphasizes the need for careful clinical separation of the functions of the second from those of the third level. We are not yet sure in how far one hemisphere may serve for the other at this level as is obviously possible in macular vision at the first level. In other words, we do not yet know how much of the agnosias result only from bilateral lesions of the secondary sensory cortices or in how far they may follow a unilateral lesion of the same cortical field if it involves the dominant hemisphere. The evidence of past studies is conflicting and it seems entirely possible that there may be wide individual differences here, dependent on physiological usage or on age and habituation.

Unilateral control is well established as the principle of physiological organization at the third or language level, but unfortunately we have no direct method of determining which hemisphere is the dominant one except through observations and tests of the side of the body preferred in certain acquired motor skills. There is no method of auditory examination for determining whether the language functions derived from this sensory system are organized in the left or in the right hemisphere, and this is true even when a lesion has disturbed this function. In vision I think that some of the testing methods which have been devised in connection with the examination of strephosymbolics give hints as to the preference for one side or the other (or, more commonly in this group, as to the degree of hemispheric ambivalence), but in general we must turn to a study of handedness which is very untrustworthy because it is so exposed to the influence of chance or of purposeful training.

When we come to evaluate the evidence as to the origin of a physiological superiority of one hemisphere of the brain on the basis of this, as yet sole-available criterion, it becomes evident that some children start out with a decided preference for the right or the left hand, as the case may be, at quite an early age, but that many are obviously indeterminate in this particular for a considerable period of their infancy or childhood. The numerical relations of right- or left-handedness in the adult, together with the familial occurrence of preference for the left, have led the geneticists to assert that these conditions follow the classic laws of heredity with right-sidedness operating as a Mendelian dominant. The occurrence of many individuals who in early life do not develop a strong preference for either side is also entirely in harmony with the hereditary viewpoint, since it has been experimentally demonstrated that repeated crossings of heterozygous stocks to not result in complete segregations of the dominant and recessive characters, but that intergrading occurs resulting in varying degrees of mixture of the two. When we approach the problem of handedness with such intergrades in mind the issue is seriously complicated by the very large part which is played by training in the acquisition of motor skills. So large indeed is this factor that an answer to the problem of handedness in many children probably cannot be obtained by tests, but requires a diagnosis based upon the findings (often contradictory) of a large series of tests and observations and upon pertinent information from the developmental history of the child in question. This obviously negates the value of a very large proportion of reported studies of the past because of their dependence on inadequate or poorly conceived initial testing.

The confusing factor of chance or purposeful training of the child operates chiefly to prevent an expression concerning the numbers of intergrades rather than their occurrence. There seems to be dependable evidence of delays in choice of a master hand and of mixtures of the sidedness patterns, which bespeak a dextral-sinistral intergrading, even after due allowance has been made for the effects of training. It is obvious that comparable variations and delays in acquiring the relations which exist between the two hemispheres of the brain in the adult would result in disorders and retardations in the development of the language faculty, and we believe that it is from among these hereditary intergrades, with some additions resultant from forceful mistraining and some which follow brain injuries or diseases at birth and in infancy, that the major part of the special language disabilities arise.

If we accept the influence of heredity as a potent factor in the development of handedness—and I believe that such acceptance will follow with anyone who has not made an intellectual assignment to the extremists of either the environmental or the hereditary schools but who still considers that both factors interplay in determining the final picture—we must, I think, accept a structural basis for this transmitted character. It is, as far as present knowledge goes, impossible to accept the transmission of a character of purely functional nature, and we must assume that a structural superiority of one hemisphere underlies the fixed physiological preference given it in the development of the third level functions in both the complete dextrals and the complete sinistrals. However, such structural superiority might quite conceivably be passed to the child in any one of three ways: first, there might be a better equipment of all of the cortical mechanisms of one side giving a complete hemispheric superiority; second, there might be a more complete or more mature structure in one major cortical division only (e.g., the auditory) with gradual spread of the physiological pattern of unilaterial use to other areas; or, third, a better structure might develop independently in the two hemispheres in connection with each major functional division. A solution to this problem will clearly not be forthcoming until much wider studies have been made, but we may tentatively review the evidence which is at present available.

The functions of word understanding and of speech (unilateral mechanisms in the adult) are frequently developed with normal progress in children before there has been a definitive choice of a master hand or in whom there are demonstrable mixed patterns of dextrality and sinistrality. On the other hand some children have clearly arrived at a selective choice of one hand or the other before spoken language has reached its expected development for their age. The complex visual integrations requisite for the understanding and reproduction of graphic language become available to the child at a much later period than the auditory background of spoken language or the motor preference for one or the other hand. The usual period at which children, by and large, can be taught to read and write seems to be about the sixth year, and it is probably this factor which has determined the beginning of formal schooling at this age. There are of course many variations from this in both directions and among these are to be found the striking retardations in otherwise normal or even superior children who suffer with minor grades of strephosymbolia. The more severe degrees of this condition illustrate clearly, as typified by in the case described above, that development may proceed normally in the auditory, kinesthetic, and motor fields, but that there may exist a very highly selective obstacle to acquiring the adult patterns underlying graphic language.

The fact that the two functions of acquiring spoken language and of making a choice of a master hand do not follow in the same sequence in all children speaks against the transmission of a total hemispheric superiority and against the consistent transmission of the dominance principle by virtue of a better structure in one area with subsequent spread of the habit through use. It suggests that cortices controlling these two functions may have a different hereditary urge toward structural complexity or toward early maturation, and this is further supported by the evidence of delay in the visual language functions in the presence of entirely competent auditory and kinesthetic mechanisms. We are therefore considering, very tentatively of course but as projecting new problems for study, this concept of separable hereditary factors in the three major fields of the language faculty.

As has been mentioned above, the problem of unilateral dominance can be raised as a clear issue only in discussing the third or language level. The clinical analysis of cases of strephosymbolia indicates a disorder of exquisite selectivity involving only the third level of visual integration. For this reason an analysis of the reading errors encountered in studies of such cases would seem to be an excellent starting point for an attack on the nature of the functional processes to which the unilateral dominance principle applies.

Our earlier studies of the errors presented by the strephosymbolics in their attempts at reading indicated the presence of two major factors in this disability: first, failure in accurate recall of details of individual symbols and, second, failure in the recall of sequences of symbols in the order of their presentation. Inaccuracies of recall leading to failure of recognition or to confusions between symbols are to be seen freely in those cases of strephosymbolia which are studied soon after this disability has become apparent, i.e., at about the age of six to seven years and before these confusions have been straightened out by repeated efforts. Here we meet errors of various types. Some are confusions due to relatively vague similarities between letters such as *e* and *a* or *l* and *k*; others are due to failure of recall of the spatial orientation of a symbol. These are of two kinds: first, where vertical disorientation occurs as when *u* is mistaken for *n* and *p* for *b*; and second, where right and left disorientation occurs as when *b* is mistaken for *d* and *p* for *q*. This latter type of error is by far the most common in practically every case and if individuals be followed during retraining experiments this sort of mistake will be found to be the most refractory. One of the interesting observations here is that this error is not a fixed one, i.e., the child does not consistently miscall *b* as *d*. If this were true, he could soon be taught to correct his mistakes. Apparently there is almost a complete equivalence in these two symbols so that at one time the letter is correctly recognized and again it is given the name of its twin. This ambivalence was one of the elements which led to my suggestion of a hemispheric rivalry as the major factor in strephosymbolia. Usually these failures to differentiate the symbols accurately, except for a minor persistence of the *b–d* and *p–q* confusion are comparatively easily overcome by proper retraining methods. When strephosymbolic children attempt to write letters, errors of this type are readily apparent in their product and among these are frequent substitutions of *b* for *d* and *p* for *q*. Apparently it is possible for the orientation of these symbols to be implanted with sufficient security to enable visual recognition of them and yet to be insufficiently linked with the kinesthetic element to assure their correct graphic reproduction. Thus some children learn to tell *b* from *d* when seen but may write *d* when *b* is dictated to them. The graphic records thus often give additional evidence of the ambivalence of antitropic letter forms.

In considering failures in recall of sequences, we find in the reading disability a wealth of suggestive material. Indeed, except in the most severe cases and those with very inadequate training, the mistakes in the recognition of individual symbols usually disappear or are reduced to a relatively unimportant place quite early and those of sequence form apparently the chief obstacle to reading. Here again as in the simpler errors, both true sinistrad reversals and more gross disorientations occur and there is again a strong suggestion of ambivalence. Thus the word *was* may be interpreted as *was* or as *saw* interchangeably at different encounters. With many children however, especially as they get older and the emotional stress of their failures becomes more severe, the reversals are less prominent in the picture than are the complete failures in recognition and the substitution of other words which often have only the scantiest of visual similarity. It is important therefore in order to get a true perspective of the problem to study cases at various stages.

Even more instructive are progress studies of the same child over a period of time and these bring out the difficulty of sequence building rather strikingly. One such child who had learned no reading up to her third year in school mastered in a comparatively short period of special retraining the sequences of combinations of three letters so that she rarely made a mistake, but when tested with the six letter word *repast* she read it as *ast-rep*. She had clearly maintained the dextrad sequence for each three letter unit but had then combined the two units in sinistrad order. For testing this sequence building capacity, phonetic nonsense syllables (i.e., devoid of meaningful associations) and nonsense words composed of two, three, or more syllables, make excellent material. One child who had considerable difficulty in her reading had reached the point where she could read correctly almost all of the test list of one- and two-syllable nonsense words, yet stumbled badly on those of three syllables and was entirely at sea with longer ones. When she was asked to read separately each of the four constituent syllables of one of the longer test combinations she did so perfectly, but a synthesis of one word from these was entirely impossible without numerous errors which were mostly elisions or confusions of the order of sounds in the syllable or of syllables in one word—some of them sinistrad reversals. This difficulty in synthesis of sounds and syllables in unfamiliar long words is often encountered in older children as a remnant of an earlier reading disability and may be a serious limitation to their acquisition of information through reading or in learning foreign languages.

Our recently reported studies of the isolated disability in spelling bear out the suggested importance of the sequence factor here also. They however add an element of interest since many pathological spellers showing a striking failure in the visual recall necessary for the spelling of many words in English are yet good silent readers. Obviously the visual engrams here are sufficiently well implanted and integrated to permit recognition but not to serve in recall.

In our studies of the special disability in writing this difficulty with sequences is again seen. Many cases of retardation in acquiring writing are associated with the reading disability or with the apraxic factor of an obviously mistrained left-handed individual, but in some the writing difficulty seems to exist in practical isolation. In the younger children of this group troubles are encountered with the recall of the patterns needed to reproduce individual symbols. The *b–d* and *p–q* confusions are among the most frequent but those of inversion, such as *n* and *u* and *m* and *w* are also met as are those dependent apparently on very slight similarities as has been mentioned above. Individual letters and also numbers are also frequently recalled and written in a sinistrad orientation; indeed on the same page one will often find a given letter written in its correct form in one place and in the reversed orientation in other, and the child will frequently show his confusion by stopping to ask, for example, "Which way does a *J* go?". Usually however this stage is passed quite early, but the easy construction of sequences of the individual symbols required for cursive writing lags sadly behind advancement in other language acquisition. That this is not a difficulty of coordination of the finer muscles of the hand as it is sometimes erroneously called is obvious from the presence of other finger skills such as drawing, piano playing, etc., in many cases. This marks the writing trouble as a specific disability in such individuals. In one case there was a considerable degree of skill with the pencil in sketching and individual letters were well drawn with the right hand, but cursive writing in the ordinary form, in spite of much practice, remained a difficult task and yielded a very poor product. There were no skills of note in the left hand, but when mirror writing was attempted for the first time with the right hand the result was so much better than the dextrad efforts as to be astonishing. This case with others of similar nature gives the most suggestive recent evidence in support of the thesis of interhemispheric ambivalence or rivalry offered as an explanation of the *b–d* and *p–q* confusions, the tendency to sinistrad sequence building, and the unusual skill in mirror reading to be found in typical cases of strephosymbolia. Cases with the writing disability are not always poor readers, and it becomes obvious therefore that the visual engrams may be brought into adequate association for recognition and yet fail to enter into the linkage with the kinesthetic necessary for graphic reproduction.

Following the leads offered by these studies of interference with the acquisition of graphic language we have begun some investigations of disorders of certain other functions which are known to be controlled in the adult mainly or exclusively from one hemisphere. These extensions are in their infancy but a brief review may be offered of the trend which they seem to be taking.

One function of great importance to the child in which unilateral dominance is the rule in the adult is that of spoken lagnuage. This naturally may be divided into the receptive and reproductive phases and we may in parallel with the aphasias thus anticipate sensory and motor types of speech delay. The difficulty of analytic separation of these will be recognized by those who have worked with the comparable disentanglement of the sensory and motor elements in the language losses in adults, but it is far more intricate in the child since these delays are usually encountered in quite young and often apparently very uncooperative children. Sensory delay, i.e., retardation in understanding speech, will obviously also retard oral speech development. The usual criterion, that of understanding speech, which serves fairly well in aphasics is often undependable since it is very difficult to evaluate the attention factor in such children. Some of them indeed seem to be particularly prone to disregard spoken words and to pay a greater degree of attention to visual and kinesthetic stimuli, resulting apparently in an investigative urge which keeps them constantly on the move inspecting and feeling objects but more or less oblivious to speech sounds. This may be in marked contrast to their quick attention to other sounds in the environment such as the ringing of the telephone bell or music played on a victrola. Another difficulty which we encounter here is the apparent intimate relation between the development of the general intellectual capacity of the child and his capacity to learn spoken symbols. Clearly, delays in learning to recognize words will result in a picture very like that of feeble-mindedness and indeed we may by studies of the language delays be approaching a better understanding of at least one type of this heterogenous group. These complexities and technical difficulties of analysis of retardations in the acquisition of spoken language are such as to make our progress here slow and laborious.

One of the first requirements in investigating the problem of these children is a measurement of their auditory acuity. Some aid is often given here by the history, but not infrequently the parents themselves are in a quandary as to how much the child actually hears and bring this forward as one of the questions for which they demand an answer from the examiner. A frequent factor encountered in the history and in clinical observation of this type of case is the great variability from time to time. Occasionally the child will respond pertinently to words spoken in a very low tone and again will pay no more attention to them than we do to the noises of passing traffic. Tests with the audiometer are of great value in children who are old enough to cooperate in them and this age may be extended downward somewhat by means of the train and tunnel adjunct devised by Dr. Ewing of England. In several of our patients whom we first thought to be cases of congenital word deafness we have found a significant drop in the auditory acuity, in both ears, in the upper ranges of the frequencies used in speech and have thus been led to consider them tentatively as cases of partial cortical deafness rather than of selective word deafness.

However children are sometimes seen having little or no evidence of a motor speech block and adequate hearing, and yet they are severely retarded in the understanding of spoken words and consequently also in learning the patterns needed for oral reproduction of them. Any opinion as to the intellectual capacities of these children must, I believe, be held in abeyance without prejudice, since it is clearly obvious that defects of language understanding will retard the apparent intellectual development of the child and that the only just measure of latent abilities will rest on an evaluation of his learning capacities by other pathways than the auditory and by the results of specially designed methods of retraining for word understanding. In certain of our cases such experiments seem to indicate fairly clearly a latent educability far beyond that which would be inferred from the word understanding.

In the efforts at speech which these children make we are finding again, I believe, factors comparable to those of the reading, spelling, and writing disabilities. Many single sounds are so poorly differentiated by these children that we may tentatively infer that they are not well recorded as auditory recall engrams and thus give rise to errors analogous to the simpler errors of recall of individual units in the reading disability. When we come to the question of sequences of sounds, however, it must be borne in mind that the situation is one in which the time factor rather than that of spatial position is of importance. In recalling visual sequences in the printed word it is the spatial relations of the letters which is important. In spoken words however it is the temporal relations of a series of sounds which interest us. This is in harmony with the obvious functional importance of space and time in vision and audition.

The reproduced sequences of children suspected of congenital word deafness exhibit a wealth of errors. Many of these are inadequate pronunciations or sound elisions from the proper sequence for a particular word. In a few instances we have recorded true temporal reversals in pronunciation of short words, such as *nap* for *pan* and *naf* for *fan*. These however are rare in our present experience. Somewhat more common are reversed reproductions of the units of compound or paired words such as *combhair* for *haircomb*. One of my boys says he lives on *Driverside River* (Riverside Drive). With older children of this general type the errors may be sufficient to result in true neologisms such as *ardless* for *astronomer* and *flooshy* for *flying ship*.

We have not yet perfected tests by which to estimate the competence of the second level of the auditory function in these children, i.e., the hearing and recognition of sounds, but their general reactions to sounds of the environment would strongly indicate that this function is normally developed, thus paralleling the situation to be found in the second level of the visual function in strephosymbolics.

Stuttering forms one of the disorders of spoken language which often expresses itself in early childhood. With adults or adolescents who have stuttered for years there is commonly so great an overlay of emotional factors as to render the picture very confusing. When however the patient is seen in childhood, soon after the disability is first apparent, he often seems singularly free of undue fears, of self-consciousness, or of the overweighted attachment to his mother which are so often interpreted as bearing a causal relation to stuttering. Examinations of such children will almost without exception show normal reflex movements of the chest and abdomen in respiration and usually normal echo repetition of individual sounds and short words but great difficulty in integrating these units into the motor sequences required for propositional speech. In stutterers seen in early childhood other dominance problems such as retarded speech development, delay in choice of a master hand, or mixed handedness patterns are frequent. With those whose speech disturbance begins between six and eight years of age, delay in reading, in spelling, and difficulty in learning to write easily are very common complications. Many stutterers are, however, bright or even precocious in their acquisition of reading skill and are apt with their hands. The great variability in their fluency of speech from one time to another is a common observation and suggests an interesting parallel to the variability in the recall of the visual and auditory engrams at the third level noted in the strephosymbolics and the word deaf children.

This group is most apt to have a strong family history of stuttering uncomplicated by other language delays and apparently passing more frequently from father to son than otherwise. We are hoping for further aid in understanding this disorder through extended studies of the bilateral action current patterns obtained by the oscillograph which are at present under way and will be reported upon later, but we are tentatively interpreting stuttering as a failure in the kinesthetic or premotor integrations requisite for combining the simpler reflex units of the breathing mechanism, the larynx, the tongue, and the lips into the extremely complex sequence of movements which are necessary for fluent speech.

Our studies have in the main been centered about the language faculty and its disorders, but we have naturally encountered deviations in the acquisition of other functions which in the adult are known to be under unilateral cerebral control, occurring as complications of speech and reading disorders. Among these is the difficulty met by some children in learning intricate movements and this is occasionally of such severity as to merit classification as congenital apraxia. In such cases there is an unusual difficulty in learning those motor patterns which are not of the simple bilateral or alternative type of long phylogenetic ancestry, but which require a recombination of fractions of these simpler reflex acts into more complex movements and particularly those movements which depend more or less on mimicry and hence on a repicturing of the motions of others. Thus, we would not include here standing, walking, crying, laughing, swimming, and postural control but would include throwing, drawing, writing, dancing, and a great range of other acquired skills and especially those in which the hand is used. It seems probable that it is this condition which has given rise to the implications in the use by the French of the word *gaucherie*. It is unfortunate that this should bear the connotation of awkwardness for while this is often to be observed in the left-handed it seems in our experience to be more frequent in those with mixed-handedness. Many left-handed individuals are exceedingly skillful in athletics, in mechanics, and in art. The problem of the *gaucher* therefore seems to be not that of left versus right but that of lack of predominant skill in either.

Naturally the prosecution of these studies in the language delays is having it repercussion on our approach to the alpha-privative syndromes. It has long been apparent that the extent of the functional losses in the language faculty cannot be brought into correlation with the extent of the structural damage which has produced them. A very small lesion in the angular gyrus region in one patient, for example, may result in as widespread a disturbance in reading and writing as a much larger destruction of the same area in another case. This bears equally heavily against the mass action theory of cerebral function as propounded by Lashley from his studies of rat brain exsections and against the theorem of the precise pigeon-holing of functions of the older localizers. It is however conformable to the concept of a reduction of physiological supremacy of the master hemisphere for those integrative processes which are dependent on the integrity of the affected cortical locus. This makes of the aphasias as much of a physiological as an anatomical problem. The practical equivalence in structure of the third level cortices of the two hemispheres raises the intriguing question of the possible latent physiological potencies of the undamaged nondominant hemisphere in cases of aphasias resultant upon unilateral lesions. Here the problem of rivalry between a damaged active area and an intact though previously inactive area is pertinent. Our own studies of the alpha-privative syndromes are as yet too few and incomplete to be of much value in answering these questions, but a number of our observations suggest the occurrence of rivalry and show the presence of disorders in the process of recall and reproduction of sequences.

DISCUSSION

The following questions submitted to Dr. Orton before the Commission, together with the answers to them, are here reported verbatim.

Dr. Frederick Tilney: I simply want to express my great appreciation to Dr. Orton for his presentation of this subject. I have been in fairly close contact with him for several years now and know the kind of work that he is doing. I think from what he has done so far, that it looks very much as if the principles which he is establishing are going to extend themselves far beyond the speech function and take us into much broader, deeper fields of psychology, at least that it is the way this work appears to me.

Dr. Bernardus Brouwer: I appreciate very much the work of Dr. Orton but I have not so much experience in this line. I would ask only one question. There are some findings in literature about these children from the anatomical side. Can you give some important data of these cases, chiefly of the inborn speech disturbances? There are some I remember but they are not in my conscious knowledge.

Dr. Samuel T. Orton: My impression is that those who have shown that have shown also difficulties demonstrable at the lower levels, in other words, the cases of defect in hearing, auditory defect, also show a reduction in the hearing acuity, and that type of case we have seen also.

Hinshelwood's original idea of congenital word blindness, as he called it, or strephosymbolia, as I have called it, was that it was due to a true defect in development, an agenesis of what he calls the area for word memories or visual word centering. Of course, we have given up the exact pigeon-holing of the localizers of that day. We do not feel there is such a predestined area, and even if there was an agenesis there, adjacent areas would probably take on that function if it were an agenetic phenomenon. The thing that interests me is this, that if that were true, we would certainly find those agenetic areas in a great many brains, because we have rather definitely decided they are definitely determined. The reading disability is present in a demonstrable grade enough to be a serious obstacle to the start of the child's reading in about 6 per cent of the total school population.

SPECIAL DISABILITY IN SPELLING

♦   ♦   ♦

As the writer has previously emphasized (1929) a large part of early academic education is, from the neurological standpoint, a building of associations between visual symbols and previously acquired auditory memories of words. In almost every child a very considerable development of the language function has taken place before he encounters any academic training. Before he enters school he has spent several very active years in the acquisition of verbal memories and the building of linkages between these and the object or concept which they represent and in developing as the motor counterpart thereof his own powers of reproducing these auditory engrams in speech. In school he is faced, usually for the first time, with the task of learning to arouse these word storages and their accompanying meanings through a series of symbols, each of which, in a language based on a phonetic alphabet, represents one sound of a series which constitutes the spoken word. At the same time or shortly thereafter he is introduced to the reproductive component of written language, that is, to the translation of the sound sequences of words into their corresponding letter names, as in oral spelling, or into their graphic symbols, as in writing.

The process of learning to read, which plays so critical a part in all academic training, is subject to marked variations which cannot be correlated with the general intellectual powers of the individual child, and the writer has called attention under the name of strephosymbolia (1925) to a specific obstacle in learning to read which exhibits itself in certain characteristic errors and which is believed to represent one expression of an heredity variation in the establishment of the complete unilateral cerebral dominance which obtains normally in the physiological control of the language function.

Reprinted from Bulletin of the Neurological Institute of New York, June 1931 Vol. 1, No. 2

Current neurological practice recognizes an exceedingly precise localization of certain brain functions. This applies particularly to the functions which belong to the lower levels of cerebral elaboration, i.e., those pertaining to the projection systems. Uncomplicated lesions occurring in these fields express themselves in such symptoms as Jacksonian attacks, upper motor neurone paralyses, central anesthesias and, hemianopsias, which play a most important and trustworthy part in localizing diagnosis.

In the higher elaborations, however, there has been a change from the older views of an exact, circumscribed, and constant localization of these more complex functions. Particularly is this true of the very intricate patterns underlying the language faculty, and there is now a tendency to look upon language as a complex tripartite associative process in which data of visual, auditory, and kinesthetic[1] origins are brought into varying relationship. Pending the acquisition of more exact knowledge the cortical field in which this process is carried out is accepted as the rather wide zone of the third level cortices which occupies a considerable area in the temporo-parietal regions. Opinions vary strikingly among neurologists as to how far a fixed pattern of localization may exist within this zone. This forms one of the most challenging problems of present neurological science and practice. Regardless, however, of the ultimate solution of this question there is one major variable which is universally recognized. This is the fact that in a given individual one hemisphere—which is designated as the dominant one and which may be either the right or the left—plays a part of much greater functional importance in the language faculty than does the other. It is cardinally important to our studies of cerebral physiology, however, to recognize that this concentration of functional values in one hemisphere is not a universal rule in all cerebral functions but appears only at the highest level of cortical elaboration to which we also ascribe the language faculty. As the writer has pointed out elsewhere (1928) there are striking differences in the interhemispheric relations at the same level of integration in different functions as well as at different levels of any one function. The motor cortices and the lower kinesthetic levels operate as independent unilateral organs. This arrangement is in harmony with the physiological requirement of separate motor control of the two sides of the body and equally so for the need of separate recording of the exteroceptive and proprioceptive sensations from each half of the body. Thus it is cardinally important to the organism that pain stimuli, for example, received by the brain from the right hand, be differently perceived and separately recorded from those arising in the left, in order that motor responses resulting from such stimuli be related to the proper side. This functional separation is of course clearly exhibited in the unilateral effects of lesions in the precentral and postcentral gyri of one hemisphere. A very different physiological need, however, exists in the case of two of the projicient exteroceptors—vision and audition. Here the independent recognition of stimuli received by each of the two symmetrical receptor organs would lead to confusion, and some mechanism must be established to permit of the correct interpretation of the stimuli originating in a single point of light, for example, but relayed simultaneously from both retinae to both cerebral hemispheres. Two sorts of physiological mechanisms would be theoretically possible to meet this need: first, the two hemispheres might operate by rivalry with one attuned to the incoming stimuli and the other inhibited or, second, they might operate as a unit by a process of physiological fusion. There is evidence to suggest that in certain animals the principle of rivalry exists, but Sherrington has convincingly shown that in human vision there is complete bilateral fusion. The visual function cannot, however, be looked upon as a unit in this regard since peripheral vision is differently innervated and differently affected by a unilateral destructive lesion in the brain that is macular vision. Macular vision is not lost in a unilateral lesion and there seems to be no striking difference in this regard whether the lesion occurs in the dominant or in the subordinate hemisphere. The plan of bilateral fusion seems to be the rule in audition also, although I am aware of no such concrete studies of this topic as Sherrington has given us for vision.

At the second level of cerebral elaboration there seems to be evidence of a bilateral fusion in vision and audition. The severe disturbances of these two functions resulting in mind blindness and mind deafness apparently occur only in the presence of extensive bilateral lesions of the corresponding sensory fields.

From this and other evidence it may be tentatively assumed that in man the lower platforms of the two hemispheres act independently in kinesthesis, while in vision and audition they act together as a functional unit and this introduces the very interesting relation existing between the two hemispheres at the third or language level. Neither the principle of independent action which is seen in the lower levels of kinesthesis nor that of fusion which is seen in the lower levels of vision can be applied to this zone, since in this higher function one hemisphere seems to be of prime importance while the activity of the other is almost if not entirely negligible. Lesions of the language zone in the dominant hemisphere give rise to a large group of symptoms—the alpha-privative group (aphasia, alexia, agraphia, etc.)—while those in the subordinate hemisphere remain silent.

It should be remarked, however, that there is no such contrast in structure of the two hemispheres as is seen in function. Certain differences have been noted by various authors.and held to explain the superiority of the left or right hemisphere, but such differences are exceedingly small when compared with the overwhelming functional importance of the dominant side. The third level cortices of the subordinate hemisphere seem about as well developed in extent and in detail as do those of the dominant side. Certainly there is, in the subordinate, a mechanism capable of receiving neural irradiation and registering it, and it seems logical to suppose that the much greater importance of the dominant hemisphere rests on the establishment of a physiological habit of use of that side rather than on any great anatomical inferiority of the other. Failures in the acquisition of this habit of exclusive use of one hemisphere would lead to the conflicting persistence of the records in the other and to consequent confusion.

The existence of unilateral dominance in man raises a question of sufficient theoretical interest to warrant a slight digression, viz., What is the mechanism in all of the symmetrically built axial animals which serves to prevent ambivalent confusion? That ambivalence of sufficient degree to cause motor antagonisms between the two sides does not occur to any striking degree is evinced by the ease with which both instinctive and adaptive reactions are carried out by such animals, and such an adjustment must indicate either an alternating dominance (i.e., a rivalry) or a fixed unilateral dominance such as is seen in man. The principle of phylogeny of the central nervous system is demonstrably one of superposition of new levels of neural mechanisms on those of earlier establishment, with the maintenance of a large degree of autonomy at the lower levels but a subordination to a measure of control by the highest. Obviously a more or less complete bilateral equivalence would be a functional possibility at all of the lower levels and theoretically dominance, either transitory or fixed, need reside only at that critical level where a reaction must be determined on the basis of the importance to the animal of various simultaneously arriving stimuli, or, in other words, where a choice of alternative motor responses may be made. This critical level is in the cortex in mammals, and in the human brain it would seem possible to still further delimit its residence to the third level of cortical integrations which constitutes the seat of higher mental functions and which, as outlined above, is the first point at which definitive unilateral dominance emerges in man's brain. The question of whether or not a unilateral control exists in animals of lower cerebral organization than man must be approached with due regard to the critical isolation of reaction patterns which are under the sole control of the highest neural mechanism of that particular animal.

Either hemisphere in man may play the dominant role although the left functions in this way much more frequently. The two most readily observable diagnostic signs of left or right cerebral dominance are the master hand and the master eye. The more skillful use of the right hand in trained acts and particularly in those requiring a high degree of associative integration, such as writing, is usually held to be sufficient evidence as to the existence of a left hemispheric dominance. Obviously, however, the influence of training, either consciously or unconsciously applied by parent or teacher, may in many instances modify the native patterns of a particular child so that the value of this single observation is largely nullified. Moreover an encouraged or enforced shift to the right hand in writing has been so common a practice in the past and still exists in so many localities that the record of the hand used for writing is an exceedingly untrustworthy guide to dominance. Frequently mixtures of handedness patterns appear under observation and by test which leave the investigator quite in the dark as to how far the natural or inherent master hand has been influenced by the training to which the individual has been exposed.

The master eye has been held by some to be a safer guide to native dominance than the master hand. The master eye may be defined as the eye chosen by habit when for any reason there is an enforced use of one or the other eye, as when peeking through a small hole or sighting along a straight line such as an arrow or a rifle barrel. Tests for eyedness are simple and very easy to carry out but, as with handedness, too much dependence should not be placed upon a single method. Since the master eye occasionally exhibits the greater visual defect, it would appear that this phenomenon does not rest on visual acuity but is an expression of motor control of the eyeball in sighting, comparable to handedness. The occurrence of left-eyedness in an individual with a distinctly greater skill in the right hand in trained movements is fairly common. This is especially true of those who give a history of left-handed tendencies in infancy and a shift to right-handedness by training and it has been held by some writers that since eyedness is less subject to modification by training than is handedness, the master eye of a given individual will serve as a diagnostic index of his inherent pattern and that all right-handedness in left-eyed people results from training. The occasional finding of a clear-cut right-eyedness in a person who uses the left hand by preference in all skilled acts tends to negate this assumption and supports the thesis that these two motor patterns may occur as inherently separate functions.

Left-handedness has been the subject of studies in inheritance and has been held by geneticists to be transmitted as a Mendelian recessive. Since left-handedness is merely one of the expressions of right cerebral dominance this may then be restated in this form: The selective use of the right hemisphere in control of highly skilled movements is determined by heredity as a recessive character. However, strict Mendelian segregation between dominant and recessive characters can be expected only when dealing with matings of homozygous stocks. In other circumstances intergrades between the dominant and recessive characters are to be expected, and the expression of this principle of intergrading in the inheritance of right or left cerebral dominance might readily explain delays in the choice of a master hand and interference with the development of skill in either. Moreover, one might well anticipate disturbances in the acquisition of other functions, such as the various components of the language faculty, which are normally dependent on the selective use of one cerebral hemisphere, and one might expect to encounter these variants more frequently in families in which left-handedness occurs. These expectations seem to be abundantly supported by the facts. The writer has elsewhere reported (1930) a series of family studies showing in different members of three generations of eight families the occurrence of language disturbances such as delayed speech, stuttering, strephosymbolia, and pathological writing. In the same families there were also, as might be expected, numerous instances of left-handedness without language disturbance. Numerical studies of the distribution of strephosymbolia between the two sexes have brought out the fact that this condition is more frequent in boys than in girls by a ratio of about three and a half to one and it has long been noted that stuttering also is more common in males. These facts seem to suggest that the inheritance of some, at least, of these special disabilities in language follow a partial sex-linked type of heredity rather than the strict Mendelian distribution.

The various special disabilities in language acquisition all bear the common hall mark of a failure in building facile associations between the various sensory engrams employed in the language structure. One of the most prominent obstacles to this easy association building is, as has been shown in the case of reading (Orton 1925), the condition of strephosymbolia which is characterized by a confusion between a given symbol and its mirrored counterpart, by a tendency toward reversal of direction in reading so that words are read in part or as a whole to the left instead of to the right, and by a facility in mirror reading. All of these symptoms stand in fairly definite quantitative relationship to the severity of the disability (Monroe 1928).

Recognition of a symbol such as the letter *b* entails the comparison of the visual sensation aroused by that symbol with previous implantations (i.e., engrams) which have been built into a fixed association with the name of the letter or its sound or both. When, however, the recall of the implanted engram is not constant but may be either the dextral form (*b*) or its mirrored counterpart (*d*), and where the recall of a previously seen group of letters may be in either the dextrad or sinistrad order (as when *was* is read as either *was* or *saw*), it is clear that rapid and fixed associations between letters and sounds and groups of letters and their corresponding sound sequences (words) cannot be readily built, and there results a considerable degree of delay in learning such associations and many faults in the linkages which are established. This view that the confusions so arising do not rest on disturbances in the visual process but rather on an ambivalence or variability in the engrams with which the visual experience is to be compared forms the crux of the explanation which I have offered for strephosymbolia. It elucidates the great instability which characterizes mistakes between *b* and *d* for example, and explains the complete interchangeability of these two letters which is often seen, as when *rudder* is reproduced as *rubder*. Moreover the occurrence of these mistakes in writing would seem to be rather conclusive evidence that this confusion exists in the registered engrams and not in the visual experience. I believe that the children with these confusions see as others do but fail to learn to elide completely one of the two antitropic engrams registered as a pattern for the later comparison which forms the basis of recognition. This view is derived from the neurological thesis of fused bilateral function at the lowest visual levels and complete unilateral dominance at the language level and would tend to minimize the importance of eye movements, minor degrees of eye muscle imbalance, and minor visual defects which have been so much emphasized by certain other workers in the field of reading disabilities.

Children with a marked reading disability are almost always bad spellers. Occasionally a poor reader will learn to spell fairly readily by rote auditory memory and when examined upon recently acquired lists of words will show a fair degree of skill. These implants, however, if not reinforced by the visual recall, are evanescent and if such a child be examined upon a list of words one or two years below his current efforts he will generally be found to have lost many of the words which he knew at an earlier period. One such boy was reported by his teachers as attaining consistently high grades in the spelling of sixth grade words but when examined by graded tests he failed completely at the fourth grade level. A similar discrepancy may often be seen between a child's ability to pass spelling tests in school and his ability to make use of the same words in propositional writing. More commonly, however, spelling and reading skills are acquired at about an even rate and educational profiles show them keeping closely together. This is shown graphically in the profiles of three cases reproduced in Figure 1.

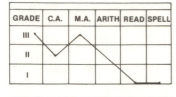

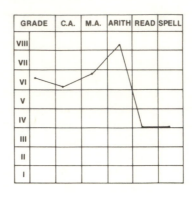

Fig. 1. Educational profeles of three boys with a special disability in reading, showing how spelling parallels the reading defect
C. A.—Chronological age.   M. A.—Mental age

Reading, however, requires a much less accurate degree of visual representation in the associative process than does spelling, and it is therefore not surprising to find individuals whose visual engrams are adequate for the recognitive associations required in reading but quite inadequate for recall and hence are not serviceable for spelling. In such cases the special disability in spelling may stand out as an isolated defect although not infrequently the history of the child's progress in school gives evidence of an earlier reading disability. Here also the method of instruction in reading seems to play an important part, and many of the children with isolated spelling disabilities are found to have been taught to read by the whole word or sight method which has failed to establish the sound association with individual letters necessary for the reproduction of the word in spelling. An educational profile of a spelling disability without a reading defect is given in Figure 2.

Occasionally, bad spelling seems to be derived from a difficulty in association between the visual and the kinesthetic engrams which results in marked retardation in writing skill. Apparently, the exceedingly slow and laborious writing of such children may have a secondary effect on spelling, especially where this is taught exclusively as a written exercise. In such instances there is at times a noticeable difference in ability between oral and written spelling. The cases of pathological writing cannot be reviewed here in detail but will form the basis of a later paper. Not infrequently, however, they occur in naturally left-handed children who have been subjected to an enforced shift to the use of the right hand for writing. This was the case with the boy whose educational profile is shown in Figure 3.

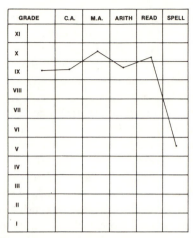

GRADE	C.A.	M.A.	ARITH	READ	SPELL
XI					
X					
IX					
VIII					
VII					
VI					
V					
IV					
III					
II					
I					

Fig. 2. Educational profile of a boy with a highly selective disability in spelling
C. A.—Chronological age.   M. A.—Mental age

Usually an inability to spell is treated as of more or less minor importance, in sharp contrast to a reading disability. Occasionally, however, it reaches such a degree of severity, even where it exists in isolation, as to form a definite scholastic handicap, as was the case with the boy whose educational profile is shown in Figure 2, who was refused admission to the school of his choice solely on the basis of his spelling deficiencies.

The recognition of the existence of a spelling disability offers no difficulties, but the accurate diagnosis of the character of the faulty associations which underlie the disability and which must form the

GRADE	C.A.	M.A.	ARITH	READ	SPELL	WRIT'G
X						
IX						
VIII						
VII						
VI						
V						
IV						
III						
II						
I						

Fig. 3. Educational profile of a boy with a marked disability in writing and a moderate defect in spelling
C. A.—Chronological age.   M. A.—Mental age

basis of rational reeducational efforts is somewhat more complex. Where it is associated in a young child with a typical strephosymbolic obstacle to reading, the special methods devised for the correction of this difficulty will also improve the spelling to a marked degree although it is probable that skill in spelling will be acquired more slowly than in reading. In the cases where an isolated spelling defect exists, an analysis of the errors must precede any attempt at retaining.

The analysis which follows does not attempt a complete compilation of the types of spelling errors at large but merely a classification of those which have appeared most strikingly in the children whose retraining has been proceeding under my direction. The errors used as illustrations have been taken from the records of children with spelling disabilities of both categories—some with reading disability and some without it—and are drawn from both written and oral spelling of words and from sentences, usually given by dictation, although some are from propositional writing.

Confusions resulting from reversals of orientation of symbols whose mirrored form closely simulates another symbol are frequent in the younger children and in those presenting a severe reading disability. Such confusions between *b* and *d* are shown in Figure 4, which is reproduced from traced replicas of written exercises in spelling.

In some instances the error was seen and corrected by writing over the mistake; in others it passed unnoticed. Since the child sometimes recognizes such errors after they are written and makes erasures and corrections, it is important for the examiner to watch the child at work as well as to study the finished product to determine the confusions that may be present. Some children spontaneously resort to a kinesthetic test and may be observed tracing both forms of the letter in the air to obtain a clue as to which orientation is correct.

Evidence of the complete interchangeability of these two letters is found in four efforts of a girl of ten to spell *because*. All of these occurred within five lines of a school exercise and were *decose, becars, decars,* and *becard*.

The comparable confusion between *p* and *q* is shown graphically in Figure 5. At 1 is a tracing of the effort of the seven-year-old child whose educational profile is shown in Figure 1 to write a *p* from dictation, at 2 the product of a ten-year-old child in trying to write the word *spoil*, and at 3 a boy's spelling of *stop, soap* and *camp*.

The confusions arising between *b* and *d* and between *p* and *q* through comparison with the reversed or antitropic engrams are obvious. Certain other confusions are less easy to see but are understandable when the letters are examined in a mirror or by looking through the page. Thus the lower case *f* when seen in mirrored form somewhat

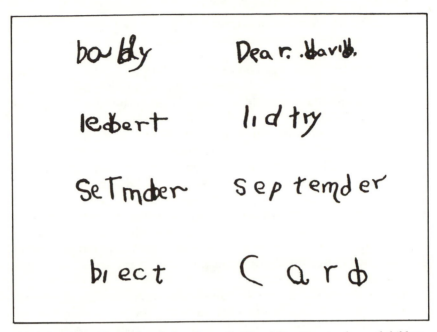

Fig. 4. Graphic evidence of confusions in recall of *b* and *d* in attempts of several children to write the words *baby*, *David*, *liberty*, *September*, *direct*, and *card*

resembles a *t*. This confusion has been encountered a number of times in reading and is exhibited in writing in the work of a girl who wrote *transfer* as *transter* and *suffer* as *sutFer* although orally she spelled both words correctly. The mirrored form of a lower case *a* is somewhat like

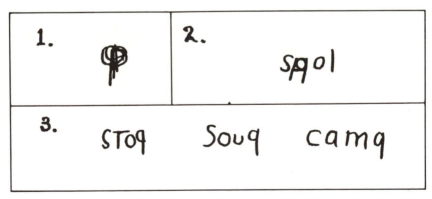

Fig. 5. Graphic evidence of confusion between *p* and *q* At 1, writing *p* to dictation. At 2, writing the word *spoil* to dictation. At 3, writing the words *stop*, *soap*, and *camp* to dictation.

an *s*. Confusions between these two letters have been encountered in reading but I have not yet found them in writing. In children who have been taught manuscript writing *g* and *q* are sometimes confused as illustrated by a thirteen-year-old boy's spelling of *guess* as *quess*. The use of capital letters to avoid the difficult choice between letters whose lower case forms are antitropic occasionally points out the existence of a confusion. This is shown in the word *sutFer* and it also is seen to good advantage in the product of a seven-year-old boy when attempting to write the alphabet from memory, as shown in figure 6. He started with a capital *A* and followed this with a capital *B*, thus avoiding the issue of differentiating the lower case forms. A small *c* follows but he returned to a capital at *D* and then when requested to make small letters he miswrote *b* for *d*. He recognized his error, cancelled it and then wrote a small *d*. The *b-d* and *p-q* confusions rest apparently on an ambivalence of antitropic engrams. In this there seems to be no progressional element and I have therefore listed this type in my records as static reversals.

There is a second and more frequently encountered form of reversal in which the fault lies in the direction of progress rather than in orientation of the symbol. Here there is a tendency to assemble the letters in sinistrad or alternating sinistrad and dextrad order. This type I have designated as kinetic reversals. As in the reading disability this tendency may exhibit itself in only a few letters of the word or in a syllable or in a whole word. (This is to be differentiated from mirror writing in which there is sinistral orientation of all the letter forms as well as sinistrad progress in writing.) The following list gives typical examples of misspellings due to kinetic reversals.

warm	wram	orphan	rophan
night	inght	idleness	dileness
girl	gril	accomplish	accompilsh
the	hte	improvement	emporvemet
afraid	afard	teeth	theet

Fig. 6. Use of capital *B* and *D* to avoid confusion between the small letters

eight.................. ieght	difference .... drifence
elect ....elcet	target ....tagret
particular........... particalur	direct ....dierct
John ....Jhon	expedition......... expetidion
station ....statoin	testimony ....testominy

An interesting variant of the kinetic type I have recorded as an in-and-out reversal in which the child starts in from one end of the word, which may be either the right or the left end and after spelling through part or all of it then turns around and spells back again over the same letters. Thus *how* becomes *wow* if started at the right and spelled by this in-and-out method, or becomes *hoh* if this order of progress be reversed, and I have had both of these responses. Other suggestive variants of this process are seen in *gone* written as *goneg*, *green* as *greer*, *able* as *ablbe*, *retire* as *reteter*, *had* as *hah*, *good* as *goog*, and finally, as the most perfect example, *rag* spelled as *garag*.

Figure 7 illustrates kinetic reversals in writing. On the upperline are shown three words in which the final letter has been written first. In two of these the error was recognized by the boy who wrote them and would have been erased had he not been asked to leave them. The second line shows the product when a ten-year-old girl was asked to write *green*, *of* and *oh* to dictation. In these examples the first attempts were erased but "ghosts" were left which could be readily seen. In attempting *green*, as will be noted from the figure, this child first wrote n e e r and saw her error only when she reached the final letter *g*. In writing *of* she produced *Fo* and then corrected it. This was one of the children to whom *f* and *t* were equivalent and the one who wrote *sutFer* for *suffer*. It is interesting to note in figure 7 the use of a capital *F* in *of* to avoid this dilemma.

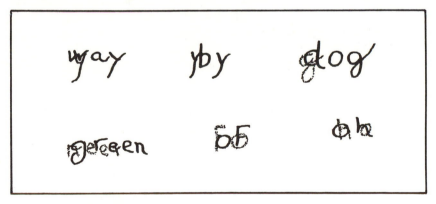

Fig. 7. Kinetic reversals shown in the words *way, by, dog, green, of,* and *oh* written to dictation. Explained in the text.

The proportion of static to kinetic errors is markedly variable in different cases. In the younger children both may be found, but apparently the static reversals are the more easily corrected since the older children usually show few or no reversals of this type.

Lack of constancy in the recall of either the sinistrad or dextrad engram as evinced in the two types of reversals is held to be the chief source of failure in establishing a quick association between the visual engrams of the letters of a word and their sounds. When this failure is severe it serves as an obstacle to the acquisition of both reading and spelling. Apparently it may exist, however, in a lesser grade which does not prevent the establishment of engrams sufficiently clear and constant for recognition and hence for reading. Such engrams however may not be adequate for the accurate recall of the look of a word necessary for the spelling of nonphonetic words or for the easy recognition of errors after they have been made. Not infrequently such a child will say of his own product, "That doesn't look right but I can't see what's wrong with it."

Naturally this failure to incorporate the visual element into the association throws most of the burden of spelling upon the auditory memory with consequent attempts at phonetic spellings. This results in many errors due both to the lack of a consistent phonetic structure in English and to specific false associations between letters and sounds operative in a given individual.

The vowels are a particularly fertile source of errors in spelling as they are in the reading disability. With a few exceptions the consonants require the building of but one association between the symbol and its sound and hence present a much easier task than do the vowels where multiple linkages are needed. The vowel *a* forms one of the best illustrations of this. Not only may this symbol stand for a wide variety of sounds as in *ale, senate, care, am, final, arm, ask,* and *sofa,* but one of its sounds ā may be represented by *a, e, ey, ay, ai, ea, eigh,* etc. In reading, a fair approximation of the exact sound is often quite adequate for the recognition of words. In my experience with retraining drills for the correction of the reading disability I find three sounds for the letter *a* are usually sufficient. These are sounds which this letter represents in the three words *hat, face* and *arm.* This illustrates the wide difference in the complexity of associations required for reading and for spelling and explains, I believe, why a disability may persist in spelling after reading is mastered. Difficulty with the vowels may result in their complete elision as when *work up* is spelled as *wkrp* and *express* as *xprs,* or in the ommission of the muted or unstressed vowels as in *favor* spelled as *fawr, summer* as *sumr,* and *comfort* as *comfrt.* It may produce substitutions between vowels whose sounds in common usage are conflicting, as where *e* acquires the short *u* sound from its common pronounciation in *the* as shown in spelling *elect* as *ulect*. Another source of vowel confusions, when the visual recall is deficient, is found in words where the sound, even by correct usage, might be expressed by either of two vowels as when *warm* is spelled as *worm*, *afraid* as *ufrad*, *ball* as *boll*, etc. Where simple sounds are represented by diphthongs or phonograms errors are fairly common, as in *sope* for *soap*, *sup* for *soup*, *fit* for *fight*, etc.

Other examples of vowel errors of various types are:

actor	acter	cellar	celler
blossom	blossam	another	unother
elect	ealkt	visitor	visiter
church	chirch	guides	gides
illustrate	elistrate	merchant	merchent
husband	husben	say	sae
aroma	eroma	custom	costum
eight	eaght	costume	custom

While vowel errors are much more frequent in misspellings than errors in consonant sounds the latter often occur, and this seems to be particularly true of those children who have been taught in schools which stress the sight or flash method of teaching reading with more or less neglect of training in phonetics. Such confusions are to be seen occasionally in young children, apparently because of vague similarities of form other than those explained by static reversal. Mistakes of *h* and *k*, *m* and *n*, and *h* and *b* are probably of this origin. These seem to be comparatively unimportant, however. Confusions are more frequent between two letters representing somwhat similar sounds. Thus *k* and *g* are often mixed, leading to the spelling of *think* as *thing* and *thankful* as *thangful*. The hard (or *k*) sound of *c* is likewise mixed with *g* giving *cown* for *gown*, *croup* for *group*, and *gomming* for *coming*. *D* and *t* are confused resulting in *trawn* for *drawn* and *breat* for *bread*. *V* and *f* form another difficult pair and their interchange results in spelling *vavorite* for *favorite* and, in the reverse order, *abofe*, for *above*, and, for complete security, *half* is written as *havf*. *X* is another letter that frequently makes trouble when its phonetic equivalent *ks* is not known. Very often the *x* represents only a *k* sound to the child and an additional symbol must be used to bring in the *s* sound. Thus we find *express* spelled as *exsprs* and *examination* as *exzamination*.

The *w* and *wh* sounds are frequent stumbling blocks and one twelve-year-old boy has accomplished a certain linguistic economy by reducing both *weather* and *whether* to *wether*. The sound of *w* is often taught as *oo* and the child is instructed to pronounce *went* as *ooent*. This linkage sometimes becomes fixed with the resultant spelling of *school* as *skwl*, and *suit* as *swt*, etc.

Occasionally multiple false associations may be built. One boy when shown a *j* and asked to give its sound, responded somewhat hesitatingly with *jŭ*. He had, however, written *began* as *bejan* so I asked him whether *j* might have any other sound in order to see if it were also liked with the hard or gutteral *g*. He answered, unexpectedly, "Yes, pŭ." Further analysis revealed a loose linkage between *j* and *g* based on sound similarity, between *j* and *g* based on sound similarity, between *g* and *q* based on a visual similarity in the manuscript writing which he had been taught, and between *q* and *p* by static reversal. The result was that any of these four letters when encountered in reading might bring to him either its own sound or that of any of the others, and in written spelling the sound of any one might recall the proper graphic symbol or that of any of the other three.

When the early teaching of reading has been exclusively by the sight method to the complete neglect of phonetic training, children with-even a relatively mild degree of strephosymbolic confusion may fail entirely to learn that a sound may be represented by a single letter and will fall back on the nearest whole word to express that sound. These errors I have designated as sight implants. Thus, such a boy who did not know the sound of the letter *u* but had been taught to recognize the word *you* made quite correct application of what he had been taught in spelling *document* as *dockyoument*. Other examples of these sight implants from my records are:

taxation	tacksaytion	education	egyoucation
appal	abhaul	plagiarize	playjurise
appal	apaul	theivish	thevefish
example	exsampull	frequently	freakwently

Some children seem particularly prone to substitute a whole word with a somewhat similar configuration for the one given. Examples of this are:

suit	shout	soap	shop
walk	work	fight	faith
walk	wake	eight	night

Poor visual recall of the letters in words not only limits spelling to a phonetic basis but interferes with the natural aid to pronunciation which comes from a knowledge of how a word is spelled and habitual mispronunciations in their turn may be carried over into spelling with resulting errors which are quite exact phonetic reproductions of the incorrectly spoken words. Thus one of my patients spells *lonesome* as *losome* and pronounces it so. Another, a boy of seventeen, talks of the *"sopperntendnt"* of his school and spells it so. Other examples of spelling which seem to be exact phonetic equivalents of the way the word was pronounced are: *speculating* as *specalatin, gyroscope* as *garowscope* and *dangerous* as *dangerss.* Not infrequently the spelling of a word quite accurately reflects common errors of pronunciation, as *libury* for *library, pixure* for *picture, easly* or *easily,* and telphone or *telephone.* The effects of venacular pronunciations are also to be seen at times in spelling.Thus it is not surprising to find Boston boys writing *invertation, estermate, celerbration, intervidual, perculiar,* nd *bananer.*

As might be expected, omissions of letter groups, other than the dropping of muted vowels as discussed above, are frequent. They seem to be particularly common in written spelling when the act of writing is very slow and laborious. Additions are also encountered frequently, chiefly in the younger children.

A rarer form of error in spelling, encountered somewhat more frequently in reading, is apparently the result of a perseveration of parts of a previous word in the production of a following word of a series. An example of this is *afraid* spelled as *afraight* immediately after spelling *eight* correctly.

When various intermixtures of the errors listed above occur in one word the analysis of the sources of the mistakes is often quite intriguing. In a written composition of a ten-year-old girl is found the word *wart* in a context which makes it seem to be a word substitution. However *water* would fit perfectly and later in the same composition *water* is spelled *watr. Wart* is obviously *water* with an elision of the second vowel and a kinetic reversal of the *t* and *r. Nuls* is a phonetic contraction of *unless* with a kinetic reversal of the *u* and *n. Qulkey* is the result of omissions and a kinetic reversal in *quickly. Stashne* is a phonetic spelling of *station* with a kinetic reversal of the last two letters. *Appear* by a phonetic contraction and a kinetic reversal becomes *apre. Beng* results from an omission and kinetic reversal of *began. Blo* is the result of a vowel error and kinetic reversal of *ball. Stut* may be constructed from *suit* y an omission and an in-and-out reversal. *Direct* becomes *draxt* when the slurred *i* is dropped and the *e* and *a,* and the *c* and *x* sounds a printed *x* and asked its sound responded, *"ĕk,"* and there was practically no difference between her sounds for short *a* and short *e. Thol* was offered by a girl of ten for *fell.* She proved to have a confusion between *f* and *th* sounds and to have associated *e* with a short *u* sound, probably from her pronunciation of *the* as *thŭ* and this was in turn mixed with the short sound of *o.* A comparison between the sentence or word dictated and the written response is often quite essential to the interpretation of errors. Such a comparison is shown below:

"Heih bi yon lue hte sumr?
"How did you like the summer?"

Several types of errors can be recognized here and a relationship traced between the product and the work attempted, but without the guide sentence such interpretation would be impossible. The struggle of an eleven-year-old boy with three types of errors is shown graphically in Figure 8. In writing *liberty* from dictation he first produced a vowel error (*e* for *i*) and a static reversal of *b*. He saw the reversal, scratched it out-and started again. This time he corrected the reversal but entered another vowel error (*a* or *e*) and a kinetic reversal of the *rt*. Again he saw the reversal and struck out the word. His third attemp contained only the two vowel errors one of which he saw and corrected by writing an *e* over the *a*.

As in some of the examples interpreted above, the word written may bear so little relation to the one dictated that it justifies the characterization of a neographism. Examples of these with the words which were dictated are listed below:

propellor	paloler	ask	anec
insurance	ubscgebscge	educational	eadyouchnall
microscope	micsiocep	motion	mothing
century	schere	pouches	pousesc
scrupulously	squpsly	eat	etye
enormous	enmouse	elect	eelkl
ran	ralnd	another	aghera

Fig. 8. Facsimile of the efforts of an eleven-year-old boy in writing *liberty*. Explained in the text.

> zaki pek danged ya Till beyend the valr avatte intrudisige trab topes

Fig. 9. Neographisms and misspellings produced by a ten-year old girl writing from dictation the following sentences: "Expect danger until beyond the valley." "Avoid introducing trade topics"

Where neographisms constitute the bulk of the written work the product has a bizarre appearance and often is quite unintelligible although it may be legible. Figure 9 is a copy of such a specimen. This was written from dictation by a ten-year-old girl who also had a marked reading disability. The sentences dictated to her are given in the legend.

When such neographisms are produced in propositional writing and the content forgotten by the writer an understanding of the words thus misrecorded is quite impossible. This is illustrated in the classic written by a seventeen-year-old strephosymbolic, which I have used as an illustration in an earlier article but which is reproduced here (Fig. 10) to show misspelling at its best. This is a composition describing the English campaign of 1777 in the American Revolution.

In the foregoing description of symptomatology no effort has been made to construct an exhaustive list of misspellings or to place them in order of frequence or importance since they vary so much from case to case that generalizations are of little value. This bears with equal

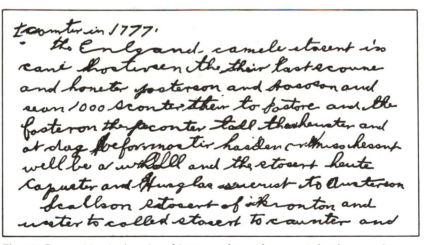

Fig. 10. Composition in American history made up almost entirely of neographisms

weight on the question of retraining. No one procedure can be advised for bad spellers in general and reeducation must partake of the nature of an individual prescription based on a critical analysis of the error types in each case. A series of simple and practical tests to reveal defects is given below together with suggestions for a remedial approach to each. Again no claim is made for completeness and they are intended merely as a record of tests and methods which are in successful use and under trial in current experiments. Many of the tests as well as some of the retraining measures are applicable to disorders of language other than pathological spelling and particularly to the reading disability.

TESTS AND METHODS OF RETRAINING

Tests of auditory acuity should be carried out in all cases where there is any question as to the competence of this function. However, in the great majority of cases it will be easily apparent without special tests that auditory sensitivity is quite adequate.

Rough tests for the accuracy of auditory differentiation of speech sounds may be made by asking the child to repeat the sound of each letter of the alphabet after the examiner. Usually it will be clear that the sounds are accurately reproduced. Where trouble exists a cursory estimate of the relative part played by the sensory and motor fractions can often be reached by repeating the sound as the child gives it and asking if it is correct. For example, one small boy who consistently spoke of his brother as "Wobert" would shake his head in disapproval when I used "Wobert," and would approve only Robert. Clearly the auditory patterns of the r sound were correctly registered in his brain and served for recognition but not for control of the motor response. Motor speech difficulties are apt to appear as residuals of infantile speech involved, particularly the consonants r,l,s, and w. Lack of clear-cut separation of the short sounds of the vowels is often found also. Where these difficulties are revealed the orthodox methods of lip and tongue training in use by speech teachers are recommended.

As a rule the individual letter sounds are well repeated and tests may then be extended to short sound sequences. Here I use both short, one-syllable words and nonsense syllables. The latter would seem, a priori, to be valuable since they exclude the practice effect in known words and they do at times serve to show a lack of clear-cut separation in the enunciation of the sounds of the short vowels which might be missed were familiar words used exclusively. Most children of the special disability group, however, are able to carry out this echo repetition accurately when short units are presented. The words given them to repeat may then be gradually increased in length and as the patterns offered them become progressively larger, difficulty in reproduction becomes obvious. In one recent case, this occurred with a rather abrupt transition when four-syllable words which were unfamiliar to the child were attempted and in efforts to repeat still longer words there occurred translocation of the sounds, perseverations, and a few clear-cut verbal reversals. With all single letter sounds and with shorter words and syllables, repetition was practically perfect. No trouble was encountered until the sound sequence became too long to be reproduced by an echolalic type of response, so that registration and recall became necessary for reproduction. Then the difficulty rested on a faulty order of recall. This factor in the auditory function seems to parallel the reversals found in reading and has implications which will be mentioned later. When this type of distortion of words is present I have recommended practice in syllabic dissection of verbally presented long words and their later synthesis from these syllables with care as to order and accuracy of pronunciation.

In all cases of bad spelling as well as poor reading it is important to listen very carefully to the patient's propositional speech for inaccuracies, omissions, and sound confusions. Sometimes this type of error is very hard to detect; for example, in the boy who spells *dangerous* as *dangerss*. This substitution of *ss* for *ous* has been heard a number of times and one must listen with considerable care and attention to recognize it. Clearly a knowledge of how such a word is spelled would aid in correcting the pronunciation but the reverse is equally true—where the spelling is sadly at fault an exact memory of the sounds in a given word will be of aid in spelling it. For this reason, training by the usual methods for accuracy of enunciation is recommended.

The acuity of the visual function, like that of audition, should be carefully examined and refractive errors corrected. As a rule the children with a selective retardation in reading or in spelling will be found to have a normal visual acuity and normal power of visual discrimination. Many of them have far keener vision than others of their school group who have learned to read and spell accurately.

Eye dominance, as well as handedness, is a variable in the bad spellers and should be determined, as a matter of interest, in each case. In the reading disability the right-eyed and right-handed children far outnumber those with other patterns. In the children who have a selective spelling disability, the left-eyed and left-handed or left-eyed and right-handed pattern seems to be somewhat more frequent proportionately than the others, but there is no consistency in this. Some children of the sinistral or of the mixed types are excellent in spelling and others who are consistently of the dextral type are poor enough to warrant their inclusion in this special disability.

Tests of the association between letters and sounds should begin with the individual letters of the alphabet. The majority of the older children have learned to give the name of each letter on visual presentation of its symbol. Occasionally, however, even the names of *b's* and *d's, p's* and *q's* will be miscalled, and with the younger children and those with the more severe degrees of strephosymbolia there are often quite a number of letters for which the name is not readily forthcoming. When the child is asked to give the sound of each letter instead of its name, failures, delayed responses, and confusions are exceedingly common. Occasionally this reveals interesting evidence of former static reversals in that a child may give the correct name for a printed letter and yet give the sound of its mirrored opposite. Thus a boy when shown a printed *b* and asked its name responded promptly with the correct name but when asked how it sounded offered *dŭ*.

Phonetic knowledge of the alphabet is held to be unnecessary by many schools and this may be true for some children, but for those who have a tendency toward strephosymbolic confusions it is, I believe, an essential. Training in fundamental phonetics may be carried out to advantage by the usual teaching methods except where confusions of the static reversal type occur. The ordinary process of linking a sound to a printed symbol by repeated exposures fails rather strikingly here, and residual confusions between *b* and *d* may remain in spite of much effort. As in the training of the reading cases, simultaneous tracing over a pattern while saying the name (and alternately the sound) of the letter is recommended to establish the association between the name (and the sound) and the proper orientation of these reversible figures by means of kinesthetic reinforcement. This method is often spontaneously adopted by children to differentiate *b* from *d* and they can be seen to try out the direction by finger movements before coming to a decision. Tests for the recognition of *b* and *d*, etc., such as are used in the diagnosis of the reading disability, are of very limited value in estimating the part which this confusion plays in spelling since they are selectively measures of recognition rather than of recall. In several instances static reversals of this type have been found to persist in writing long after correct recognition has been established.

The kinetic reversals are of much greater importance in spelling than are the static. These form a factor which comes into play when the sequences of sounds are to be translated into sequences of symbols and may be present to a considerable degree long after the individual letter-sound linkages are correctly established. The presence of kinetic reversals in spelling can be readily recognized but where a tendency toward this is present but masked, and exhibits itself in a confused order of letters rather than in recognizable reversals, it is sometimes of value to test for reversals in reading. For this purpose the test material should be unfamiliar, and foreign languages of which the child has no knowledge may be used to advantage here. Miss Anna Gillingham, psychologist at the Ethical Culture Schools in New York has suggested Esperanto words for this purpose and they have proven very useful. These serve as glorified nonsense syllables and exclude sight recognition and thus test the basic capacity to derive sounds from letter sequences, so necessary in the adequate implantation of newly encountered words.

The remedial measures recommended for the correction of kinetic reversals presuppose an adequate grounding the phonetic equivalents of individual letters, diphthongs, diagraphs, and phonograms. When this has been acquired the sequence reversals may be directly approached by training in syllabic synthesis of long words. As an aid to this, following with the finger or pointing with the pencil is to be highly recommended.[2] Its application to oral reading has a definite influence on spelling since it serves to impress the proper order of symbols and to fix the associations between these and the auditory sequences. Practice in oral synthesis of long unfamiliar words and multisyllabic nonsense material is also recommended. Letter and word games such as anagrams, cross word puzzles, "ghosts," and "the minister's cat" are often valuable training adjuncts.

In considering spelling errors which appear in writing it is often somewhat difficult to evaluate the motor element. Some help is forthcoming here from the history of the development of motor skills in the patient, i.e., crawling, walking, running, talking, etc., and from careful historical and observational studies of the handedness pattern of the child. These factors cannot be reviewed in detail here. Not infrequently, however, it is possible to show that a child with a history of normal development of the motor functions, a well established handedness pattern, and an average or even superior skill in other manual activities still has great trouble in the acquisition of writing, and occasionally it appears that insecurity in spelling is the main obstacle. My analysis of the interrelation between spelling and writing is far from complete but some description of the test methods employed will serve to indicate the lines of investigation.

Since the basic process of written spelling in a language using a phonetic alphabet consists in drawing the appropriate symbol for the sound of each letter, the linkages which exist between sounds and their graphic symbols may be advantageously explored. This may be done by dictating the phonetic equivalents of letters to the child and asking him to write the corresponding letter. Pertinent delays and errors are often revealed. The training methods applicable to their correction are obvious. Such direct phonetic training is not of course adequate in English spelling, but certain obvious consonant confusions can often be corrected by practice in writing letters from dictated sounds. Among these mistakes in consonants may be found evidence of static reversals expressed in writing only. The linkages may have been properly established between the visual symbol and its name and its sound, and yet a reversal may occur in writing it. Thus a boy when shown a letter *p* was able to give the correct name and the correct sound for it but reproduced it in mirrored form in writing as shown at *3* in Figure 7. Comparative tests of the ability to copy in writing and to write from dictation (where the factor of spelling also enters) and spontaneously (where both spelling and constructive effort play a part) are sometimes revealing, i.e., a fairly neat and accurate product when copying and a page covered with erasures, alterations, or neographisms when writing from dictation indicates that the spelling of the words rather than the motor element in writing them is at fault. Figure 11 shows such a comparison. Here it is obvious that the remedial attack should be directed primarily at spelling.

In writing, however, the kinesthetic component is of prime importance and it is quite conceivable that an interference with the written reproduction of words might rest on an inadequate integration of the kinesthetic patterns with those of audition and vision. This would

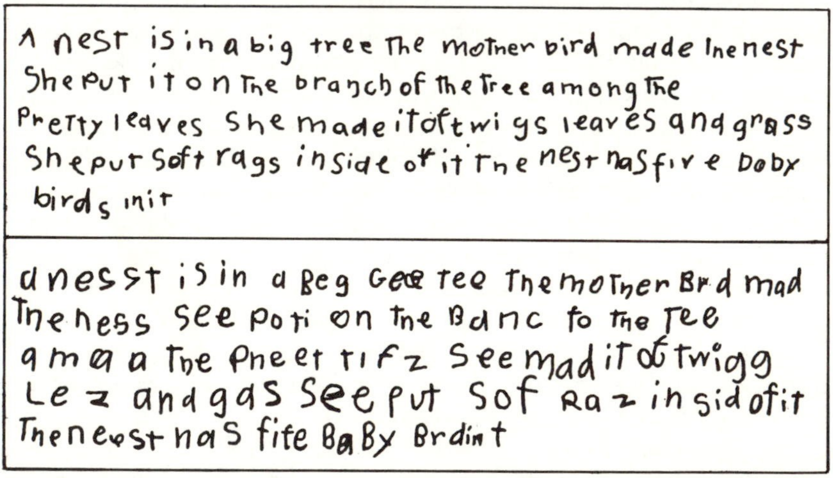

Fig. 11. Comparison between copying (above) and writing the same material from dictation (below)

seem to be the case with those children whose oral spelling is very much better than their written spelling. One outstanding example of this was the case of a girl who had led her class in spelling in Texas but on moving to another state was failing consistently in this subject. Inquiry revealed that in Texas the spelling exercises were oral while in her new home each day's list of words had to be written. In many schools of today oral spelling has been largely abandoned. Apparently this rests on the assumption that if a child knows how to spell a word he can also write it. This is probably true for the majority, but it overlooks the fact that there are many children who vary somewhat from the common pattern in their learning processes and that restriction to a single method of teaching is apt to work a hardship on them. Moreover the two processes—oral and written spelling— employ widely different nervous mechanisms and we would expect to find differences in facility in these functions such as our cases seem to present. Where there is a markedly greater facility in oral than in written spelling the fundamental linkages between individual sounds and kinesthetic letter patterns should first be examined as outlined above. After the correction of such errors as are found the child will frequently improve very rapidly if taught to spell aloud while writing.

The methods of retraining outlined above are most applicable to younger children. With the older ones there is usually some resistance to going back to lessons in the alphabet for example. In such cases oral reading with attention to the accuracy of enunciation has been found to be of great value. Reading aloud is usually quite difficult and often is exceedingly faulty with bad spellers. This is especially true with those who have been taught to read exclusively by the sight or flash method. Very often indeed a child so taught has literally no equipment with which to approach the sounding of a newly encountered English word or the strange letter combinations of the test material except for large letter groups such as have been quoted above in discussing sight implants. His stumbling efforts at pronouncing long and unfamiliar words bring to light the inadequate associations between the look of a word and its sound. Reading aloud to a teacher, parent, or tutor who has a good ear for pronunciation and who is alert to the importance of slight variations from accurate sounding is a very valuable training method. The teacher should follow the text by eye in order to assure the reading of every word and to correct misreadings. If this be not done word substitution such as *house* for *home*, *syrup* for *sugar*, *place* for *palace*, etc., may occur without disturbing the meaning of a sentence sufficiently to be noted by the listener.

In this oral reading, stress by overpronunciation should be laid on the sounding of all of the letters in a word. Thus *favor* is read with an overemphasized *or* as *favOR, husband* as *husBAND, library* as *libRARY* and *picture* as *picTURE*. This stress on the muted sounds of words is apt to seem stilted at first and may require some coaxing to accomplish. As one boy remarked, "That sounds awful high hat." Very little of it is carried over into ordinary speech, however, and the child soon learns that such emphasis serves to fix certain letters in his memory. Care must be taken that the proper pronunciation or its purposely over-stressed exaggeration be kept in linkage with the meaning which often has attached itself to a somewhat or entirely different sound equiv-alent. *FavOR*, for example, must not be planted as a new word but must be built into the association already surrounding *favr*. Certain difficult spellings can often be securely implanted in older children who are studying other languages by explaining their origin. Thus *lieutenant*—"the place holder"—and *peninsula*—"almost an island"—can be readily fixed with students of French and Latin.

So intimate is the interlinkage between the various functions enter-ing into the language faculty that in addition to specific training to establish the correct associations between sounds and letters any general improvement in skill in reading, speech, or writing may be counted upon to lead to an improvement in spelling.

The psychiatric effects of the presence of a disability in spelling except when it is extreme seem to be relatively mild as compared with those which accompany the reading disability. This we would expect from the fact that bad spelling does not form by any means so great an obstacle to education as does poor reading and errors in spelling are largely condoned. Some children show moderate degrees of inferiority reaction. With many, however, there results merely a disinclination toward writing which may serve as an obstacle to the development of a real facility of expression. Because there is less punishment inherent in spelling failures than in poor reading there is usually not the same incentive to work toward its correction, although usually the children have labored hard enough in school at the task of rote memorizing of words to be ready and willing to apply themselves to other methods of procedure. They very commonly become much interested in the test-ing program and in the explanation of their errors and often are quite convinced of the pertinence of the recommendations for retraining. When this occurs they are most cooperative and as they begin to note improvement they often take a very active interest in their retraining and often apply its principles for themselves.

In the review of the subject of pathological spelling, attention had centered, as in previous studies in reading, on the process of building associations between visual, auditory, and kinesthetic engrams. These studies have led to the opinion that the chief obstacle to the ready formation of the proper associations is an inconstancy of recall of the previously implanted engrams with which a sensory experience must be compared in order to permit recognition and, further, that this inconstancy rests on the failure to establish the usual pattern of complete unilateral cerebral dominance.

The dominance problem is pertinent to all expressions of the language function. In written language (reading and writing) the factors concerned are spatial, i.e., it is the capital orientations and spatial sequences which are subject to confusions such as we see in the two types of reversals. In spoken language (verbal understanding and speech) the sequences are temporal rather than spatial. Traces of confusion in temporal sequnce of sounds have been observed a number of times in these studies. One such instance is mentioned in this report. Confusions of sequence in the recall of auditory engrams might quite conceivably lead to an obstacle to the recognitgion of the spoken word and to its reproduction in speech. Thus fators comparable to those which underlie the selective disabilities in reading and spelling may also operate in congenital word deafness and retarded speech. The challenging implications of this possible extension of the concept of strephosymbolia into the auditory field have led to the establishment, under the direction of the writer, of a research project supported by a grant from the Committee on Research and Publication of the Neurological Institute. This program has already been started with an intensive study of a case of congenital word deafness.

SUMMARY

Selective disability in spelling usually accompanies the reading disability. It may however exist as an isolated defect.

Inconstancy of recall of visual, auditory, and kinesthetic engrams probably interferes with the establishment of the fixed associations needed for correct spelling.

Faulty spelling like other expressions of a language defect is found in certain families in association with left-handedness, reading disability, and speech disorders and is considered to be the result of variations in the establishment of unilateral cerebral dominance.

Analytical tests and retraining methods are discussed.

NOTES

1. For the sake of simplicity the term kinesthesis will be used throughout this article to designate the function of the area immediately back of the Rolandic fissure. It should be remembered, however, that kinesthesis, strictly speaking is probably only one part of the function subserved by this cortical field and that we are here dealing with an aggregate of the epicritic fractions of all of the sensory relays which find their way from the surface of the body by way of the spinal pathways—not only, as the term would imply, those from muscles, joints, and tendons. Thus we include here that fraction of all of the non-projicient exteroceptors—touch, pain, and temperature—as well as the proprioceptors—the true kinesthetic. I know, however, of no inclusive term which delimits this aggregate of fractions.

2. I appreciate that in making this recommendation I am waving the red flag to many educators who hold that it has been statistically "proven" that finger following makes for slow reading. In this I believe there has been a fundamental misinterpretation. I am convinced that the tendency to slow and insecure reading rests on a lack of acquisition of dominance in one hemisphere, that this is determined largely be heredity and tht the use of the finger is a spontaneous remedial effort adopted by those who suffer from this difficulty of maintaining direction and as such it is to be encouraged. In simpler words, I believe that these children are not retarded in reading speed because they use their fingers but they use their fingers because they are retarded in reading by direction confusions.

SPECIAL DISABILITY IN WRITING*
with Anna Gillingham

◆　　◆　　◆

Writing, like other fractions of the language faculty, is intimately related to the problem of unilateral cerebral dominance since it is frequently lost in the adult as a result of destructive lesions of the dominant hemisphere and is not disturbed by lesions of comparable extent and locus in the subjugate hemisphere.

Previous communications by one of us (Orton 1925) have offered the hypothesis that failure to acquire the usual cerebral pattern of the adult, i.e., unilateral dominance, lies at the bottom of the selective retardation in learning to read occurring in children who are otherwise able, and studies of children who have unusual difficulty in learning to write offer an additional approach to this problem.

Although there are published standards for judging writing quality, its exact evaluation is difficult if indeed not impossible. The factors of appearance or style and of legibility cannot be rated with accuracy and only that of writing speed can be numerically compared with the product of others, and for this reason no exact statement can be made concerning the limits within which the term special disability in writing can be said to apply. We have come to use the term for those children who, in spite of adequate or even extensive training, are lagging far behind their accomplishment in other academic lines in learning to write, with average speed for their age, in a legible, reasonably well formed hand. Figure 1 gives the educational profile of such a case. It is not quite pure since this boy's spelling was also somewhat

*This report is based in part on work done under a grant from the Committee on Research and Publication of the Neurological Institute of New York.

The cases of congenital word deafness which we have studied are omitted here since they are few in number and have not progressed in their education far enough to be judged critically for the presence or absence of a true writing disability.

Reprinted from Bulletin of the Neurological Institute of New York, Vol. III, Nos. 1 and 2, June, 1933

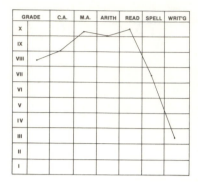

GRADE	C.A.	M.A.	ARITH	READ	SPELL	WRIT'G
X						
IX						
VIII						
VII						
VI						
V						
IV						
III						
II						
I						

Fig. 1. Educational profile of a fifteen-year-old boy with a marked writing disability. C.A., chronological age: M.A., mental age

behind his achievement in his other studies, but this was making him relatively little trouble in school while his writing speed (circa 40 letters per minute) was so low as to form an almost insuperable obstacle in written examinations and in the taking of notes on class assignments, etc.

When a child is first learning to write, distortions both of form and orientation of the letters are very frequent in his efforts. One of common occurence is that of mirror writing. Occasional reversed letters are so frequent at this stage as to be almost universal. The consistent sinistrad orientation of all letters and sinistrad progression in words, i.e., true mirror writing, is far less common but by no means rare. When this occurs in a left-handed child writing with the left hand it probably represents merely the natural reversal of pattern which results from the antitropism of the two sides of the body and is not considered to be of much moment. When, however, mirror writing is spontaneously produced by the right hand, it suggests a twist in reproduction of considerable interest and probably of some prognostic value as most children whom we have seen who have exhibited this initial tendency have experienced considerable difficulty with reading later. Occasionally a vertical inversion is also seen so that the child writes all letters upside down, and, rarely, inversion and mirror writing are combined. As a rule the inversions are rapidly corrected either spontaneously or under guidance but the tendency to reversals is much more difficult to eradicate. These earlier aberrations are not of course to be looked upon as writing disabilities although they do, we believe, indicate certain tendencies which may in some cases persist sufficiently to interfere with the easy acquisition of a writing skill.

Among the older children who have been exposed to training in writing for several years and yet who have made very indifferent progress in it, several groups may be recognized.

The first group is that in which there is clinical evidence of damage or injury to the pyramidal or prepyramidal motor systems. Here are to be found particularly the dystonias of the birth injury type, spasticity of Little's disease, etc. In these cases the difficulty in writing is to be looked upon chiefly as an expression of the general motor disintegration although the question of establishment of normal dominance in these injured brains is far from settled. This is notably so when we consider the problem of an apraxic factor dependent on damage of the thalamus or the posterior limb of the internal capsule or the postcentral cortical fields and accompanying a more overt motor lesion. An extensive series of autopsy studies of such cases will be required to evaluate this factor. In general, however, the difficulty in learning to write experienced by these children is so in harmony with the rest of the motor dysfunction that it need not detain us here.

The second group is made up of certain obvious sinistrals who have met difficulty because of training unsuited to their needs. Of these there are two types: first, those who have been permitted to use their left hands in writing but who have been trained with the paper in the right-hand position or have been forced to acquire a slant which is abnormal for them, and, second, those who have been taught to write with their right hands but who have been permitted to retain the use of the left hand in all other activities and who show little or no evidence on examination of confused or mixed dominance. The first group will be discussed more in detail in the section of this paper dealing with retraining. The second may well be further elaborated here.

The large number of left-handed individuals who have acquired a satisfactory writing with the right hand demonstrates without question that this is possible in many instances, but certain cases seem to indicate clearly that in some individuals the use of the wrong hand will lead to serious difficulties. One such case is that of the boy whose educational profile is shown in Figure 1. He was recognized from infancy as being strongly left-handed but he had been trained to use his right hand for both eating and writing. As he went forward in school his difficulty in learning to write legibly and with acceptable speed became an increasing handicap so that by the time he had reached the eighth grade, his writing speed as shown in Figure 1, had progressed only to the normal rate for third grade children. Figure 2 shows at *A* a sample of this boy's right-hand writing at this time. At *B* is a tracing of his product with his left hand in a trial at the same time. As will be noted, the latter without previous training is better formed than

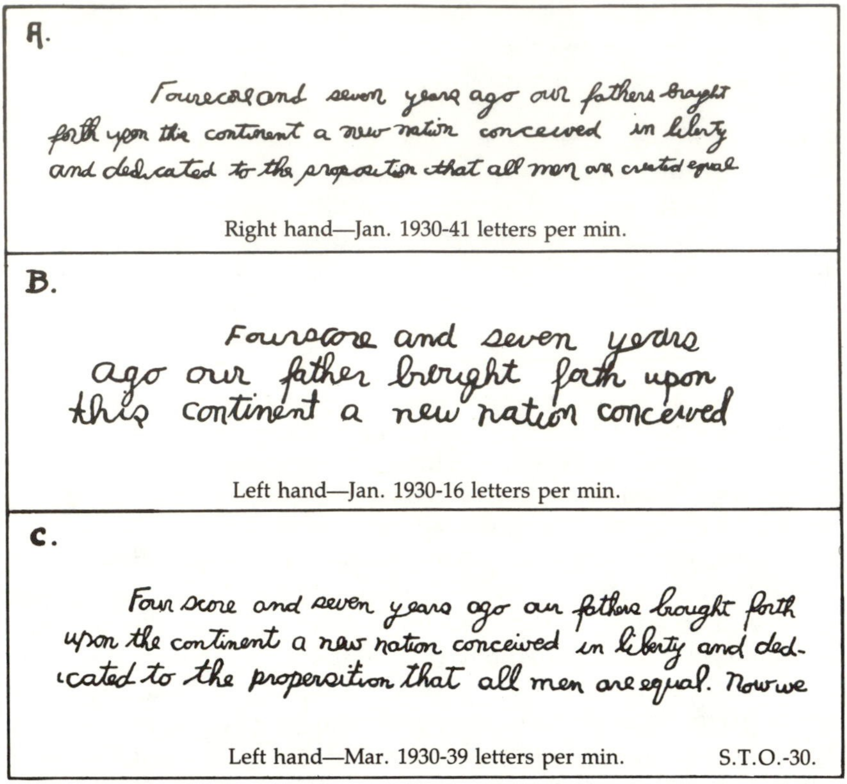

A.

Fourscore and seven years ago our fathers brought forth upon the continent a new nation conceived in liberty and dedicated to the proposition that all men are created equal

Right hand—Jan. 1930-41 letters per min.

B.

Fourscore and seven years ago our father brought forth upon this continent a new nation conceived

Left hand—Jan. 1930-16 letters per min.

C.

Four score and seven years ago our fathers brought forth upon the continent a new nation conceived in liberty and ded-icated to the proposition that all men are equal. Now we

Left hand—Mar. 1930-39 letters per min.   S.T.O.-30.

Fig. 2. Three samples of the writing of a left-handed boy of fifteen who had been taught to use his right hand for writing

that of the right. It was, however, only about one-third as fast. In spite of the years of training of the right, it was recommended that he be taught to use his left hand for writing and within three months as shown at C he had acquired a speed with the left practically equal to that previously attained with the right and a much better quality.

Figure 3 gives another example of this. This is taken from the work of a left-handed boy of superior mental ability, thirteen years of age, who was forced by his school to use his right hand during the first six grades. Near the end of the sixth grade training of the left was instituted but with insufficient time to establish a facility, and in the seventh grade due to pressure of work he shifted back to the more experienced hand because of its greater speed. In the eighth grade because of persistent poor writing, left-handed training was revived and he was given many hours of practice. At A in the figure shown his right-hand writing when in the seventh grade while at B is shown the improvement accomplished in a year and a half of practice with the left

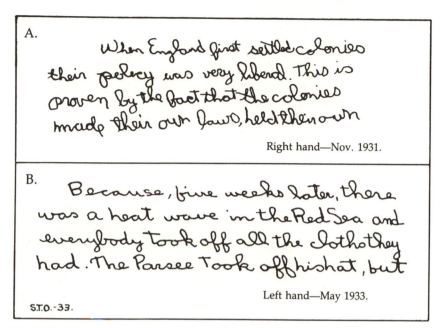

Fig. 3. Improvement in writing resultant on retraining the master hand (left) in a boy of thirteen

hand. Other cases of this type indicate that while a true writing disability may not result from an enforced use of the less skillful hand, such training may in many instances lead to a much greater difficulty in writing and a much less legible product than probably would have resulted had the master hand been trained for the intricate motor integrations of this fraction of the language function. Occasionally injury or peripheral paralysis of the master hand or arm may dictate training of the other for writing. When this occurs it is wise to bear in mind that writing may be slow and difficult of acquisition and that special methods of training may be highly profitable.

A third and by far the largest group is composed of those children whose difficulty in writing coexists with other problems which we relate to delays or failures in acquisition of clear-cut unilateral dominance. These are the cases which we consider to be intergrades between the dextrals and the sinistrals and which, from the results of other studies which will be published later, seem to form a very large group constituting a graded sequence between the pure dextrals and the pure sinistrals.

Several subgroups may be tentatively segregated under this head, viz.: those associated with strephosymbolia (reading and spelling disabilities), those occurring as a part of the picture of congenital apraxia, those accompanying stuttering, and a group who show none of the above syndromes but do give evidence of confusions or crossed patterns on tests of their handedness and eyedness.

The association with strephosymbolia is often close. The majority of cases of marked delay in learning to read show a comparable delay in learning to reproduce the letters in writing, and with some of these the writing difficulty remains as a more or less isolated disability after a reasonable degree of reading skill has been acquired. The pathological spellers likewise very often suffer from a measure of writing disability. As has been pointed out elsewhere (Orton 1931) one factor in this may be the great uncertainty in how to spell the word and the consequent distraction from the mechanics of writing. When this is suspected, a test of the child's ability to copy from print into his own handwriting compared with his efforts when writing to dictation or in composition will usually clearly indicate the potence of this element. Figure 4, reprinted from an earlier article, illustrates this. The boy whose work this is suffered from a considerable degree of strephosymbolia and in this connection it is of particular interest to note the use of the capital B when writing from recall and the correct use of the lower case letter while copying.

There is an interesting group of children who in spite of good intelligence and good muscular strength encounter an unusual degree of difficulty in learning any motor patterns which require a high degree of complexity of muscular movements. Such individuals we interpret as cases of congenital apraxia. They usually learn the simpler move-

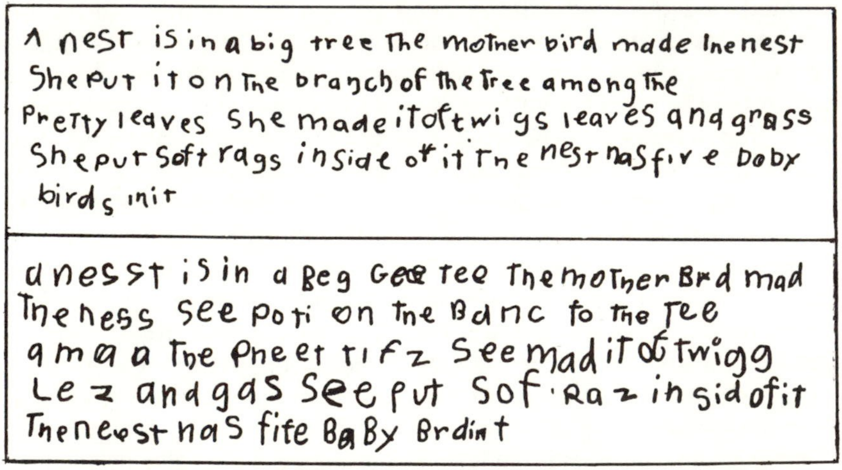

Fig. 4. Contrast between copying and writing to dictation showing the influence of a spelling disability

ments which have a longer phylogenetic ancestry, such as walking, running, grasping, tossing, swimming, etc., with fair skill, although often without much grace, at about the usual age, but they are exceedingly slow and clumsy in learning to recombine units of those movements into such activities as dancing, skating, tennis, over hand throwing, sewing, etc. One such child recently studied was a girl of ten with a good intelligence who was competing easily in school with girls older than herself in arithmetic, reading, spelling, and the other academic subjects of her grade but who was left sitting on the mourners' bench when the period for athletics and physical training came around. At home she was a confirmed bookworm and made exceedingly slow progress in skating, riding horse back, tennis, etc., and enjoyed none of them. In many settings this would have carried little penalty but she was unfortunately a member of a family group that valued these activities very highly. On neurological examination she showed no pathological reflexes, no dystonia, and no sensory changes. She did show however marked difficulty and slowness in rapid successive movements, such as repetitive apposition of the thumb and first finger, rapid pronation and supination of the hand, and hopping. She could hop, with difficulty, on the right foot but not on the left. Moreover she was very slow and clumsy in carrying out many practiced movements such as buttoning clothes, opening and closing a safety pin, tying her shoes, etc. It is worthy of note that these difficulties seemed to be of an apraxic rather than of an ataxic nature. Her handwriting, while not pathological, was yet poor enough in contrast with her accomplishment in the rest of her school work to warrant classification as a special writing disability. Her difficulty in this we interpret as a part of the general apraxic disorder.

There is a fairly frequent association of exceedingly poor handwriting with stuttering, although it is by no means the rule since many stutterers develop a good handwriting. Some of those who both stutter and have trouble in writing are sinistrals who have been taught to write with the right hand, and many others are those who give a history of a clearly expressed preference for the left hand in infancy which was cured by early and insistent training so that later they, externally at least, appear entirely right-handed. It seems probable therefore that many of the bad writers who also stutter should be transferred to our earlier group of those who have encountered trouble due to training unsuited to their particular needs. Exact comparison of the quality of the product in writing is difficult or impossible, but as far as our observations go there does not seem to be any special characteristic of the bad writing of stutterers which marks it off from that of other pathological writers. Occasionally their writing shows a certain degree of tremulousness on long strokes, but neither the clonic nor the tonic spasms which form so prominent a part of the stuttering episode are as a rule to be observed in their writing. Occasionally we see a considerable amount of movement of the lips, mouthing of words, while writing, but the motor overflows of this character are by no means so striking as the grimaces of the facial muscles or the even grosser face or body movements which so often accompany stuttering.

The fourth and final subgroup is that of those children who in addition to very poor writing show evidence of intergrading other than strephosymbolia, apraxia, or stuttering. Here we include those who show mixed hand and eye patterns, i.e., right-handed and left-eyed, or vice versa, those who show variations in a series of tests for eyedness or in the same test at different times, indicating a failure to have established a clear-cut choice of a master eye, and those who in their history or by test show that neither hand has developed an exclusive predominance for all skilled acts or who show a decided preference for one hand in spontaneous acts, combined with a greater skill in the other hand for some or all of the motor patterns which have been exposed to the influence of training.

METHODS OF TESTING

As with all the problems of delay in development of the language faculty, the family history is of interest. Occasionally direct heredity (as in the case described below in connection with figure 9) is found. More commonly this is not so, but we are becoming increasingly convinced that children with any of these specific delays are much more apt to spring from family stocks in which other evidence of dominance problems can be obtained by careful inquiry. Since the possible relationship of such disorders as bad spelling or stuttering to poor penmanship is not an obvious one, this information can usually be obtained only by direct questioning. For this purpose, queries should be directed toward the existence in the family of left-handedness, ambidexterity, reading disabilities, speech delays and disturbances, apraxic disorders, and pathological spelling, as well as of other cases of bad writing.

Obviously the problem of whether the right or left hand should be used for writing is of fundamental importance in the individual case, and in determining this the personal history of the patient is often of great value. Inquiry should be made of the parents concerning tendencies noticed in infancy or early childhood toward selective use of either hand and toward a possible prolonged period of indifferent use of both. Questions should also be asked as to whether training was specifically directed toward one side (almost invariably the right in such cases) and if so how much pressure was used and how long it was continued. Similarly, the child's training at school in this respect must be determined. The examiner should also inquire from the patient as to which hand is used by preference in a large range of activities; too small a group may easily prove misleading. Tests for handedness skills are also strongly indicated since frequently training will have resulted in habituation so that the natural latent skills are obscured. Figure 5 gives a good example of this. This was a boy of eleven who had been shifted in infancy from a well expressed tendency to use the left hand and at the time he entered school was looked upon as entirely right, handed. He used his right hand in throwing, eating, writing, and most other

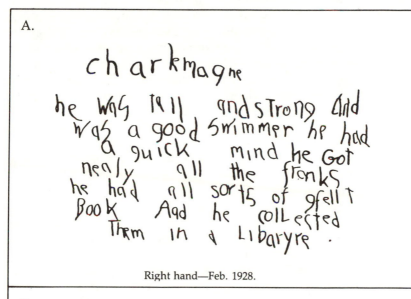

Fig. 5. Serious writing obstacle due to mistraining. Sample at *A* was after five years of intensive effort with the right hand in a boy of eleven. *B* shows the result of one year's retraining of the left.

trained acts although in many simpler movements he volunteered the left. He was definitely left-eyed and in simultaneous blindfold writing with both hands the left gave much the firmer and better formed product. He also was a moderate stutterer, a pathological speller, and writing was said to be beyond him after extended drill. On the basis of this and other evidence, retraining of the left hand was recommended. Figure 5 shows at *A* the skill he had acquired in writing after five years of labor with the right hand and at *B* the result of one year's training of the left. No attempt will be made here to describe the tests we use for either handedness or eyedness since these will form the basis of later reports, but it may be well to emphasize that a large number of such tests are advisable since the findings by one method are not infrequently contradictory to those of another.

To determine writing speed we use the standardized Gettysburg Edition of the Ayres Scale for Measuring Handwriting except that we present it as a typewritten copy rather than the script as in the original test since many of our patients have considerably greater difficulty in reading script than in reading print. This is especially true of those children who have been taught manuscript writing and have had little experience in reading cursive script. We occasionally further modify the original plan in the case of younger children by giving them much simpler material to copy. Copying is the best test of the simple mechanics of writing, since it excludes the distraction due to spelling which is present in writing to dictation and in composition and in the propositional element in composing. It seems wise however to obtain samples of all three, copying, writing to dictation, and original composition, since one frequently finds a pertinent difference between the writing speed in these tasks and occasionally a somewhat comparable deviation in the writing quality (e.g., Figure 4).

Our studies have not concerned themselves greatly with the question of the quality of writing as estimated by measuring scales but certain obvious faults have been observed in children who have been slow in learning this function. These are chiefly gross crudities in letter forms leading to confusions such as those between *o*, and *a*, *b* and *f*, *m* and *n*, etc., marked irregularity in height, depth, or width of letters and especially of the loops, tremulousness, angular distortions of sweeping curves, and marked variability in the slant of the axes of letters. A lack of precise motor control may also show in the numbers of blots with ink or erasures with pencil, and faults in the general distribution of the material on the page so that spacing of words and paragraphs is apt to be poor.

One interesting exploratory test is to ask the child to write his name or some familiar material such as "United States of America" with each hand in each lateral orientation, i.e., in the dextrad (to the right)

direction with first the right and then the left hand and then in the
sinistrad (or mirrored) direction with each hand, keeping a record of
the time required for each product. For recording, the four specimens
may be easily earmarked by the following symbols in which the letter
indicates the hand used and the arrow the direction followed:

⊣L ⊣L⟩ ⟨R R⟩

It is also an aid to have the mirrored samples written on the back of
the test sheet with a sheet of carbon paper face up beneath it, thus
reversing on the face of the test sheet the two sinistrad efforts so that
they may be more directly compared with the dextrad. A number of
interesting observations have been collected by this method. Some
children (and some adults) have a rather striking degree of equivalence
of all four patterns. Two such instances are shown in Figure 6 and are

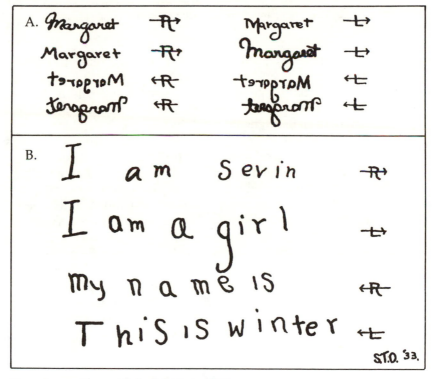

Fig. 6. Practically equal skill in all four ways of writing. At *A* are shown examples in both
manuscript and cursive styles. The mirrored samples have not been reversed. The two
mirrored samples in *B* have been reversed in reproduction for ease in comparison. The
letters indicate the hand used and the arrows the direction of writing.

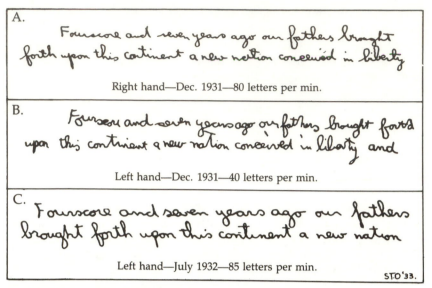

Fig. 7. Writing samples of a left-handed youth of seventeen who had always written with his right hand

explained in the legend. Our case material is not yet extensive enough to permit of any conclusion from such findings but it is our impression that these children have a good manual dexterity as a rule.

Occasionally the left-hand dextrad writing, when first attempted, is of better quality than the right although its speed is less. This is to be seen in Figure 2, *A* and *B*. The speed ratio here was R:L::1:3. More commonly the trained hand shows much the better qualitative product, but the relative speed may indicate a considerable latent skill in the left. This was the case with a youth of seventeen who came for examination because of stuttering. He was left-handed in all spontaneous activities. Figure 7 shows the superiority of his right hand (*A*) over his left hand (*B*) writing. The speed ratio however was R:L::1:2, an unusual relation since the right hand had been trained for writing for eleven years and the left hand had had no training in this function. He also reported a subjective feeling of greater ease in the left-hand trial. An experiment in training of the left hand for writing was recommended for its influence both on speech and on facility in writing and at the end of seven months he had acquired a left-hand writing better in both speed and quality than his right as shown at C in the figure.

Not infrequently all four samples are poor (Figure 8). Here again only a tentative opinion is warranted, but we feel that the individuals who give this result are apt to be quite poor in all finer muscular integrations of the hand and many represent the apraxic group.

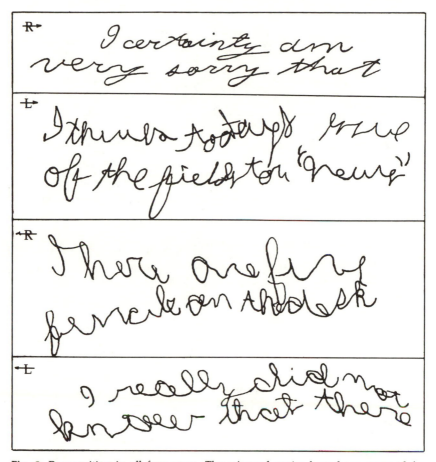

Fig. 8. Poor writing in all four ways. The mirrored copies have been reversed for reproduction. This was the work of a thirteen-year-old boy with an intelligence quotient of 144.

In a number of cases we have found a marked facility in mirror writing with the right hand in the presence of a striking difficulty with dextrad writing. The most startling case of this sort was that of a twenty-one-year old medical student who had never been able to learn to write with sufficient skill to permit him to read his own product unless it was done very slowly and painstakingly. He gave the history that his father had had great difficulty in learning to write and what writing he had acquired was done with the pencil held in a midline position between the two hands and that his paternal uncle, an able lawyer, had found the acquisition of writing an insuperable obstacle. Figure 9 shows at *A* the dextrad writing of this medical student. This was written to dictation and is better than his usual efforts in prop-

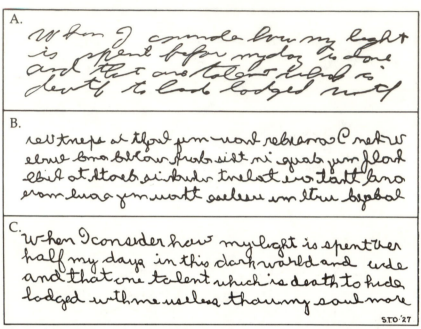

Fig. 9. Almost illegible right-hand dextrad writing as shown at *A* but with latent mirrored skill with right hand as shown at *B*. *C* is *B* reversed for convenience in comparison

ositional writing. At *B* is shown his mirror writing with his right hand. This was also written to dictation and was made within a few days after this sinistrad ability had been discovered so it represents an untrained latent skill. He was quite unskillful in writing with his left hand in both the dextrad and sinistrad directions. At C is a replica of the mirrored writing reversed by a tracing process so that its character may be more easily compared with that at *A*. This case was also interesting in that he had acquired a considerable dexterity in other acts. He was interested in bacteriology and was an accomplished technician in this field. Varying degrees of this mirrored skill in the right hand have been found in quite a number of our cases of very poor writers and another illustration of similar type is shown in Figure 12.

We have found a number of cases in which the left-handed mirror writing was the best of all four ways but we have not yet encountered a case, comparable to that recorded above, in which the only pattern easily available was the mirrored form produced by the left hand, although such cases may be anticipatéd.

Occasionally there is a very striking difference in the superficial appearance of the dextrad writing produced by the two hands due to differences in slant. A good example of this is shown in Figure 10. These were made by a college student who was rather markedly

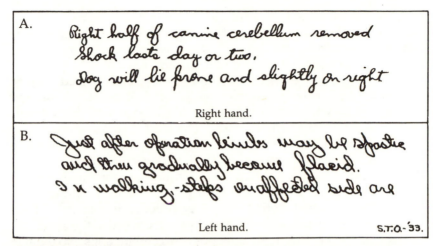

Fig. 10. Right- and left-hand writing of a college student who had trained both hands and used them on alternating sides of the sheet in his notebook

left-handed although he threw and wrote with his right hand. He reported that in a course in engineering drawing he used the ruling pen with the left hand but changed to the right for lettering. He was strongly left-eyed. There was no history of any effort at training the right hand for either the throwing or the writing. His writing was acceptable but it was a somewhat fatiguing process and he felt that he did not do himself justice in written examinations. He was interested in the possibility of developing a more automatic and less fatiguing handwriting by training his master hand (the left) for this purpose and undertook to train himself by copying with his left hand from a printed text for a few minutes daily. A left-hand skill developed with surprising rapidity. At A in Figure 10 is shown a facsimile of his right-hand product, while at B is that of his left produced after less than a year of training. He had lost none of his former skill with the right and capitalized this double gift by taking notes in class with the right hand on one side of the sheet in his notebook and with his left on the reverse. The two samples shown in the figure are taken from the two sides of one of these sheets from his notebook.

There is a general tendency for the dextrad writing produced by the left hand to have a backhand slant in contrast to that of the right and the mirrored forms, when well produced, seem more apt also to follow this tendency. There is however no consistent similiarity in slant or in form shown between any two or the four types. Frequently the two mirrored forms are much more alike than are the two in the dextrad direction and often both the mirrored patterns tend to be more like the left-hand dextrad than like the right-hand dextrad, although the comparison is scarcely safe since we are recording here one pattern (i.e., dextrad with the right hand) which has almost always been exposed to considerable training and three which are untrained and hence prob- ably represent a more natural motor pattern.

A test which is somewhat akin to the one last described may be carried out by giving the patient a piece of chalk in each hand and asking him to write his name on the blackboard with both hands simultaneously, with his eyes closed. The most common spontaneous pattern is for both hands to travel together in the dextrad direction (Ŀ R⁺) but it is not uncommon to find the right traveling to the right and the left producing mirror writing (Ŀ R⁺). Much less commonly the left may travel to the right while the right produces mirror writing (Ŀ⁺R⁺) and very occasionally both hands may produce the sinistrad form (Ŀ⁺R⁺). After the spontaneous pattern has been recorded the child may be asked to try the three remaining possible combinations. No definite interpretations are put on the results of this test except that the master hand is apt to produce much stronger and more regular strokes and achieve a much more even spacing of letters even in cases in which the opposite hand has been trained for writing. Confused patterns such as reversals of one or more letters of a series consistently oriented are tentatively considered as evidence of failure to develop a strong uni- lateral lead. Some children have been found who are entirely unable to write with both hands at the same time in any of the four combinations and these seem to fall in the apraxic group. The large blackboard writing may be traced for preservation by means of thin tissue paper sheets and a crayon. Caution is indicated in evaluating this blackboard writing in terms of ordinary writing with pen or pencil since it makes use of a very different set of muscular integrations (arm and shoulder vs. hand). Dr. Earl Chesher of the Language Research Project of the Neurological Institute has recently demonstrated in one intergrade a much greater skill in movement of the shoulder group on the left side than on the right but a reversal of this when finer finger movements were tested. This was uncovered by an apparatus of his own designing which is to be described later.

Writing with a pencil while blindfolded is another method of probe which has yielded suggestive results. In this test we have the patient again try writing in all four ways as outlined above. The commonest result is a much poorer product than writing in the accustomed manner, together with comments from the child that it is much harder than with the eyes open. Occasionally a child writes about as well with the blindfold as without except for difficulty in maintaining a horizon- tal line. The mirrored form likewise has been found in an occasional child to be surprisingly well produced with either the left or the right

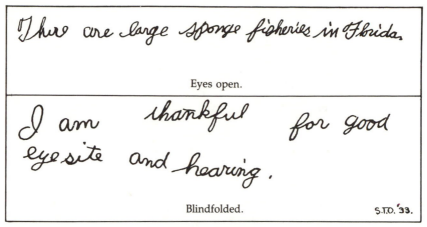

There are large sponge fisheries in Florida.

Eyes open.

I am thankful for good eye site and hearing.

Blindfolded.

S.T.O. '33.

Fig. 11. Contrast between writing while watching paper and while blindfolded produced by a thirteen-year-old boy.

hand or with both. Figure 11 shows a comparison between writing with the eyes open (at *A*) and when blindfolded (at *B*).

As opposed to the above test which aims at testing the importance of the visual factor in writing we have attempted to evaluate the kinesthetic element in some children by putting the child's hand, carrying a pencil or a stylus, through the passive motions required for the production of certain letters while his eyes are closed or covered and asking him to tell what letter has been traced. In some of the bad writers we have uncovered an almost total inability to recognize such motions.

With many cases a study of the ease of acquisition and the skill attained in fine coordinations of finger movements other than writing will expose a sharp contrast between them and those used for writing. Inquiry will not infrequently reveal a considerable degree of skill in shop work, sewing, drawing, piano playing, etc., entirely out of harmony with the disability in writing. Figure 12 gives an excellent example of this. This was the work of a twelve-year-old girl who preferred her right hand in all practiced acts although she was definitely left-eyed and showed a high degree of equivalence between the two sides in tests of untrained skills. At *A* in the figure is a sketch made by her in her own home showing, we think, an entirely adequate skill in the use of the pencil. At *B* is a representative sample of her dextrad writing. *C* shows her skill in mirror writing with her right hand, which had been tried only a few times before this experiment, and at the bottom of the figure is the mirrored writing reproduced in reverse to permit an easier comparison with the dextrad sample.

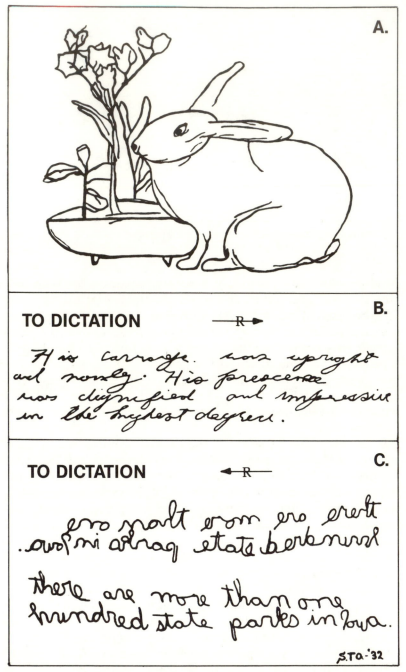

Fig. 12. At *A* copy of a sketch to indicate skill with pencil. At *B* representative sample of right-hand dextrad writing. At *C* right hand mirror writing and below this the same reversed. Eleven-year-old-girl.

DISCUSSION

Clearly the most usual pattern of learning to write is first the establishment of a visual engram of the letter form, then the gradual association of this record with the kinesthetic engram necessary for its reproduction, and finally a progressively increasing facility of control by the kinesthetic fraction until the writing process becomes semiautomatic. Intimate associations are also obviously formed with the auditory engrams, completing the three-fold integration pattern which seems to underlie the whole of the language function. That neither the visual nor the auditory fraction is essential to this process is convincingly demonstrated by the fact that Helen Keller has learned to write without the aid of engrams implanted through either the visual or the auditory pathways. Miss Keller has been kind enough to supply an example of her writing for an illustration in this article, which is reproduced in Figure 13. The part commonly played by the visual element, however, even when writing has been cultivated to the point where it has been invested with well nigh automatic facility, is shown by the almost constant occurrence of agraphia as an accompaniment of alexia due to lesions in the angular gyrus region and without complicating paralysis or demonstrable kinesthetic losses.

We have encountered no cases in which we were able to trace the disability in writing to disturbances of the visual implant alone although such cases with uncorrected visual errors undoubtedly exist. In those children who show a striking defect in recognition of the passive movements of tracing letters and in those whose writing trouble is part of a general apraxia but without organic motor symptoms, unusual difficulty in learning to write may be tentatively ascribed to a failure of establishment of the usual kinesthetic patterns. In the rare cases where blindfold writing is as good or better than writing with the eyes open the assumption seems justifiable that there has been a failure to establish the normal facile association between the visual and the

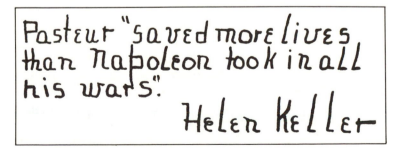

Fig. 13. A sample of Helen Keller's writing.

kinesthetic engrams, resulting in a measure of conflict. One of our boys who showed this characteristic said of the experiment, "It's easier that way because you don't have to look at the letters." This suggestion of rivalry between the arriving visual sensations and the recall patterns necessary for reproduction was also strongly suggested by our observations in an unreported case of alexia. This man had suffered from a fracture in the left parieto-occipital region. When asked to copy figures he was quite unable to do so while looking at them although he could reproduce them after observing them for a moment and then closing his eyes while he made the copy.

The number of children who are very poor writers and yet have an uncultivated skill in mirror writing is impressive although contrast as great as that shown in Figures 9 and 12 is unusual. The existence however of a highly organized though undiscovered sinistrad skill in the presence of a marked dextrad disability seems to add considerable weight to the thesis of interhemispheric rivalry resultant on failure to acquire the complete unilateral pattern of the normal adult. Additional weight is given to this in the two cases quoted above in both of which motor skills below the language level of cortical integration were well developed, since it is at this third level that the problem of unilateral dominance is most securely established.

One obvious result of these studies, which confirms our findings in strephosymbolia and in our studies of handedness, is the conviction that all of these faulty integrative patterns show a very wide variability in both the qualitative and quantitative sense. The highly individual character of the organization of skills and disabilities in a given child emphasizes again the need of full analysis of each case and an approach to treatment without fixed methods but rather as an experiment. It should also be remembered that many normal writers show on test good mirror writing and an occasional one a practical equivalence in all the four ways of the test. The finding of mirror writing or other unexpected skill therefore in a child can only be interpreted as part of the whole picture and not as a rigid diagnostic sign.

We have no opinion to offer on the debated question of manuscript versus cursive writing except that it is clear that in children who have a native difficulty in establishing the kinesthetic engrams required for writing, training should be consistent and one method should be maintained. Some of our patients have been changed back and forth from one method to the other with change in school as many as three or four times and have failed to gain an acceptable skill in either or have acquired a succotash of letter forms. Figure 14 shows an example of this. The custom existing in some schools of training in the manuscript style for several years in the lower grades and then starting over with

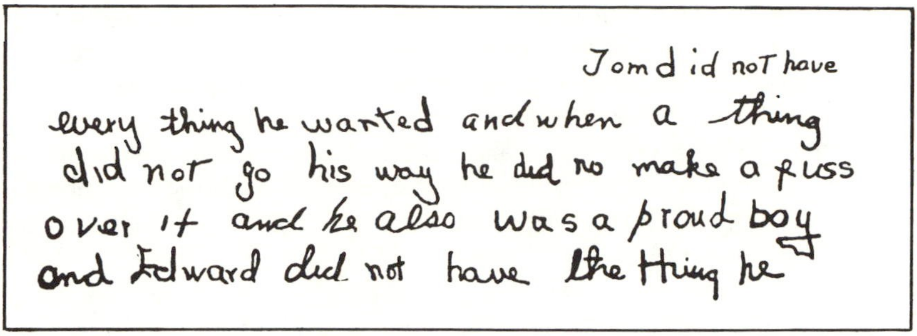

Fig. 14. Mixture of cursive and manuscript letter forms. This was produced by a thirteen-year-old girl who was taught in manuscript writing for the first four school grades and then for three years in the cursive.

the cursive has been followed in some observed children by almost as much trouble in learning the new forms as they had in the beginning. Indeed mixtures such as that produced in the figure, which are particularly prone to appear when the child is tired or hurried, suggest that the existence of a double set of engrams may in some children serve as an added liability. This is particularly true of children in those schools in which the shift to the cursive writing is required in a certain grade but is not accompanied by adequate training to establish the new forms.

As in all of the special disabilities the emotional factors are of prime importance in evaluating the severity of the condition and in outlining treatment. As a resultant of the presence of the writing disability we see as a rule much less marked emotional upheavals than those which follow severe strephosymbolia, but a considerable measure of a feeling of inferiority which often carries over into other academic work, is often engendered by a serious failure in writing after a conscious effort has been made. Conversely a striking improvement in other subjects is not an unusual result of the return of self confidence which comes with successful training. The child's own attitude toward the difficulty and that which he has absorbed at home have a considerable influence on his spontaneous efforts to correct his trouble. Where he has heard that "No business man has to write his own letters," he is not apt to be impressed by the need of learning to write. A very slow penmanship may however form a real obstacle to success in school work as in the case of one of our boys who consistently was able to finish only about one half of his examination questions in the allotted time and was failing in all of his examinations as a result, although his papers were almost perfect as far as he went. This experience gave him a deeply ingrained feeling of hopelessness about the scholastic hurdles ahead of him. Any undue emotional factors operating at home or in school may appear as contributing elements in the disability. This seems to be particularly true of the type of child who is in need of rather rigorous discipline to encourage much output of effort and who is not receiving this adequately. In other children, the writing disability may serve as a real block to their written verbal expression and may reduce the quality as well as the quantity of their output in written compositions, letters, etc., and engender an emotional bias against all situations in which writing is required.

As with the reading and spelling disabilities, there remains for a long time a tremendous variability in the child's product after the retraining has been undertaken. When such a selective difficulty has existed, apparently the older distorted patterns are still apt to recur after new and correct habits have been established by properly designed retraining, so that ground won by patience and persistence may seem to have been completely lost almost overnight when new emotional or physical stresses arise. One boy who had been making good progress with his writing suffered a broken leg and his mother reported that his writing had gone "all to smash." Such slumps are usually transitory, however, and the lost ground is generally very quickly regained.

The writing disability is much more frequent in boys than in girls. This conforms to findings in other special language delays and suggests a sex influenced hereditary factor. In a series of thirteen children selected because of bad writing from the Ethical Culture Schools, eleven were boys and only two were girls. A direct hereditary history of writing trouble is not common but the frequence of left-handedness and of other language disabilities in the families of our cases is significantly high and the disorder is looked upon as one of the variants of the dominance problem resting largely on an hereditary basis.

The much discussed question as to whether it is wise to train a left-handed child to write with the right hand cannot be answered as a generality with any assurance. Many left-handed individuals have been so taught with no obvious ill effects, but it can scarcely be gainsaid in the light of some of our material that difficulty may follow both in speech and in writing, and there remains moreover the possibility that even those who have escaped complications might have written better and with more ease had their native tendencies been cultivated. Studies along the lines of the examination suggested here would be of interest, for example, in cases of writer's cramp.

TRAINING PROCEDURES

With left-handed children who have been trained to write with the right hand and who are failing rather badly to gain speed and legibility with this hand, an experiment in retraining the left hand is justified even though the writing with the left hand is unpromising at first attempts. In this event, as indeed with all left-handed writers, the position of the paper and the slant of the letter axes in writing are very important to prevent the awkward positions so often assumed and so difficult to eradicate. The problem of the position of the paper seems so simple that one wonders at the number of times that left-handed children are allowed to hold the paper in the position which is correct for right-handed children but not for them. Easy right-handed writers usually carry the weight of the arm at the elbow using the internal condyle as a pivot with the paper in such a position that the swing of the forearm from this fixed point will permit the hand to follow across the sheet with a minimal shift of arm or body posture (hunching). The top of the sheet is toward the left and the angle which the paper makes with the mid-plane of the body naturally varies somewhat with the individual to permit the hand to traverse the sheet horizontally while pivoting on the condyle. Obviously, to adapt this position to the left-handed person the top of the sheet must be toward the right and the paper must make an angle to the body plane exactly the opposite of that for the right-handed person.

Our experiences in training the bad writers lead us to place emphasis on the need of determining the natural slant of letter axes for each individual. This appears from our present work to be of paramount importance in both right- and left-handed children as a preliminary to further training efforts, and indeed in some cases the adoption of the natural slant has been the only training factor necessary to produce an almost magical betterment in the penmanship. The backhand slant is generally accepted as the usual pattern for left-handed writers but it is not so widely recognized that it may be the facile method for certain right-handed people. To ascertain the natural slant, specimens of the child's attempts at writing, especially those toward the end of an assignment when fatigue is beginning to set in, are examined carefully to see whether there is a greater tendency toward one deviation from the vertical than toward the other. Freehand exercises with the eyes closed may also be tried to determine whether lines in any one slant tend to maintain their parallelism better than in others. Pages ruled with parallel lines in the vertical and in exaggerated right- and back-hand slants are inserted on different days beneath translucent paper and the child is asked to write between them, and the product is examined to see which he has followed most closely. It sometimes is necessary to overcome a prejudice derived from previous teachers or from parents before thorough cooperation can be obtained and it is essential to have the child understand that this is an attempt to capitalize native talents which will result in easier and more fluent writing. Even in the face of a strong prejudice most children can be led into trying a new angle for a time "just to see how it will work" and once an improved skill is demonstrable the prejudice usually completely evaporates.

In the younger children and in the older ones with more severe degrees of the disability, training for fixation of proper letter forms is important. For this purpose patterns carefully drawn on coordinate paper and copied by the child on similar paper are advantageous. If this be presented as drawing, not writing, it often aids by relieving the feeling of need for speed which has usually been engrafted on writing. When the form has been copied a variable number of times, the child may be asked to attempt it again with the eyes closed or looking away from the paper. This training of the motor patterns with the visual sensory element excluded has proven of great value. Indeed this procedure has formed the mainstay in the successful retraining of a number of cases which had proved obdurate to extended drills in previous years by ordinary methods. The exclusion of the current visual sensory impressions of the work being produced may be accomplished by imposing a barrier between the eyes and the page, or by drawing the letter from memory with the eyes closed, or by looking at a pattern on the blackboard at a distance without lowering the eyes to the paper. In some cases we have drilled the child for several weeks by these methods before permitting him to look at the page on which the writing was being done and when this was permitted he was told that it was only for the purpose of following lines and margins and not to direct the pencil by sight. Usually it is easy to obtain free, well-formed letters in this way and the cramp in the fingers, the clenched jaws, the mouthings, and stiff body postures so common to the bad writers often almost immediately disappear. This procedure, as will be seen, is analogous to the touch method of teaching typewriting.

With very young children and especially with those who suffer from the not infrequent combination of strephosymbolia or its derivative, the spelling disability, it is doubly advantageous to combine a measure of phonic training with the writing by teaching the child to write the letter from its dictated phonic equivalent (i.e., its sound rather than its name) and it is often of further value to have the child repeat the sound and at another time, the name, of the letter while he forms it. This double training will aid in establishing the consistent recall of the letter form in one orientation, essential for reading acquisition, and will also serve to prevent the occasional failure of linkage between the sounds of the letters and their proper graphic reproduction which underlies the cases of good oral spellers who make many errors in written spelling. At the beginning of this training, it may prove helpful to have the child trace the letter forms over copies made by the teacher, which will insure the establishment of the kinesthetic engram in its proper orientation, and similar tracing and sounding of letters combined into syllables and phonetic words will aid the formation of the habit of consistent progression to the right for both reading and writing. When the word stage is reached, copying from the blackboard or from printed text may be added, but it should be remembered that copying is advised in all training for writing rather than writing to dictation or in composition. At first the aim in this should be accuracy and neatness rather than speed and later an increased speed may be encouraged as fast as can be achieved with maintenance of quality.

The retraining lessons are laborious work for the child and it is deemed unwise to make the lesson periods too long. Indeed frequently repeated short periods seem to return a better yield. No statement can be made as to optimum time here since this varies with the age and temperament of the child and with the severity of the disability. With young adults who wish to undertake their own retraining we advise starting with copying for ten minutes daily at first, increasing this as rapidly as possible without inducing undue fatigue until one-half hour per day is reached, maintaining this until a good speed and quality are gained before undertaking propositional writing. Daily practice is highly advisable as even the interruption of the training over a weekend may show itself in a regression to the older patterns when the child returns to school on Monday morning. In those children who have a severe handicap it is important to relieve them from all other writing except that during the retraining period. Otherwise the pressure for speed in class work, examinations, etc., often largely negates the value of the special training. Various provisions may be made to accomplish this. All written work may be omitted, oral examinations may be substituted for written, work to be prepared out of class may be dictated to parent or teacher, or, if the child has learned to use the typewriter this may be substituted for handwriting. We feel it important to stress this point of relief from other writing pressures until a reasonable skill has been gained, as we have seen failures and regressions which we believe to have been directly due to neglect of this precaution. For this reason, the summer vacation period may prove an excellent time for the initiation of the retraining program provided that adequate supervision can be secured.

Above all it is important for the teacher to appreciate that the rebuilding of a facile set of controlling patterns which are not spontaneously forthcoming must be done slowly and that the child must be encouraged continually by pointing out his improvement rather than his mistakes. Our experiments are not yet of long enough standing to evaluate the end results of special training. We feel secure in saying that a legible handwriting can be secured in almost every case, but it seems probable that those who have had a marked disability will always carry a measure of the handicap, expressed in lack of ease of writing, in inferior writing speed, or in regressions under pressure for too great speed or in examinations or at times of emotional or physical stress. In this again the writing disability cases are closely akin to the cases of the reading and spelling disabilities.

Finally, in fairness to both child and teacher it must be remembered that this special obstacle may exist as an isolated phenomenon unrelated to the general intelligence or to other academic skills and that to judge such a child solely on his written work will result in an unjust estimate both of the child's acquisitions and of his teacher's success in training him.

SUMMARY

Cases of marked retardation in learning to write are described and discussed.

They are tentatively grouped as cases with predominating motor difficulty, cases largely dependent on an apraxic factor, and cases in which the visuo-kinesthetic association process is disturbed or retarded.

Except for those cases accompanying demonstrable motor system disease, they are considered to result from failure to establish the adult pattern of unilateral cerebral dominance.

Cases are reported with a persistent difficulty in learning to write in the dextrad direction but with a latent skill in mirror writing with the master hand. These cases show good manual dexterity except in writing and their symptoms are held to be added evidence of inter-hemispheric rivalry.

Methods of examination and training are described.

The Development of Speech Understanding in Relation to Intelligence

◆　　◆　　◆

The origin of human speech is lost in the shades of antiquity. We have no very clear idea of the source of human speech as a particular function, but I think there are some things we can derive from biological parallels by studying the situation in animals.

Man is the only speaking animal, but as a matter of fact, all animals have means of communicating with each other; while not speech in the true sense of the word, yet means which do carry from one animal to the other a great deal of the emotional tone of the situation, so that the mother hen has an entirely different cluck for her chicks when she wants to feed them than when she is urging them to hide from the oncoming hawk. Again the dog's tone of voice, so to speak, carries a very different implication if he is on the trail of a rabbit than when he is whining for the favor of his master. There is a great deal that can be communicated by animals to each other in this sense of carrying feeling tones of a situation. The striking difference between human speech and this communication of the animal is that the human has learned to substitute a meaningful word or symbol for the object itself, and that the animals do not have. I say "do not have" advisedly, because we do find that a good many animals can be taught the meaning of certain sounds to serve as symbols. There are many trained dogs that can be sent from one room to the other to get a specific article, e.g., to fetch the master's gloves, and they will not come back with anything but the gloves.

So it is quite possible to train a certain measure of symbolic registration in some of the brighter and more intelligent animals, but they do not serve as symbols which an animal can reproduce in order to pass on its meaning to others of its own kind. It is only in man that we find true symbolic speech actually developed.

Reprinted from Child Research Clinic Series, The Woods Schools, November, 1934 Vol. 1, No. 6

We do not know much as yet about the age of symbolic speech. It has been estimated roughly by anthropologists, largely on the basis of the brain case capacity of fossil man, that the brain was not large enough to serve the function of speech until approximately a half-million years ago, and that is a comparatively short geological period when you realize that the mammalian series of animals alone runs back two hundred million years.

Meaningful speech is a thing in which we should have particular interest because it is the function which is exclusively human and is our measure, very largely, of what we know generally as intelligence.

There is, I think, to be seen in every youngster a parallel evolution in the individual to the phylogenetic parallel. The infant at first understands keenly the emotional tone of things that are said to it long before it recognizes any of the meanings of the words said. The child knows when the mother is frightened without any knowledge of the meaning of the word which the mother is using. Indeed, the word might be left out entirely and the feeling tone of the voice would carry over the emotional set of the instant without any true meaning whatsoever. I think we can see there an evolution in the beginning of the child's history quite parallel to that of animal speech which we can recognize so clearly in the animals below man's grade.

Gradually this emotional speech is supplanted by meaningful speech as the child learns to recognize or is taught to recognize the meanings of the individual word, thoughts, and associations of the word which correspond with the given object or situation or duty or need of the moment. That that is purely a matter of teaching or of conditioning may be readily enough seen by the fact that the child learns the language to which it is exposed. There is nothing inherent in the word or its associated meaning except that which is taught to the child by the parent or teachers who are working with him; so that the child will learn English, French, or Swahili with equal facility, depending on which he hears.

Obviously it is the language itself which is an artificial structure built to indicate certain meanings and which is implanted in the child gradually by experience as he goes forward. The word, when it is learned by the child, rapidly becomes a handle by which that individual child can communicate with others. Almost without exception the child begins with certain nouns, often with the pronouns *I* and *we* in certain types of children, but more commonly with nouns having concrete meanings. Gradually to the learning of the names of objects around him is added the learning of abstract and derived meanings of words which carry so much of the meaning of our ordinary conversation and communication with each other. Indeed, I think one might say that intelligence, as we recognize that intangible and very difficult subject, is merely the soil in which the language function can be grown. There must be a certain degree of ease of adaptability of the individual in order that the language may be implanted there, and the ease with which the language function is picked up by various children is very strikingly variable.

If there be a definite sensory defect of intake and if that defect be obvious, we have a problem which can then be approached through some other sensory pathway. I can never think of defective situations without thinking of what was done in the case of Helen Keller. Deprived of both vision and audition, she was educated in a marvelous manner merely by substituting the sense of touch. Many of us would think immediately that she probably had a highly exaggerated sense of touch. One would think that there must be some kind of compensation where both vision and audition are lost and she would have probably developed the sense of touch above that of others. That has been disproved. My friend and colleague, Dr. Frederick Tilney, has studied Miss Keller's sense of touch critically and found it actually to be below that of the average individual.

Where it is obvious that the child is blind or deaf from the beginning, the problem is not so complex; it is not so hard to understand and not so hard to approach. Fairly adequate institutions have been built up for the handling and special education of both those groups. If, however, the sensory defect is masked and is not so easy to recognize, then the problem becomes one in which there is much more complexity and it is more difficult to understand what should be done and how to approach it.

The first requirement for the development of spoken language is obviously hearing. If the child be completely deaf the spoken language is going to be strikingly difficult to acquire and can be taught only in such a roundabout way as the speech taught to Helen Keller. Yet it is sufficient for her to serve as a means of communication. She has been taught through the kinesthetic pathways how to place her lips and tongue for the sounding of certain vowels and sounds and in that roundabout way has been taught to make speech sounds which, though defective, are definitely understandable. It is where there is a clear defect that it is rather easy to understand what we are dealing with. But there are certain other types of sensory defects which are not so clear, and which I think we must view with considerable hesitation before we accept them entirely, but which certainly are open to investigation and deserve careful further study.

There are two of these types of masked hearing defects which would not be obvious to the superficial examination which we have been working with a great deal of interest in our research laboratories at the Neurological Institute. One of these is a type of deafness which is known as high frequency deafness. We do not like that term high frequency because we have found a number of cases in which a comparative defect is found in the lower frequencies of the hearing range rather than in the higher frequencies; but the commonest form is a case in which audition is entirely normal or practically normal for all the lower ranges of sounds which the normal human ear can receive, but in which there is a distinct loss of acuity of reception at the higher frequencies. If that loss is in only the extremely high frequencies, it does not interfere in the least with the speech mechanism. If, however, it happens that the loss in acuity falls between 512 and 2048 double vibrations per second, that field in which most of the human speech sounds fall, the patient will have distinct difficulty in understanding the spoken word and, even more strikingly, difficulty in reproducing it in speech.

I have seen, for example, two little girls, sisters of six years and eight years of age, both of whom had very striking defects in their speech. They had almost no s, th, or f, etc. They would occasionally get them into a word and some of these sounds they had learned by watching the lips of others. They had become rather proficient lip-readers by themselves.

In studying their audiograms, we found both of them to have a striking loss of hearing in the higher frequencies only. The lower frequencies—ordinary sounds of the environment and deeper sounds—were heard with fair accuracy and yet when it came to the high frequencies, to the pitches of notes which are necessary for the differentiation, e. g., of s, th, f, etc., these children could not hear them and consequently they could not reproduce them.

Finding two youngsters in the same family with the same speech defect, the question immediately arose as to whether or not the younger one was copying the older one. However, when we finally had their completed audiograms, we found that both had approximately a similar defect. One had a 28 percent loss within the speech range and the other a 32 percent loss in the same range. We immediately suspected a family difficulty and so we brought the father and mother in to have their hearing also tested by the audiometer. The mother's hearing was absolutely normal at all frequencies. The father rather pooh-poohed the test and said, "I was in the aviation service overseas in the War and I had my ears extensively tested before I was admitted. There can't be anything wrong with my ears." Each of his ears had been tested largely for the functioning of the semicircular canal rather than from the auditory acuity standpoint and he had never had a selective audiogram of this nature. When we finished his audiogram we found that he had a high-frequency deafness almost exactly like that of his two daughters, except that his was further up in the range of frequencies and had not affected the speech range. His difficulty began at the pitch of 2048 double vibrations per second and from there on up he was partially deaf, whereas with his daughters that same gap occurred lower down the scale so that they missed many sounds spoken to them which were important in understanding spoken words and in reproducing them.

Instead of the term high frequency we would rather substitute the term regional deafness as a deafness within a certain region of the hearing spectrum. This type of partial deafness or regional deafness does not, as a rule, influence very strikingly the understanding of the spoken word. A child gets enough of the skeleton of the word to attach a meaning to it, and hence the defect does not interfere with the general intellectual development.

There is, however, another type of deafness which I think is very meaningful indeed from the standpoint of the development of the intelligence and that is congenital word deafness, a condition which leads us immediately into deep and pretty largely uncharted waters. We do not really know very much about the story. It is a novel research field and yet a field in which there appears to be so much promise that it seems more than worth while to study it very intensively.

The concept is drawn largely from cases of individuals who have formerly known how to talk and then because of injury or damage to the brain by reason of a hemorhage or growth of a tumor have lost the capacity to understand the spoken word. There are very few cases in adult life that are entirely pure. There is generally a good deal more lost than the understanding of the spoken word. In certain cases, it can be shown that these people who have had the ability to understand what is said to them still have entirely normal hearing and still have a normal capacity to understand sounds other than speech. There is no loss of hearing; they are not deaf. There is no loss of the second level function of the hearing capacity. They still know the difference between the telephone bell and the dinner bell; they still know sounds apart and know the meaning of those sounds accurately and with entire ease and skill, but the meaning of the intricate series of sounds which constitute the spoken word is gone from their minds.

That is an exact parallel to the situation which we see in the visual sphere in the reading cases where an adult has lost his reading skill. It is an exact parallel to the situation we see as developmental alexia or congenital word blindness in the developing child, a youngster who has normal vision but cannot learn to understand the printed word.

Carrying that same concept over from this double source, that is, from the ideas derived from adult cases with an acquired word deafness, and from comparison with children who have a congenital word blindness, we anticipated that we would find a considerable number of children whose difficulty was due to congenital word deafness, i.e., to an inability to recall the previous exposures to word sounds with sufficient accuracy so that they could recognize them again when they heard them. If recognition does not come and the handle for various concepts is lacking, the word does not come and intelligence is going to lag. This concept of word deafness is not new and yet we do not know how many cases there are. There have been cases recorded in the literature for a great many years past, but very sparsely, and it has generally been looked upon as an exceedingly rare condition. As a matter of fact, from our own studies, I believe there are a great many more cases than we have yet recognized and the reason they have been looked upon as so rare is because the majority of cases with this difficulty have been allotted to one of two other groups. They have been looked upon either as fundamentally defective, and hence not developing their language function, or as deaf and have drifted into deaf and dumb asylums. It may be that many of those to be found in deaf and dumb asylums are cases of congenital word deafness.

When it comes to a selection, to a diagnosis as to whether in a given child we are dealing with a total intellectual defect or with an expression of this special language delay or congenital word deafness, I must confess that we are quite at a loss. We have, as yet, no accurate diagnostic criteria by which we can say whether we are dealing with a specific language delay or with a general intellectual retardation. Our best approach to that, I believe, is in the matter of retraining. When we come to study other developmental delays in language and in the learning of motor skills, as in the developmental alexia or congenital word blindness and in the apraxia of childhood, we find that the best approach and the one which yields the best return for teaching efforts is to find the smallest possible unit which the child can handle and begin a gradual reconstruction of the sequences or series of the smaller units; e.g., in the reading disability cases, we frequently have to go back to a simple phonetic structure, teaching the phonetics of every single letter of the alphabet and then gradually blending these in sequences.

We have a twenty-five-year-old carpenter who has never learned to read beyond second grade skill, yet even in these days of depression he has a job and has three men working under him, so that one must say that there is some intelligence and some manual skill available in that man's mind, yet his reading has never gone beyond second grade. It is marvelous to note the rate at which the man is taking hold of the learning of reading by a simple reduction to the smallest roots, not throwing the whole word at him at once, but rather a synthetic building up of words from their phonetic units. It took only one session to give him the rule for the final *e*, to show him how it affects a preceding vowel sound.

When we stop to think of the latent possibilities in teaching the reading cases, it may be worth while to carry that same concept over into the field of teaching speech cases delayed in the understanding of words and consequently drifting gradually toward a defect by deprivation and becoming obviously feeble-minded. In selective cases of this sort, I think an effort to teach language by reducing it to the simplest possible forms, to the simplest possible phonetic units, and gradually building up the capacity to remember and reproduce sequences of articulatory sounds is, without much question, the most profitable attack on the whole problem.

I do not know where we are going with all these studies, but we have seen some cases in which we feel there was a great deal to be gained by teaching language on the oral or spoken side in that general way. The limitation of the understanding of the spoken word, obviously, will have a direct and immediate effect on intelligence, since without the word, without the handle for the concept, the concept itself will not be planted and the youngster will not have the intellectual material either to work with inside or to communicate with others on the outside. The reading disability cases where there is no difficulty in spoken language are seriously handicapped academically but not intellectually. Some youngsters who would never learn to read without very special teaching have very high intelligence quotients. We have seen reading disability cases who have spent three years in school with no progress whatsoever in being able to read or write, with intelligence quotients of 135, 140 and 145. I think that a latent intelligence may coexist with a comparable difficulty in understanding the spoken word of such a degree that it will make the child appear to be defective. I have a feeling that it will be more than worth while as we go forward to undertake constructive and selective training to see whether we cannot, by encouraging the language function, develop an intelligence which might otherwise remain latent.

VISUAL FUNCTIONS IN STREPHOSYMBOLIA

◆   ◆   ◆

Children who make little or no progress in learning to read during their first two or three years in school quite naturally are often referred to the ophthalmologist, and some of them undoubtedly need corrective lenses. However, many, if not the majority, of them have adequate vision and in reality present neurologic problems. One owes a considerable debt to two English ophthalmologists—Morgan, who described the first case of congenital word blindness in 1896, and Hinshelwood, who published a small monograph on this subject in 1917. In his report Hinshelwood included several cases of acquired word blindness, as well as a group of the congenital type, and emphasized the striking parallelism between them; because of this likeness, he ascribed the occurrence of the syndrome in children to a failure of development of the cerebral cortex in the neighborhood of the angular gyrus.

In 1925 I studied several cases of delay in learning to read and was struck by the inability of the children to differentiate *b* and *d* and *p* and *q* and their tendency to read many words from right to left, instead of in the usual direction, which led to uncertainty in their distinguishing such words as *was* and *saw* and *on* and *no*. I found, also, that some of them showed an unexpected facility in reading mirrored print and that some also had a native skill in producing mirror writing. To account for these observations and to bring the whole syndrome into better consonance with advancing neurologic views concerning cerebral localization, I offered the theory that the condition in these cases was not the result of a pathologic factor, such as Hinshelwood's cortical

Read at a meeting of the New York Academy of Medicine, Section of Ophthalmology, on Feb. 15, 1943.

The Rockefeller Foundation is furnishing aid for the research program on which this work is in part based.

Reprinted from the Archives of Ophthalmology, December, 1943, Vol. 30, pp. 707–713

agenesis, but a physiologic deviation due to failure of aquisition of the normal adult pattern of complete dominance of one hemisphere of the brain.

In cases of loss of acquired visual functions, three distinct steps or levels of elaboration in the brain can be recognized. The first permits only the seeing of objects of the environment but does not tell the meaning of the things seen; the second adds the meaning of objects, maps, pictures, etc., but it requires a third step, or relay, to permit the reading of words. These three steps are recognized by neurologists in the three clinical syndromes of cortical blindness, mind blindness, and word blindness. It is generally believed that it is only at the third level that the principle of unilateral dominance applies, and there are reasons for believing that at this level the records, or engrams, in the two hemispheres of the brain are opposite in sign, or antitropic, to each other and that one engram must be elided to prevent confusion. This elision of the engram of the nondominant hemisphere seems to occur only at the third, or mnemonic level, since only here does a unilateral lesion completely destroy function, as can be seen in cases of acquired alexia. Learning to read, therefore, according to this envisagement, entails the elision of one of the two antitropic records, or engrams, and faulty or incomplete elision would result in uncertainty in mnemonic recall of orientation and progression, such as is seen in children with congenital word blindness.

It should be remembered that these reversals of form and direction are to be seen best during the first few years of learning to read, and that after continued exposure they largely disappear, although frequently in an older child the tendency to reverse can be demonstrated by using unfamiliar letter combinations, such as nonsense syllables. The confused memory patterns which interfere with recognition in reading are also to be seen in the same children when they attempt to spell, and reversals in spelling persist after the child has learned to read. The most striking evidence of antitropism comes from some persons with special writing disability in whom skill in mirror writing lies dormant and unsuspected. One of my patients who could not learn to write legibly in the common, or dextrad, direction could produce creditable mirrored script with the first attempt at sinistrad progression.

This physiologic theory offers a much more favorable prognosis than did its predecessor, and the work of my associates and myself in retraining, as well as extended observations during the last eighteen years, has, I believe, substantiated it. As descriptive of this syndrome in cases of reading and spelling disability I offered the term strephosymbolia, or twisted symbols, as being less misleading, especially

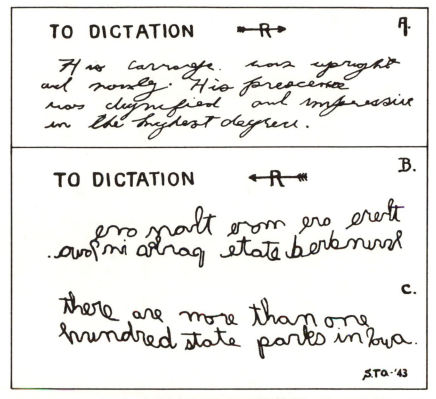

Fig. 1. *A,* tracing of the handwriting of an eleven-year-old girl, written to dictation with her right hand; *B,* a tracing of her mirror writing, also made with her right hand, after only two or three trials of this procedure, and *C,* a tracing of *B* reversed by printing through the back of a negative, so that the product can be more readily compared with *A.*

to the layman, than the older term congenital word blindness. To the neurologist the term word blindness means a loss or lack of the ability to recognize words although vision may be intact, but to the layman the term infers an inability to see. Moreover, I believe this disorder is hereditary rather than congenital, and I much prefer to call it developmental than either congenital or hereditary.

One of the visual functions which is often discussed in connection with reading is that of eyedness. There is a common misconception that the eye selected for sighting, the master eye, is the eye with the better vision. This is not always true. As an example, one of my patients wore a + 2.00 D. sphere and a + 1.00 D. cylinder for his right eye, while for his left eye a + 1.25 D. sphere and a + 0.50 D. cylinder was prescribed. In spite of the greater errors in his right eye, he used this eye consistently for sighting. The master eye is usually on the same side as the master hand, but cross preferences in either direction are to be found. Sighting is a function of the extrinsic ocular muscles which act to bring the object observed, the pupil, and the fovea centralis into line. These muscles are of the striated, or voluntary, type and are under the control of the motor centers of the brain adjacent to those which control handedness. It is possible that the right or left homonymous parts of the peripheral portion of the retina might have a superior equipment and so determine the eye most apt to be attracted to a distant object and thus fix the eyedness in early infancy before binocular fusion has begun. However, the frequency with which left-eyedness and ambiocularity occurs in families in which there is also a preference for the left hand in some members leads me to the belief that eyedness is dependent on hereditary factors which govern the choice. It must be noted, however, that the many crossed patterns of eyedness and handedness would imply separate hereditary factors for the areas of the brain which control the eyes and those which control the arm.

The handedness pattern is open to much greater environmental influence than is eyedness, although there is evidence that the native eyedness pattern can be shifted also. Shooting a rifle was the factor in one such case, and my colleagues and I have observed children in whom a spontaneous shift from the left to the right eye has been noted in repeated examinations over a period of years. Some left-eyed persons can aim a rifle with the right eye only if the left eye is closed or covered, while right-eyed persons usually learn to disregard the image in the left, or nondominant, eye and can aim a rifle with both eyes open. In the case of a shotgun the situation is different, since without sights on the gun it may be aimed with the left eye. A priori, one might think that in aiming at a distance this would be a negligible factor, but that it does influence the accuracy of aim is recognized by gunsmiths who build special stocks with a slight offset for those who shoot from the right shoulder but aim with the left eye. Accuracy in the use of a shotgun is said to be much improved by this procedure, and the same principle may apply in certain types of machine guns.

Some of the simpler tests of eyedness are not entirely trustworthy when used alone, and as a consequence my associates and I make use of a battery of tests to determine eyedness. In this connection it is interesting to note that the manoptoscope devised by Parsons, in our experience frequently gives results out of harmony with those of other tests. Parsons used this instrument in his examinations on which he based his conclusion that left-eyedness is evidence that a given child was originally intended to be left-handed and, further, that eyedness determines which side of the brain shall be the dominant one. He held that when left-eyedness is found in a right-handed person it is evidence that training has influenced the handedness pattern and that the right-handed pattern is implanted in many naturally left-sided children because the right hand is used habitually by so large a proportion of both mothers and teachers. However, we have seen a number of left-handed children who are right-eyed, whereas training right-handed children to use the left hand, either purposively or accidentally, is rare. Many persons, moreover, are neither definitively right-eyed nor left-eyed, and may be termed ambiocular.

In 102 patients with reading disabilities whose records I have recently reviewed, the following distribution of eyedness patterns was found: right-eyedness, 40 patients; left-eyedness, 37 patients, and ambiocularity, 25 patients.

The left-eyed and the ambiocular persons together numbered 62, as against 40 who were right-eyed, obviously a much higher proportion than one would expect in the population at large. Of the 40 patients who were right-eyed, 12 were either left-handed or had mixed right-handed and left-handed habits. Of the 37 who were left-eyed, only 5 were left-handed, but 17 showed a mixture of handedness patterns or gave a history of having been shifted to right-handedness in childhood. Of the whole group of 102, 69 showed a crossed or mixed pattern of handedness and eyedness, and 83 gave a family history of left handedness or of language disorders.

My interpretation of these results is that left-eyedness is not the cause of the reading disability but rather indicates that there is present in these persons a tendency toward use of the right hemisphere of the brain, i. e., left-sidedness. This tendency may or may not involve those parts of the brain which are of primary importance in reading. The symptoms seen in the left-eyed and in the ambiocular patients do not differ from those seen in the right-eyed persons, and while covering the eye might lead to a change in eyedness, one would not expect any influence on the higher centers of the brain which are involved in strephosymbolia. Each macula is connected with both calcarine areas, and Sherrington's flicker experiments demonstrated that functionally the two eyes are interchangeable; it would seem therefore to make no difference which eye is used for sighting, since the image from either eye is probably relayed to the higher centers on both sides.

A second group of visual functions which is to be considered in connection with the reading disability includes the various refractive errors. There is no question that serious refractive disorders will interfere with reading, but many persons with minor degrees of myopia, hyperopia, and astigmatism learn to read easily. Moreover, many persons with reading disability have normal refraction. When more serious errors are present, not only does their correction with appropriate lenses fail to enable the child with strephosymbolia to read without special instruction, but even while he is wearing such lenses such a child exhibits the same errors of orientation and progression as do other children with strephosymbolia. This is, I believe, what one would expect on theoretic grounds. I have already mentioned the tendency to reversals in the mnemonic recall of previous exposures to the word, which must be used in order that it be recognized when it is presented again. This point is often difficult for the layman to grasp, since recognition of a word at sight seems to be simultaneous with seeing it. This, of course, is because the transmission of nerve impulses from the arrival platform to the region of the angular gyrus is too rapid to be registered in consciousness. The existence of a special zone of the cortex of primary importance in the function of word recognition is, however, clearly demonstrated in cases of acquired alexia, in which selective loss of the ability to read occurs without loss of the ability to see or of the capacity to recognize objects, diagrams, maps, etc. These last functions are sometimes disturbed in cases of large occipital lesions which have involved the rest of the occipital coretx of both hemispheres, and acquired alexia is rarely, if ever, pure. A homonymous hemianopsia is frequent, but acquired hemianopsia can occur without alexia, and alexia is combined with it only when it involves the master hemisphere and when the lesion extends far enough forward to cut both the homolateral path from the calcarine cortex to the region of the angular gyrus and the heterolateral path from the opposite calcarine cortex by way of the corpus callosum (subcortical word blindness of Dejerine). This, again, demonstrates the adequacy of one hemisphere, since a lesion which cuts only the homolateral pathway does not cause alexia even though it is in the master hemisphere. While hemianopsia is the most common complicating picture, other symptoms, such as agraphia and varying degrees of aphasia, are also often found; indeed, in the acquired case pure alexia is so rare that some neurologists have questioned its occurrence. Persons with strephosymbolia, on the other hand, often show the alexia syndrome in exquisite purity. Handwriting may or may not be affected, and when it is not, an illuminative demonstration of the mnemonic character of the disturbance and the adequacy of vision can be made by comparing the child's ability to copy accurately with the errors he makes in attempts to read or to write to dictation. In both these processes he calls on his visual memory, and in both he makes the typical errors of reversal. It is difficult to see how reading *was* for *saw*, *ratshin* for *tarnish* or *astrep* for *repast*, or how writing *ti* for *it* or *stpo* for *stop* could result from any refractive error.

The foregoing comments may, I think, be applied equally well to the heterophorias.

In a case in my experience, the diagnosis of hyperphoria was made at about the same time that I first saw the boy, when he was eleven years of age, but his family did not follow the ophthalmologist's advice and neither glasses nor treatment was provided. The boy had been in school most of the five preceding years, and while he did not have a very good basic equipment, he nevertheless had a mental age of 9 years when he was first seen and should have been able to read at the third or fourth grade level. He manifested, however, definite strephosymbolia, and his reading and spelling abilities were below the first grade norms. An intensive course of phonic retraining was instituted; after two and a half years of this treatment he had gained about a fifth grade skill in silent reading, and his oral reading and spelling were at about the fourth grade level. At this time he was seen by Dr. Conrad Berens, who found exophoria of 8 prism diopters and right hyperphoria of 1 prism diopter at 25 cm. The gain in reading previously recorded had, however, taken place before treatment for his heterophoria was begun.

In another case, that of a boy seen recently in Philadelphia, a diagnosis of exophoria was made, and sight reading methods were recommended, with definite prohibition of the phonic training which has been found so serviceable in retraining persons with strephosymbolia. This boy's father and paternal grandfather were left-handed, and his mother had been a poor student, although we were unable to determine whether or not this had been due to a reading disability. The boy himself definitely favored his right hand in almost all activities but was left-footed and left-eyed. He was twelve years old and had been in school the usual period of years. Psychometric examinations by a battery of tests gave mental age ratings varying all the way from 9 years 7 months to 13 years 2 months. Even at the lowest of these ratings, he should have been able to read at third or fourth grade levels, but his reading achievement was that of a very low first grade level. He copied a second grade paragraph without errors, but he misread *left* as *felt*, *was* as *saw*, *on* as *no*, *nip* as *pen* and *ton* as *not*. In attempting to spell to dictation a column of simple words, he wrote *ol* for *low*, *sa* for *ask*, *egt* for *get*, *bolg* for *belong* and *awy* for *way*. When he was asked to read a simple paragraph printed in mirrored type, he accomplished this almost as rapidly as he read the ordinary print, whereas a boy of his age who had gained normal reading skills would require at least ten times as long for the mirrored passage. At the time of these examinations he was wearing the glasses prescribed for him by the ophthalmologist who advised the sight reading teaching and interdicted the phonic training. I believe that with continuance of that proceeding the boy's directional confusion will persist and that he can be taught to maintain consistent dextrad progression only by phonic training and dextrad analysis and synthesis of words from their phonic equivalents.

I am not personally familiar with the aniseikonic disturbances, but I understand from others that patients with such disorders are by no means all nonreaders, nor do the nonreaders all show that disorder (Imus, Rothaey, and Bear 1938).

Much attention has been paid to vacillating movements of the eyes, and while bad habits in this regard might easily interfere with easy and fluent reading, it is also obvious that such a boy as the one last mentioned would scan a word from either direction in his confusion as to which way it should be read and would therefore exhibit back and forth movements of the eyes as the result of his uncertainty as to direction. Moreover, such vacillating movements would scarcely account for the confusion such children show between single letters, such as *b* and *d* and *p* and *q*, or for the facility in reading mirrored print, in which constant sinistrad progress rather than alternating ocular movements is required.

Finally, the data we have assembled from the study of left handedness and of various language difficulties in the family stock of children who have a specific disability in learning to read and show the strephosymbolia syndrome give what to me is convincing evidence that such children represent intergrades between right-sided and left-sided familial tendencies and that the reading disability follows fairly definite hereditary trends. In this connection it is interesting to note that the reading disability and other language disorders are much more frequent in boys than in girls. In the current sample of 102 patients, 84 were boys and 18 girls. About the same distribution occurs for stuttering. In families with this disturbance there are also more than the expected number of left-handed members and persons with delayed speech, stuttering, reading, writing and spelling disabilities, and abnormal clumsiness (developmental apraxia). In the childhood histories of children who come to attention as presenting reading and spelling problems we not infrequently find indications of developmental deviations in their acquisition of speech and motor patterns which bear out the belief expressed herein that the strephosymbolia syndrome can best be explained on the basis of confused cerebral dominance rather than of abnormal vision.

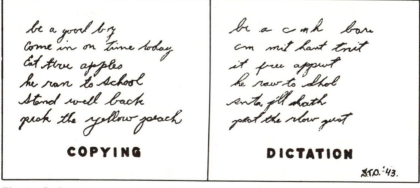

COPYING   **DICTATION**

Fig. 2. Carbon paper tracing of the writing of a twenty-one-year-old patient with strephosymbolia, showing the contrast between copying and writing to dictation (see *Addendum*).

Addendum.—After this paper was presented at the meeting of the academy, but before it was completed for publication, I studied the case of a man aged 21 with the strephosymbolia syndrome who, in spite of having "served time" through eight grades of the public schools in New York state, had acquired less than first grade reading skill. Figure 2 shows (1) his ability to copy from print into script, demonstrating that there was no agraphia, and (2) his floundering efforts to write from dictation. This contrast demonstrates clearly that the confusion lies in the mnemonic recall and not in visual distortions. This patient is now being given remedial instruction, and his eyes are being studied by Dr. Conrad Berens. A complete report of this case, together with the results of the remedial work and of Dr. Beren's study, will be published later.

Some Disorders in the Language
Development of Children

◆   ◆   ◆

The production of the spoken language which, of course, is about the first evidence of language development in children is so simple that it seems almost automatic. Speech seems to come to the child without instruction but if you will think a moment, you will appreciate that everything which a child learns in the way of language is taught to him. We do see idioglossia, as Dr. Robbins pointed out, particularly in cases of twins who often develop a language of their own, having no meaning to others but fully understood between themselves. On the whole, however, the language that the child first speaks is that which he has learned from his mother or his nurse. He is being instructed constantly through what he hears. The development of his speech is a learning process and one that is approachable from the standpoint of teaching. There has been too little emphasis placed on the teaching of the spoken word in the preschools and kindergartens. Much stress has been placed on various activities but little on purposive language development. The fact that speech appears so early in the average child chronologically is probably related to the race development. We have quite good evidence from fossil man that man has had brain capacities adequate for speech, and therefore possibly some kind of verbal communication with others, for approximately five hundred thousand years. On the other hand, our reading dates back scarcely five thousand years. Even in that time it was available to only a few priests and others of the educated group. Reading as a general function for human beings is very recent indeed and, even today, is far from universal even in the most civilized parts of the world.

Deviations in the development of the spoken word are to be expected. We find no consistent development which we can call normal for all children and deviations may express themselves in a number of

Reprinted from Proceedings of Child Research Clinic Conference, The Woods Schools, May, 1946

ways. We may see delay, in various degrees, in the onset of speech but in some such cases, when it does come it is quite normal. We may see defects of articulation, defects of grammatical construction, defects in vocabulary and so on—all of these are evidence of some difficulty in the acquisition of language or, in other words, they are developmental difficulties. I think in the past they were wrongly called "congenital" or "hereditary" defects, although strong hereditary factors can be seen operating in certain families.

The language function at large, however, includes not only the understanding and the reproduction of the spoken word, which may be called sensory and motor speech, but also reading and writing which are respectively the sensory and motor components of graphic language—printed or written language, if you wish—and finally, there is a third form of communication of ideas, i.e., sign language. You might hesitate about accepting the sign language but when you think of what talking is to the deaf and dumb, you see it is a very serviceable method of communication. It is one way of telling another person what one feels and is thinking about, and that, of course, is the fundamental basis of all language. It is a choice of the substitute—be it the printed word or the spoken word or gestures—for an object or a feeling in order to communicate what is going on in one individual's mind to that of another, so I like to include sign language for the sake of scientific completeness.

In practice, however, we find that the two important functions of language are the spoken and the graphic. Personally, I have spent much time on the visual language and feel that I know it better. For many years, I served an apprenticeship in the autopsy room, studying brain lesions and associating them with speech disturbances which had previously been observed in the patients on the hospital wards. Then, some twenty years ago when I was starting mental hygiene clinics for children in one of the middle-western states, I became very much interested in some youngsters who were having trouble in learning to read—trouble out of all proportion to their general intelligence and to their age and to their school training—and I have been particularly interested in this problem ever since. From my studies of these children, I feel that we can exclude the field of organic defects of the brain such as those so well discussed by Dr. Robbins and Dr. Phelps. We can assume that many of these reading cases develop on the basis of a strictly functional disorder. I cannot go into the details of that here but there are good neurological reasons for making such a statement. The functional explanation I have offered is that of a faulty establishment of dominance in the reading centers of the brain. Let me stress that: *reading* centers of the brain. I emphasize that here because many of these children are quite bright with good I.Q's before they enter school. They learn quickly, have a good vocabularly, good auditory understanding, and good speech.

Such a youngster, for example, after three years in a well-known private school was reading nothing although he obtained an I.Q. of 142 on standard tests. Now there is something odd if a boy with an I.Q. of 142 cannot learn the very simple process of reading. This boy had mastered his arithmetic. He knew the arithmetical combinations and had learned the numerals, but he could not be sure of his words. Among his troubles were the constant reversals and twists in the order of letters to which I have called attention in many of these cases and from which is derived the term strephosymbolia as a descriptive word. This youngster was given some remedial work after school by an especially trained tutor. The school, in this instance, was rather resentful of anything being done outside of their classrooms but the parents insisted upon having the retraining undertaken. It was carried on at home and the school knew nothing as to what was being done for the boy. However, at the end of the school year they wrote a very self-congratulatory letter to the parents as to the improvement in the boy and the success of the school's training. That youngster has gone on with little academic trouble. He is a college graduate now and has held a commission in the armed services. We have seen a similarly successful outcome in many of our reading cases during the past twenty years.

The process of reading in the adult is controlled or initiated or overseen, if you prefer, largely, if not entirely, from one hemisphere in the brain. In other words, only one hemisphere functions in the process of reading or writing. We do not know why this should be but it is true and can be observed where fractions of the language function are damaged by a stroke or other injury to the brain. In these cases any injury to the dominant half of the brain will result in extensive damage to the language function, while injury in exactly the same locus in the brain but in the opposite side or nondominant hemisphere will give no specific language symptoms whatsoever. In right-handed people, the left hemisphere of the brain is almost always the dominant one and vice versa. Whether or not our theory is right, I do not know, but I do know that the methods of retraining which we have derived from that viewpoint have worked. I do not claim them to be a panacea for reading troubles of all sorts but I do feel that we understand the blockade which occurs so frequently in children with good minds and which results in the characteristic reading disability of the strephosymbolic type of childhood.

Studies of the language function in the adult show, however, that it is not only reading which may be damaged by a unilateral brain lesion. Loss of the spoken word, motor and sensory aphasia, is much more common and that gives us evidence that the same principle is at work in speech as we have found in reading. Therefore we forecast quite early in our studies that speech disorders in children would be found comparable to these two types of language losses in adults. Subsequent studies have shown this probably to be true. There appears to be a marked difference in children with delayed or defective speech according to whether their understanding of the spoken word of others is or is not impaired. In some speech cases the understanding of the speech of others seems to develop nearly or entirely as well as in the average child. These are the children whom we have classified as motor speech delay cases. They are the youngsters who come nearest to warranting the advice so often given to parents to "Let him alone— he'll outgrow it." I cannot completely subscribe to this advice for although spontaneous improvement often occurs, it is much more rapid and more complete, in our experience, under expert guidance by a trained teacher. In general, however, the outlook for recovery in this type of case is quite good.

There is another group of children with speech difficulties for whom the prognosis is less favorable with our present limited knowledge of training procedures. These are similar to the sensory aphasia cases among adults in that they fail to understand much of what is said to them. They are sometimes called word deaf children. These children are not deaf in the ordinary sense of the word. It is often possible to demonstrate that they can hear everything in their environment and that they respond naturally and normally to sounds other than speech. In other words, they recognize the telephone bell and the door bell and can differentiate between them. Although their reactions show that they are receiving these sounds and interpreting them correctly, they do not understand words that are spoken to them. This is a difficult concept to grasp until you know something about the intricacy of the understanding of language within the brain. There must be at least three processes at work; first, the hearing itself; second, the understanding of the sound, and third, the understanding of the meaning of the word. The situation in the auditory field is much like that which we find in the visual functions of the children with the reading disability or, as it is sometimes called, developmental word blindness. These children show no consistent visual disorder other than the lack of a quick recognition of the printed word. They see well and often make good use of visual memories of objects and even of pictures and maps. It is only in the more complex function of word recognition from print that any obstacle is encountered. There is likewise no evidence of any peculiarity in the way in which they see things; they do not see backwards or in mirrored fashion. They often show superior visual-motor coordinations in games and in various manual skills. We have many times asked for complete eye examinations by the best trained ophthalmologists. Their reports have indicated that there was nothing wrong whatsoever with the vision of the patient.

Two such cases come to my mind. They presented such a severe degree of reading disability that we had them studied carefully from every angle to be sure that we had left no stone unturned. One was a young man of twenty-two with an I.Q. of 100 who had spent ten years in the public schools in New York State and was still completely illiterate. We have also recently seen a twenty-one-year-old veteran who had been graduated from the eighth grade in a parochial school in Cincinnati, Ohio, through his ability to learn by ear, but who was unable to read or write a single word except his own name. He also had an average I.Q. In both cases we had the eyes carefully examined and the reports were entirely negative. I think there is a demonstrable type of reading disability which has no relation to vision but which is essentially a matter of the recall of previous visual impressions.

This is a point which may bear some elaboration for in the adult who is alexic, i.e., who has lost his reading as the result of a stroke or other brain injury, there is often no loss of vision. He is frequently as good as ever in interpreting pictures and visual materials of various kinds but he cannot get any meaning from looking at a printed word. It is astounding to see a man look at *c-a-t* and shake his head and say, "I don't know what it means." Sometimes he will read off the letters one by one and then say, "That means *cat*," but as a group of letters it had no meaning at all to him; yet that same person could see perfectly and had no visual trouble. He was able to make use of what we call neurologically the first and the second levels of vision. He was able to see and to make use of maps and pictures and diagrams but he could not read a simple printed word. In other words, only the third or word level of vision showed an interruption of function. Similarly in the developmental word-blind and word-deaf cases of language disturbances in children, I believe that there is a functional difficulty, acting selectively at the third or word level, in the visual or auditory areas of their brains.

I am afraid that my topic has made it necessary for me to introduce a number of things that are difficult to understand. However, I believe that in these twenty years we have gained a good insight into the background of the specific reading disability and know a good deal about the training of the strephosymbolic cases. The work in developmental word deafness (sometimes called, wrongly I think, congenital sensory aphasia) is not so advanced but it has given us promise and considerable hope for the future. I am hopeful that in many of these cases which, if uncorrected, would go on to become feeble-minded by defect, we will be able to bring about marked improvement if we are clever enough to devise the proper methods of teaching them.

Another of our early forecasts was that certain children would have great difficulty in acquiring motor skills although they were not spastics or suffering from motor disabilities in the ordinary understanding of the term. This anticipation was based on the study of adults in whom a one-sided brain lesion will not infrequently wipe out an earlier acquired skill of some kind, producing the condition known as apraxia. As an example, a person accustomed to write on the typewriter so extensively that the matter of finding the keys was entirely automatic, had, following a very minor brain lesion with only a suggestion of paralysis, a complete loss of her ability to typewrite. She could no longer remember the position of the letters on the keyboard and had to go back to the simple hunt and peck system of beginners.

Our studies of similar developmental apraxic conditions in children have been very fragmentary. It is a field that is still uncultivated and still open to research, but such as they have been, they seem to have led us to the recognition of a sensory and a motor type of apraxia. With the sensory type, the child does not apparently understand the motions he wants to make and with the motor type he knows what he wants to do but cannot carry out his idea. Perhaps the best description of this condition in children is clumsiness. I wonder whether the awkwardness referred to by some observers as double left-handedness might not be better explained on this basis. In any case, we have found that by special training methods much can be done to help such children. They are constantly under a tremendous handicap because they cannot compete successfully in any sort of athletics, but often they can be taught to do one thing pretty well. In the case of one boy of this type, the athletic master of his school came to me for instructions. I suggested that he pick out one activity which none of the other boys could do well and try to train the boy so that he could excel in that. He chose quoits and after teaching the boy how to pitch horseshoes successfully he turned him loose among his schoolmates. His success in this one skill was a great lift to his morale. In such cases, training which we have found most promising is based upon the analysis of the more complex activity into the simplest component units. For example, in baseball, you cannot teach a boy how to pitch until you teach him how to stand properly, how to balance his weight, how to get his arm back for a long swing, etc. By separating the patterns which you wish to teach him into units, working on each one separately, and finally putting them together in a given sequence, I feel that much may be accomplished for these youngsters. Although it is too soon to make positive statements on the basis of completed studies, the viewpoint that many of these difficulties may be due to a failure in the establishment of dominance gives us at least reason to hope that we can work out successful methods of treatment.

The only general process which seems to relate to all three of these developmental difficulties of childhood—the reading and the speech disabilities and the apraxias—is that of sequence building. In reading, the individual must recall the exact sequence and order in which the letters of the word occur in space. In the spoken language, he must recall the exact sequence and order in time in which the sounds occur in a word so that he can understand it and reconstruct it. In the speech errors of many of these children there is a confusion in the order of the sounds which belong in the word. For example, one small boy told me that he lived on *Driverside River* in New York. Similarly, the apraxic cases often have no trouble in learning the simpler units of a motor skill but they have great difficulty in putting them together in sequences. It seems to me quite probable that this problem of remembering and reproducing sequences in their proper order in space and in time is associated with the problem of cerebral dominance.

SOME STUDIES IN THE READING DISABILITY

◆　　　◆　　　◆

In any review of the evolution of the nervous system it is evident that there are several places in which there has been a distinct leap forward by the introduction of a decidedly new pattern of organization of nerve tissues without however discarding the older patterns. The most recent such evolutionary saltation is that which is accomplished in the vertebrates by the establishment of the dorsal Chord of nervous tissues which form the central nervous system. From this point onward there is no such total revision of the building plan but rather a progressive growth and increase in importance of the head end of the dorsal Chord structures. It is interesting to note that there is no major change in architecture to differentiate man's most important organ, his brain, from that of his nearest animal competitors, the great apes. The differences to be found here are, first, an enormous overall increase in size of the brain and, second, a relative increase in size of certain areas which are represented in the chimpanzee's brain, for example, by only a relatively small space, but which in man's brain are so expanded as to cover the larger part of the lateral surface of that organ.

The great overall enlargement of the brain would of course increase tremendously its functional capacities merely by the provision of so many more brain cells and so many more interconnecting fibre systems, but the differential growth of the lateral areas also suggests the possibility that new functions might arise there. These areas are described by the anatomists as the great association zones and there is added interest to be gained when we observe that damage or destruction in specific parts of these zones has been related to losses in functions which are exclusively human—communication by speech and by graphic means and great manual dexterity.

The animals have developed means of communicating their emotional status to others of their kind and to their enemies by means of

An unpublished address by Samuel T. Orton, M.D., presented at the Medical Convocation of the University of Pennsylvania, June 18th, 1945, upon receiving the Honorary Degree of Doctor of Science.

vocal processes and bodily postures—thus the snarl and bared teeth of an angry dog or the bay of a trailing hound are distinctly indicative of their reactions of the moment—but it is man alone who has learned to use a fixed sequence of sounds as a symbol or substitute for an object or an action, to use graven or written symbols to replace the spoken words as in the phonetic languages or to indicate an idea as in the Chinese written language, and finally, to develop manual dexterity to the high degree that is represented in the finger movements of the trained typist or the pianist, for example. These three major functions—spoken language, graphic language, and superior skills— are naturally grouped together as the three outstanding abilities which are distinctively human and they are further associated by the fact that the newly expanded cortices of the association zones of the brain play an important part in their integrity. One other fact and a curious one links them and that is that they are all under the exclusive control of one hemisphere of the brain. Thus in these functions not only must injury or disease of the brain affect a given area, but it must lie in the dominant or master half of the brain while an exactly similar injury or disease in the opposite hemisphere will give no symptoms of language disorders or of apraxia, the loss of skilled movements.

This peculiarity of the brain's action is spoken of as unilateral cerebral dominance. No comparable superiority of one half of the brain is found in the animals nor does it affect the older parts of man's brain. Both hemispheres are operative together in seeing and in hearing and each operates independently in touch, and there is no evidence of any greater importance of either side. As yet no adequate explanation of this new principle of operation has been forthcoming although there is room for interesting conjecture. The controlling or master hemisphere of the brain is usually, although not always, on the side opposite to the master hand—thus, in a right-handed person the left brain hemisphere is commonly the important one.

One small area of one of the association zones is known to be very important in reading and a relatively small amount of damage, providing it affects the master half of the brain, will result in complete loss of the ability to recognize a word at sight in a patient, although before the injury, he had been a competent reader. There is no interference with vision as the patient still sees the word but has no idea of its meaning; visual interpretation of objects of the environment and even of pictures, maps, diagrams, etc., may also be intact, and, not infrequently, the individual letters can be named correctly although when in sequence in a word there is no recognition of it as a whole. Occasionally the spelling out of the letters in a word will identify it. It is an illuminating experience to see an educated man completely baffled by the word *cat* until he spells out the three letters *c-a-t* and then exclaims, "Oh, that spells *cat!*" This is the condition known as alexia and for emphasis let us repeat that had the patient's injury involved the half of his brain other than it did he would have experienced no trouble with his reading. Cases of alexia cannot write spontaneously although many of them can copy from print into their own characteristic script, indicating that there has been no interference with the mechanics of writing but only with the recall of the letters of a word in their correct order.

This skeleton outline of the loss of reading skill because of brain damage in the adult is given here because of the rather striking similarity such cases show to the picture presented by some children in learning to read. There is a considerable variability in the ease with which school children acquire reading and there are quite a number who find this accomplishment difficult or well nigh impossible in spite of good general intellectual equipment. Extreme cases of this disability are rare but in lesser degree it forms an obstacle to the easy acquisition of this most important subject which is sufficiently frequent to form a challenge to educators. Our own studies indicate that about ten per cent of the total school population suffer from it enough to retard their reading advancement one full school grade below that to be expected from their age and intelligence. All degrees of severity between a comparatively benign difficulty and an apparently insurmountable handicap have been observed. As an extremely severe case may be cited that of a man of average intelligence and good vision, twenty-one years of age, who had attended public schools in New York State until he was sixteen but nevertheless came out an illiterate, unable to read even first grade material and unable to write anything that would carry meaning to another.

Such marked trouble with learning to read has naturally attracted considerable attention and a number of theories as to its causation have been advanced. Perhaps the most widely accepted medically was that of Hinshelwood, an English ophthalmologist, who called attention to the striking similarity of symptoms between these children who were failing to acquire reading and those adults who had suffered a loss of reading through brain injury affecting the critical locus for this function. On this basis, supported by the fact that occasionally more than one member of a family suffered from the same trouble, Hinshelwood offered the hypothesis that these children suffered from a congenital lack of development in the brain area critical for reading.

Twenty years ago the writer, in the course of an experiment in extending neuropsychiatric service into the community, encountered several children with severe reading disabilities in the school of a county seat town in central Iowa and felt that there were sound neurological reasons for challenging Hinshelwood's hypothesis although his observations were confirmed. Like the alexia cases, these children had adequate vision and made good use of visual material of simpler organization, such as pictures and maps, and could often name the letters of a word correctly, yet they were very deficient in recognizing words at sight in spite of frequent previous exposures. Moreover, copying correctly from print into script was possible even in those whose attempts at spontaneous writing were unintelligible. While certain other considerations seemed to exclude the brain defect hypothesis in these children, the close agreement between the symptoms they exhibited and those of alexia in the adult called for a theory which would include some interference with a physiological pattern common to them both, and this brought the unusual plan of unilateral cerebral dominance, or one-sided brain control, up for consideration, and the thesis was tentatively considered that some factor was causing an interference with establishment of the exclusive one-sided control in reading which had long been demonstrated as the normal adult pattern. This viewpoint—that the trouble might be the result of a functional deviation rather than an anatomical defect—altered the whole outlook and gave immediately added impetus to further careful clinical observations and to experiments in educational retraining with the hope of overcoming the handicap.

When seen during the first few years of their exposure to reading, children with the special disability in this subject show a marked difficulty in differentiating the lower case letter *b* from *d* and *p* from *q* and are often puzzled as to whether *w-a-s* spells *was* or *saw*. Such children also frequently reverse groups of letters or whole syllables not only in their attempts at reading but in their written spelling as well. Some of them find mirror writing comparatively easy and some can read mirrored print almost as well and occasionally even better than they can the ordinary form. In spelling, the same reversals and confusions in sequence of letters are to be seen and when the disability is marked there is evidence of a very faulty linkage between the letters and their appropriate sounds so that the written letters bear little or no relation to the constituent sounds of the word. Bizarre misspellings leading at times to completely unintelligible writing occasionally result. Conversely, the deficient or erroneous linkages between sound and the corresponding printed symbol can frequently be shown to be a factor in producing reading errors. Later observations in cases of isolated writing disability offered further instructive material. Two such adults—both physicians as it happened—who had labored conscientiously and long but unsuccessfully to acquire a facile and legible handwriting in the ordinary or left-to-right direction, were found when first tested and without any practice to be able to write in mirrored characters, proceeding from right to left, and to produce easily thereby a well formed script.

Together these varied observations led to a reconsideration of the possible functions of the inert or nondominant hemisphere. Its capacity for retraining has frequently been the subject of discussion and conjecture in connection with recovery from the symptoms of aphasics who have lost the function of speech through injury or disease in one hemisphere, but apparently very little attention has been paid to what it may be doing in the normally functioning brain. Obviously since the large areas corresponding to the language zones of the dominant hemispheres do not give comparable symptoms when damaged or destroyed, they must be functionally inactive and it is safe to assume therefore that such activity as may be present there is suppressed or deleted since it plays no part in the functions of the corresponding areas of the controlling half. However, such suppression of this activity must be purely a functional phenomenon since structurally the two sides are equivalent and alike except that they are the right and left counterparts of each other. As yet no distinct anatomical superiority of the dominant over the nondominant hemisphere has been demonstrated by autopsy studies and while there may be such differences in the finer structure and almost innumerable interconnections present in the cortex, yet we must acknowledge that the nondominant hemisphere is adequately equipped as far as structure goes to function as a control mechanism were it not for the established habit of action whereby the master hemisphere takes full command. However, its inactivity as a controlling mechanism does not exclude a considerable measure of activity of its own below the control threshold. Thus its connections with the sensory receiving stations are intact and abundant and it seems evident that sensory data such as those furnished to the dominant side are constantly irradiating the nondominant side as well and I believe that we may assume that they are being recorded there although this it not readily demonstrable since such records are not used for responses. There will be one major difference however, and that is that they will all be of opposite sign, that is, right-left counterparts of each other. This will be obvious from the structural relations of the two hemispheres as well as from their connections with the muscles and sensory systems of the body.

From these and other considerations the theory was offered that the special reading disability which serves as a serious handicap to academic advancement in many children may be explained as a failure in complete elision of memory records of the nondominant hemisphere

and as a persistence therefore of two more or less equipotential records, thus explaining both the nature of the early symptoms and the
failure of prompt recognition of words at sight; in other words, a
physiological failure to establish the normal pattern of unilateral cerebral dominance in control of graphic language, reading, spelling, and
writing. To delimit this group of children with failures and delays in
learning to read from those where other factors were operative, the
term strephosymbolia was suggested. Derived from the Greek, this
means twisted symbols and was offered as a descriptive term because
of the reversals and confusions in direction which characterize the
early errors in attempting to read and spell exhibited by this reading
disability group.

These studies have been intensively followed throughout the entire
twenty year period since the initial observations and the results of this
extended program have abundantly demonstrated our earlier belief
that these children with strephosymbolia are not lacking in intelligence,—some indeed have unusually good minds—are retrainable in
reading even after several years' failure in this subject, and that
methods already available are serviceable when properly applied and
conscientiously carried out to correct the disability.

Handedness, the commonly accepted measure of the native laterality of an individual, does not apparently determine the dominant side
of the brain but handedness itself is probably determined by the
brainedness in the majority of individuals. In other words, the superiority of one side of the brain probably leads to greater skill with the
opposite hand and foot and to choice of the opposite eye as the master
or sighting eye, as well as determining the locus of the control centers
for the language functions, but in all of these statements exceptions
must be expected. Handedness is possibly the least trustworthy of
these guides since it is so open to accidental or purposive training in
infancy. By and large however, the laterality of a given individual is
probably governed by hereditary factors but it is abundantly clear that
this is not a simple Mendelian pattern. The geneticists have demonstrated for us that when interbreeding occurs over a considerable
period between stocks carrying antagonistic traits, a certain amount of
mingling of such traits may occur. The inheritance of laterality is far too
complex to be analyzed from our present information. However, our
current belief is that our cases of disordered cerebral dominance may
be tentatively considered to be intergrades between left and right
dominant patterns. Clinical findings of mixtures of handedness, eyedness and footedness, as well as many carefully garnered family histories
have yielded much supportive evidence of this view.

Since the principle of unilateral brain control operates not only in reading and writing but also in the understanding of speech and in speaking and in learning to carry out skillfully many motor acts, our attention has also been directed to certain delays and defects in spoken language and to the abnormal clumsiness of some children, and interesting and instructive observations have been forthcoming here also. This extension of a promising field of study has been only surveyed and an opportunity for much profitable investigation undoubtedly exists here.

One striking yield of the successful remedial program in children who have suffered from any of these special disabilities is the improvement in the personality of the child. This often affects the child's interest, his self-confidence, his attention, and his willingness to work and frequently offers a corrective to misbehavior which arises as a reaction to his academic failures. Thus these studies offer marked promise in the fields of child psychiatry and education as well as in that of brain physiology.

References

Apert, E. (1924). [Title not available.] *Bulletin Médical, 38*(9).

Bachmann, F. (1927). *Ueber kongenitale wortblindheit.* Berlin: S. Karger.

Berkhan, O. (1885). Ueber die störungen der schriftsprache. *Archiv für Psychiatrie und Nervenkrankheiten, 16.*

Brodmann, K. (1909). *Vergleichende localizationslehre.* Leipzig: Johann Ambrosius Barth.

Caetani, G. (1924). Myriad-minded Leonardo da Vinci. *The Scientific Monthly, 19,* 449.

Campbell, A. W. (1905). *The localization of cerebral function.* Cambridge: Cambridge University Press.

Claiborne, J. H.(1917). Stuttering relieved by reversal of manual dexterity with remarks on the subject of symbol amblyopia. *New York Medical Journal, 105,* 577.

Fildes, L. (1923). Some memory experiments with high-grade defectives. *British Journal of Psychology, 12*(3).

Fildes, L. & Myers, C. S. (1921). Left-handedness and the reversal of letters. *British Journal of Psychology, 12*(3).

Golla, F. L. (1921). The objective study of the neuroses. *The Lancet, 2,* 115.

Gordan, H. (1920). [Title not available.] *Brain, 43*(4).

Harman, O. B. (1915). *Kelynack's defective children.* New York: William Wood.

Head, H. (1920). Aphasia: an historical review. *Brain, 43,* 390.

Hinshelwood, J. (1917). *Congenital word blindness.* London: H. K. Lewis.

Huelson, C. (1909). *The roman forum.* Trans. J. B. Carter. New York: G. E. Stecgart.

Imus, H. A., Rothney, J. W. M., & Bear, R. M. (1938). *An evaluation of visual factors in reading.* Hanover: Dartmouth College Publications.

Javal, L. E. (1906). Physiologie de la lecture et l'ecriture. *Anales d'Occustistique, 82,* 242.

Kerr, J. (1896). *The Howard Price essay of the Royal Statistical Society.*

Kussmaul, A. (1881). *Ziemmsens enclopaedia der speciellen pathologie und therapie.* Leipzig: F. C. Vogel.

Lyday, J. F. (1926). The Greene County mental clinic. *Mental Hygiene, 10,* 759.

McCready, E. B. (1926). Defects in the language zone in children. *American Journal of Psychiatry, 18.*

Marie, P. (1922). Existc-t-il dans le cerveau humaine des innés ou préformés du language? *Presse Medicale, 30,* 177.

Monroe, M. (1928). Methods for diagnosis and treatment of cases of reading disability. *Genetic Psychology Monographs 4*(4 & 5).

Morgan, W. P. (1896). A case of congenital word blindness. *British Medical Journal, 2,* 1378.

Nice, M. M. (1918). Ambidexterity and delayed speech development. *Pedagogical Seminary and Journal of Genetic Psychology, 25,* 141.

Orton, S. T. (1925). "Word blindness" in school children. *Archives of Neurology and Psychiatry, 14,* 581–615.

Orton, S. T. (1927). Training the left handed. *Hygeia, 5,* 451.

Orton, S. T. (1928). A physiological theory of the reading disability and stuttering in children. *New England Journal of Medicine, 199*(21).

Orton, S. T. (1929). The neurological basis of elementary education. *Archives of Neurology and Psychiatry, 21,* 641–646.

Orton, S. T. (1930). Familial occurrence of disorders in the acquisition of language. *Eugenics, 3*(4).

Orton, S. T. (1931). Special disabilities in spelling. *Bulletin of the Neurological Institute of New York, 1*(2), 159–192.

Orton, S. T. (1943). The philosophy of psychiatry. In F. J. Sladen (Ed.), *Psychiatry and the War.* Springfield, IL: Charles C. Thomas.

Orton, S. T., & Travis, L. E. (1927–29). Studies in stuttering. *Archives of Neurology and Psychiatry, 18,* 673, 998, 1014; *21,* 386.

Pick, A. (1924). [Title not available.] *Medizinische Klinik, 20,* 20.

Parson, B. S. (1924). *Lefthandedness.* New York: Macmillan.

Sereni, E. (1923). Contributo all 'analisi della scrittua speculare. *Revista de Psicologia i Pedagogia, 19,* 135.

Sherrington, C. S. (1906). *The integrative action of the nervous system.* New Haven: Yale University Press.

Thomas, C. J. (1908). Congenital word-blindness and its treatment. *Public Health.*

Warburg, F. (1911). Ueber die angeborene wortblindheit. *Zeitschrift für Kinderforsch, 4.*

APPENDIX 1

◇————————————————◇

A Glossary of Some Technical Terms as They Are Used in This Volume

ACTION CURRENT—An electric current occurring during action of a nerve or muscle.

AGE—1. *Chronological*—Age in years and months as usually calculated.

2. *Mental*—A rating, expressed in years and months, of the development of the intelligence of an individual as measured by certain standardized tests.

AGENETIC—Defective development—as applied to the brain, a failure in growth of certain parts of the brain.

AGNOSIA—Loss of the power to recognize the import of sensations. The varieties correspond with the several senses and are distinguished as auditory, visual, gustatory, tactile, etc. Visual agnosia is equivalent to mind-blindness, auditory to mind-deafness. *Astereognosis* is a special form of this condition in which there is loss of ability to recognize objects by handling them without seeing them.

AGRAMMATISM—Inability to utter words in their correct sequences; impairment of the power to speak grammatically and syntactically due to brain injury or brain disease.

AGRAPHIA—1. *Acquired*—Loss of a previous ability to write resulting from brain injury or brain disease.

2. *Developmental (Congenital)*—Unusual difficulty in learning to write which is out of harmony with the other intellectual accomplishments and manual skills of the individual.

ALEXIA—1. *Acquired*—Loss of a previous skill in reading which follows disease or damage to certain parts of the brain.

2. *Developmental (Congenital)*—Inability to learn to read with the rapidity and skill which would be expected from the individual's mental age and achievements in other subjects.

AMBILEVOUS—Poor in manual dexterity with both hands; "doubly left-handed." *cf.* Ambidextrous.

AMBIVALENCE (a. Ambivalent)—Having equal power in two contrary directions.

AMNESIA—Loss of memory.

AMPHIOCULARITY (a. Amphiocular)—Using either eye for sighting without consistent preference. *See* Master Eye.

ANGULAR GYRUS—*See* Gyrus.

ANTITROPE (a. Antitropic)—Alike except for opposite orientation, as, for example, a pair of gloves.

APHASIA (a. Aphasic)—1. *Acquired*—A loss in the power of expression by speech, writing or signs or of comprehending spoken or written language, due to injury or disease of the brain centers.

2. *Developmental (Congenital)*—A failure in development of speech or speech understanding which is not the result of deafness or of defect in the peripheral speech mechanism.

APRAXIA (a. Apraxic)—1. *Acquired*—The loss, as a result of injury or disease of parts of the brain, of previously acquired skilled acts, not dependent on paralysis.

2. *Developmental (Congenital)*—A failure in development of normal skills—abnormal clumsiness.

AREA (As applied to the brain—Area may designate an anatomical region of the brain, as when we speak of the frontal area, or it may be restricted to parts of the brain which have a common function as in the term *motor area (q.v.)* or it may be used in describing a part of the brain which has a characteristic microscopic structure such as the *area striata (q.v.)*.

Area, Motor—That part of the brain cortex in which lie the giant nerve cells which are in direct command of voluntary motion and whose destruction results in paralysis of voluntary motion, but without loss of reflex or involuntary movements.

Area Striata—That part of the brain cortex which is characterized by a heavy band of nerve fibers not found elsewhere so strongly developed. The white line formed by these fibers is prominent enough to be seen by the naked eye, and the cortex so marked is the terminus of the nerve paths coming from the eyes and forms an important part of the visual center of the brain.

ARRIVAL PLATFORM—That part of the brain cortex to which the nerve fibers carrying a given sensation are distributed. Thus we recognize an arrival platform for vision, for audition, etc. As a rule the microscopic structure of these areas is quite different from those surrounding them. *See* Area Striata.

ASSOCIATION—The process by which a stimulus becomes connected with previous experiences or other stimuli. *Associative linkages*—the connection existing in memory between two associated stimuli.

AUDIOGRAM—*See* Audiometer.

AUDIOMETER—A device to test the power of hearing. As generally used this instrument can be used not only to test hearing in general but to compare the acuity for each of a number of pitches, and the record made from such a test of a considerable pitch range in a given individual is called an *Audiometer-Curve* or simply an *Audiogram*.

BASE DEAFNESS—*See* Deafness.

BLEND, PHONETIC—The fusion of individual letter sounds as they are combined in ordinary speech.

BLINDNESS—1. *Cortical-Blindness*—Loss of vision resulting from destruction of the visual center (arrival platform) in the brain, but without disease or disorder of the eyes or optic nerves.

2. *Mind-Blindness (Visual Agnosia)*—Loss of the ability to recognize objects by sight although they are still seen.

3. *Word-Blindness*—(a) Acquired—Loss of the ability to recognize the meanings of printed or written words.

(b) Developmental (Congenital)—Inability in learning to read which is out of harmony with the individual's general intelligence and ability to learn by other channels.

BRAIN CENTER—A part of the brain which is devoted to one function, as, for example, the *motor center. See* Area.

CEREBRAL—Pertaining to the cerebrum or main portion of the brain.

CEREBRAL DOMINANCE—*See* Dominance.

CEREBRAL LOCALIZATION—The study of the part which various brain areas play in its functions.

CLINICAL—The study of the living patient (literally at the bedside) as contrasted with autopsy and laboratory studies.

CLONIC SPASM—*See* Spasm.

CONGENITAL—Belonging to one from birth, as differentiated from *acquired* which is the result of some influence acting after birth.

CONVOLUTIONS, BRAIN—*See* Gyrus.

CORTEX, BRAIN (pl. Cortices, a. Cortical)—The outer surface of the brain which contains the nerve cells and most of their inter-connections. It is grayish in color as compared to the underlying white matter which contains no nerve cells and which is made up almost entirely of nerve fibers connecting various areas. It is the cortex which is referred to as the "gray matter" of the brain. The various cortices may be referred to according to their function, as, for example, *the motor cortex*, or by anatomical location as in the *parieto-occipital cortex*.

DEAFNESS—1. *Cortical-Deafness*—Loss of hearing as a result of destruction of the auditory arrival platforms but with no disease of the ears or auditory nerves.
2. *Mind-Deafness (Auditory Agnosia)*—Loss of the ability to understand the meaning of sounds of the environment although they are heard.
3. *Word-Deafness*—(a) Acquired—Loss of the ability to understand the spoken word.
(b) Developmental (Congenital)—Difficulty in learning to understand spoken words.
4. *Regional Deafness*—Lowered acuity of hearing in a part only of the normal range of pitch. This may include chiefly the lower range when it is called *bass deafness*, but more commonly the higher range is affected, resulting in *high-frequency deafness*.
5. *Peripheral Deafness*—Deafness due to disease of the ear or auditory nerve as contrasted with that due to brain lesions as described above.

DEMENTIA—A degradation from a previously acquired mental level.

DEVELOPMENTAL—Incidental to growth. As used in this volume in connection with the various language disorders this term is intended to include intrinsic factors—both hereditary and congenital, and extrinsic influences of the environment, such as training, which play a part in the development and evolution of the language faculty in the individual, thus giving a somewhat broader range to the expression *developmental alexia*, for example, than was true of its predecessor *congenital alexia*. The *developmental disorders of language* are those in which there is exhibited a specific difficulty in acquisition or learning as contrasted to the *acquired* in which there is a loss of a previously acquired skill.

DEXTRAD—Toward the right side or hand or in the right-hand direction.

DEXTRAL—Right. Also used as an abbreviation for a right-handed person.

DIGRAPH—A group of two letters representing a single speech sound, as, for example, *th*.

DIPHTHONG—A union of two vowels forming a compound sound such as *oy*. Where two vowels represent one sound as in *ea* they constitute, strictly speaking, a digraph, and are sometimes called *improper diphthongs*.

DOMINANCE (a. Dominant)—1. *Cerebral Dominance*. When used by physiologists without further qualification this refers to the increasingly important role played by the cerebral cortex, as the animal scale is ascended, in controlling and integrating the activities of the lower nervous centers such, for example, as the cerebellum and the spinal cord.

2. *Unilateral Cerebral Dominance*. When used with this qualifying adjective the expression refers to the concentration of functional control of language in one half of the brain such as is revealed by the fact that speech, for example, may be entirely lost although only one hemisphere of the brain has suffered injury.

3. *Eye Dominance. See* Master Eye.

4. *Mendelian Dominance*. The tendency of one character to mask or hide its opposite when both are present in the parents. Thus, for example, if one parent comes from a family who are without exception brown-eyed and the other comes from a comparable blue-eyed family, all the children of the first generation will be brown-eyed and for this reason brown eye color is said to be dominant over blue, which is called a recessive character. The tendency to blue eyes is not entirely lost in such a situation since some of the brown-eyed children of the first generation are able to transmit blue eyes to their own offspring if they mate with other hybrid individuals like themselves, or if they choose blue-eyed mates.

DYNAMOMETER—As used herein, an instrument for testing the strength of the hand grip.

ECHOLALIA—Echo speech. A stage in the development of speech in the child when he repeats words said to him with no understanding of their meaning. It also is an occasional symptom in some cases of mental disease in adults.

ELECTROENCEPHALOGRAPH—An instrument for amplifying and recording the very weak electrical currents which occur in the brain.

ENGRAM—The physiological record of a previous stimulus left in the brain or other nerve centers.

ETIOLOGICAL—Causative. In medicine, pertaining to the cause of disease.

EYEDNESS—*See* Master Eye.

FOOTEDNESS—Consistent preferential use of either the right or left foot for such unilateral functions as kicking, hopping, starting upstairs, etc.

FUSION, BINOCULAR—The combination of the image produced by the two eyes into one sensory impression.

GALVANOMETER—An instrument for detecting or recording electrical currents.

GENETICS—The study of heredity. Experimental genetics has become a highly specialized field of biology in which the laws of heredity are studied by controlled matings of animals and plants.

GRAPHIC LANGUAGE—The use of drawn or written symbols to record or transmit ideas.

GYRUS (pl. Gyri)—The surface of the brain in all the higher mammals, including man, is marked by an intricate pattern of flat-topped ridges called *gyri or convolutions*, which are separated by narrow clefts called *sulci*. Angular gyrus—the brain cortex surrounding the end of the first temporal sulcus. It is the "critical area" for reading and is shown at 1 in Figure 3.

HANDEDNESS—*See* Master Hand.

HEMIANOPSIA—Blindness for one half the field of vision.

HEMIPLEGIA—Paralysis of one side of the body.

HEMISPHERE, CEREBRAL—Either lateral half of the brain.

HEREDITY—1. *Mendelian*—Following the laws of heredity as described by Mendel. *See* under Dominance.
2. *Sex-Linked*—A character or hereditary disease or defect which is transmitted consistently to children of one or the other sex only. The most commonly quoted disorders of this nature are *hemophilia* and *color blindness*, which are transmitted by unaffected mothers to their sons.
3. *Sex-Influenced*—A less rigid transmission to one sex than the *sex-linked*.
4. *Hereditary Lading*—The degree of taint or tendency toward the transmission of a disease or defect.

HOMOZYGOUS—Having exactly the same heredity. The nearest approach to this condition in experimental genetics is produced by many generations of very close inbreeding of animals or plants.

HYPERKINESIS—Overactivity or excessive movement.

INFANTILISMS, SPEECH—Persistent childish defects in speech. Of these the lisp, the substitution of *w* for *r* and of *f* or *v* for *th* are common.

INTELLIGENCE QUOTIENT (I.Q.)—The ratio between an individual's mental age and his chronological age (*q.v.*).

INTERGRADES—1. Genetic—Various degrees of intermingling of hereditary characters.
2. *Motor* (as used herein)—Intermixtures of right- and left-sidedness, as, for example, an individual who is right-handed and left-eyed, or one who performs some skilled acts with the left hand and others with the right.

KINAESTHESIS—Sensations from the muscles, tendons and joints by which muscular motion, weight, position, etc., are perceived. It is also from these sensations that new patterns of movement are in large part established.

LABIAL (As applied to speech)—Sounds in which movements or position of the lips play a part, such as *p, b, m*.

LATERAL (As applied to the brain)—The outer or convex surface of either hemisphere.

LESION, BRAIN—Damage to the structure of any part of the brain from injury or disease.

LINGUAL (As applied to speech)—Sounds which are formed with the aid of the tongue, such as *t, d*.

LINKAGES—*See* Association.

LOBE—One of the major anatomical subdivisions of the brain. The five lobes are indicated in Figure 1.

LOCALIZATION—*See* Cerebral Localization.

MASTER EYE—The eye which is habitually used for sighting.

MASTER HAND—The hand which is used by preference in skilled acts.

MASTER HEMISPHERE—The dominant half of the brain. *See* Dominance (2).

MEMORY—1. *Recognition memory* is that degree of familiarity with a given stimulus which permits its recognition when exposed again.

2. *Recall memory* is the somewhat greater degree of familiarity which permits the reviving of a stimulus in memory without renewed exposure.

MESIAL (As applied to the brain)—The inner or flat surface where the two hemispheres of the brain come together.

MNEMONIC—Pertaining to memory.

MOTOR AREA—*See* Area

MOTOR NERVE CELLS—The large nerve cells in the spinal cord from which fibers run to the muscles and which directly control muscular movements. Also the giant nerve cells of the motor cortex in the brain which direct the activity of the spinal motor cells in voluntary movement.

MOTOR OVERFLOW—The term used in this volume to include involuntary movements of muscles, other than those directly concerned, during the spasms of stuttering and stammering. Some of the facial grimaces of many stutterers fall into this group.

MUSCLES, EXTRAOCULAR—The muscles on the outside of the eyeball which serve to turn it in its socket, as contrasted with the *intraocular* muscles whose duty is that of focusing the lens and changing the size of the pupil.

MYELIN (Myelin Sheaths)—The fat-like substance which forms an insulating sheath around the nerve fiber.

NEGATIVISM—A propensity to do the opposite of that which is requested.

NEOGRAPHISMS—The graphic equivalent of *neologisms (q.v.)*.

NEOLOGISMS—The invention of new words and particularly the use of word sounds in meaningless new combinations.

ONTOGENETIC—Origin and development of the individual, and thus to be contrasted with *phylogenetic* which is the evolution or ancestral history of a race or group of animals.

PATHOLOGICAL—Abnormal or diseased.

PARAGRAMMATISM—The type of errors seen in some cases of aphasia, characterized by confusion in the use and order of words and grammatical forms. *cf.* Agrammatism.

PARAPHASIA—The use of wrong words to express meaning as seen in some aphasics.

PHONETIC—Of or pertaining to speech sounds and their relation to graphic symbols.

1. *Phonetic Synthesis*—The building up of a word from its phonetic units.

2. *Phonetic Analysis*—The dissection of a spoken word into its component sounds.

PHYLOGENETIC—*See* Ontogenetic.

PHYLUM—One of the primary or main divisions of the animal or vegetable kingdoms.

PROPOSITIONAL SPEECH—Purposeful expression as contrasted with repetition of memorized material.

RECESSIVE HEREDITARY CHARACTER—*See* Dominance—Mendelian.

REVERSALS (As used in this volume)—1. *Kinetic*—Confusion or misreading a series of letters or words in which a progressional element enters, as when a whole word is read backward.

2. *Static*—Confusion or mistakes in recognition of single letters which are alike except for their orientation, such as *b* and *d*.

SECLUSIVENESS—The tendency to withdraw from social contacts.

SEX-INFLUENCED—*See* Heredity.

SEX-LINKED—*See* Heredity.

SINISTRAD—To or toward the left.

SINISTRAL—Left. Also used as an abbreviation for a left-handed person.

SPASM—A sudden involuntary contraction of a muscle.

1. *Clonic Spasm*—When characterized by alternating contraction and relaxation.

2. *Tonic Spasm*—When persistent in contraction.

SPEECH MECHANISM—This consists of two parts, the *peripheral* and the *central*.

1. The *peripheral* mechanism is made up of the lips, tongue, glottis, larynx, breathing apparatus and all of the nerves controlling these parts.

2. The *central mechanism* is not so thoroughly understood but requires the collaboration of a number of areas in the cerebral cortex, notably those devoted to hearing and Broca's area, which is the brain center for motor control of speech.

STEREOPSIS (Stereoscopic Vision)—Perception of the third dimension in objects so that they appear as solid instead of as flat pictures.

STREPHOSYMBOLIA—A delay or difficulty in learning to read which is out of harmony with a child's general intellectual ability. At the outset it is characterized by confusion between similarly formed but oppositely oriented letters, and a tendency to a changing order of direction in reading.

SUSPENOPSIA—A tendency for the image arising in either eye to be entirely disregarded for a short period of time so that the individual is using one eye only for the time being.

SYNDROME—A complex of symptoms; a group of symptoms which occur together.

THERAPY (a. Therapeutic)—The treatment of disease.
TIMBRE—The quality of a tone or sound.
TONIC—*See* Spasm.

UNILATERAL CEREBRAL DOMINANCE—*See* Dominance.

VIBRATO—Slight variations in pitch, less striking than the termulo, which
    characterize emotional expression in speech and in singing.
VISUO-MOTOR CO-ORDINATION—The accurate adjustment of movement
    to accord with the incoming visual stimuli.

WORD-BLINDNESS—*See* Blindness.
WORD-DEAFNESS—*See* Deafness.

APPENDIX 2

◇————————————————————————————◇

Works by Samuel Torrey Orton

A study of the pathological changes of some mound-builders' bones from the Ohio Valley, with especial reference to syphilis. (1905). *University of Pennsylvania Medical Bulletin, April.*

With Edwin A. Locke, M.D. The pathological findings in two fatal cases of mycosis fungoides. (1907). *Journal of the American Medical Association, 48.*

Report of a case of chorion epithelioma of the testicle. (1907). *Journal of Medical Research, 17(2).*

A pathological study of a case of hydrocephalus. (1908). *American Journal of Insanity, 65(2).*

With Walter L. Dodd. Experiments on transmission of bacteria by flies with special relation to an epidemic of bacillary dysentery at the Worcester State Hospital, Massachusetts, 1910. (1910). *Boston Medical & Surgical Journal, 163(23).*

Note on an anomaly of the postcentral sulcus simulating the double rolandic of giacomini. (1911). *The Anatomical Record, 5(4).*

A case of extensive brain disease from endarteritis probably of syphilitic origin. (1912). *Journal of the American Medical Association, 59.*

Further observations on the fly problem at the Worcester State Hospital, Massachusetts, 1911. (1912). *Boston Medical & Surgical Journal, 166(6).*

Some technical methods for the routine examination of the brain from cases of mental disease. (1912). *American Journal of Insanity, 69(2).*

An analysis of the errors in diagnosis in a series of sixty cases of paresis. (1913). *Journal of Nervous and Mental Disease, 40(12).*

A note on the occurrence of B. aerogenes capsulatus in an epidemic of dysentery and in the normal. (1913). *Journal of Medical Research, 29(2).*

A study of the brain in a case of catatonic hirntod. (1913). *American Journal of Insanity, 69(4).*

Ed. Worcester State Hospital papers, 1912–13. (1913). *Massachusetts State Board of Insanity, Series 1913, Nos. 4–19.*

The distribution of the lesions of general paralysis. (1914). *American Journal of Insanity, 70(4).*

A note on the circulation of the cornu ammonis. (1914). *The Anatomical Record, 8(4).*

A study of the satellite cells in fifty selected cases of mental disease. (1914). *Brain, 36, Pts. 3 & 4.*

The present status of the application of the Abderhalden dialysis method to psychiatry. (1915). *American Journal of Insanity, 71(3).*

The relation of syphilis to mental disease. (1916). *Boston Medical & Surgical Journal, 174(15).*

A review of the histological lesions of syphilis of the nervous system. (1916). *Interstate Medical Journal, 23(8).*

Some considerations of general paresis from the histological standpoint. (1916). *American Journal of Insanity,* 73(1).

Some observations of the influence of angle of section on measurements of cortex depth and on the cytoarchitectonic picture. (1918). *Journal of Nervous and Mental Disease,* 47(4).

Histologic evidence of the path of invasion of the brain in general paresis. (1919). *Archives of Neurology and Psychiatry, 1.*

On the classification of nervous and mental diseases. (1919). *American Journal of Insanity,* 86(2).

General paresis. (1924). *Journal of the Iowa State Medical Society, August.*

The problem of the feebleminded: A mobile psychiatric unit as the most feasible method of meeting Iowa's mental hygiene needs. (1924). *Twenty-Fifth Iowa State Conference of Social Work.*

Negative histological findings in experimental organic processes. (1925). *American Journal of Psychiatry, 60.*

The pathology of the hereditary and familial nervous and mental diseases. (1925). *Archives of Neurology and Psychiatry, 13.*

Neuropathology—lecture notes I. (1926). *Archives of Neurology and Psychiatry, 15.*

Neuropathology—lecture notes II. (1926). *Archives of Neurology and Psychiatry, 16.*

Studies in stuttering, introduction. (1927). *Archives of Neurology and Psychiatry, 18.*

Training the left handed. (1927). *Hygeia, September.*

An impediment to learning to read—a neurological explanation of the reading disability. (1928). *School and Society,* 28(715).

Foreword. In Marion Monroe, Methods for diagnosis and treatment of cases of reading disability. (1928). *Genetic Psychology Monographs,* 4(4 & 5).

Certain failures in the acquisition of written language: Their bearing on the problem of cerebral dominance (Transactions, Philadelphia Neurological Society). (1929). *Archives of Neurology and Psychiatry, 22.*

The need of consolidation of psychiatric thought by a broad program of research. [Presidential address of the 85th annual meeting of the American Psychiatric Association, May, 1929]. (1929). *American Journal of Psychiatry,* 9(1).

The neurologic basis of elementary education. (1929) *Archives of Neurology and Psychiatry, 21,* 641–646.

The relation of the special educational disabilities to feeblemindedness. (1929). *Proceedings of the Fifty-Third Annual Session of the American Association for the Study of the Feebleminded, May 13–15.*

With L. E. Travis, Ph.D. Studies of action currents in stutterers. (1929). *Archives of Neurology and Psychiatry, 21.*

The three levels of cortical elaboration in relation to certain psychiatric symptoms. (1929). *American Journal of Psychiatry, 8.*

Some neurologic concepts applied to catatonia. (1930). *Archives of Neurology and Psychiatry, 23.*

A clinical and pathological study of two cases of obstruction of the aqueduct of sylvius. (1931). *Bulletin of the Neurological Institute of New York, 1(1).*

With Lauretta Bender, M.D. Lesions in the lateral horns of the spinal cord in acrodynia, pellagra, and pernicious anemia. (1931). *Bulletin of the Neurological Institute of New York, 1(3).*

With Abner Wolf, M.D. The occurrence of intranuclear inclusions in human nerve cells in a variety of diseases. (1932). *Bulletin of the Neurological Institute of New York, 2(2).*

With Joseph Post, B.A. Some experiments with a new embedding material. (1932). *Bulletin of the Neurological Institute of New York, 2(2).*

With Abner Wolf, M.D. Intranuclear inclusions in brain tumors. (1933). *Bulletin of the Neurological Institute of New York, 3(1 & 2).*

Behavior disorders associated with developmental disorders in language acquisition. (1934). *Connecticut State Medical Society Journal, 3,* 12–14.

An hypothesis concerning the neural mechanism of stuttering. (1934). *Journal of Nervous and Mental Disease, 98,* 188–193.

Ed. *Localization of function in the cerebral cortex.* (1934). Baltimore: Williams and Wilkins.

Three levels of cortical elaboration in relation to certain psychiatric symptoms. (1934). *American Journal of Psychiatry, 8,* 647–659.

A neurological explanation of the reading disability. (1939). *The Educational Record* (Suppl. 12).

Word-blindness and other papers on strephosymbolia (specific language disability—dyslexia). (1966). *Orton Society Monograph No. 2.*

AUTHOR INDEX

345

SUBJECT INDEX

Page numbers in italics refer to information in illustrations and tables.

Abnormal clumsiness. *See* Apraxia, developmental

Academic achievement
developmental agraphia and, 58, *59*
developmental alexia and, 53-57, 163
early education and, 175-76
emotional problems and, 78-81
~ handedness and, 145
mixed syndromes and, 75
treatment and, 103, 105

Age
chronological/mental, and educational profile, 42-43
critical periods for language development, 36, 37
language acquisition and, 9
stuttering and, 74, 117, 119
teaching of reading and writing, 9

Agrammatisms, 27, 151

Agraphia. *See also* Writing
academic achievement and, 58, *59*
behavioral/emotional problems and, 81
brain damage and, 64-65
developmental, 58-66
handedness and, 58-64, *60-65*, 65
letters and, 58-64, *60-65*
mirror writing and, 60-64, *61-65*, 90, 91
motor, 25-26
purity of syndrome, 65
treatment for, 107-10, *109*
types of, 58
vision-averted writing and, 64-65, *65*
visual material and, 225-26

Alexia (word blindness). *See also* Word blindness
academic achievement and, 53-57
acquired, 127, 165, 166, 169, 170, 219
analysis of, 87
apraxia and, 214, 235
arithmetic and, 48-49
auditory development and, 43-45
~ brain lesions and, 153
~ brain structure and, 185-91, 188-89
case studies of, 131-44, 222-25
characteristic forms of, 41
confusions in alphabetical letters, 137-38, 176-78, 182, 195-97, 204, 208, 213, 229-30, 244-45, 301, 322
~ congenital, 129, 130, 131, 150-59, 165, 166, 170, 181, 200, 219
definition of, 20-22
developmental, 40-58
diagnostic tests for, 170, 171
early studies of, 40-41, 165-67
emotional/behavioral problems and, 79-81, 160-61, 172, 179, 197-98, 206, 325
eye movements and, 307-308
eyedness and, 303-305
failures in recall of sequences, 230
foreign language study and, 55
graded severity of, 170
hearing and, 233
~ hereditary factors and, 303
higher education, 53, 54, 57
indications of, 42, 105-106, 168, 204, 301-302

347